MODERN TREATY LAW
AND PRACTICE

ANTHONY AUST

CAMBRIDGE
UNIVERSITY PRESS

PUBLISHED BY THE PRESS SYNDICATE OF THE UNIVERSITY OF CAMBRIDGE
The Pitt Building, Trumpington Street, Cambridge, United Kingdom

CAMBRIDGE UNIVERSITY PRESS
The Edinburgh Building, Cambridge CB2 2RU, UK
40 West 20th Street, New York, NY 10011-4211, USA
477 Williamstown Road, Port Melbourne, VIC 3207, Australia
Ruiz de Alarcón 13, 28014 Madrid, Spain
Dock House, The Waterfront, Cape Town 8001, South Africa

http://www.cambridge.org

First published 2000
Fifth printing 2006

Printed in the United Kingdom at the University Press, Cambridge

Typeset in Minion 10.5/14 pt   *System* QuarkXpress®   [SE]

A catalogue record for this book is available from the British Library

Library of Congress Cataloguing in Publication data

Aust, Anthony.
Modern treaty law and practice / Anthony Aust.
p.   cm.
Includes bibliographical references and index.
ISBN 0 521 59153 8 (hardbound)
1. Treaties. I. Title.
KZ1301.A93   2000
341.3'7–dc21   99-33753   CIP

ISBN 0 521 59153 8 hardback
ISBN 0 521 59846 X paperback

For Katie and Sophie

CONTENTS

FOREWORD

The law of treaties is one of the branches of international law whose roots go back furthest in time. With the emergence of political communities came the need for them to deal with each other, to settle questions in dispute without having to go to war, to arrange the consequences of success or failure after a war had been fought, to strike alliances, organise matters of trade, settle territorial limits to their power, and so on. For such matters they needed from early times some accepted rules covering two matters, the sending of envoys and the making of agreements. Both have remained central to the conduct of what we now call international relations.

Over centuries the rules and practices governing those agreements have evolved into the modern law of treaties. The evolutionary process is a continuing one. A book on the law of treaties written at the end of the nineteenth century is recognisably about the same subject as its equivalent written today. Yet, while the general body of the law remains broadly stable, times change and bring with them changes in the law. International organisations have emerged as significant actors in the treaty-making process; multilateral treaties are nowadays concluded more frequently, and have more parties, than used to be the case – a reflection of the enormous increase in the number of states during the course of the present century – and there have been great technological changes, especially in communications, which have noticeably affected the process by which treaties are negotiated and concluded.

The modern law is now authoritatively set out in the Vienna Convention on the Law of Treaties 1969, and in its parallel Convention of 1986 on treaties made by international organisations. They are, however, not only far from a complete code on the subject, they are also not free from continuing controversy even in respect of matters which they do deal with (such as the vexed topic of reservations, which the International Law Commission is presently studying once again, having previously reported

xv

on the matter in 1951). Moreover, as is so often the way, new issues have arisen which were not envisaged when the principal Vienna Convention of 1969 was concluded. A new book on the law of treaties, surveying the subject some thirty years after the Vienna Convention was concluded, is timely.

What, however, makes the present volume particularly welcome is its manifest concern with the practical aspects of the law of treaties. Undoubtedly the law of treaties exercises a great intellectual fascination. Many issues directly or indirectly raise large questions of legal theory. Furthermore, some treaties are of enormous historical significance, like the Peace of Westphalia of 1698 and the Treaty of Rome of 1957. But it must always be recalled that treaties are essentially instruments for regulating by agreement the myriad day-to-day affairs of states. International travel and broadcasting, international posts and telecommunications, international trade – these and many other matters, which are usually taken for granted, are dependent upon a network of often very detailed treaties, both bilateral and multilateral.

For this array of treaties – essential for the conduct of international relations, but seldom eye-catching – the negotiating process is well established. So too are most of the relevant legal rules. But however well developed international rules and processes may be, they have a practical dimension to which much less attention is usually paid. This is doubly unfortunate. The true significance of many rules is illuminated by being seen in the perspective of their application in practice, while the steps which need to be taken in applying the rules can be as important as the rules themselves, going far to explain why many things are as they are.

It is the great virtue of this volume that, in looking at the law *and* its practical context, it grounds the treatment of the law of treaties firmly in the real world of international relations, foreign ministries and diplomacy. That is the world about which Mr Aust is exceptionally well qualified to write. As one of the senior legal advisers in the Foreign and Commonwealth Office, who has served not only in London but also in diplomatic posts abroad (including as Legal Adviser to the United Kingdom Mission to the United Nations in New York from 1988 to 1991), he brings to this book a wealth of experience on all aspects of treaty law and practice. That experience, and the insights which flow from it, pervade every chapter.

Everyone concerned with treaties and the law relating to them, whether on a day-to-day basis, occasional practitioners in the field, or as outside observers of the treaty process, will benefit greatly from Mr Aust's up-to-date and practical treatment of the subject. I warmly commend this volume, which is a welcome addition to the literature in this field.

Sir Arthur Watts KCMG QC
London, January 1999

ACKNOWLEDGMENTS

I have first to thank Kirsten Kaarre Jensen. It is not easy for a wife to share three years of her life with that unholy pair, Toshiba and Gates. But she has done so uncomplainingly, at least most of the time. She also read and commented on the manuscript from the perspective of a former diplomat. But I value even more her understanding and support.

Next I must express my great appreciation to Arthur Watts, not just for the foreword, but for suggesting that I write this book. Without his encouragement I doubt it would have been written.

Although this book reflects my own experience, in certain areas I have inevitably also drawn upon that of my colleagues past and present in the Foreign and Commonwealth Office (FCO). Several of them have supplied texts or taken time to read and comment on various parts. It is always invidious to pick out names, but special thanks must go to Michael Wood for reading the complete manuscript (twice), and making many helpful suggestions to improve it. My youngest colleague at the time, Ruma Mandal, also read the whole text. Her searching questions showed me where I had to explain rather better what I had assumed the reader would know. The book has benefited also from the fruits of the superlative research into some of the more perplexing treaty questions done for the FCO legal advisers by Susan Hulton; as well as Andrew Young's special knowledge of Hong Kong. And, of course, my thanks must go to Frank Berman for supporting me in this endeavour.

No lawyer can work effectively without a well-run library. Susan Halls, the librarian, as well as Anne Sutton, Jane Crellin and other staff of the FCO Legal Library, helped enormously by searching out material for me. Isabel Warner and her staff of the FCO Treaty Section read the draft and contributed much practical information from their personal and collective knowledge.

Others, both at home and abroad, commented on certain passages in the manuscript or supplied material. They include Andrew Barlow,

Alan Boyle, Irene Cacic, James Crawford, Francis Delon, Christopher Greenwood, Jan Klabbers, Palitha Kohona, Martti Koskenniemi, Gerard Limburg, Borut Mahnic, Nicolas Michel, Sally Morphet, Richard Nzerem, Riina Pihel, Bette Shifman, Peter Slinn, Eric Suy, Berte Timm, Peter Tomka and Rüdi Wolfrum.

John McHugo was good enough to read the manuscript and made perceptive comments from his perspective as a commercial lawyer.

Last, but by no means least, thanks must go to my editor, Finola O'Sullivan, and to Martin Gleeson and Caroline Murray, for guiding me through the mysteries of publishing in the most painless way.

I must express my appreciation to the following for giving permission to reproduce certain Appendices: K, P and Q (the UN Secretary-General); H, I and L (the Foreign and Commonwealth Office); and C (the Austrian and British Ministries of Defence). Appendices A, B and E are Crown copyright protected material reproduced with the permission of the Controller of Her Majesty's Stationery Office.

Needless to say, the opinions expressed in this book do not necessarily reflect those of the British Government.

TABLE OF TREATIES

Where appropriate either a treaty is listed under the name or acronym by which it is commonly known, or the subject matter is mentioned first. If a UN registration number is given, but no UNTS reference, the treaty will not have been published in the UNTS at the time of writing (December 1998).

Multilateral treaties

Additional Protocols of 1977 to the Geneva Conventions (1125 UNTS 3 (No. 17512); ILM (1977), p. 1391; UKTS (1999) 29 and 30)

AETR II Agreement 1970 (993 UNTS 143 (No. 14533))

American Convention on Human Rights 1969 (ILM (1970), p. 673; UKTS (1980) 58)

Antarctic Marine Living Resources Convention (CCAMLR) 1980 (402 UNTS 71; ILM (1980), p. 837; UKTS (1982) 48; TIAS 10240)

Antarctic Mineral Resources Activities Convention (CRAMRA) 1988 (ILM (1988), p. 865)

Antarctic Treaty 1959 (402 UNTS 71 (No. 5778); UKTS (1961) 97)

Antarctic Treaty, Environmental Protocol 1991 (ILM (1991), p. 1460; UKTS (1999) 6)

ASEAN Framework Agreement on Intellectual Property Cooperation 1995 (ILM (1996), p. 1074)

ASEAN Framework Agreement on Services 1995 (ILM (1996), p. 1077)

Austrian State Treaty 1955 (217 UNTS 223 (No. 2249); UKTS (1957) 58; TIAS 3298)

Bribery Convention 1997 (ILM (1998), p. 1)

Cambodia Agreement 1991 (ILM (1992), p. 1820)

CEDAW (Convention on the Elimination of Discrimination Against Women) 1979 (1249 UNTS 13 (No. 20378); ILM (1980), p. 33; UKTS (1989) 2)

CERD (Convention on the Elimination of All Forms of Racial
   Discrimination) 1966 (660 UNTS 195 (No. 99464); UKTS (1954) 39)
CFE (Conventional Forces in Europe) Treaty 1990 (ILM (1991), p. 6)
CFE, Document of the States Parties 1993 (UKTS (1994) 21)
CFE, Document Agreed 1996 (ILM (1997), p. 878)
Chemical Weapons Convention 1993 (CWC) (ILM (1993), p. 804; UKTS
   (1997) 45; UN Reg. No. 33757)
Chicago Convention 1944 (15 UNTS 295 (No. 102); UKTS (1953) 8)
Chicago Convention, Article 3*bis* Protocol (ILM (1984), p. 705; UKTS (1999)
   68)
CITES (Convention on International Trade in Endangered Species) 1973
   (993 UNTS 243; ILM (1973), p. 1085; UKTS (1976) 101)
Climate Change Convention 1992 (ILM (1992), p. 851; UKTS (1995) 28; UN
   Reg. No. 30822)
Commonwealth of Independent States (CIS) Charter 1993 (ILM (1995),
   p. 1282)
Comprehensive Nuclear-Test-Ban Treaty 1996 (CTBT) (ILM (1996), p. 1443)
Congress of Vienna, Acts (64 CTS 454)
Constantinople Convention 1888 (171 CTS 241)
Conventional Weapons Convention 1980 (1342 UNTS 137 (No. 22495); ILM
   (1980), p. 1523; UKTS (1996) 105)
Dayton Agreement 1995 (ILM (1996), p. 75)
EMEP Protocol 1984 (ILM (1988)), p. 701; UKTS (1988) 75)
ENMOD Convention 1977 (1108 UNTS 151; ILM (1977), p. 16; TIAS 9614)
Espoo Convention 1991 (ILM (1971), p. 802)
Estonia Agreement 1995 (*Finnish Treaty Series* 1995, No. 49) and with
   Additional Protocol 1996 (UKTS (1999) 74)
Eumetsat Convention 1983 (UKTS (1990) 32)
Eurocontrol Convention 1960 (523 UNTS 117 (No. 7557); UKTS (1963) 39)
Eurocontrol Convention, Amending Protocol 1981 (UKTS (1987) 2)
European Convention on Extradition 1957 (359 UNTS 273 (No. 5146);
   UKTS (1991) 97)
European Convention on Human Rights (ECHR) 1950 (213 UNTS 221 (No.
   2889); UKTS (1953) 71)
European Convention on Human Rights, Protocol No. 11 (ILM (1994),
   p. 960)
European Convention on Nationality 1997 (ILM (1998), p. 44)
European Convention for the Peaceful Settlement of Disputes (820 UNTS
   102)

Bilateral treaties

TABLE OF MOUs

For an explanation of the term 'MOU' see pp. 17–18 below.

Multilateral

Commonwealth Secretariat Agreed Memorandum 1965 (ILM (1965), p. 1108)

Helsinki Final Act 1975 (ILM (1975), p. 1293)

Memorandum of Understanding on Port State Control in the Caribbean Region 1996 (ILM (1997), p. 237)

OSCE Charter of Paris 1990 (ILM (1991), p. 193)

OSCE Document on Confidence and Security Building Measures and Disarmament in Europe 1987 (ILM (1987), p. 191)

Paris Memorandum of Understanding on Port State Control 1982 (ILM (1982), p. 1)

Rio Declaration on Environment and Development 1992 (ILM (1992), p. 876)

UNCED Non-Legally Binding Authoritative Statement of Principles regarding Forests (ILM (1992), p. 882)

Bilateral

The shortness of this list is merely due to the fact that, although there are many more bilateral than multilateral MOUs, very few are published even if they are not confidential.

Argentina–UK Joint Declarations on the Falkland Islands 1989 and 1995 (ILM (1990), p. 129 and ILM (1996), p. 304)

Austria–UK Memorandum of Understanding on Defence Contracts and Cooperation (see Appendix C)

Israel–US Declaration on Trade in Services (ILM (1985), p. 679)

NATO–Russia Founding Act 1997 (ILM (1997), p. 1007)

Russia–US Charter of Partnership and Friendship 1992 (ILM (1992), p. 782)

UK–US Memorandum of Understanding on User Charges 1983 (102 ILR 561)

TABLE OF CASES

Permanent Court of International Justice and International Court of Justice

Other international courts and tribunals

Arbitrations

National courts

GLOSSARY OF LEGAL TERMS

The terms used most frequently in this book are italicised.

acceptance, approval	Same effect as ratification (q.v.).
accession	Same effect as ratification (q.v.), but not preceded by signature.
adherence	Shorthand term for consent to be bound (q.v.).
consent to be bound	To sign a treaty not subject to ratification or to ratify, accept, approve or accede to a treaty.
contracting state	A state which has consented to be bound by a treaty, *whether or not the treaty has entered into force* (Article 2(1)(f)).
customary international law	Rules derived from general practice among states together with *opinio juris* (q.v.), and see p. 10 below.
domestic law	Law of a state (sometimes called 'municipal' or 'national' law).
erga omnes	Valid for all.
estoppel	The principle that a state cannot act inconsistently with what it has acquiesced in or taken a particular position with respect to (see p. 45 below).
exchange of notes	Two or more instruments which constitute either a treaty or an MOU.
Final Act	Formal document recording the results of a diplomatic conference, especially one to adopt a multilateral treaty (see p. 73 below).
full powers	Formal document authorising a person to sign a treaty or do other acts with respect to a treaty (Article 2(1)(c)) (see Chapter 5).

international law	The body of rules binding on states and other subjects of international law (q.v.) in their relations with each other.
international legal personality	Being a person or legal entity to which international law attributes legal rights and obligations (mainly states and international organisations).
jurisdiction	The right in international law for a state to exercise authority over its nationals and persons and things in its territory, and sometimes abroad (extraterritorial jurisdiction).
memorandum of understanding	Name given to both treaties and MOUs (see p. 20 below).
MOU	A non-legally binding instrument (see Chapter 3).
negotiating state	A state which took part in the drawing up and adoption of the text of a treaty (Article 2(1)(e)).
opinio juris	General belief by states that a non-treaty rule is legally binding on them (see p. 10 below).
party	A state which has consented to be bound by a treaty *and* for which the treaty is in force (Article 2(1)(g)).
primary legislation	Law made by a national legislature (cf. secondary legislation (q.v.)).
private international law	The domestic law dealing with cases with a foreign element (also known as conflict of laws).
ratification	Following signature, the expression of a state's consent to be bound by a treaty.
reservation	A unilateral statement, however phrased or named, made by a state when consenting to be bound by a treaty by which it purports to exclude or to modify the legal effect of certain provisions of the treaty in their application to that state (Article 2(1)(d)) (see Chapter 8).

secondary legislation	Legislation by the executive under power given by primary legislation (q.v.).
signatory	Not a precise term. Should only be used to describe a state which has signed a treaty which is subject to ratification but has not yet ratified; but best avoided (see p. 91 below).
sovereignty	The right of a state to act independently of other states, subject only to such restrictions as international law imposes.
state	See p. 47.
state responsibility	Responsibility of a state in international law for its wrongful acts (see p. 300 below).
subject of international law	Possessor of rights and obligations in international law (mainly states and international organisations).
subordinate or subsidiary legislation	Secondary legislation *(q.v.)*.
third state	A state which is not a party (q.v.) to a treaty (Article 2(1)(h)) (see Chapter 14).
travaux préparatoires (or travaux)	Preparatory work of a treaty (see pp. 197–9 below).
treaty	See Chapter 2.

ABBREVIATIONS

Most often used in this book

'the Convention'	Vienna Convention on the Law of Treaties 1969
'the 1969 Convention'	Vienna Convention on the Law of Treaties 1969
'the Convention itself'	Vienna Convention on the Law of Treaties 1969
'the Vienna Convention'	Vienna Convention on the Law of Treaties 1969
'the 1978 Convention'	Vienna Convention on Succession of States in respect of Treaties 1978
'the 1986 Convention'	Vienna Convention on the Law of Treaties between States and International Organisations or between International Organisations 1986
'Article'	An article of the 1969 Convention (unless otherwise indicated)
Blix and Emerson	H. Blix and J. Emerson, *The Treaty Maker's Handbook* (1973)
ILC Commentary	Commentary of the International Law Commission on its final draft articles on the Law of Treaties (YBILC (1964), II, pp. 173–274)
ILM	*International Legal Materials* (published by the American Society of International Law)
McNair	A. McNair, *Law of Treaties* (2nd edn, 1961)
MOU	Memorandum of understanding (see pp. 17–18 below)
Oppenheim	*Oppenheim's International Law* (9th edn, 1992)

Sinclair	I. Sinclair, *The Vienna Convention on the Law of Treaties* (2nd edn, 1984)
UKTS	*United Kingdom Treaty Series*
UN Depositary Practice	*Summary of Practice of the Secretary-General as Depositary of Multilateral Treaties* (1994)
UN Multilateral Treaties	*Multilateral Treaties Deposited with the Secretary-General*
UNTS	*United Nations Treaty Series*

Other abbreviations

AFDI	*Annuaire français de droit international*
AJIL	*American Journal of International Law*
All ER	*All England Law Reports*
ASIL	American Society of International Law
Aust YBIL	*Australian Yearbook of International Law*
BFSP	*British and Foreign State Papers*
BYIL	*British Yearbook of International Law*
CEDAW	Convention on the Elimination of All Forms of Discrimination Against Women
CERD	International Convention on the Elimination of All Forms of Racial Discrimination
CLR	*Commonwealth Law Reports*
Cm, Cmd, Cmnd	Command Papers (official UK publication)
CMLR	*Common Market Law Reports*
CoE	Council of Europe
CTBT	Comprehensive Nuclear-Test-Ban Treaty 1996
CTS	*Consolidated Treaty Series*
EC	European Community
ECHR	European Convention on Human Rights
ECJ	European Court of Justice
ECOSOC	UN Economic and Social Council
ECR	*European Court Reports*
ECSC	European Coal and Steel Community
EEC	European Economic Community
EJIL	*European Journal of International Law*
EURATOM	European Atomic Energy Community

FAO	Food and Agriculture Organisation
FCO	Foreign and Commonwealth Office, London
Hague Recueil	*Recueil des cours, Académie de Droit International de la Haye*
Hansard	Record of UK Parliamentary debates (Lords or Commons)
Hertslet	Hertslet, *Commercial Treaties* (reprinted in ten vols., 1970)
HKSAR	Hong Kong Special Administrative Region
HMSO	Her Majesty's Stationery Office
IAEA	International Atomic Energy Agency
ICAO	International Civil Aviation Organisation
ICCPR	International Covenant on Civil and Political Rights
ICJ	International Court of Justice
ICLQ	*International and Comparative Law Quarterly*
ICRC	International Committee of the Red Cross
ILA	International Law Association
ILC	International Law Commission
ILO	International Labour Organisation
ILR	*International Law Reports*
ITU	International Telecommunications Union
LNTS	*League of Nations Treaty Series*
LQR	*Law Quarterly Review*
MacLeod	MacLeod, Hendry and Hyett (eds.), *The External Relations of the European Communities* (1996)
MLR	*Modern Law Review*
Monroe Leigh	M. Leigh (ed.), *National Treaty Law and Practice* (1995)
NATO	North Atlantic Treaty Organisation
NILR	*Netherlands International Law Review*
NYIL	*Netherlands Yearbook of International Law*
O'Connell	D. O'Connell, *International Law* (2nd edn, 1970)
OECD	Organisation for Economic Co-operation and Development
OJ	*Official Journal of the European Communities*

OSCE	Organisation for Security and Co-operation in Europe
PCA	Permanent Court of Arbitration
PCIJ	Permanent Court of International Justice
PLO	Palestine Liberation Organisation
Reuter	P. Reuter, *Introduction to the Law of Treaties* (2nd English edn, 1995)
Satow	*Satow's Guide to Diplomatic Practice* (5th edn, 1984)
SI	statutory instrument (UK secondary legislation)
TIAS	*Treaties and other International Agreements Series* (US)
UK	United Kingdom of Great Britain and Northern Ireland
UN	United Nations
UNCIO	UN Conference on International Organisation
UNCLOS	UN Convention on the Law of the Sea 1982
UN Doc.	UN official document
UNESCO	UN Educational, Scientific and Cultural Organisation
UNGA	UN General Assembly
UNJurYB	*UN Juridical Yearbook*
Whiteman	M. Whiteman, *Digest of International Law*
WLR	*Weekly Law Reports*
YBIL	*Yearbook of International Law*
YBILC	*Yearbook of the International Law Commission*
ZaöRV	*Zeitschrift für ausländisches öffentliches Recht und Völkerrecht*

Introduction

Experience is the name everyone gives to their mistakes.[1]

In writing this book my purpose is to meet a long-felt need for a new work on the law of treaties which deals with the subject in a comprehensive, up-to-date and practical way. The making and operation of treaties is a daily occurrence. Understanding treaty practice enhances knowledge of the law of treaties. With very few exceptions, international law cannot be practised full-time except in a foreign ministry or an international organisation. Just as with domestic law, legal concepts and rules only become truly meaningful when one has drafted and worked with legal texts. A close involvement in the practice of treaties and the intricate procedures surrounding them leads to a fuller appreciation of their true nature.

I am very fortunate to have been able to practise international law in a foreign ministry. My perspective is therefore that of a practitioner; and this book is very much a distillation of some thirty years' experience. My aim is to inform the reader about all aspects of treaty law and practice by collecting the necessary information in one place. Although I have tried to avoid using too many British precedents, many examples are drawn from personal knowledge and experience. Whenever possible I have used primary sources. I have also tried to present the material, including the index, in a way which will help to answer questions like: What is an MOU? Where can I find the text of a treaty? Can part of a state make a treaty? When are full powers needed? What is consensus? What does Article 18 mean? How does 'dualism' work? Can a state withdraw an instrument of ratification? What is the status of treaties in the law of the United States? What does a depositary do? Can Hong Kong enter into treaties? How do I to set about drafting a treaty?

But this is not just a book by a legal practitioner for legal practitioners.

---

[1] Oscar Wilde, *Lady Windermere's Fan*, Act I.

1

Although legal advisers in foreign ministries and international organisations will, it is hoped, find it helpful, it has been written with a particular
eye to the needs of diplomats generally. All of them have to deal with treaties. Some will have had legal training; many not. Yet, there are few foreign
ministries which have a legal department staffed by professionally
qualified, full-time lawyers. Many will have diplomats with varying
degrees of legal training, but who will during their career do other jobs
with little legal content; and a lot of legal work has to be done by diplomats
with no legal training at all. Inevitably, their work will include treaties.

Like contracts in ordinary life, treaties are an indispensable tool of
diplomacy. Although the concepts of sovereignty and jurisdiction are
basic to a proper understanding of international law, problems involving
them do not constantly arise in the work of a diplomat. But every day a
treaty is being drafted, negotiated, concluded, signed, ratified, interpreted
and – it is hoped more rarely – breached. Many ordinary human activities
are governed by treaties, although usually without those affected (including most diplomats) being aware of it. Some activities are possible only
because they are authorised by treaties. The operation of civil aircraft
engaged in international transport is regulated by a vast and complex
network of multilateral and bilateral treaties.

Although this book does not presume to be a scholarly work, I hope it
will be of value to writers, teachers and students of international law.
Those who deal in specialised subjects, such as economic law, environmental law, EU law and human rights law, may also find things to interest
them. They, and students of politics and international relations, need to
have an understanding of the international legal framework within which
their field of study operates, and treaties are an essential part of that
framework.

Existing works in English on the law of treaties are either out-of-date,
cover only certain aspects of the subject, or are largely theoretical. The
scholarship and lucid style of McNair's Law of Treaties (2nd edn, 1961) can
still be read for its brilliant insights, but relies heavily on precedents from
the distant past, and from my country. McNair also published just five
years before the draft of what was to become the Vienna Convention
emerged from the International Law Commission. O'Connell's
International Law (2nd edn, 1970) suffered the disadvantage of being published just after the adoption of the Vienna Convention; and his chapters
on treaties rely heavily on judicial decisions rather than the practice of

states. Nevertheless, it is a masterly summary of the essentials of the law of treaties, and of problems which are still with us today. Blix and Emerson's *The Treaty Maker's Handbook* (1973) is limited to precedents of treaty forms and clauses, and is now rather dated. The chapters on treaties in *Satow's Guide to Diplomatic Practice* (5th edn, 1979) cover only a small part of the subject, and often more from an historical perspective. Sinclair's *The Vienna Convention on the Law of Treaties* (2nd edn, 1984) is an essential guide to the negotiation of the Convention, and explains with characteristic clarity the difficult issues which faced the negotiators and how they were dealt with, if not always resolved. But it is not, and does not purport to be, a comprehensive guide to treaty law and practice. Reuter's *Introduction to the Law of Treaties* (2nd English edn, 1995) is good to read and thought-provoking, but idiosyncratic. The best concise modern guide to the law of treaties is in Jennings and Watts' ninth edition of *Oppenheim's International Law* (1992), but, although the incomparable footnotes are a valuable source of material, many practical aspects are not covered. I have, however, benefited greatly from that work and Sinclair's.

As far as possible this book illustrates law and practice by reference to precedents drawn from the last quarter of the twentieth century. Older precedents are cited only if they are still clearly relevant or instructive.

The Vienna Convention on the Law of Treaties is now thirty years old, and is likely to remain unchanged for many decades yet. Like the United Nations Charter, the intelligence of its drafting has enabled states to adapt their practice without distorting or departing from the Convention. The Convention codified, and to some degree developed, the law as it had evolved through the practice of states. But practice has not stood still since 1969. The Convention's rules provide a framework which is sufficiently flexible to accommodate important developments in state practice. Many of the provisions expressly envisage states agreeing to depart from the rules of the Convention. Article 7(1) requires the representative of a state to produce full powers in order to adopt the text of a treaty, but then immediately makes an exception in recognition that states may agree to dispense with full powers. This is just one, small example; in many other places the Convention recognises that states will depart from the Convention's rules.[2] The rules are thus largely residual, leaving treaty

---

[2] See also Articles 9(2), 10(a), 11, 12(1)(b), 13, 14(1)(b), 15, 16, 17(1), 20(1), (3) and (4)(b), 22, 24, 25, 28, 29, 33(1) and (2), 36(1), 37(1), 39, 40, 41, 44(1), 55–60, 70(1), 72(1), 76–78 and 79(1).

practice very much in the hands of states – as it should be. I do not therefore subscribe to the view that the Convention has had its day, that it is
incapable of coping with the demands of the twenty-first century. In my
experience, which I believe is shared by other practitioners for whom the
Convention is their 'bible', it does not need mending, or rather, amending.
As I will seek to demonstrate, it has proved itself to be a most adaptable
tool, well able to deal with the challenges to treaty-making presented by
the changes in international life in the last thirty years.

Because of the central role played by the Convention, a good deal of the
book is a commentary on it. I know only too well the frustration of trying
to find out – and under pressure – precisely what an article of the
Convention means and how it has been applied. I hope this book will go
some way to help.

How to use this book

Unless the context indicates otherwise, references to 'the Convention',
'the Vienna Convention', 'the 1969 Convention' or 'the Convention itself'
are to the Vienna Convention on the Law of Treaties 1969; and, unless
otherwise indicated, a reference simply to, for example, 'Article 18' is to
an article of the Convention. The term 'MOU' refers to a non-legally
binding instrument.[3] There is a list of other abbreviations at pages
xxxvi–xxxix above.

The footnotes

The footnotes are for the most part not substantive, but are there to make
it as easy as possible for the reader to check a statement or follow up a point
by further reading. The book can be read and understood without reading
any of the footnotes.

Other aids

A glossary of legal terms on pages xxxiii–xxxv above has been included to
help those who are not lawyers, or at least not international lawyers. The
table on page 432 below lists where in this book particular articles of the

---

[3] For a fuller explanation of the term, see pp. 17–18 below, and Chapter 3.

Vienna Convention on the Law of Treaties are cited, and may prove useful when the reader is in a hurry.

Emphasis

When words in a quotation are *emphasised*, the emphasis is mine unless otherwise indicated.

Errors and omissions

Inevitably you will find mistakes and omissions, and no doubt disagree with my views. Your suggestions and comments would be much appreciated, and can be sent to me at home or at work, or c/o CUP, Publishing Division, Cambridge CB2 2RU, United Kingdom (fax ++44 (0)1223 315052; e-mail information@cup.cam.ac.uk).

The Vienna Convention on the Law of Treaties

> The Convention clearly marked the beginning of a
> new era in the law of treaties.[1]

A large part of this book is necessarily devoted to the Vienna Convention on the Law of Treaties. Although the Convention does not occupy the whole ground of the law of treaties, it covers the most important areas and is the starting point for any description of the modern law and practice of treaties. It thus merits a short introduction. The other purpose of this chapter is to define the scope of this book by mentioning briefly those aspects of the law of treaties which the Convention does not deal with, but which will be covered in this book.

The Convention is one of the prime achievements of the International Law Commission. The Commission was established by the UN General Assembly in 1947 with the object of promoting the progressive development of international law and its codification. The law of treaties was one of the topics selected by the Commission at its first session in 1949 as being suitable for codification. A series of eminent British international legal scholars (James Brierly, Hersch Lauterpacht, Gerald Fitzmaurice and Humphrey Waldock) were appointed as Special Rapporteurs. The Commission adopted a final set of draft articles in 1966. They were considered by the United Nations Conference on the Law of Treaties in Vienna in 1968 and 1969. The Convention was adopted on 22 May 1969 and entered into force on 27 January 1980. By the end of 1998 it had only eighty-four parties out of the some 190 states there are today.[2] Some of the reasons for this will be discussed below.

The full text of the Convention is at Appendix A.

[1] P. Reuter, *Introduction to the Law of Treaties* (2nd. English edn, 1995), para. 32.
[2] The 188 members of the United Nations do not include, for example, the Holy See, Switzerland or Tuvalu, although Andorra, Liechtenstein, Monaco and San Marino became members in the early 1990s and Kiribati, Nauru and Tonga in 1999.

Scope of the Convention

The Convention sets out the law and procedure for the making, operation and termination of a treaty. The Convention does not apply to all international agreements, only those between states (Article 1). Nor is it concerned with the substance of a treaty as such. That is a matter for the parties to the treaty.

Oral agreements

For reasons of clarity and simplicity oral agreements were excluded from the Convention. But this does not affect their legal force, or the application to them of any of the rules in the Convention to which they would be subject under international law independently of the Convention, such as customary international law[3] (Article 3(a)). Oral agreements between states, although rare, are not unknown even today. The dispute between Denmark and Finland about the construction of a Danish bridge across the Store Bælt (Great Belt) was settled in 1992 by a telephone conversation between the Danish and Finnish Prime Ministers, in which, in return for a payment by Denmark, Finland agreed to discontinue its case before the International Court of Justice. There is no joint record of the agreement.[4] US law requires an oral agreement to be reduced to writing by the US Government.[5]

Treaties with or between other subjects of international law

States do not enter into treaties only with other states; they enter into treaties with other subjects of international law, in particular international organisations; and international organisations enter into treaties with each other. The Convention does not apply to such treaties, which are the subject of the Vienna Convention on the Law of Treaties between States and International Organisations or between International Organisations 1986,[6] which, in effect, applies to such treaties the provisions of the 1969 Convention, suitably adapted. Although the 1986 Convention is not yet in force, there can be little doubt that its provisions,

---

[3]   See p. 10 below for an explanation of customary international law
[4]   *Finnish Yearbook of International Law* (1992), pp. 610–13, and ILM (1993), p. 103.
[5]   See pp. 32–3 below.   [6]   ILM (1986), p. 543.

following closely as they do those of the 1969 Convention[7], are generally accepted as the applicable law. Although the 1969 Convention does not apply to treaties between states and international organisations, such as a host country agreement, in so far as the rules of the Convention reflect the rules of customary international law applicable to treaties with international organisations, they will apply (Article 3(b)). Where states which are parties to the 1969 Convention are parties to a treaty to which other subjects of international law, in particular international organisations such as the European Community, are also parties, *as between the states parties* it is the 1969 Convention which applies, not customary international law (Article 3(c)).

No retrospective effect

The Convention applies to only those treaties which are concluded by states after the date the Convention enters into force for those states (Article 4).[8] There is no problem in applying this rule to bilateral treaties. In the case of a multilateral treaty, the Convention will apply to those states which participated in the conclusion of the treaty after the Convention entered into force for them, but not for other states.[9] The Convention entered into force on 27 January 1980. The UN Convention on the Law of the Sea (UNCLOS) was concluded on 10 December 1982. Thus for those states which were parties to the Convention on that date, its rules will apply as between them with regard to UNCLOS. Article 4 provides, however, that the rule against retrospection is without prejudice to the application of any rules in the Convention to which treaties would be subject under international law independently of the Convention. Thus, those rules of the Convention which reflect customary international law apply (but as customary law) to treaties concluded before the entry into force of the Convention, or concluded afterwards but before the Convention entered into force for parties to those treaties.[10]

---

[7] The first seventy-two articles deal with the same subjects as Articles 1–72 of the 1969 Convention.

[8] For an account of the negotiation of Article 4, see Sinclair, p. 230. See also P. McDade, 'The Effect of Article 4 of the Vienna Convention on the Law of Treaties 1969', ICLQ (1986), pp. 499–511; and E. Vierdag, 'The Time of the "Conclusion" of a Multilateral Treaty', BYIL (1988), pp. 75–111.   [9] See Sinclair, pp. 8–9.   [10] As to the *Gabcikovo* case, see p. 11 below.

International organisations

Since the constituent instrument (i.e., the constitution) of an international organisation and a treaty adopted *within* the organisation are made by states, the Convention applies to such instruments, but this is without prejudice to any relevant rules of the organisation (Article 5). Those rules may, for example, govern the procedure by which treaties are adopted within the organisation, how they are to be amended and the making of reservations.[11]

State succession, state responsibility and the outbreak of hostilities

For the avoidance of doubt, Article 73 confirms that the Convention does not prejudge any question that may arise in regard to a treaty from a succession of states,[12] from the international responsibility of a state (for breach of a treaty),[13] or from the outbreak of hostilities.[14] The Convention does not deal with these matters, which are largely governed by customary international law, and are discussed here in later chapters.

Bilateral and multilateral treaties

The term 'bilateral' describes a treaty between two states, and 'multilateral' a treaty between three or more states. There are, however, bilateral treaties where two or more states form one party, and another state or states the other party.[15] For the most part the Convention does not distinguish between bilateral and multilateral treaties. Article 60(1) is the only provision limited to bilateral treaties. Articles 40, 41, 58 and 60 refer expressly to multilateral treaties, and the provisions on reservations and the depositary are relevant only to such treaties.

The Convention and customary international law

The various provisions mentioned above, and the preamble to the Convention, confirm that the rules of customary international law continue

---

[11] See, for example, p. 109 below on the rules for reservations to ILO Conventions.
[12] See pp. 305–31 below.
[13] See pp. 300–4 below, and the *Gabcikovo* judgment, para. 47 (ILM (1998), p. 162).
[14] See pp. 243 below.   [15] See p. 19 below.

to govern questions not regulated by the Convention. Treaties and custom are the main sources of international law. Customary law is made up of two elements: (1) a general convergence in the practice of states from which one can extract a norm (standard of conduct), and (2) *opinio juris* – the belief by states that the norm is legally binding on them.[16] Some multilateral treaties largely codify customary law. But if a norm which is created by a treaty is followed in the practice of non-parties, it can, provided there is *opinio juris*, lead to the evolution of a customary rule which will be applicable between states which are not party to the treaty and between parties and non-parties. This can happen even before the treaty has entered into force.[17] Although many provisions of the UN Convention on the Law of the Sea 1982 (UNCLOS) went beyond mere codification of customary rules, the negotiations proceeded on the basis of consensus, even though the final text was put to the vote. It was therefore that much easier during the twelve years before UNCLOS entered into force in 1994 for most of its provisions to become accepted as representing customary law.[18] This was important since even by the end of 1998 UNCLOS still had only 127 parties.

An accumulation of bilateral treaties on the same subject, such as investment promotion and protection, may in certain circumstances be evidence of a customary rule.[19]

To what extent does the Convention express rules of customary international law?[20]

A detailed consideration of this question is beyond the scope of this book, but it is, with certain exceptions,[21] not of great concern to the foreign ministry lawyer in his day-to-day work. When questions of treaty law arise during negotiations, whether for a new treaty or about one concluded before the entry into force of the Convention, the rules set forth in the Convention are invariably relied upon even when the states are not parties to it. The writer can recall at least three bilateral treaty negotiations when he had to respond

---

[16] See M. Shaw, *International Law* (4th edn, 1998), pp. 54–77.
[17] See H. Thirlway, 'The Law and Procedure of the International Court of Justice', BYIL (1990), p. 87.
[18] See T. Treves, 'Codification du droit international et pratique des Etats dans le droit de la mer', *Hague Recueil* (1990), IV, vol. 223, pp. 25–60; and H. Caminos and M. Molitor, 'Progressive Development of International Law and the Package Deal', AJIL (1985), pp. 871–90.
[19] See Thirlway, 'Law and Procedure', at p. 86.   [20] See Sinclair, pp. 10–24.
[21] See p. 127 below about the time limit for notifying objections to reservations.

to arguments of the other side which relied heavily on specific articles of the Convention, even though the other side had not ratified it. When this happens the justification for invoking the Convention is rarely made clear.

Whether a particular rule in the Convention represents customary international law is only likely to be an issue if the matter is litigated, and even then the court or tribunal will take the Convention as its starting – and normally also its finishing – point. This is certainly the approach taken by the International Court of Justice, as well as other courts and tribunals, international and national.[22] In its 1997 *Gabcikovo* judgment (in which the principal treaty at issue predated the entry into force of the Convention for the parties to the case) the Court brushed aside the question of the possible non-applicability of the Convention's rules to questions of termination and suspension of treaties, and applied Articles 60–62 as reflecting customary law, even though they had been considered rather controversial.[23] Given previous similar pronouncements by the Court, and mentioned in the judgment, it is reasonable to assume that the Court will take the same approach in respect of virtually all of the substantive provisions of the Convention. There has been as yet no case where the Court has found that the Convention does not reflect customary law.[24] But this is not so surprising. Despite what some critics of the Convention may say, as with any codification of the law the Convention inevitably reduces the scope for judicial law-making. For most practical purposes treaty questions are resolved by applying the rules of the Convention. To attempt to determine whether a particular provision of the Convention represents customary international law is now usually a rather futile task. As Sir Arthur Watts has said in the foreword to this book, the modern law of treaties is now authoritatively set out in the Convention.

Effect of emerging customary law on prior treaty rights and obligations

Most treaties are bilateral, and most multilateral treaties are also contractual in nature in that they do not purport to lay down rules of general

---

[22] Numerous examples, particularly concerning Articles 31 and 32 (Interpretation) are to be found in *International Law Reports* (see the lengthy entry in the ILR Consolidated Table of Cases and Treaties, vols. 1–80 (1991), pp. 799–801).

[23] At paras. 42–6 and 99 (*ICJ Reports* (1997), p.7; ILM (1998), p. 162).

[24] M. Mendelson in Lowe and Fitzmaurice (eds), *Fifty Years of the International Court of Justice* (1996), at p. 66, and E. Vierdag (note 8 above) at pp. 145–6. See also H. Thirlway, 'The Law and Procedure of the International Court of Justice', BYIL (1991), p. 3.

application. But, since 1945 so-called 'law-making' treaties have become so numerous that a sizeable number of topics have come to be regulated by both customary law and treaty law. Whether the emergence of a new rule of customary law can supplant a prior treaty rule seems to have been studied in depth only quite recently.[25] The view has been expressed that international law has no hierarchy of sources of law, custom and treaty being autonomous; and that, even when custom has been codified, it retains its separate existence. This is a controversial theory,[26] and does not reflect the approach to legal problems taken by foreign ministry legal advisers, who, when dealing with an actual problem, naturally give more weight to an applicable treaty rule than a different customary rule. Nevertheless, new customary rules which emerge from economic changes or dissatisfaction with a treaty rule can result in a modification in the operation of a treaty rule. In the *Fisheries Jurisdiction* cases (*United Kingdom* v. *Iceland*; *Federal Republic of Germany* v. *Iceland*) in 1974, the International Court of Justice decided that, since the adoption in 1958 of the High Seas Convention, the right of states to establish twelve-mile fishing zones had crystallised as customary law, despite the provisions in that Convention regarding freedom of fishing on the high seas.[27]

Nor does international law contain any *acte contraire* principle by which a rule can be altered only by a rule of the same legal nature. Article 68(c) in the International Law Commission's 1964 draft of the Convention provided that the operation of a treaty may be modified by the 'subsequent emergence of a new rule of customary international law relating to matters dealt with in the treaty and binding upon all the parties'.[28] Although the article was not included in the final text of the Convention, this was only because the International Law Commission did not see its mandate as extending to the general relationship between customary law and treaty law.

Reference material on the Convention

The single most valuable source of material on the meaning and effect of the articles of the Convention remains the Commentary of the

---

[25] See M. Villiger, *Customary International Law and Treaties* (2nd edn, 1997); K. Wolfe, 'Treaties and Custom: Aspects of Interrelation', in Klabbers and Lefeber (eds.), *Essays on the Law of Treaties* (1998), pp. 31–9; and *Oppenheim*, pp. 31–6.

[26] See *Nicaragua* (*Merits*), *ICJ Reports* (1986), p. 92, paras. 172–82; and H. Thirlway, 'The Law and Procedure of the International Court of Justice', BYIL (1989), pp. 143–4.

[27] *ICJ Reports* (1974), p. 3 at pp. 13 and 37.   [28] YBILC (1964), II, p. 198.

International Law Commission on its draft articles and contained in its final report on the topic.[29] The history of the drafting of the articles is in the Yearbooks of the Commission beginning in 1950. However, since the Vienna Conference naturally made changes to the draft articles, one needs to refer also to the summary records of the Conference.[30] A comprehensive guide to the negotiating history (*travaux*) has been produced by Rosenne.[31] This should be used in conjunction with Wetzel's book, which has the text, in English, of all the most important *travaux*.[32] There are useful accounts of the negotiations in Sinclair and by Kearney and Dalton,[33] who took part in the Vienna Conference.

---

[29] YBILC (1966), II, pp. 173–274. See now A. Watts, *The International Law Commission, 1949–1998* (1999), vol. II, Chapter 8.

[30] UN Doc. A/Conf. 39/11 and Add. 1. The *documents* produced at the Conference are in A/Conf. 39/11/Add. 2.   [31] S. Rosenne, *The Law of Treaties* (1970).

[32] Wetzel and Rausching, *The Vienna Convention on the Law of Treaties: Travaux Préparatoires* (1978).   [33] AJIL (1970), pp. 495–561.

2

What is a treaty?

the intolerable wrestle with words and meanings.[1]

Like the Vienna Convention, this book is primarily concerned with treaties between *states*. Article 2(1)(a) defines a 'treaty' as:

> an international agreement concluded between States in written form and governed by international law, whether embodied in a single instrument or in two or more related instruments and whatever its particular designation.

As with most of the Convention, although the definition is expressed to be for the purposes of the Convention and is limited to treaties between states, its elements now represent customary law. As we shall see, the difficult question is not with the definition itself, but whether a particular instrument or transaction falls within the definition.[2] An examination of the elements of the definition will go some way to answer that question, as well as illustrating some of the key principles underlying the law of treaties.

Definition of 'treaty'

'an international agreement'

To be a treaty an agreement has to have an international character. When we examine the other elements of the definition we will see what that means. The Convention uses 'treaty' as a generic term. The constitution, law or practice of some states divide treaties variously into categories such as inter-state, inter-governmental, inter-ministerial or administrative.[3]

---

[1] T. S. Eliot, *East Coker*, Part 2.
[2] H. Thirlway, 'The Law and Procedure of the International Court of Justice', BYIL (1991), pp. 4–5.   [3] See Chapter 10 on treaties and domestic law.

The Convention does not recognise such distinctions. Treaties can also be described as 'universal' or 'regional', but this has no legal significance.[4] The term 'plurilateral' is, however, relevant in relation to reservations to treaties.[5]

The International Law Commission's Commentary makes it clear that the definition of treaty includes those international agreements which by the 1960s were increasingly being drafted in a less formal manner.[6] For example, there is no difference in legal effect between a treaty contained in a single instrument and one constituted by an exchange of notes, provided it satisfies the other elements of the definition (see the examples in Appendices B and E). In 1945 there was still some uncertainty whether international agreements drafted in a less formal way could properly be called treaties, and this was reflected in Article 102 of the United Nations Charter which requires the registration of 'every treaty and every international agreement'. By the 1960s there was no longer any doubt on the matter.

'concluded between states'

A treaty can be concluded between a state and another subject of international law, in particular an international organisation, or between international organisations, but this is outside the scope of the Convention, and of this book. An agreement between international or multinational companies, or even between a state and such a company, is not a treaty. The International Court of Justice has held that an oil concession granted by a state to a foreign company was not a treaty because the state of nationality of the company was not party to the concession.[7] Even when, as sometimes happens, an agreement between a state and a company provides that it shall be interpreted in whole or in part by reference to rules of international law, that does not make it a treaty.[8] There are, however, a small number of agreements between states to which non-state entities are also parties, but this does not affect their status as treaties.[9]

---

[4] But see McNair, pp. 739–54, on the differing legal character of treaties.
[5] See p. 112–13 below.   [6] YBILC (1966), II, p. 173 at pp. 188–9.
[7] *Anglo-Iranian Oil Company* (*United Kingdom* v. *Iran*) (*Preliminary Objections*) *ICJ Reports* (1952), p. 93 at p. 112.
[8] See C. Greenwood, 'The Libyan Oil Arbitrations', BYIL (1982), pp. 27–81. See pp. 24–5 below about agreements between states which are governed by domestic law.   [9] See p. 53 below.

In the nineteenth century agreements between imperial powers and the representatives of indigenous peoples, such as the Treaty of Waitangi 1840 by which Maori chiefs ceded New Zealand to the British Crown,[10] were often drawn in the same form as a treaty and described as such.[11] But, since the land occupied by such peoples was not considered at the time to be a state, such agreements are not treaties, even if they had, and continue to have, effects in domestic law.[12]

But a treaty does not have to be expressed to be between states as such. Since a state is a legal concept, not a natural person, its head of state, its government or some other agency of the state has to act on behalf of the state. A treaty may therefore be expressed to be concluded by heads of state, governments, ministries or other state agencies.[13]

'in written form'

The Vienna Convention does not apply to oral agreements.[14] But, even though the modern practice is for the original text of a treaty to be typed or printed, there is no reason why a treaty should not be contained in a telegram, telex, fax message or even e-mail, or, rather, constituted by an exchange of such communications. Provided the text can be reduced to a permanent, readable form (even if this is done by down-loading and printing-out from a computer), it can be regarded as in written form. The absence of original signed copies is not a problem, provided there is a means of authenticating the 'signature'.[15] In September 1998 a Communiqué on Electronic Commerce was issued by US President Clinton and Irish Prime Minister Ahern by electronic means. They did so by each operating a separate computer terminal and, using an electronic signature, that is a signature in digital form which is in, attached to or associated with the data (in this case the Communiqué) and used to indicate the approval by the 'signatory' of the content of the data. The 'signature' must therefore be uniquely linked to the signatory, identify him, be created by means under his sole control and connected to the data in a way

---

[10] 6 Hertslet 579; 29 BFSP 1111.

[11] See the 1815 Treaty between the United States and the Sioux and other Indian tribes (65 CTS 81).

[12] See McNair, pp. 52–4; *Oppenheim*, para. 595, note 2; D. O'Connell, *International Law* (2nd edn), vol. 1, p. 440.   [13] See also pp. 47–8 below.   [14] See p. 7 above.

[15] Cf. section 5 of the (UK) Arbitration Act 1996 (ILM (1997), p. 165); and see p. 24 below.

which would reveal if it were to be subsequently altered unilaterally. This can be done with a 'smart card'.[16] Although the Communiqué was not a treaty, it may not be too fanciful to envisage full powers, instruments of ratification or even treaties being signed and deposited electronically. One should not, however, get too excited with such developments. Given the mistakes made now in treaties and treaty procedures, there is no reason to suppose that information technology will necessarily improve matters.[17]

'governed by international law'

According to the International Law Commission's Commentary, the phrase 'governed by international law' embraces the element of an *intention to create obligations under international law*. If there is no such intention the instrument will not be a treaty. In the *Aegean Sea Continental Shelf* case, the International Court of Justice considered the terms of a joint communiqué issued by the Greek and Turkish Prime Ministers, and the particular circumstances in which it was drawn up, in order to determine its nature. The Court found that there had been no intention to conclude an agreement to submit to the jurisdiction of the Court.[18] Thus intention must be gathered from the terms of the instrument itself and the circumstances of its conclusion, not from what the parties say afterwards was their intention.[19]

Although the law of treaties does not require a treaty to be in any particular form or to use special wording,[20] lawyers practising in foreign or other ministries deliberately utilise instruments which employ carefully chosen terminology to indicate that, rather than creating international legal rights and obligations, the intention of the participants is to record no more than mutual *understandings* as to how they will conduct themselves (see Appendices C and D). The existence of such instruments, and the extent to which they are a significant vehicle for the conduct of business between

[16] Unfortunately the President and the Prime Minister were in the same room: see *Financial Times*, 7 October 1998, IT review, p. xv, which, uncharacteristically for that paper, described the 'document' as a treaty. The European Community is drafting a directive on a common framework for electronic signatures, from which these technical details have been taken.

[17] See pp. 270–3 below on the problem of errors.

[18] *ICJ Reports* (1978), p. 3 at pp. 39–44. See H. Thirlway, 'The Law and Procedure of the International Court of Justice', BYIL (1991), pp. 13–15.

[19] *Qatar v. Bahrain, ICJ Reports* (1994), p. 112 at paras. 26–7.

[20] See the *Temple of Preah Vihear (Preliminary Objections) ICJ Reports* (1961), pp. 31–2.

states, is not well known outside government circles. In fact, a large number of such instruments, bilateral and multilateral, are concluded every year covering a wide range of subjects. Most are never published. A recent (published) example of such a multilateral instrument is the Memorandum of Understanding on Port State Control in the Caribbean Region 1996.[21]

Such instruments have been variously described as 'gentlemen's agreements', 'non-binding agreements', 'de facto agreements' and 'non-legal agreements'. These non-legally binding instruments are most commonly referred to by the initials 'MOU'. This is short for 'Memorandum of Understanding', since this is the name most often given to them. However, as will be explained shortly, calling an instrument a 'Memorandum of Understanding' does not, in itself, determine its status, since – and most confusingly – some treaties are also given that name.[22]

How to distinguish between a treaty and an MOU, how and why MOUs are used, and their possible legal consequences, is discussed in detail in the next chapter.

'whether embodied in a single instrument or in two or more related instruments'

This phrase recognises that the classic form for a treaty – a single instrument (Appendix B) – has for a long time been joined by treaties drawn in less formal ways, such as exchanges of notes. These play an increasingly important role. An exchange of notes usually consists of an initiating note and a reply note (Appendix E). But in 1994, in *Qatar v. Bahrain*, the International Court of Justice had to consider the legal effect of a *double* exchange of letters between (1) Qatar and Saudi Arabia and (2) Bahrain and Saudi Arabia.[23] Saudi Arabia, having agreed to use its good offices to help solve certain territorial disputes between the other two states sent each of them letters in identical terms proposing certain settlement procedures. Each wrote to Saudi Arabia accepting the proposal. Saudi Arabia then announced that the two states had agreed to go to arbitration. This complicated scheme was necessary because of political sensitivities, but the text of each letter and of the announcement were agreed in advance;

---

[21] ILM (1997), p. 237. See also the list of MOUs at p. xxx above
[22] See pp. 20–1 below.   [23] *ICJ Reports* (1994), p. 112; ILM (1994), p. 1461 (see para. 17).

and although three states were involved there were only two parties, Qatar and Bahrain. Although the form of a double exchange was unusual, there are several examples of treaties being constituted by three or more principal instruments (important treaties may have several subsidiary instruments).[24] The arrangements for dealing with claims between Iran and the United States, including the establishment of the Iran–US Claims Tribunal, were established in 1981 by (1) a Declaration by the Algerian Government setting out the formal commitments which had been made to it by Iran and the United States (a similar arrangement to that used later by Saudi Arabia); (2) an Iran–US Agreement which entered into force on receipt by Algeria of a 'notification of adherence' by each party; and (3) an Escrow Agreement between the United States, the Federal Reserve Bank of New York, Bank Markazi, Iran and the Central Bank of Algeria, as escrow agent.[25]

A treaty which is part bilateral and part multilateral can be constituted by a series of parallel exchanges of notes, all identical in substance, between one state and a number of states (A–B; A–C; A–D etc.).[26] In such a case it is important to make clear in the notes who are the parties. In an exchange between, say, four states there could be four parties (A, B, C and D), or two (A and B+C+D).[27] In such a case, when there are only two parties it may also be necessary to make clear whether the treaty can be terminated only by one of the parties, or whether one of the states constituting a party can, by denouncing the treaty, bring about its termination.

The drafting of normal exchanges of notes is discussed in the final chapter.[28]

'whatever its particular designation'

One of the most mystifying aspects of treaty practice is the unsystematic way in which treaties are designated (named). Writers have sought to explain, sometimes at great length and not very convincingly, why certain

---

[24] For an example of a triple exchange, and other multiple exchanges, see *Satow*, para. 29.38.

[25] ILM (1981), p. 230; 62 ILR 599; AJIL (1981), p. 418.

[26] See the six parallel Exchanges of Notes between Germany and Belgium, Canada, France, Netherlands, United Kingdom and United States (ILM (1991), pp. 415 and 417; and McNair, pp. 29–30).

[27] See the two Memoranda of Understanding on the Avoidance of Overlaps and Conflicts relating to Deep Seabed Areas of 1991 (UKTS (1991) 52 and UKTS (1995) 4).

[28] At pp. 355–6 below.

names are given to particular categories of treaty.[29] That task has become even more difficult today, the names chosen being even more confusing, inconsistent and changeable than in the past. It is often more a matter of the practice of international organisations or groups of states, or political preference, which determines how a treaty is named. But, whatever the position may have been in the nineteenth or early twentieth centuries, the name does not, in itself, determine the status of the instrument; what is decisive is whether the negotiating states intended the instrument to be (or not to be) legally binding. Thus, just as one should never judge a book by its cover, one should not assume that the name given to an international instrument automatically indicates its status either as a treaty or an MOU. Although it is reasonable to assume that an instrument called a treaty, agreement or convention is a treaty, one should nevertheless examine the text to make quite sure. Most other names are problematic. Both the UN Charter and the Charter of the Commonwealth of Independent States 1993 (CIS)[30] are treaties, but the OSCE Charter of Paris 1990[31] and the Russia–United States Charter of Partnership and Friendship 1992[32] are MOUs.

Memorandum of understanding

One must be especially careful about the status of any instrument called 'Memorandum of Understanding'. This designation is most commonly used for MOUs in the sense described above, but occasionally one will find a treaty called a Memorandum of Understanding. Only by studying the terms of an instrument can one determine its status. Some have been misled into believing that because an instrument is called a Memorandum of Understanding it cannot be a treaty. Conversely, others have mistakenly assumed an instrument designated Memorandum of Understanding must be a treaty because several bearing that name have been registered as treaties.

The practice of designating a treaty a Memorandum of Understanding appears to have started in a small way after the Second World War, three being concluded in the 1950s in connection with the Treaty of Peace with

---

[29] See *Satow*, paras. 29.9–29.33, 30 and 31.1–31.22.   [30] ILM (1995), p. 1282.
[31] ILM (1991), p. 193; A. Bloed (ed.), *The Conference on Security and Co-operation in Europe* (1993), pp. 537–50.   [32] ILM (1992), p. 782.

Italy.[33] The reason may have been a desire, perhaps for political reasons, for a less formal appearance. More recent examples of treaties designated as Memorandums of Understanding are the Memorandum of Understanding relating to the Implementation of the Guidelines for Transfers of Nuclear-Related Dual-Use Equipment 1992;[34] the two Memorandums of Understanding of 1991 on the Avoidance of Overlaps and Conflicts relating to Deep Sea-Bed Areas;[35] and the Memorandum of Understanding concerning the establishment of the Inter-Organisation Programme for the Sound Management of Chemicals 1995.[36] The United Nations frequently concludes treaties called Memorandum of Understanding, for example, the (ill-fated) Iraq–UN Memorandum of Understanding 1998 concerning weapons inspections.[37] An even more misleading name for a treaty is the *Provisional Understanding* regarding Deep Seabed Matters 1984.[38] On the other hand, the Paris Memorandum of Understanding on Port State Control 1982 is unquestionably an MOU.[39]

Exchange of notes

Exchanges of notes (or letters) pose the same problem since they may constitute either a treaty or an MOU. Hundreds, possibly thousands, are concluded each year. If the exchange is intended to be a treaty it is customary to provide expressly that it '*shall constitute an agreement* between our two Governments' (see Appendix E). If intended to be an MOU, it is usual to specify that the exchange '*records the understanding* of our two Governments', or a similar formula (see Appendix F). Although exchanges of notes tend not to be on matters of major political importance, or only supplementary to a treaty, a few have been substantial. The 1940 'Lend-Lease Agreement' between the United Kingdom and the United States, under which the United Kingdom was lent 60 badly needed destroyers in return for leases of bases, was constituted by an exchange of notes.[40]

---

[33] UKTS (1956) 52 and UKTS (1957) 51. See also the Memorandum of Understanding regarding German Assets in Italy 1947 (138 UNTS 111; UKTS (1947) 75) and the Memorandum of Understanding on the Application of the MFN Agreement 1949 to the Western Sectors of Berlin (42 UNTS 356; UKTS (1950) 7).   [34] ILM (1992), p. 1097.
[35] UKTS (1991) 52 and UKTS (1995) 4.   [36] ILM (1995), p. 1315.
[37] ILM (1998), p. 501. See also the Iraq–UN Memorandum of Understanding 1996 (ILM (1996), p. 1097).   [38] ILM (1984), p. 1354; UKTS (1985) 24.   [39] ILM (1982), p. 1.
[40] 203 LNTS 201 and 204 LNTS 15.

Guidance on drafting both types of exchange of notes is at pages 355–8 below.

Less usual treaty names

Treaties have always been given a variety of names, including less usual ones like Compact, Solemn Declaration, Administrative Agreement,[41] Protocol of Decisions, Platform, Concordat,[42] Agreed Minute[43] and Terms of Reference.[44] In 1992 a treaty between Lithuania and Russia on the withdrawal of Russian forces from Lithuania was concluded with the name 'Timetable', its substance consisting of detailed tables of military assets. The document was originally annexed to a treaty on the same subject. There was a political problem over signature of the treaty, but, since it was important that the withdrawal should proceed on a proper basis, the 'Timetable' was signed, and later registered as a treaty with the United Nations.[45] A supplementary treaty to the Comprehensive Nuclear-Test-Ban Treaty 1996 (CTBT), adopted by a resolution of the signatory states, is called simply 'Text'.[46]

Titles can be enigmatic, sometimes deliberately. The Joint Declaration of China and the United Kingdom on the Future of Hong Kong 1984 is clearly a treaty, and was registered as such with the United Nations by both parties.[47] The title was chosen for political reasons. On the other hand, since 1989 Argentina and the United Kingdom have made various 'Joint Declarations' and 'Joint Statements' recording the outcome of meetings between their representatives on matters concerning the Falkland Islands, including fishing and oil exploration in the south-west Atlantic. These documents sometimes include substantial provisions. Although they occasionally use some treaty-type terminology ('agree' and 'shall'), they are not otherwise in normal treaty form.[48] Further evidence that these

---

[41] See UKTS (1999) 5.   [42] See *Satow*, paras. 30.11–30.15.

[43] Canada–EC Agreed Minute on Conservation and Management of Fish Stocks 1995 (ILM (1995), p. 1262).

[44] Agreement establishing the International Copper Study Group in 1989 (1605 UNTS 211 (No. 28026)).

[45] UN Reg. No. 29146. Unpublished so far in English; English translation on file with the author.

[46] UKTS (1999) 46.

[47] 1399 UNTS 33 (No. 23391); ILM (1984), p. 1366; UKTS (1985) 26.

[48] See the Argentina–United Kingdom Joint Declaration on Co-operation over Offshore Activities in the Southwest Atlantic 1995 (ILM (1996), p. 304; and p. 301 which refers to earlier Joint Declarations).

Joint Declarations were not intended to create legal obligations is that they usually provide that they will be sent to the UN Secretary-General for distribution as official documents of the General Assembly, thus implying that the two states do not intend that they should be registered with the Secretary-General as treaties,[49] and none have been registered. While Argentina continues to assert its claim to the Falkland Islands it may be reluctant to enter into treaties with the United Kingdom about the territory, even though it did so before 1982.[50]

In the distant past a Final Act occasionally constituted a treaty,[51] but this is no longer so.

Colloquial names

The Convention on International Civil Aviation 1944 was adopted in Chicago, and is more usually referred to as the Chicago Convention.[52] Sometimes a treaty which is adopted in one state but signed in another will be known – at least colloquially – by the name of the place where it was adopted. The General Framework Agreement for Peace in Bosnia and Herzegovina 1995 is generally, and most conveniently, referred to in English as the Dayton Agreement after the place it was adopted, though it was signed in Paris.[53] The Landmines Convention 1997 is known also as the Ottawa Convention, since it was conceived and opened for signature there, although adopted in Oslo.[54] The Locarno Pact 1925[55] was negotiated at Locarno but signed in a room in the Foreign Office in London, and which has been known ever since as the Locarno Room. There are other examples.[56] And the media have much to answer for. A treaty is rarely called a Pact, but this term is regularly used by journalists as convenient shorthand, and who can blame them? The Locarno Pact was a series of treaties. The famous Kellogg–Briand Pact of 1928 was the General Treaty for the Renunciation of War.[57]

Unless it is clear from the context which treaty is being referred to, one should avoid shorthand terms such as 'Hague Convention', 'Geneva

---

[49] See the first Joint Declaration (of Madrid) 1989 (ILM (1990), p. 129, para. 13).
[50] For example, the Exchange of Notes of 1971 concerning Communications between the Falkland Islands and the Argentine Mainland (825 UNTS 143 (No. 11824); UKTS (1972) 64).
[51] *Satow*, para. 31.11.   [52] 15 UNTS 295 (No. 102); UKTS (1953) 8.   [53] ILM (1996), p. 75.
[54] ILM (1997), p. 1509; UKTS (1999) 18.   [55] 54 LNTS 305.
[56] See the letters page of the London *Times* for 14 December 1995.
[57] 94 LNTS 57; UKTS (1929) 29.

Convention' or 'Vienna Convention' since there are several treaties which have titles starting with those words.

A treaty does not have to be signed

There are other matters which the Convention does not deal with, at least explicitly. For example, the Convention's definition of treaty does not mention signature; and it is apparent from other provisions, such as Articles 12 and 13, that signature is not a prerequisite. A treaty can be constituted by an exchange of third-person diplomatic notes, which, according to long-standing diplomatic practice, are initialled but not signed.[58] There can be circumstances when the use of an unsigned instrument is preferred for polit-ical reasons. The Decision of the Heads of State and Government, adopted at a meeting within the European Council at the Edinburgh Summit on 12 December 1992, concerning certain problems raised by Denmark about the (Maastricht) Treaty on European Union, though not in customary treaty form is regarded by the Member States as a treaty and has been registered and published as such. Some of the leaders were reluctant to be seen to have signed it, and they were skilfully advised that they did not have to sign.[59]

A more routine example is to be found in the – otherwise uncommon – practice of the Food and Agriculture Organisation (FAO). Treaties adopted by the FAO Conference are not signed but are subject to 'accep-tance' by Member States, which is equivalent to ratification.[60] There may also be a tendency for states to conclude treaties by resolutions. As we have seen, the treaty establishing the Preparatory Commission of the Comprehensive-Nuclear Test-Ban Treaty 1996 (CTBT) was effected by a resolution of states which had signed the CTBT.[61]

Agreements between states governed by domestic law

States can also contract with each other under domestic law. They may do so if the subject matter is exclusively commercial, such as the purchase of

---

[58] See a China–UK exchange of notes of 1996 (UKTS (1996) 100).
[59] UKTS (1994) 2. It might also be seen as an agreement made in connection with the conclusion of a treaty (Article 31(2)(a)): see pp. 189–91 below.
[60] See, for example, the so-called 'Compliance Agreement' adopted at the FAO Conference in 1993 (ILM (1994), p. 968 (Article X)). See also the Convention on the Privileges and Immunities of the United Nations 1946 (1 UNTS 15 (No. 4)).
[61] See p. 22 above.

commodities in bulk. The law of the contract may be that of a third state. If a state leases land from another state for an embassy there will usually be an instrument under domestic law, such as a lease, though this may be granted pursuant to a treaty.[62] The fact that some of the provisions of a treaty refer to domestic law will not alter the status of the treaty. Treaties concerning loans may provide that the contractual arrangements for the loan shall be governed by the law of the lender state.[63]

Pactum de contrahendo

Latin phrases should always be approached with caution since they can conceal more than they reveal. This is especially so with *pactum de contrahendo*, the exact meaning of which is uncertain.[64] Fortunately, the term is rarely employed. It has been used to refer to an agreement to conclude a treaty; an agreement to include certain clauses in future agreements between the same parties; and an agreement to become party to a treaty which has already been concluded, such as the celebrated undertaking by Poland in the Treaty of Versailles to accede to the Berne Convention on Railway Transport.[65] The term should probably not be used to describe an agreement to negotiate a treaty, even though such an agreement must be carried out in good faith.[66]

Modus vivendi

A treaty is not usually so designated.[67] The term is used more to describe a treaty which is intended to be temporary.[68] It is also used for MOUs, particularly on fisheries matters.

For where to find treaties, see pages 280–4 below.

---

[62] Russia–UK Agreement on Leases of New Embassy Premises 1996 (UKTS (1997) 1). Contrary to popular belief, the land on which a state's embassy stands is *not* territory of that state.

[63] See the text of the Denmark–Malawi Loan Agreement 1966 (586 UNTS 3 (No. 8493)), Article XII; and F. Mann, *Studies in International Law* (1973), pp. 241–53. Grants by the US Government to other Governments under the Foreign Assistance Act 1961 are made under agreements governed by US federal law.

[64] McNair, pp. 27–9; *Oppenheim*, para. 599; O'Connell, p. 202.   [65] McNair, p. 29, note 1.

[66] See H. Thirlway, 'The Law and Procedure of the International Court of Justice', BYIL (1992), pp. 3–10.

[67] But see the Modus Vivendi between the Belgo-Luxemburg Economic Union and Turkey on MFN Treatment of 1947 (37 UNTS 223).

[68] See the Interim Agreement on the Fisheries Dispute between Iceland and the United Kingdom 1973 (UKTS (1973) 122), and *Fisheries Jurisdiction, ICJ Reports* (1974), p. 3 at p. 18.

3

MOUs[1]

Open covenants of peace, openly arrived at, after which there shall be
no private international understandings of any kind, but diplomacy
shall proceed always frankly and in the public view.

Since President Woodrow Wilson issued this understandable, but
slightly unworldly, appeal in 1919,[2] diplomacy has developed many new
ways of doing business. Diplomats know that it is impossible for all
international transactions, whether important or not, to be embodied
in treaties, even when the matter is proper and lawful. Hence the relent-
less rise of the MOU. As described briefly in the previous chapter, an
MOU is an instrument concluded between states which is not legally
binding.[3]

But first, a word of warning. Because the use of MOUs is now so widespread, some government officials may see the MOU as the more usual
form, a treaty being used only when it cannot be avoided. The very word
'treaty' may conjure up the fearsome formalities of diplomacy. One of the
tasks of legal advisers in foreign ministries is to explain the differences
between a treaty and an MOU, and why one might be preferable to the
other. In general, unless there is a particular advantage in having an MOU,
such as confidentiality, there may be no reason not to have a treaty. On the
other hand, there is, in principle, no reason to prefer a treaty to an MOU,
unless there is a need to create legally binding rights and obligations or,
because of the subject, there is a constitutional or other domestic legal
requirement for a treaty.

[1] This chapter is a much modified version of the author's 'The Theory and Practice of Informal
International Instruments', ICLQ (1986), pp. 787–812.
[2] AJIL (1919), p. 161. As to Wilson's naïve views concerning the Paris Peace Conference, see J. M.
Keynes, 'The Economic Consequences of the Peace', in *Collected Writings of John Maynard
Keynes*, (2nd edn, 1971), vol. II, pp. 23–34. [3] See pp. 17–18 above.

Evidence of intention to conclude (or not conclude) a legally binding instrument

The actual practice of states is to indicate their intention to conclude a treaty by consciously employing terminology such as 'shall', 'agree', 'undertake', 'rights', 'obligations' and 'enter into force'. When they do *not* intend to conclude a legally binding instrument, but rather an MOU, instead of 'shall' they use a less imperative term, such as 'will'. Terms like 'agree' or 'undertake' are avoided; the instrument is expressed to 'come into operation' or 'come into effect'; and most of the final clauses usually found in treaties, and the testimonium, are omitted or simplified. The instrument will normally be designated, in English, 'Memorandum of Understanding' or 'Arrangement'. However, as explained earlier, taken on its own the designation of an instrument can be most misleading; a 'Memorandum of Understanding' or an 'Exchange of Notes' may be a treaty or an MOU.[4] The terminology used for MOUs does not reflect practice with domestic law contracts, where the use of 'will' as opposed to 'shall' does not, in itself, necessarily denote an intention not to create a legally binding obligation. But nor should it be assumed that, just because an instrument contains treaty terminology, it is a treaty. A joint governmental statement will often utilise such language even though it is conveying only a political message, political statements being sometimes more impressive if couched in more assertive terms.[5]

A table comparing treaty and MOU terminology is at Appendix G. The main differences are illustrated by the treaty (Appendix B) and the MOUs (Appendices C and D). Guidance on treaty and MOU drafting is in Chapter 23.

Content

The subject matter of an instrument is not a guide to status, since the same subject matter can be found both in treaties and in MOUs. A notable exception is when the instrument contains a clause providing for the settlement of disputes by compulsory international judicial process, the

---

[4] See pp. 20–1 above.
[5] See the Joint Statement on Terrorism by the Iranian and Russian Foreign Ministers of 26 September 1998 (UN Doc. A/C.6/53/6); the Atlantic Charter 1941 (AJIL (1941), Supplement, p. 191); and McNair, p. 6.

inclusion of such a clause being hardly consistent with an intention to enter into a non-legally binding instrument.[6]

Express provisions as to status

The states which in 1975 adopted the Final Act of the Conference on (now Organisation for) Security and Co-operation in Europe made clear their intention not to enter into a treaty by stating at the end of the Final Act that it was 'not eligible for registration [i.e., as a treaty] under Article 102 of the Charter'.[7] The OSCE Charter of Paris 1990 also provides that it is not eligible for registration.[8] The OSCE Document of the Stockholm Conference on Confidence- and Security-Building Measures and Disarmament in Europe 1987 provides that: 'The Measures adopted in this Document are politically binding.'[9] Any doubt as to the status of the Declaration on Trade in Services, signed by Israel and the United States on 22 April 1985, is dispelled by the preamble which declares that: 'the principles set forth below shall not be legally-binding.'[10] An MOU adopted in 1992 by the UN Conference on Environment and Development (UNCED) is engagingly entitled 'Non-legally binding authoritative statement of principles regarding forests'.[11] The NATO–Russia Founding Act 1997 refers in its preamble to 'political' commitments.[12] When transmitting a copy of it to the UN Secretary-General, the NATO Secretary-General stated that it was not eligible for registration under Article 102. A recent (confidential) bilateral MOU included the statement that it 'represents a political commitment by the Sides [i.e. Governments] and does not constitute a legally-binding agreement'.

Such express statements seem to be a growing trend, particularly in MOUs with the United States. They and other categorical statements are conclusive as to the intended status of the instrument. But the use of such formulas is not yet common, and omitting them certainly does not, in itself, indicate that the instrument was intended to be a treaty. One should not therefore equate their use with a formula such as 'subject to contract', which is used constantly by lawyers in common law countries to prevent a document containing proposals from being held to be legally binding.

---

[6] See H. Thirlway, 'The Law and Procedure of the International Court of Justice', BYIL (1991), at pp. 7–8.   [7] ILM (1975), p. 1293. As to Article 102, see pp. 275–80 below.
[8] ILM (1991), p. 193.   [9] ILM (1987), p. 191 at p. 195, para. 101.
[10] ILM (1985), p. 679.   [11] ILM (1992), p. 882.   [12] ILM (1997), p. 1007.

Circumstances in which the instrument was concluded

If the form, terminology or express terms of the instrument do not contain sufficient evidence of the intention of the parties as to its status, it is necessary to consider the circumstances in which the instrument was drawn up, and the subsequent acts of its authors, such as non-registration.

Registration and non-registration

Registration of an instrument with the United Nations pursuant to Article 102 of the UN Charter does not confer on the instrument the status of a treaty if it does not already have that status.[13] Nevertheless, registration is generally good evidence that the states concerned regard it as a treaty. An examination of every tenth volume of the *United Nations Treaty Series* from 1980 to 1989 (inclusive)[14] produces only four instruments which are clearly MOUs. All were registered by the United States, three at the same time.[15] A treaty (usually bilateral) is sometimes registered by one party even though another party does not regard it as a treaty. Although non-registration is less of an indication as to the status of an instrument, in the US–UK Heathrow User Charges Arbitration 1988–1992 the Tribunal held that a UK–US MOU of 1988 was not legally binding, citing, among other factors, that it had not been published or registered with the United Nations or ICAO. But failure to register a treaty does not deprive it of treaty status, even if, in theory at least, the treaty cannot be invoked before an organ of the United Nations.[16]

Disagreement as to status

A nice problem can arise when differing views are held as to the status of an instrument, though this appears to happen chiefly with bilateral instruments. The author is aware of at least two instances of this coming to light when a bilateral instrument was on the point of being signed, and four after it had become effective. In two of the latter cases the disagreement only became apparent once a dispute had arisen, and this may well have been a factor. In both cases the instrument was supplementary to a treaty.

---

[13] See p. 279 below.   [14] Vols. 1160–1550 (Reg. Nos. 18323–26961).
[15] 1550 UNTS 3 (No. 26949); 1180 UNTS 83 (No. 18881); 1180 UNTS 163 (No. 18888); 1180 UNTS 179 (No. 18889).   [16] See further pp. 278–80 below.

In 1997 a bilateral MOU concluded by a ministry of the United Kingdom was submitted to the parliament of the other state for approval as a treaty. The misunderstanding about its status was discovered only when the other state asked if the United Kingdom's treaty procedures had been completed.[17]

Difficult problems can arise when an MOU which is subsidiary to a treaty contains provisions purporting to amend, or which are otherwise inconsistent with, the treaty. This raises the question whether the inconsistent provisions have any legal effect. In certain cases the MOU might be regarded as evidence of a mutual waiver of rights under the treaty. But use of MOUs to modify treaty provisions can be dangerous and lead to uncertainty as to the precise effect on the treaty.

It is not usually necessary to determine the precise status of a subsidiary instrument which is in the nature of a statement of interpretation of a treaty. The rules in Article 31 cover most cases adequately.[18]

The practice of states

The widespread use of MOUs results solely from state practice. In the past foreign government negotiators may have been rather bemused by requests, usually from Commonwealth states, to change the title of a draft from 'Agreement' to 'Memorandum of Understanding' or 'Arrangement', and every 'shall' to 'will'. But what may in the past have been seen by some as a slightly tiresome – even quaint – obsession is now firmly established.

Commonwealth states

The fifty-four states which are members of the Commonwealth tend to use MOUs, bilateral or multilateral, even in those cases where other states might employ a treaty. The Commonwealth Secretariat was established in 1965 by an MOU called 'Agreed Memorandum'.[19] Other Commonwealth institutions were similarly established. The 1966 Scheme relating to the Rendition of Fugitive Offenders (i.e. extradition) within the Commonwealth is contained in a document adopted by a Meeting of Commonwealth Law Ministers which uses MOU terminology.[20]

---

[17] The error was partly due to the British Embassy not reporting that the MOU was being negotiated.   [18] See pp. 189–91 below.   [19] ILM (1965), p. 1108.   [20] Cmnd 3008.

European Union states

In 1996 the Secretariat of the EU Council of Ministers circulated a questionnaire to all fifteen Member States concerning 'The internal procedures of Member States for the conclusion of international agreements approved under a simplified procedure or agreements without legally-binding force'.[21] For almost all the Member States the key factor in distinguishing a 'non-legally binding instrument' from a treaty was the intention of the states. Ireland, which, like the other Member States except the United Kingdom, has a written constitution, replied that if an instrument was not intended to be binding it would be worded to reflect that intention; and that the Irish courts had distinguished between MOUs and treaties on the basis of the intentions of the governments as reflected in the language of the text and the formalities, or lack of them, associated with it. The replies of other EU Member States echoed these points and added further factors which for them distinguished MOUs from treaties: the title of the instrument; the avoidance of mandatory language; the omission of treaty-type final clauses; and, generally, the absence of a parliamentary procedure.[22]

United States

Examining the practice of the United States is valuable because it is better documented. The purpose of the US Federal Regulations dealing with international agreements is to implement the federal law known as the 'Case Act' (see below) by giving guidance to agencies of the US Government as to the types of international instruments which the Act requires to be notified to Congress. The Regulations thus cover those instruments which fall within the definition of treaty (as that term is understood by international law),[23] and lay down criteria by which to judge whether a particular instrument is a treaty.[24] The following extracts are particularly relevant:

---

[21] The replies are summarised in EU Doc. PESC/SEC 899 of 9 August 1996.
[22] See also the Opinion of the Advocate-General of the European Court of Justice in *France v. Commission* [1994] ECR V-3641 at 3654.
[23] See pp. 157–60 for an explanation of treaties and the US Constitution.
[24] 46 FR 35918, as amended by 61 FR 7071, see *Code of Federal Regulations* 22, Part 182, revised as of 1 April 1998.

(1) *Identity and intention of the parties* . . . The parties must intend their undertakings to be legally-binding, and not merely of political or personal effect. Documents intended to have political or moral weight, but not intended to be legally-binding, are not international agreements . . .

. . .

(5) *Form.* Form as such is not normally an important factor, but it does deserve consideration. Documents which do not follow the customary form for international agreements, as to matters such as style, final clauses, signatures, or entry into force dates, may or may not be international agreements. Failure to use the customary form may constitute evidence of a lack of intent to be legally bound by the arrangement. If, however, the general content and context reveal an intention to enter into a legally-binding relationship, a departure from customary form will not preclude the arrangement from being an international agreement. Moreover, the title of the agreement will not be determinative. Decisions will be made on the basis of the substance of the arrangement, rather than on its denomination as an international agreement, a memorandum of understanding, exchange of notes, exchange of letters, technical arrangement, protocol, agreed minute, or any other name.

These extracts adopt a not dissimilar approach to that of other states: there must be an intention to enter into legally binding undertakings and use of non-customary treaty form may indicate that the parties did not intend to enter into a legally binding relationship. But it is also clear that in US practice use of non-treaty language does not necessarily preclude the instrument from being an 'international agreement' if 'the general content and context reveal an intention to enter into a legally-binding relationship'. Since less weight is given to terminology, it is more difficult to predict whether a particular instrument will be regarded by the United States as a treaty or an MOU.

But it must be remembered that the purpose of the Regulations is to implement the 'Case Act'.[25] Under the Act every 'international agreement' has to be published annually and the text submitted to Congress within sixty days of entry into force. The term 'international agreement' is defined in the Act so as to exclude 'Treaties', that is those treaties which under the Constitution have to be submitted to the Senate for approval.[26] Furthermore, the Act requires oral agreements (which are not covered by

---

[25] Public Law 92–403, as amended by Public Law 95–426 (ILM (1972), p. 1117 and ILM (1979), p. 82).   [26] See pp. 157–9 below.

the Convention[27]) to be reduced to writing and notified to Congress. Also, the Act excludes any 'agreement' if its public disclosure would be prejudicial to national security. Given the obligation in Article 102 of the UN Charter to register all treaties,[28] this exclusion would seem directed at confidential MOUs.

Nevertheless, in practice the United States – or at least some US agencies – appears to regard some instruments as treaties which other states would see as no more than MOUs. This may, in part, be due to the tendency of the United States to name a treaty 'Memorandum of Understanding'. This has led to some instruments which are clearly MOUs or, perhaps only domestic law contracts, being erroneously regarded as treaties. A 1981 Memorandum of Understanding between the 15th Air Base Wing, Hickham Air Force Base, Hawaii and the Royal Air Force detachment at Hickham is drawn in the form of an agreement. But it is not expressed to have been made on behalf of the UK and US Governments or even departments of them, and the 'final clauses' are not in normal treaty form. It was signed by the US Base Commander and an RAF sergeant. The subject was the supply to the RAF detachment of various goods and services, including fuel and coffins. The preamble cites certain US federal legislation, and the parties are described as 'Host' and 'Tenant'. The inescapable conclusion is that it is no more than a contract drawn up under US law, but the United States registered it as a treaty.[29]

Whereas the practice of other states seems to be fairly consistent as to the use of particular terminology to distinguish MOUs from treaties, US practice is less consistent, and this results in some instruments having indeterminate status. The China–United States Memorandum of Understanding on Protection of Intellectual Property 1992 states that the two governments 'reached a mutual understanding' but includes some treaty language.[30] The Memorandum of Understanding between the same two governments on Prohibitions on Import and Export Trade on Prison Labour Products 1992 says in the preamble that they 'have reached the following understanding', but then says that 'The Parties agree'. The operative provisions use MOU terminology, but the final clauses and testimonium[31] are in treaty form.[32]

Most collaborative defence projects with the United States are effected

---

[27] See p. 7 above.   [28] See p. 275 below.   [29] 1285 UNTS 97.   [30] ILM (1995), p. 677.
[31] For an explanation of these terms, see pp. 345–54 below.   [32] ILM (1992), p. 1071.

by means of MOUs because of the need for confidentiality and the ease with which MOUs can be amended. But, perhaps because of requirements of US federal law, the US Government has sometimes regarded them as treaties. By 1993 the United States had some twenty-two defence memoranda of understanding with the United Kingdom.[33] Some were clearly treaties, but the rest, although only MOUs, had been registered by the United States as treaties.[34] This was unacceptable to the United Kingdom. Australia and Canada had the same problem with the United States. As a result the United States concluded a so-called 'Chapeau Agreement' with each of the three states. This is a treaty containing ready-made provisions on matters such as the legal status of armed service personnel and liability.[35] When an MOU for a collaborative defence project with the United States needs to provide for such matters, it will state that the relevant terms of the Chapeau Agreement will apply; and the United States will not register the MOU as a treaty. In a similar way, an MOU, in providing that persons specified in it will be accorded certain immunities, may make reference to provisions of the Vienna Convention on Diplomatic Relations 1961.[36]

The distinction between treaties and MOUs is reflected in a recent UK–US treaty which expressly replaced a bilateral MOU and preserved a trilateral MOU.[37] In 1991 Japan and the United States concluded a treaty to implement an earlier MOU.[38]

How and why MOUs are used rather than treaties

Today MOUs are employed in most areas of international relations – diplomatic, defence, trade, aid, transport etc. There may, in fact, be no area in which they are not found. In many cases, all things being equal, a treaty could be used. Frequently MOUs supplement treaties, like the MOUs accompanying almost all bilateral air services agreements, and which are treated as confidential. The United Kingdom has over 100 air services

---

[33] See *Treaties in Force* (1997), Office of the Legal Advisor, US State Dept, Pub. 9433, at pp. 290–3.
[34] See, for example, 1068 UNTS 437.
[35] UK/US Exchange of Notes 1993 concerning Defence Co-operation Arrangements (UKTS (1993) 69). See J. McNeil, 'International Agreements: Recent US–UK Practice Concerning the Memorandum of Understanding', AJIL (1994), pp. 821–6, though his views most be treated with some caution since they were based on a misunderstanding of the approach to Memorandums of Understanding taken by McNair and the ILC.
[36] 500 UNTS 95 (No. 7310); UKTS (1965) 19.
[37] Agreement on Suppression of Illicit Trafficking in the Caribbean 1998 (Cm 4154). See also the text of a UK–US MOU in BYIL (1997), p. 500.   [38] ILM (1992), p. 1079.

agreements, almost all of which are supplemented by confidential MOUs. But the United Kingdom is by no means exceptional in this; it has been normal practice in international civil aviation for decades.

Appendix C contains an example of an MOU which has not been published before. It may be the first time that an MOU on such an ordinary subject has been published. MOUs like the Helsinki Final Act or the NATO–Russia Founding Act were of course disseminated widely because of their political importance. Although it is such instruments which are most often cited as examples of MOUs, they are untypical of the numerous MOUs concluded each year, which are concerned with rather boring matters, and are of little importance outside the narrow circle of those who have to negotiate and implement them, but all who are interested in treaties should be aware that they exist.

The main reasons for using MOUs in preference to treaties are confidentiality and convenience, of which there are various aspects.

Confidentiality

A rather obvious reason for preferring an MOU to a treaty is confidentiality. Since an MOU is not a treaty, there is generally no national or international requirement, or need, to publish it. In the United Kingdom even a non-confidential MOU is not published unless there is a special reason, such as the political importance of the subject matter, or because it is closely associated with a treaty. Being neither a 'treaty' nor an 'international agreement', an MOU is not required by Article 102 of the United Nations Charter to be registered with the United Nations.[39] Of the many thousands of MOUs which have been concluded since 1945, only a handful appear in the *United Nations Treaty Series*, and probably in error,[40] though that does not make them treaties.[41]

Unlike Article 102 of the Charter, Article 83 of the Chicago Convention on International Civil Aviation 1944 provides that:

> . . . any contracting State may make *arrangements* not inconsistent with the provisions of this Convention. Any such arrangement shall be forthwith registered with the [ICAO] Council, which shall make it public as soon as possible.[42]

---

[39] See pp. 275–6.   [40] See p. 33 above about US practice.   [41] See p. 279 below.
[42] 15 UNTS 295 (No. 102); UKTS (1953) 8.

One might think this requirement is more extensive than Article 102. But whatever the original intention, the practice of the parties to the Chicago Convention shows that the vast majority do not consider the requirements to extend to MOUs. Very few of the MOUs which accompany air services agreements have been registered with the ICAO. The registration rules adopted by the ICAO define 'arrangements' to include arrangements between states and *airlines*, and a few of these have been registered with the ICAO.

Many arrangements, especially in the defence field, are naturally kept confidential for reasons of national security and are therefore found only in MOUs. All states do this, and no one would suggest that they should be published or registered, although it is sometimes necessary for national parliaments to be informed of their contents on a selective or confidential basis.[43] Quite often a defence treaty will have numerous MOUs supplementing it. Given the importance of the subject matter, the 1963 UK–US Polaris Sales Agreement might seem surprisingly short, just fifteen articles. But a careful reading will show that it is an umbrella treaty.[44] Article II(2), provides that each party's representatives are authorised to enter into 'such *technical arrangements*, consistent with this Agreement, as may be necessary'. This is a reference to the immensely detailed, confidential, technical and financial MOUs which were needed during the life of the Agreement. Similarly, in 1985 the United Kingdom and the United States concluded a treaty regarding arrangements for the use by UK forces of US military facilities on Ascension Island. This is even more explicit on the question of the instrument to be used for recording the detailed arrangements. The treaty has only one substantive paragraph. This provides that the arrangements:

> shall be established in a *memorandum of understanding* to be concluded between the Ministry of Defence representing the Government of the United Kingdom and the Department for Defense representing the Government of the United States.[45]

Another reason for the use of MOUs is to protect sensitive commercial information. This is particularly so when governments are involved in obtaining concessions or contracts for their companies, or where governments act as proxies for companies. The confidential MOU associated

---

[43] See p. 32 above about the Case Act.
[44] 479 UNTS 49 (No. 6871); UKTS (1963) 59. Polaris was a submarine-launched ballistic missile with a nuclear warhead.   [45] 1443 UNTS 25 (No. 24571); UKTS (1985) 39.

with an air services agreement, under which traffic rights and capacity entitlements are laid down, is a prime example.

Lack of formality

With an MOU there is no need for elaborate final clauses or the formalities (international or national) which surround treaty-making. More often than in the case of a treaty, an MOU will become effective on signature without the need for any further procedure. This factor alone can mean that an MOU can generally be negotiated, signed and come into effect more quickly than a treaty. Even when a treaty enters into force on signature, the internal procedures required before it can even be concluded may be lengthy. In some cases these problems may be such that the only practicable way of proceeding is by an MOU. Not being a treaty, an MOU is generally not subject to any constitutional procedures, such as presentation to parliament, though that will depend on the constitution, laws and practice of each state. The liberalised arrangements regarding air services which the United Kingdom negotiated in the 1980s with several European states were each embodied in an MOU called 'Agreed Record of Discussions'. This enabled the arrangements, which were experimental, to come into effect quickly; and the MOU form made it that much easier to modify them quickly in the light of experience.

Like treaties, MOUs are signed by ministers or officials, though probably more often by officials than is the case for treaties. This is, however, more a reflection of the generally lower importance of the subject matter. There are significant exceptions when the MOU is a statement of high political intent, such as the Helsinki Final Act 1975[46] and the NATO–Russia Founding Act 1997.[47]

Amendment

A distinct advantage of the MOU is the ease with which it can be amended. Since it is not a treaty, any amendment can be effected with the same ease and speed as the MOU itself. Even when a treaty has a simplified procedure for amendment built into it, it will still involve certain formalities. In the case of arrangements, such as collaborative defence projects or development aid,

---

[46] ILM (1975), p. 1293.   [47] ILM (1997), p. 1007.

involving complicated technical or financial provisions, there is often need to make frequent, and sometimes major, modifications. When the arrangements are multilateral the need for a method of amendment with the least possible formality and delay is often essential for their effectiveness. Even when the subject matter is not particularly sensitive, it may still be convenient to conclude a quite short 'umbrella' treaty, with the detailed provisions being put in one or more MOUs. Ministers prefer to be seen signing treaties rather than MOUs.

Termination

The termination provisions of many MOUs can be quite similar to those found in treaties. A period of notice is usually provided for, although this may be less than the six to twelve months commonly found in treaties. Sometimes there is no provision for termination, especially when the MOU is supplementary to a treaty. Difficult questions can then arise. A free-standing MOU can probably be terminated by giving reasonable notice, although, since it is not a legally binding instrument, failure to give due notice may, at least as a matter of *law*, have no legal consequences. On the other hand, if the MOU is supplementary to a treaty and has itself no termination clause, can it be terminated before the treaty itself is terminated? Much may depend upon its purpose. If it is essential for the implementation of the treaty, the arguments against termination of the MOU only are stronger. But again, since it is not legally binding, there should be no legal obstacle to giving immediate notice, although politically it could be damaging.[48] In certain cases such an MOU might be regarded as an instrument for the purposes of Article 31(2)(a).[49]

Dispute settlement

An MOU will usually have some provision regarding the settlement of disputes about its interpretation or application, and typically will provide that they will be settled by negotiation and not referred to any third party, court or tribunal. This provision is usually inserted as a further indication that the instrument is not intended to be legally binding. Since negotiations are always possible, such a provision is seldom found in treaties.

---

[48] See next page.   [49] See pp. 189–91 below.

Although Article 102(2) of the UN Charter provides that unregistered treaties cannot be invoked before organs of the United Nations, including the International Court of Justice, in practice they can be invoked before the Court.[50] It would therefore follow that an MOU could also be invoked, though whether this would help the legal argument may depend on whether, in the particular circumstances, the MOU has legal consequences.[51]

Interpretation

In the interpretation and application of MOUs it is convenient and reasonable to apply by analogy the rules for the interpretation of treaties in so far as they are not at variance with the non-legally binding nature of MOUs. The *travaux* of an MOU may be as important as those of a treaty, though they may be even more difficult to find.

Dangers in using MOUs

Too easy a recourse to MOUs can carry dangers. We have already seen the problem of disagreement as to status, but there are other problems.

Respect for MOUs seen as less important than for treaties

Because an MOU is not legally binding there may sometimes be a temptation not to take the commitments in it so seriously. This would be to ignore the fact that political commitments engage the good faith of governments. Even though failure to carry out an MOU does not usually have legal consequences, it does not mean that a state is free, politically or morally, to disregard them. Not only would such an attitude be dishonourable, but it could provoke a damaging political response.[52]

Possible lack of care in drafting

There might be a slight tendency among government officials to regard the drafting of an MOU as not requiring the same close attention as the

---

[50] See p. 280 below.   [51] See pp. 45–6 below.
[52] See P. Kooijmans in J. Makarczyk, *The Theory of International Law at the Threshold of the 21st Century* (1995), p. 425 at p. 430.

drafting of a treaty. If this is so, it is regrettable. In many cases the content of an MOU could equally well be put into a treaty, and errors in the drafting of an MOU could give rise to the same friction in relations as an error in a treaty. Even though the commitments in an MOU are political or moral, that is no reason for them to be expressed with less precision than they would be in a treaty.

Depending on the constitution and internal procedures of each state, it will not usually be essential for the foreign ministry to draft all MOUs. However, when another ministry drafts an MOU it should consult the foreign ministry before sending the draft to another government, and at all key stages thereafter. It is the task of the foreign ministry to explain the differences between a treaty and an MOU, and why one rather than the other may be advantageous (or not) in the particular case, and ensure that the form and wording is appropriate to whichever instrument is chosen. Unfortunately, sometimes another ministry may produce a draft which is a mixture of treaty and MOU language, or a draft which uses mostly treaty language but is headed 'Memorandum of Understanding' in the mistaken belief that this makes it non-legally binding. The foreign ministry must then advise how to put matters right.

Lack of implementing legislation

Although an MOU is not legally binding, that does not mean that it may not need to be implemented in domestic law. Perhaps surprisingly, MOUs are often used to provide for the status of armed forces in another state. Sometimes the law needed to implement such an MOU will already be in place, but, if not, care must be taken to ensure that the MOU will not come into effect until the necessary legislation has been made. This possible complication may be more important for those states with so-called 'monist' constitutions under which treaties (but not MOUs) have to be approved by parliament, whereupon they may automatically become part of the law of the state.[53] Some 'dualist' constitutions, including that of the United Kingdom, make use of 'umbrella' primary legislation which authorises the government to make secondary legislation to give effect to 'arrangements' entered into with another state, the term 'arrangements'

---

[53] See pp. 146 and 150–1 below about monism and dualism.

being chosen because it is broad enough to embrace both treaties and MOUs.[54]

Difficulty in finding MOUs

One important practical advantage of a treaty is that, being published (usually in a special series), it is much easier to find, not only by members of the public, but also by officials. MOUs are easily 'lost'. Those officials responsible for implementing an MOU should keep a copy of it (the signed text, not the final draft) somewhere easily accessible and, perhaps even more important, where their successors can find it (i.e. not only in the archives). As a fail-safe measure, since 1 January 1997 the Treaty Section of the UK Foreign and Commonwealth Office (FCO) in principle keeps a copy of each MOU concluded either by the FCO or by other ministries. This has the added advantage also of providing a set of useful precedents.

Are MOUs really treaties?

A contemporary writer on international law, Klabbers, has expressed doubts whether the distinction between MOUs and treaties is valid. He has argued that every 'agreement' concluded between states which is of a normative nature (in that it attempts to influence future behaviour), and is not made subject to another system of law (e.g. domestic), is a treaty.[55] He sees no distinction between a treaty (as defined in the Convention) and an MOU, since each embody an agreement. This sweeping assertion immediately runs up against the fact that when states do not intend to enter into a legally binding instrument they make this clear by a deliberate and careful choice of words. Klabbers argues that intention is not decisive. But to argue so ignores, first, the history behind the definition of treaty in the Convention. We have already seen that the International Law Commission saw the definition in its draft articles as including the intention to create legal obligations.[56] This vital element is confirmed by the records of the Vienna Conference. A Swiss amendment to exclude expressly 'political

---

[54] See the Visiting Forces Act 1952, section 1(2).
[55] J. Klabbers, *The Concept of Treaty in International Law* (1996), and reviews of it by I. Sinclair (AJIL (1997), pp. 748–50), P. Keller (ICLQ (1998), pp. 240–1) and C. Hopkins (BYIL (1997), pp. 278–80).   [56] See p. 17 above.

declarations and gentlemen's agreements' was rejected, apparently because it was believed to be unnecessary since such documents were not 'governed by international law' and were therefore already excluded from the definition.[57] Secondly, Klabbers' theory is also incompatible with the basic principle that a sovereign state is free to exercise (or not to exercise) its treaty-making power. We have seen how states can make agreements between themselves which are binding only in domestic law.[58] There is no principle or rule in the law of treaties or general international law that requires that every transaction between states has to be legally binding, or, more particularly, a treaty. Thirdly, the hypothesis is just not supported by the practice of states.[59] To take a recent prominent example, the NATO Member States and Russia were from the start of their negotiations at pains to ensure that there would be no misunderstanding about the status of their Founding Act 1997.[60] Since it was agreed that it should be only politically binding, it was most carefully drafted to avoid all treaty language, thus demonstrating their mutual intention not to conclude a legally binding instrument.[61]

Registration with the United Nations, although not decisive, must raise a strong presumption that the instrument is a treaty, especially if, as in 99.9 per cent of cases, the act of registration is not challenged; although non-registration is not necessarily evidence of lack of an intention to conclude a treaty.[62] Yet, if MOUs are really treaties one would expect this to be reflected in the registration practice of states under Article 102 of the Charter. MOUs are numerous, and many – possibly the majority – are not confidential. But, as we have seen, the assertion that there is no real distinction between a treaty and an MOU is not supported by the registration practice of states.[63]

Klabbers' theory, though thought-provoking, relies heavily on academic writings, interpretations of judicial decisions and philosophical argument. He finds strong support in the 1994 decision of the International Court of Justice in *Qatar* v. *Bahrain*, which held that an instrument not in customary treaty form was nevertheless a treaty.[64] The Court had to consider the legal effect of two instruments. The first was the treaty constituted by a double exchange of letters between Bahrain and

[57] See O. Schachter, 'The Twilight Existence of Non-Binding International Agreements', AJIL (1977), pp. 296–304, note 19.   [58] See p. 24 above.   [59] See pp. 30–4 above.
[60] ILM (1997), p. 1007.
[61] R. Mullerson, 'NATO Enlargement and Russia', ICLQ (1998), pp. 192–204.
[62] See pp. 278–80 below.   [63] See p. 29 above.
[64] *ICJ Reports* (1994), p. 112; ILM (1994), p. 1461.

Saudi Arabia and between Qatar and Saudi Arabia, respectively.[65] The second was the minutes of a meeting in 1990 between representatives of the three states, the minutes being signed by their foreign ministers. The minutes listed the matters which had been 'agreed' (the term, in Arabic, used in the minutes). Although the minutes were not registered with the United Nations by Qatar until six months later (and only ten days before it made its application to the Court), and Bahrain protested the registration and asserted before the Court that the minutes were not legally binding, the Court found that they constituted a treaty. Klabbers sees the judgment as 'monumental' in that, in his view, it demonstrates that any document containing commitments by states is a treaty, regardless of form or other considerations, in particular *whether or not the states intended it to be binding*.[66] Although the decision was almost certainly a compromise covering a deep division in the Court, given the particular facts of the case the Court's decision is not so remarkable. The commitments were written down, the text recording what the parties had 'agreed'. The minutes were signed by the three foreign ministers. The form of minutes of a meeting may have been unusual, but the form – as opposed to the wording – does not determine whether an instrument is a treaty. The minutes may well be at the other end of a spectrum which begins with treaties drawn up in the most formal manner, such as the United Nations Charter. Although it is not for the Court to speculate as to the intentions of the parties, it did what any court has to do, it *inferred* their intention from the text of the minutes and the surrounding circumstances, not from what the parties later asserted. The Court had previously approached the matter in various ways, and it would not be right to conclude that the judgment is a significant departure from basic treaty principles or practice.[67] The judgment will certainly be valuable if it means that in future states will be more careful in the way they express themselves, particularly when drafting minutes of meetings and diplomatic communiqués.

[65] See p. 18 above.

[66] *Archiv des Völkerrechts* (1995), pp. 361–76, and summarised in his thesis (note 55 above). See also E. Vierdag, 'The International Court of Justice and the Law of Treaties' and E. Lauterpacht, "Partial" Judgments and the Inherent Jurisdiction of the International Court of Justice' in Lowe and Fitzmaurice (eds.), *Fifty Years of the International Court of Justice* (1996), pp. 145–66 and pp. 465–86, respectively; and S. Rosenne, 'The Qatar/Bahrain Case', *Leiden Journal of International Law* (1995), p. 161 at p. 165.

[67] But see C. Chinkin, 'A Mirage in the Sand? Distinguishing Binding and Non-Binding Relations Between States', *Leiden Journal of International Law* (1997), pp. 223–47.

Klabbers seems to have assumed that state practice in the use of MOUs is neither widespread nor unambiguous. But he did not test his theory by finding out what the practice is, which is that states choose consciously and deliberately to express their intentions by using either the well-established forms and terminology of the treaty or that of the more recent phenomenon of the MOU. All too often Klabbers cites untypical international instruments, instead of the vast quantity of MOUs on ordinary subjects. And he does not address at all the point about the need to keep certain arrangements confidential. Although MOUs are, admittedly, generally not published, and therefore not easy to find, Klabbers acknowledges that he did not give much weight to state practice, finding it advisable to distance himself somewhat from it since he is not necessarily convinced of its normative effect.[68]

Are MOUs 'soft law'?

It is not easy to answer this question since there is no agreement on what is 'soft law', or indeed if it exists at all as a distinct source of law.[69] Generally, however, the term is used to describe international instruments which their makers recognise are not treaties, even if they employ imperative language such as 'shall', but have as their purpose the promulgation of norms (albeit not legally binding) of general or universal application.[70] Such non-treaty instruments are typically given names such as Guidelines, Principles, Declarations, Codes of Practice, Recommendations and Programmes. The Rio Declaration on Environment and Development 1992 is one example.[71] They are frequently found in the economic, social and environmental fields. The subject matter is usually not yet well-enough developed, or there is lack of consensus on the content of the norms, for them to be embodied in a treaty. They can therefore represent an intermediate stage in treaty-making, and sometimes never get beyond that stage. But some norms do, such as those in the Universal Declaration of Human Rights 1948 which have been the source of many universal and regional human rights treaties. All such 'soft law' instruments are MOUs in the sense that there is no intention that they should be legally binding. The main difference between them

---

[68] Letter to the author of 28 August 1996.
[69] See Birnie and Boyle, *International Law and the Environment* (1992), pp. 16–18.
[70] It can also be a description of provisions in a treaty which are of such generality that they cannot form the basis of legal rights and obligations.   [71] ILM (1992), p. 876.

and the vast majority of MOUs is that 'soft law' MOUs are invariably multilateral, seek to lay down universal norms and are published and disseminated widely. In contrast, most MOUs are bilateral, and even when multilateral they do not generally lay down universal norms, and, whether multilateral or bilateral, are seldom published.

The possible legal consequences of MOUs

Can a non-legally binding instrument like an MOU give rise to some legal consequences? The question is perplexing.

At first sight it would seem that an MOU can have effect only in the realm of politics or morals. If a state does not carry out its commitments the sanction is political (which is why MOUs are often said to be 'politically binding'); another state cannot take the matter to an international court or tribunal or impose the countermeasures it might be entitled to take in the case of breach of a treaty,[72] though the state can, of course, show its displeasure by resorting to the (much undervalued) right of retorsion.[73] But might there nevertheless be some means of legal redress?

Estoppel

The question can be posed thus: can a state conclude bilateral arrangements, about, say, status of forces, with two states using in one case a treaty and in the other an MOU (there are many examples where the difference is only in the form and terminology, the substance being the same), yet treat the MOU as no more than an expression of political will? In choosing an MOU rather than a treaty, does a state have to give up all the advantages of a legally binding instrument, in particular enforceability, in return for confidentiality, speed, flexibility, etc.? Take the case of an MOU between State A and State B under which State A expresses its 'intention' to pay State B 1 billion euros over a period of five years to help it build a dam. State B then starts building the dam, and after four years it has drawn down 500 million euros. State A then has a change of government, and the new one decides for budgetary reasons to stop the funding. Although much may depend on the circumstances and the precise terms of the MOU, the intention of State A as

---

[72] See p. 302 below.
[73] Retaliation by a state by means which are not illegal (e.g., breaking off diplomatic relations), in response to an act done by another state (see also p. 304 below).

expressed in the MOU may have legal consequences. A unilateral declaration may, depending on the intention of the state making it and the circumstances, be binding in international law. Underlying this is the fundamental international law principle of good faith.[74] Good faith also underpins the doctrine of estoppel (preclusion), which in international law is a substantive rule and broader and less technical than estoppel in the common law, being founded on the principle that good faith must prevail in international relations. The exact scope of the international law doctrine is far from settled, but in general it may be said that where a clear statement or representation is made by one state to another, which then in good faith relies upon it *to its detriment*, the first state is estopped (precluded) from going back on its statement or representation.[75] If two states choose to record the settlement of a dispute between them in an MOU rather than in a treaty – perhaps for reasons of confidentiality – they are clearly estopped from denying that the terms of the settlement are binding.[76] Where the terms of an MOU which implements a treaty are inconsistent with the treaty, estoppel may provide a basis for regarding the terms as effectively modifying the treaty. The doctrine may also help in resolving the question of whether a termination provision in an MOU has any legal effect.[77]

But if there are certain cases where the conclusion and operation of an MOU could give rise to legal consequences, does it make sense not to regard it as a treaty? The distinction between a treaty (which creates legal rights and obligations) and an MOU (which does not, but which may in certain circumstances have legal consequences) may seem rather subtle, but in law and diplomacy subtlety is a necessity. No state is obliged to conclude a treaty.[78] Each state is, in the exercise of its sovereignty, free to deny itself the benefits – such as they are – of a treaty in exchange for the advantages offered by an MOU. The MOU has shown itself to be essential for the efficient conduct of business between states. Used properly the MOU poses no threat; rather it has been proved to be an indispensable complement to the process of treaty-making.

---

[74] See *Oppenheim*, pp. 1188–93; and A. Watts, 'The Legal Position in International Law of Heads of States, Heads of Government and Foreign Ministers', *Hague Recueil* (1994), III, pp. 114–28.

[75] See *El Salvador–Honduras Land, Island and Maritime Frontier, ICJ Reports* (1990), p. 92, at para. 63; *Oppenheim*, p. 527, note 6; and H. Thirlway, 'The Law and Procedure of the International Court of Justice', BYIL (1989), at p. 36.

[76] See the award in the *UK–US Heathrow User Charges Arbitration*, 102 ILR, pp. 261–564.

[77] See p. 38 above.   [78] But see p. 25 above about *pactum de contrahendo*.

4

Capacity to make treaties

The making of treaties is one of the oldest and most characteristic exercises of independence or sovereignty on the part of States.[1]

Treaties are made between subjects of international law, in particular between states, between states and international organisations and between international organisations. This book deals primarily with treaties between states. Every state possesses the capacity to conclude treaties (Article 6). By 'state' is meant a sovereign independent state. This requires territory with a settled population, a sovereign government and independence from any other state.[2] Applying such generally accepted criteria is not always easy. All Members of the United Nations can now be regarded as states, though in the past this was not so. Even when they were still republics of the Soviet Union, the Byelorussian SSR (now Belarus) and the Ukrainian SSR (now Ukraine) were able to become parties to at least UN treaties, though this was only because of a political deal under which they were Members of the United Nations from the beginning.[3] But, this chapter is not concerned with the quality of statehood, or whether a particular entity, such as Palestine, is a state,[4] but rather with how treaty-making power is exercised by a unitary state; by parts of a state (such as the constituent units of a federal state) or by, or on behalf of, overseas territories of a state.

A treaty made between states may be expressed to be made by heads of state, or on behalf of the states, their governments or, less often, their ministries.[5] A heads of state treaty is used when the subject matter is of exceptional political importance, such as the various constituent treaties of the European Community, though it is not necessary for heads of state to sign

[1] McNair, p. 35.   [2] See *Oppenheim*, para. 34.
[3] Goodrich and Hambro, *The Charter of the United Nations* (3rd edn, 1969), pp. 81–3.
[4] On, for example, the Vatican City (Holy See), see *Oppenheim*, para. 102.
[5] See Article 3(2) of the Russian Law on Treaties (ILM (1995), p. 1370).

in person.[6] There is no difference in international law between a treaty concluded on behalf of states and one concluded on behalf of governments or their ministries,[7] since a treaty entered into by a government or ministry binds the state, and changes of government will not affect its binding force. However, under some constitutions it may be necessary or desirable to use the inter-state form when the provisions of the treaty need to be given full effect in domestic law.

A treaty expressed to be concluded on behalf of ministries may be chosen in order to avoid constitutional procedures. In principle, however, treaties should not be concluded by ministries when they include matters for which other ministries are responsible in domestic law. A treaty on, say, the status of armed forces will normally include provisions on, among other things, jurisdiction and tax exemption. Since these are not matters for which a defence ministry would have domestic responsibility, the treaty should be expressed to be between the governments. Although this should make no difference to the respective rights and obligations of the states parties, it is a useful reminder of the need to consult other ministries before concluding the treaty. Similar considerations apply to MOUs.

Federations[8]

Some states have constitutions under which the state is divided into political sub-divisions. The constituent units of a federation are the typical case, though this and other terms used to describe the constitution of a state must be treated with caution; no two constitutions, and especially federal constitutions, are the same, although certain patterns can be discerned.[9] The constituent units of a federation do not have territorial sovereignty, but, as a matter of constitutional law, they have exclusive competence over certain matters, share competence with the federation on some matters, and have no competence on all other matters. Federal constitutions vary on the question whether the constituent units have the power to enter into treaties. The Australian states and Canadian provinces have no such power.[10] Although the US Constitution prohibits the states

---

[6] See *Satow*, paras. 29.11–29.13; and McNair, pp. 18–19.

[7] For this purpose the term includes other agencies of the state, but generally not public bodies which have legal personality separate from that of the state. See *Oppenheim*, pp. 346–8.

[8] See also pp. 169–72 below.   [9] McNair, p. 36.

[10] B. Opeskin, 'Federal States in the International Legal Order', NILR (1996), pp. 353–86 (note 45, and generally).

of the Union from entering into agreements with foreign states, they have in fact entered into such agreements, particularly in recent decades, though most appear to have been with the constituent units of other federations, or not to have been in legally binding form. The subjects have been largely in the fields of trade, development, finance and culture.[11] It is doubtful if any are treaties as that term is defined in the Vienna Convention.

On the other hand, some federal constitutions authorise their constituent units to enter into agreements on matters within their legislative competence or if they have the specific approval of the federation, though it is generally in respect of a limited range of subjects.[12] Under the German Constitution (Basic Law), the *Länder* have limited power to conclude agreements in their own name on matters relating to *Land* legislation.[13] Nevertheless, the prior consent of the federal government is needed for each agreement. Since 1949 the *Länder* have concluded over eighty agreements, mostly with neighbouring states, concerning technical matters such as border arrangements.[14] Under the Swiss Constitution the federation has comprehensive treaty-making power, but the cantons may conclude treaties within the area of their competence. These can be negotiated by the cantons, but must be approved by the Federal Council before they can be signed. Some 100 such treaties, mostly of a technical nature, have been concluded with neighbouring states.[15]

Neither of these examples suggests that such agreements are binding only on the constituent unit. Given the need for federal consent, they may be properly regarded, in international law at least, as ultimately the responsibility of the federal state. This is not surprising. Most states are unitary with one government and one legislature. They do not look with much favour on federations which seek special treatment for their constituent units. It is not enough for a federal constitution to purport to confer on the constituent units the power to conclude treaties, or for the federation to assert it. When another state concludes a treaty with a constituent unit of a federation, it is not that state's responsibility to acquaint itself with the – inevitably complex – rules governing the relationship between the federation and its constituent units. The main concern of a state dealing with a constituent unit is the problem of implementation and, if

[11] Michelmann and Soldatos (eds.), *Federalism and International Relations* (1990), pp. 279–80 and 283.   [12] *Oppenheim*, paras. 75–6.   [13] See Article 30 of the *Grundgesetz* (Basic Law).
[14] Monroe Leigh, pp. 54–6.   [15] *Ibid.*, pp. 152–5. See also pp. 149–50 below.

necessary, enforcement. It is therefore right to be cautious about entering into a treaty with a constituent unit without an assurance that it is acting on behalf, or with the authority, of the federation. There will then be no doubt that it is a treaty and that the federation will be ultimately responsible in international law. If a constituent unit has not been duly authorised by the federal government, the legal status of the instrument may well be problematical. Unless it is governed by, say, domestic law – in which case it would be a contract – it may be no more than an MOU. The same would apply to agreements between governments and municipalities of other states.

Such sharing of power, and particularly legislative power, between a federation and its constituent units can cause huge problems for the federal state when it wishes to become party to a treaty which will require to be implemented also in the law of the constituent units. This can be dealt with to some extent by the use of territorial and federal clauses, and federal reservations and declarations.[16] Alternatively, a state can always conclude an MOU with a constituent unit of a federation. The Canada–United Kingdom Social Security Convention 1997 provides for the United Kingdom to conclude 'understandings' (i.e., MOUs) with a Canadian province on matters within the latter's jurisdiction and consistent with the Convention.[17]

Belgium

The Agreement on the Protection of the Meuse 1994 was concluded between France, the Netherlands *and* the Walloon, Flemish and Brussels-Capital Regions of Belgium, *each* as equal parties.[18] Since 1993 Belgium has had a particularly complex federal structure. It is now composed of the three Regions and three 'Communities' (Flemish, French and German). Each Region has exclusive competence for a wide range of matters, including water resources and the environment in its area, and is empowered to enter into treaties on such matters. In 1995 the Flemish Region entered into two treaties with the Netherlands regarding the Meuse and the Scheldt. These were published in the Belgian Official Gazette (*Staatsblad*) and registered with the United Nations, the registration being done by the

---

[16] See pp. 169–72 below.   [17] UKTS (1998) 43 (Article 13).
[18] ILM (1995), p. 854. The Agreement entered into force on 1 January 1998.

Netherlands because the Region is, of course, not a Member of the United Nations.[19]

However, the provisions of the Belgian Constitution do not mean that Belgium is not responsible in international law for the carrying out of treaties entered into by its Regions. On signing the 1994 Treaty of Accession of Austria, Finland and Sweden to the European Union, Belgium made a declaration that it *and* the Communities and Regions had 'entered into an undertaking at the international level'. The other Member States made a counter-declaration, which Belgium confirmed was correct, that the Belgium declaration was an explanation of Belgian constitutional law, and that Belgium alone was responsible for discharging the obligations of the Treaty.[20] When signing the Amsterdam Treaty 1997, Belgium stated that its signature also bound the Communities and the Regions, but confirmed that Belgium alone 'would bear full responsibility for compliance with the obligations entered into in the Treaty'.[21] Belgium has also made a similar statement in respect of treaties concluded both by the European Community and its Member States ('mixed agreements').[22]

Scotland and Northern Ireland

The United Kingdom is still essentially a unitary state, but constitutional changes which came into force in 1999 devolved certain legislative and executive powers to Scotland and Northern Ireland. Although the Scotland Act 1998 reserves to the United Kingdom the power to make treaties, their observation and implementation in relation to matters transferred to Scotland is within the competence of the Scottish Administration and Parliament.[23] Nevertheless, the United Kingdom remains solely responsible internationally for all treaty obligations. The Northern Ireland Act 1998 has similar provisions, and permits Ministers of the Northern Ireland Government to enter into certain informal arrangements (i.e., MOUs) with the Government of Ireland.[24] Administrative procedures on the conduct of international relations, in so far as they affect the Scottish and Northern Ireland Administrations are set out in separate

---

[19] See Alen and Peeters, 'Federal Belgium within the International Legal Order', in *International Law: Theory and Practice, Essays in Honour of Eric Suy* (1998), pp. 123–43; *Revue belge de droit international* (1997) 1, pp. 337–8. [20] OJ (1994) C241/402. [21] OJ (1997) C340/307.
[22] OJ (1995) C157/1. For mixed agreements, see pp. 55–6 below.
[23] Section 30 and Schedule 5, para. 7. [24] Sections 4(1) and 53, and Schedule 2, para. 3.

'concordats' agreed between the Foreign and Commonwealth Office and the Administrations.[25]

Bosnia and Herzegovina, Republika Srpska and the Federal Republic of Yugoslavia

The parties to the Dayton Agreement 1995[26] are the states of Bosnia and Herzegovina, Croatia and the Federal Republic of Yugoslavia (FRY). The preamble notes an agreement of 29 August 1995, 'which authorised the delegation of the FRY to sign, on behalf of the Republika Srpska, the parts of the peace plan concerning it, with the obligation to implement the agreement that is reached strictly and consequently [sic]'. Annexed to the Dayton Agreement are several detailed agreements to which Republika Srpska and the Muslim–Croat Federation are expressed to be parties even though they are constituent parts of Bosnia and Herzegovina, and ones between Bosnia and Herzegovina, Republika Srpska and the Muslim–Croat Federation. Given the very special circumstances, the FRY 'endorsed' the agreements and, in the case of two of them, the FRY Foreign Minister gave a written assurance that the FRY would 'take all necessary steps, consistent with the sovereignty, territorial integrity and political independence of Bosnia and Herzegovina, to ensure that the Republika Srpska fully respects and complies with' them. Thus, one state gave, in effect, undertakings to another state for the performance of an agreement by a constituent part of that other state.

Overseas territories

Overseas territories, that is to say colonies and other dependent territories, do not have the power to conclude treaties, but they may be authorised by the state to which they belong to enter into them either *ad hoc* or in certain specific subject areas. The United Kingdom has conferred a limited general power on Bermuda by means of an 'Instrument of Entrustment'. Under this Bermuda has concluded several treaties with Canada and the United States, with which it has close economic ties. But the United Kingdom remains ultimately responsible for the performance of the treaties. In the past similar entrustments were given to Hong Kong. States do not of

---

[25] See also pp. 154–5 below.   [26] ILM (1995), p. 75.

course have to enter into treaties with an overseas territory rather than the 'parent' state, but if they do they will look to the parent state for redress if the territory does not carry out the treaty, since the territory acts in effect as agent for the parent state.

A more satisfactory procedure may be for the parent state to enter into a treaty with another state expressly for the territory. The New Zealand–United Kingdom Social Security Agreement 1994 applies only to the British territories of the Channel Islands.[27] In 1996 France and the United Kingdom concluded a treaty concerning maritime delimitation in respect of the French metropolitan *département* of Guadeloupe and the British territory of Montserrat.[28]

Where a multilateral treaty provides that 'any state' may become a party to it, whether a state can become a party only in respect of an overseas territory will depend on the nature and geographical scope of the treaty. The United Kingdom became party to the 1947 Agreement establishing the South Pacific Commission (now the Pacific Community), the territorial scope of which is limited to the non-self-governing territories in the South Pacific administered by the parties.[29] The Indian Ocean Tuna Commission Agreement 1993 was ratified by the United Kingdom in respect of the British Indian Ocean Territory 'only'.[30]

Some multilateral treaties permit territorial entities which are not independent to be parties. Article 305 of the UN Convention on the Law of the Sea 1982 permits certain self-governing associated states and internally self-governing territories to become parties, provided they have competence over matters governed by the Convention, including competence to enter into treaties on such matters.[31] The Hong Kong SAR is party in its own right to several such treaties.[32]

Agreements with the parent state or between its overseas territories

As between a parent state and one of its territories, or between its overseas territories, there can be no international relations, since only the parent is sovereign; and any agreement between them will not be legally binding. When there is need for an agreement, it may be convenient – and will avoid

---

[27] UKTS (1995) 92.   [28] UKTS (1997) 28.   [29] 97 UNTS 227 (No. 1352); UKTS (1952) 21.
[30] Cm 2695.
[31] ILM (1982), p. 1261; UKTS (1999) 81. The Cook Islands (see Appendix R) is a party.
[32] See pp. 325 and 327–30 below.

any mistaken implication that it is legally binding – to draft it as if it were an MOU between states. An agreement between an overseas territory and a company or individual will be binding under domestic law.

International organisations

For the purposes of the law of treaties, an international organisation may be roughly defined as a non-state entity with international legal personality separate from that of the states which established it. The World Health Organisation is an international organisation, the International Commission of Jurists is not.[33] The constituent instrument (i.e., the constitution) of an international organisation is almost always a treaty,[34] and if it was concluded after the entry into force of the Vienna Convention for the states the Convention will apply to it (Articles 4 and 5). An international organisation has the capacity to conclude treaties if this is provided for in its constituent instrument or if it is indispensable for the fulfilment of its purposes.[35] With the rapid growth since the Second World War of international organisations, there are now numerous treaties between international organisations and states (e.g., headquarters agreements), and between international organisations. The rules governing them are set out in the Convention on the Law of Treaties between States and International Organisations or between International Organisations 1986,[36] which adopted the rules of the 1969 Convention, modifying them to take into account the different nature of international organisations.

Increasingly multilateral treaties, especially in fields such as the environment, trade and commodities, provide for certain international organisations to become parties. The UN Convention on the Law of the Sea 1982 permits international organisations to become parties if their member states have transferred competence, including the competence to enter into treaties, over matters governed by the Convention.[37] This applies to the European Community because of its exclusive competence for fisheries in the waters of EC Member States and for high seas fisheries. Many treaties are, however, not suitable for the participation of international organisations; for example, most of them have no, or only very limited, powers to enforce in the territory of their member states the pro-

---

[33] See Article 2(1)(i).   [34] But see p. 30 above about the Commonwealth Secretariat.
[35] *Reparations* case, *ICJ Reports* (1949), p. 174.   [36] ILM (1986), p. 543.
[37] See Article 305(1)(f) and Annex IX.

visions of human rights treaties. This is true even of the most highly developed of international organisations. The European Community does not have internal competence to pursue human rights in general.[38] When an international organisation and its member states both become parties to a treaty, the treaty will usually make special provision as to how the organisation and its member states are to exercise their rights and perform their obligations. It will, for example, provide that together they shall have no more votes than the total votes of the member states.[39]

The European Communities

Anything to do with the European Communities is complex, and this is particularly so for the law governing their external relations. Because of the significant and increasing involvement of the Communities in treaty-making it is necessary to know something of the relevant law, but a detailed account is outside the scope of this book.[40]

The European Economic Community (EEC) was established by the Treaty of Rome 1957. There are two other Communities, the European Atomic Energy Community (Euratom) and the European Coal and Steel Community (ECSC). The name of the EEC was changed to European Community (EC) by the Maastricht Treaty 1992. There is also the European Union (see below). Each of the three Communities has international legal personality, and therefore the capacity to enter into treaties with states and other international organisations. However, because the EC has *exclusive* competence for certain subjects, such as fisheries and trade in goods, the Member States can no longer conclude treaties which deal only with those subjects.[41] It is now for the EC alone to enter into such treaties, provided of course that the negotiating states agree. But where competence is *shared* between the EC and its Member States, such as on the environment, trade in services, competition, telecommunications and

---

[38] And is not therefore empowered under the EC Treaty to enter into negotiations to accede to the European Convention on Human Rights (see ECJ Opinion 2/94).

[39] See Article 4 of Annex IX to the UN Convention on the Law of the Sea (note 31 above). See also Article XII of the Convention on the Conservation of Antarctic Marine Living Resources 1980 (CCAMLR) (402 UNTS 71; ILM (1980), p. 837; UKTS (1982) 48; TIAS 10240).

[40] See generally, Chapter 9 of MacLeod, Hendry and Hyett, *The External Relations of the European Communities* (1996), which is the leading work on this perplexing subject; also the concise account in D. McGoldrick, *International Relations Law of the European Union* (1997).

[41] See p. 176 below about treaties entered into by Member States before they joined the EC. Euratom and ESCS have exclusive competence for certain matters.

development aid, or where the area of application of a treaty includes overseas territories of Member States,[42] both the EC and the Member States (though not necessarily all of them) can become parties. Such a treaty is known as a 'mixed agreement'. There are some treaties, such as ILO Conventions, to which Member States are parties but which do not permit an international organisation to be a party, even if it has exclusive or shared competence for the subject. In such a cases, those EC Member States which are parties to the treaty have an obligation to protect the interests of the EC. But these internal matters are not of direct concern to the other parties.

Where there is shared competence, such as for social security matters, the Member States can still conclude bilateral treaties with third states, or even with each other, though in doing so they must of course ensure the treaty is consistent with EC law. To protect Member States' rights when the EC alone concludes a treaty on a subject of shared competence, the Member States will usually insist on the inclusion of what is known as a 'Canada Clause'. This declares that the Member States retain power to enter into treaties on the subject.[43] Some treaties contain a provision under which the EC can make a 'declaration of competence' about the respective competences of itself and its Member States with regard to the matters covered by the treaty.[44]

The European Union

Unlike the European Community, the European Union (EU) has, as yet, no international legal personality.[45] It may not therefore enter into treaties. When the Member States wished to conclude a treaty with a third party in connection with the EU's Common Foreign and Security Policy (CFSP) or Justice and Home Affairs (JHA), the treaty had to be concluded by the Member States. However, since the Treaty of Amsterdam 1997 came into force the Council of the European Union is able to conclude treaties within the CFSP and JHA fields.

---

[42] For example, the Convention on the Conservation of Antarctic Marine Living Resources 1980 (note 39 above).
[43] See MacLeod, pp. 234–5. The name of the clause has nothing to do with Canadian federalism, but because the clause was first used in a Canada–EC treaty of 1976 (OJ (1976) L260/1).
[44] See Article 5 of Annex IX to the UN Convention on the Law of the Sea (note 31 above); and Article 47 of the Straddling Stocks Agreement 1995 (ILM (1995), p. 1542).
[45] See McGoldrick, *International Relations* (note 40 above), pp. 36–9.

5

Full powers

> We have judged it expedient to invest a fit person with Full Power to
> conduct negotiations on Our part in respect of Our United Kingdom
> of Great Britain and Northern Ireland: Know, therefore, that We,
> reposing especial Trust and Confidence in the Wisdom, Loyalty,
> Diligence and Circumspection of our Trusty and Well-beloved Sir
> Patrick Henry Dean, Knight Commander of Our Most Distinguished
> Order of Saint Michael and Saint George . . .[1]

The quotation is but a small extract from an old-style full powers in use
until quite recently by the United Kingdom. Other states also used, and
some may still use, similar antiquated nonsense. It is therefore not so surprising that an air of mystery still surrounds the topic. Full powers are no
more than a document produced as evidence that the person named in it is
authorised to represent his state in performing certain acts in relation to
the conclusion of a treaty, in particular its signature. The production of
full powers is a fundamental safeguard for the representatives of other
states that they are dealing with a person with the necessary authority. This
is equally important for the depositary of a treaty in view of the heavy
responsibilities he has to discharge. But, given the purpose of full powers,
before doing any act covered by them the holder must still obtain specific
instructions from his government.

In the past full powers were invariably required. The growth of treaties in
simplified form, such as exchanges of notes, and the general trend towards
informality in treaty-making, might lead one to think that the need for full
powers is not so great today.[2] That is not so. With the substantial increase
in the number of states, and the enormous growth in treaty-making,

---

[1] For the whole ghastly text, see Blix and Emerson, pp. 40–1. Note: that, even when the document is in respect of only one treaty, it is now referred to in the plural: full powers.
[2] For the origins of modern full powers see D. O'Connell, 'A Cause Célèbre in the History of
Treaty-Making', BYIL (1967), p. 156.

especially multilateral, full powers have assumed a renewed importance. Whether a treaty is bilateral or multilateral, it is therefore *essential to know in each case whether or not full powers will be needed* and, if so, to ensure that they are provided *in good time.*

Credentials

A delegate attending an international conference at which a multilateral treaty is to be negotiated needs to submit to the government or organisation hosting it a document, known as 'credentials', issued by his state authorising him to represent it.[3] They will be issued, in accordance with the rules applicable to the conference, by or on behalf of the head of state or government or, more usually, the foreign minister or a person authorised by him (see Appendix H). But the representative, by virtue of his credentials, does *not* have the authority to do more than adopt the text of a treaty and sign the Final Act. This is so even if the treaty is subject to ratification. He always needs specific instructions from his government before he can sign a treaty, as well as full powers if these are required. The same applies to a duly accredited representative to an international organisation, and even with respect to a treaty adopted within the organisation unless he has *general full powers* (see below). Full powers and credentials can, however, be combined.

Meaning of full powers

Article 2(1)(c) defines 'full powers' as:

> a document emanating from the competent authority of a State designating a person or persons to represent the State for negotiating, adopting or authenticating the text of a treaty, for expressing the consent of the State to be bound by a treaty, or for accomplishing any other act with respect to a treaty.

Although the definition refers to several different acts, it is only those which are actually specified in the document which will be authorised. The phrase 'any other act with respect to a treaty' includes:

(1) acts with respect to treaty status, such as acts declaring invalid, terminating or withdrawing from, or suspending the operation of, a treaty (see Article 67);

---

[3] For credentials, see R. Sabel, *Procedure at International Conferences* (1997), pp. 43–51.

(2) declarations or notifications in the nature of binding instruments which extend or modify the obligations of the state, such as a notification of provisional application or territorial extension; and

(3) declarations under Article 36(2) of the Statute of the International Court of Justice.[4]

More to the point, the phrase also includes signatures *ad referendum* or signatures subject to ratification.[5]

The general rule

A person is considered as representing a state for the purpose of adopting or authenticating the text of a treaty, or for the purpose of expressing the consent of the state to be bound by it, if (a) he produces appropriate full powers, or (b) it appears from the practice of the states concerned, or from other circumstances, that their intention was to consider the person as representing the state for such purposes and thus to *dispense* with full powers (Article 7(1)(b)). Unless withdrawn, full powers remain valid indefinitely, that is to say so long as there is outstanding an act covered by them.

Bilateral treaties

The ability to dispense with the production of full powers is important for bilateral treaties. The general practice today is to dispense with full powers if the other side has not requested them, though it is only prudent to seek confirmation that the other state is similarly willing, especially if the treaty is to be signed at a level below that of foreign minister; and if the treaty is to enter into force on signature it is prudent to obtain assurance that the person signing for the other state has authority to do so. In principle, full powers could be required even for a note which is to form part of an exchange of notes, but in practice this is not done. If states are content to enter into treaty relations by using simplified forms, it would be inconsistent to require such a formal document as full powers. Also, where a bilateral treaty is subject to ratification or similar procedure the states may more readily agree to dispense with full powers.

---

[4] *UN Depositary Practice*, para. 105.   [5] See p. 81 below.

Multilateral treaties

Today credentials are usually sufficient authority for all acts connected with the conclusion of a multilateral treaty, including signing the Final Act,[6] but *not* for signature and subsequent acts with respect to the treaty. Full powers are required to sign a multilateral treaty, even if it is subject to ratification, unless the negotiating states agree to dispense with them. This may happen if the number of states involved is small, but the UN Secretary-General, and the chief administrative officer of any other international organisation, will insist on full powers being produced for the signature of treaties for which he is to be the depositary. When full powers are required, the state or international organisation convening the conference must verify that they are valid and consistent with accepted depositary practice, even if it is not to be the depositary of the treaty.[7] The host state or organisation, and later the depositary, must also check that each state is entitled to become a party to the treaty. Even if a representative has valid full powers it does not follow that his state is entitled to become a party, in which case it should not of course be invited to sign the treaty.[8]

When full powers are never required

Article 7(2) contains exceptions to the general rule that full powers are required. Because of their functions, the following are considered as representing their state and do *not* have to produce full powers:

(1) Heads of state, heads of government and foreign ministers, for the purpose of performing *all acts relating to the conclusion of a treaty.* Because of their ostensible authority, these three categories of persons (which we will refer to as 'the Big Three') are not required to produce full powers for the purpose of adopting, authenticating or signing the text of a treaty or of expressing consent to be bound by it.

(2) Heads of diplomatic missions, for the purpose of *adopting the text of a treaty* between their state and the state to which they are accredited. Article 3(1)(c) of the Vienna Convention on Diplomatic Relations 1961 provides that the functions of a diplomatic mission include negotiating with the government of

---

[6] See pp. 73–4 below about the relative insignificance of signing a Final Act.

[7] Norway convened the conference which adopted the Landmines Convention in 1997, but it was opened for signature in Ottawa and the depositary is the UN Secretary-General.

[8] See pp. 92–3 below.

the receiving state, and thus the head of mission may adopt the text of a treaty between the two states.[9] Although Article 7(2)(b) of the 1969 Convention does not refer to authenticating the text, it is unlikely that a state would require production of full powers for this purpose. However, unless full powers have been dispensed with, they are required for the purpose of signing a treaty even if signature will not constitute consent to be bound.

(3) Representatives accredited by states to an international conference or to an international organisation or one of its organs, for the purpose of *adopting the text of a treaty* in that conference, organisation or organ. For a long time most multilateral treaties have been drawn up and adopted at international conferences or within international organisations and, provided a representative has been duly accredited, there is no need for him to have full powers for the adoption of the treaty. Permanent representatives to international organisations may have general full powers.

General full powers

In order to avoid having to produce full powers on each occasion that a treaty is to be signed within an international organisation, a state may issue its permanent representative to the organisation with general full powers. This is common for permanent representatives to the United Nations, and sometimes their deputies. General full powers can be issued either separately or combined with credentials. A model of the former for a permanent representative to the United Nations is at Appendix J.[10] Unless specifically provided for, general full powers will not authorise acts in relation to a treaty adopted at a conference *convened by the organisation*, rather than a treaty adopted *within the organisation* (e.g., by an annual or special assembly).

Granting a person general full powers does not, of course, empower that person to do as he likes; as with special (i.e., ordinary) full powers, he will need to seek specific instructions from his government before doing any act in relation to a treaty. The way these are given depends on the constitution and practice of his state, and is of no concern to other states or the depositary.

General full powers should be deposited with the secretariat of the organisation as soon as possible, and a copy (preferably certified by the secretariat as a true copy of the deposited original) retained by the permanent mission in case there is any question in future as to whether general full

---

[9] 500 UNTS 95 (No. 7310); UKTS (1965) 19.   [10] See also Blix and Emerson, pp. 40–1.

powers were deposited, or as to their precise terms. Experience teaches that the copy should be kept on a special file for easy retrieval at short notice.

Procedure

Although the form and content of full powers, and the issuing of them, will depend on the constitution and practice of each state, they must, in the words of the definition in Article 2(1)(c), emanate (issue) from the competent authority of the representative's state. In accordance with recognised international practice, this means one of the Big Three, though it is generally the foreign minister.

If the treaty is between heads of state, the competent authority to issue the full powers will be the head of state, unless he is to act in person. Although presidents often sign politically important treaties (and occasionally even MOUs), these days monarchs (or at least the constitutional variety) seldom sign treaties even if they are expressed to be between heads of state.

The wording of full powers does not have to be elaborate, but it must confer in an unambiguous manner authority for the person named to do the act in question, such as sign the treaty, and must include the following:

(1) Full names of the person authorised. An authority issued simply to 'the Ambassador of Nirvana' is not sufficient.

(2) Full title of the treaty. If it is not yet clear what it will be, the treaty should be identified by reference to its subject matter and the name of the conference or international organisation where the negotiations are taking place. There is no need to specify the expected date or place of signature of the treaty.

(3) Signature of one of the Big Three. A facsimile signature is not acceptable. Nor is it sufficient for full powers to be signed 'on behalf' of one of the Big Three. Full powers may not be issued by, say, a deputy foreign minister, unless he is in charge of the foreign ministry *ad interim* or is acting foreign minister. Nor will they be acceptable if issued by another, albeit cabinet, minister, apart that is from the prime minister.[11]

(4) Date and place of signature.

(5) Official seal. This is optional, but is usual.

A simple formula is at Appendix I.[12]

---

[11] *UN Depositary Practice*, paras. 31, 32 and 36.   [12] See also Blix and Emerson, pp. 38–9.

Full powers cannot be used by a deputy, or person acting for the person named in the full powers, unless he is also named in the full powers. It is therefore prudent to name at least two persons, especially if the leader of the delegation is a minister who may be called home at short notice.

Full powers are not needed when a representative deposits an instrument signed by any of the Big Three, such as an instrument of ratification.

The provision of full powers may take some time. Since these days foreign ministers are increasingly, and annoyingly for treaty departments, abroad, those responsible for the negotiation of a treaty should keep in mind the possible need for full powers. Today, negotiations are often not led by the foreign ministry. It is then the responsibility of any foreign ministry representative on the delegation to ensure that matters such as full powers are dealt with in good time. Advice should be sought from the foreign ministry treaty experts on whether full powers will be required. If the foreign ministry is content to dispense with them for a bilateral treaty, this should be proposed to the other side. If one side requests full powers this should not be seen as in any way casting doubt on the status or authority of the persons on the other side: it may well be either a domestic requirement of the other state or just its normal practice.

In the case of multilateral treaties concluded at international conferences or within international organisations the rules of procedure of the conference or organisation generally do not make provision for full powers. Therefore, unless there has been an express agreement to dispense with them, the general rule applies and full powers will be needed for signature, and the UN Secretary-General will insist on them if he is to be the depositary of the treaty.

Sending full powers by telegram or fax

Should the need for full powers have been overlooked, or there has been a delay in obtaining them, some secretariats may, in exceptional circumstances, accept full powers conveyed by a telegram sent in the name of the person who has granted the full powers. However, this will not be acceptable if the treaty is to enter into force on signature. The telegram would have to contain the same information as the full powers.[13] The original *must* be lodged with the secretariat as soon as possible thereafter. But

[13] See also ibid., pp. 42–4.

today it is better – and much simpler for all concerned – for the original signed text to be faxed, the original being sent on as soon as possible. The UN Secretary-General will accept a faxed copy of the signed original; he will not accept telegraphic full powers. He has a duty to the other negotiating states to do his best to ensure that only duly appointed representatives sign. With the rapid expansion of the international community, and with it a significant increase in the number of diplomats and other officials attending international meetings and conferences, it is that much more difficult to verify whether each representative is duly authorised. There has also been some difficulty in obtaining the signed original afterwards.[14] Other depositaries would do well to follow UN practice.

Full powers issued by an international organisation

If an international organisation is entitled to take part in the adoption and signature of a multilateral treaty it will have to provide full powers for its representative to sign, although with a bilateral treaty full powers may be dispensed with. Who within the organisation is authorised to issue full powers depends on its rules and practice. In the case of the European Community they are issued, as appropriate, by the General Secretariat of either the Council of Ministers or the Commission.[15]

Proxy signature

Although it is exceptional, a state may authorise a minister or official of another state to sign a treaty on its behalf. Unless the negotiating states agree otherwise, the principal state must provide the proxy with full powers.

Invalid acts

Article 8 provides that an act relating to the conclusion of a treaty which is performed by someone who cannot be considered under Article 7 as authorised to represent a state for that purpose is without legal effect unless it is confirmed by the state. Ratification of the treaty will constitute

---

[14] Information supplied by the UN Treaty Section.
[15] MacLeod, Hendry and Hyett, *The External Relations of the European Communities* (1996), pp. 116–17.

confirmation, as will conduct by the state which evidences the acceptance by it of the act, such as publication by it of the treaty or its implementation. However, if the authority of a representative to express the consent of his state to be bound (e.g., by signature alone) has been made subject to a specific restriction, his failure to observe that restriction cannot be invoked as invalidating the consent of the state, unless the restriction was notified to the other negotiating states before the representative expressed consent (Article 47).

Similarly, a state cannot invoke Article 46 by claiming that its consent to be bound by a treaty has been expressed in violation of its internal law regarding competence to conclude treaties if the consent has been expressed by one of the Big Three, since under Article 7(2)(a) each of them has indisputable authority to express consent.

6

Adoption and authentication

And where, though all things differ, all agree.[1]

Adoption

Once the negotiations are complete it is necessary for the states which took part in the drawing up of the treaty to express their agreement with its form and contents by adopting the text. Unless the circumstances suggest otherwise,[2] the act of adoption does not amount to consent to be bound by the treaty. A state which takes part in the drawing up and adoption of the text of a treaty is known as a 'negotiating State' (Article 2(1)(e)).

The rules on adoption are in Article 9, which embodies the classic principle that, unless otherwise agreed, adoption needs the consent of all the states which participated in drawing up the text. Until recent times this was the norm. The article, however, recognises that, since the Second World War, in drawing up treaties in large international conferences or within international organisations, the practice had been for adoption by the affirmative vote of a specified majority of the states. The unanimity rule is now restricted to the adoption of bilateral treaties or treaties drawn up by only a few states (plurilateral treaties). However, consensus is now frequently sought for multilateral treaties, though not always attainable (see below).

Bilateral treaties

Adoption of the text of a bilateral treaty is often done by initialling, though even then it may not always be easy to establish the precise time at which the text can be said to have been adopted, since the text may not be finally settled until shortly before it is to be signed. In that case adoption is, in

---

[1] Alexander Pope (1688–1744), *Windsor Forest*, 13.   [2] See p. 90 below.

effect, by signature, which will often express also consent to be bound. This telescoping of the stages of treaty-making is normal for bilateral treaties, but rare for multilateral treaties.

Treaties adopted at international conferences

The adoption of the text of a treaty at an international conference requires the vote of two-thirds of the states 'present and voting' (which excludes abstentions) unless, by the same majority, they decide to apply a different rule (Article 9(2)). These rules were formulated by the International Law Commission on the basis of general practice at the time. Many treaties are adopted by conferences convened under a UN General Assembly resolution, for example, the UN Convention on the Law of the Sea 1982, or for that matter the Vienna Convention itself. The UN Secretariat will prepare, in consultation with the states concerned, draft rules of procedure, including a rule for voting. One of the first tasks of the conference will be to adopt the rules. It is not clear by what majority this must be done. Some argue that a simple majority is sufficient, other say a two-thirds majority is necessary. In practice, the rules are almost invariably adopted by consensus.[3]

The term 'international conference' is not defined in the Vienna Convention and is not a term of art, but it is probably safe to say that, at least for present purposes, any meeting of more than two states to negotiate a treaty is a conference. The smaller the number of negotiating states, the less likely it is that they will agree to accept less than unanimity. In addition, the subject matter may be such as to require unanimity, either for political reasons, or because without unanimity the treaty might be ineffective because a key state or states which might be outvoted would decide not to become a party.[4] The negotiation of texts in the UN Disarmament Commission is done on the basis of unanimity.

Consensus

Since the text of the Vienna Convention was adopted in 1969, the wheel has come almost full circle. The two-thirds majority rule, or similar rules, were felt at the time to be necessary to protect the interests of states which

---

[3] R. Sabel, *Procedure at International Conferences* (1997), pp. 25–9.   [4] See p. 70 below.

would be in a minority at a conference. But with the rapid rise in the number of states the rule became insufficient to protect important minority interests which are often represented by less than one-third of the membership of the United Nations. For example, in the 1970s the developed countries were regularly outvoted when multilateral treaties were adopted at conferences convened by the United Nations. The conference which drew up the Vienna Convention on the Representation of States in their Relations with International Organisations of a Universal Character 1975 was a failure because that Convention was found to be unacceptable to most states which host international organisations.[5] The contentious parts having been voted through against those states' objections, the Convention has not been adhered to by any major host state. Even were it to enter into force it is unlikely to have much practical effect.[6]

This and other examples eventually led to the realisation that for a multilateral treaty to be effective the substance has to be generally acceptable to the negotiating states.[7] This is especially so for law-making treaties, such as those prescribing human rights norms, and treaties establishing international organisations. Thus, the concept of consensus (sometimes referred to as 'general agreement') began to gain ground in the 1970s, and is now often incorporated in rules of procedure.[8] There is no agreed definition of this procedural innovation, the formulation of the concept differing according to the circumstances, but the three main features of consensus are:

(1) it is not the same as unanimity;
(2) a state can join a consensus even if it could not vote in favour; and
(3) it is not incompatible with 'indicative voting' (a straw poll).[9]

For the purposes of decision-making in the Council of the International Seabed Authority, consensus is defined in Article 161(8)(e) of the UN Convention on the Law of the Sea 1982 as 'the absence of any formal objection'.[10] The Rules of Procedure of the Conference on (now

---

[5] AJIL (1975), pp. 730–58; *Digest of US Practice in International Law* (1975), p. 40.
[6] As at 31 December 1998, twenty-three years later, thirty states had adhered to the Convention, yet only thirty-five are required for entry into force.
[7] See H. Schemers and N. Blokker, *International Institutional Law* (3rd edn, 1995), pp. 781–6.
[8] See generally R. Sabel, *Procedure at International Conferences* (1997), pp. 303–13.
[9] Evensen, 'Working Methods and Procedures in the Third United Nations Conference on the Law of the Sea, *Hague Recueil* (1986), vol. IV, pp. 483–6.
[10] ILM (1982) p. 1261; UN Reg. No. 31363; UKTS (1999) 81.

Organisation for) Security and Co-operation in Europe define consensus as:

> the absence of any objection expressed by a representative and submitted by him as constituting an obstacle to the taking of the decision in question.[11]

Some regimes, such as that of the Antarctic Treaty System, always proceed by unanimity or consensus when treaty-making. Even when rules of procedure provide for adoption by a specified majority, it is normal for there to be first an attempt to reach consensus, voting being used only as a last resort. Retaining majority voting as a fall-back can, at least in the final stages of negotiations, help to promote consensus, since a state which might otherwise be considering blocking consensus will know that it could be outvoted. The rules of most conferences therefore still provide for voting. The Third United Nations Conference on the Law of the Sea 1973–1982 proceeded on the basis that:

> The Conference should make every effort to reach agreement on substantive matters by way of consensus and there should be no voting on such matters until all efforts at consensus have been exhausted.

This was not written into the rules of procedure, but contained in a declaration, which was itself adopted by consensus. The voting rules were also made much tighter.[12] In the event, the Conference proceeded by way of consensus right up to its final substantive session, when there was voting on a number of amendments and on the adoption of the Convention as a whole. Rule 33 of the UN Conference on Straddling Stocks 1993–1995 provided that:

> The Conference should conduct its work on the basis of general agreement. It may proceed to vote in accordance with Rule 35 only after all efforts at achieving general agreement have been exhausted. Before doing so, the Chairman shall inform the Conference that all efforts at achieving general agreement have been exhausted.[13]

The use of consensus does, however, mean that because some – perhaps many – states will still be unhappy with the result, they will be more likely to try to modify the application of the treaty to them by means of reservations or interpretative statements.[14] It also means that the quality of the

---

[11] Rule 6(4); see A. Bloed, *The Conference on Security and Co-operation in Europe* (1993).
[12] Sinclair, pp. 37–9.   [13] UN Doc. A/CONF. 164/6 (1993).   [14] See pp. 100–7 below.

text may suffer. The lengthy process of seeking consensus can result in texts of considerable complexity or obscurity. The negotiation of only one new article for the Chicago Convention (Article 3*bis*), took up the whole three weeks of a conference.[15] But this is the price one has to pay for achieving a text which will have a better chance of obtaining wide adherence.

If the support of a state which is blocking consensus is critical for the success of the treaty, voting the text through may prove to be a pyrrhic victory. India blocked adoption of the Comprehensive Nuclear-Test-Ban Treaty in the Committee on Disarmament, which operates by consensus.[16] The matter was then taken to the UN General Assembly where the treaty was adopted by a vote of 158 to 3 (Bhutan, India and Libya) with 5 abstentions. The treaty cannot enter into force until forty-four (named) states (including India, North Korea and Pakistan) have ratified it.[17] The Landmines Convention 1997[18] was negotiated under considerable pressure, and produced a text which was, at least technically, not entirely satisfactory. The basic proposal had been developed by a relatively small group of states, which did not include the United States. Because it became clear to the United States that it could not obtain consensus for its amendments, or even a two-thirds majority, it did not call for a vote, but announced that it would be difficult for it to become a party. The Convention entered into force on 1 March 1999, but without the United States (or China and Russia, which did not take part in the conference) as a party. Some of its effectiveness may therefore be lost. These remarks might also be made about the Statute of the International Criminal Court (ICC),[19] which was adopted by a vote, the United States voting against. The outcomes in such cases are partly due to (largely domestic) political factors, and partly to pressure to complete negotiations by a fixed deadline. In contrast to other important treaty negotiations, most of the participants in the ICC conference were opposed to having a second session (as happened in the case of the Vienna Convention) or prolonging the session ('stopping the clock').

Treaties adopted within an international organization

Article 9 does not deal as such with treaties drawn up within an international organisation, as distinct from those drawn up at a conference,

---

[15] ILM (1984), p. 705; UKTS (1999) 68; and see pp. 198–9 below.
[16] Not to be confused with the UN Disarmament Commission (see p. 67 above).
[17] ILM (1996), p. 1443.   [18] ILM (1997), p. 1509; UKTS (1999) 18.   [19] ILM (1998), p. 1002.

including those convened by an international organisation, but Article 5 provides that the Convention is without prejudice to any relevant rules of an international organisation.[20] Accordingly, if the organisation has specific rules for the adoption of treaties, they will apply.

Many treaties are drawn up within the United Nations and the specialised agencies. In the United Nations they are normally negotiated in the Main Committees of the General Assembly, and particularly in the Sixth (Legal) Committee in the case of law-making treaties. A Committee recommends the treaty to the General Assembly for adoption, which is done by means of a resolution to which the text of the treaty is annexed.[21] The resolution will be adopted in accordance with the Rules of Procedure of the General Assembly, which for this purpose probably require only a simple majority. But, in practice, a draft treaty is not presented for adoption unless there is consensus or near consensus.

Authentication

Before a negotiating state can decide whether to consent to be bound by a treaty, it needs to have the final text. The process by which this is established is known as authentication, and consists of the certification that a document contains the definitive and authentic text, and is thus not susceptible to alteration. Although, at least in theory, the text could still be changed at any time before signature, for multilateral treaties it is important that there should be a point of no return so far as the text is concerned.

Authentication is done by an act or a procedure.

Bilateral treaties

Initialling the text of a bilateral treaty is normally regarded as amounting both to adoption *and* authentication, at least if the treaty is to be in only one authentic language. However, in practice each state is free to suggest technical, or even substantive, changes at any time before signature.

---

[20] See p. 9 above.
[21] See UNGA Res. 52/164 (A/RES/52/164), adopting the International Convention for the Suppression of Terrorist Bombings 1997. For the text only of the Convention, see ILM (1998), p. 251.

Multilateral treaties

For a multilateral treaty, a formal procedure of adoption followed by authentication is important. In the past authentication was usually done by signing the text. This was possible when the number of states involved was quite small and the authentic text was in only one language, usually French. But today multilateral treaties nomally have several authentic languages, and so other methods are needed. The business of negotiating a multilateral treaty is often a confused affair, as demonstrated in the recent case of the Statute of the International Criminal Court. Even when one has the services of a highly experienced secretariat, the final stages of what is usually a lengthy process are hectic, and errors and inconsistencies invariably creep into the text due to the pressure to adopt it by a certain date. It is not unusual for the basic negotiating text to be only in English, and for some of the other language texts to be available in final form only at the end of the conference. There is then a need not only to check the adopted text for typographical inconsistencies and errors (i.e., copy-edit), but to translate it, or complete its translation, into other authentic languages.

Article 10 therefore provides that the text of a treaty is established as authentic and definitive by such procedure as may be provided for in the text or agreed upon by the states participating in its drawing up. In the absence of such procedure, authentication is by signature, signature *ad referendum* or initialling of the text or the Final Act incorporating the text. Initialling is probably the most usual way of authenticating the text of a multilateral treaty which is to be between only a few states. For other multilateral treaties initialling is usually replaced by a formal procedure.

Treaties adopted within an international organisation

Article 10 does not govern the authentication of treaties adopted within an international organisation as such, since Article 5 preserves the applicability of the rules of the organisation. It is common practice for a treaty adopted within an international organisation to be authenticated by the adoption of a resolution by an organ of the organisation, such as an assembly of the member states, or by an act of authentication performed by a duly authorised authority of the organisation, such as the president of the assembly or the chief executive officer. The Constitution of the Food and Agriculture Organisation provides that the text of a treaty adopted by the FAO Conference is authenticated by the certification of two copies of the treaty in all the FAO languages by the Chairman of the FAO Conference and the FAO Director-General. One certified copy is deposited in the FAO archives once the treaty has entered into force; the other is sent to the UN Secretary-General for registration. Authentic copies, certified only by the Director-General, are sent to the FAO members.[22]

It is usual for a treaty which has been negotiated by a subsidiary body of the UN General Assembly to be adopted and authenticated in one step. Once negotiations have been completed, a cleaned-up text in the six official United Nations languages will be prepared by the Secretariat. A draft resolution with the text annexed will then be presented to the General Assembly. Adoption of the resolution amounts to adoption and authentication of the text.

When a treaty has been adopted and authenticated at a conference convened by the United Nations the Secretariat will prepare an authentic text in all six official UN languages, and the Secretary-General will usually send certified copies of the authentic text to members when the treaty is opened for signature.[23] This procedure is much to be preferred. In recent years a small number of important treaties were, for understandable political reasons, signed immediately on adoption. Inevitably this prevented the text from being properly checked, with the result that numerous errors then had to be corrected by a cumbersome procedure; sometimes the errors raised points of substance.[24]

Final Act

The Convention mentions Final Acts only in Article 10(b). A Final Act is a formal statement or summary of the proceedings of a diplomatic conference. It will include basic facts about the conference, such as its purpose, which states attended, who presided, who chaired the various committees and their composition. Treaties adopted by the conference and other related documents, such as resolutions and agreed or national interpretative statements will be attached. A good example is the Final Act of the Vienna Conference on the Law of Treaties (Appendix K).[25] It is usual for each negotiating state to sign the Final Act, but this is optional, and anyway does *not* commit the state to sign or ratify any treaty attached to it.

---

[22] UKTS (1961) 11. Article XIV(7). WHO has a similar procedure.
[23] As to opening for signature, see p. 77 below.   [24] See pp. 270–3 below.
[25] See also the Final Act of the 1996 Special Meeting of Contracting Parties to Consider and Adopt a Protocol to the London Convention 1972 (ILM (1997), p. 4).

Nevertheless, and depending on what is decided at the conference, signing the Final Act may have certain consequences, such as entitlement to membership of a preparatory committee.

Full powers are not needed to sign a Final Act, the credentials of the representative being enough.[26]

The Final Act of the Helsinki Conference on Co-operation and Security in Europe 1975 had no treaty attached to it. But, because it, unlike most Final Acts, contained lengthy, substantive (though not legally binding) provisions of great political importance, and thus might have been mistaken for a treaty, the Final Act contains a statement that it 'is not eligible for registration under Article 102 of the Charter of the United Nations'.[27] It is, in effect, an MOU.

When is a treaty 'concluded'?

The Convention refers to the 'conclusion' of a treaty twenty-three times, but does not define that term[28] (treaties may also be said to have been 'made', or 'entered into', but these are equally imprecise terms). The absence of a definition does not cause problems in the day-to-day work of a foreign ministry. For most purposes, a bilateral treaty is regarded as having been concluded when it is signed by both states. Depending on the circumstances, a multilateral treaty is generally regarded as having been concluded on signature of the Final Act (or other means by which it is adopted) or, if applicable, on the date the treaty is opened for signature, whichever is the later. For example, the Convention on the Elimination of All Forms of Racial Discrimination was adopted (but the text not authenticated) on 21 December 1965. It was opened for signature on 7 March 1966, and it is this latter date by which it is known. Although it has been suggested that 'concluded' refers to the entry into force of the treaty, this cannot be sustained as a general proposition, except when a treaty is brought into force by signature. The date of conclusion may be of some importance in the application of the rules in Article 4 (non-retrospection),[29] Article 30 (successive treaties)[30] and Article 59 (termination of a treaty by conclusion of a later treaty).[31]

---

[26] See p. 58 above.   [27] ILM (1975), p. 1293. And see p. 28 above and pp. 275–8 below.
[28] E. Vierdag, 'The Time of the "Conclusion" of a Multilateral Treaty', BYIL (1988), pp. 75–111.
[29] See p. 8 above.   [30] See p. 173 below.   [31] See p. 235 below.

7

Consent to be bound

and here is the paper which bears his name upon it as well as mine.'[1]

The term 'contracting state' describes a state which has consented to be bound by a treaty, even though it may not yet have entered into force (Article 2(1)(f)). A 'party' is a state which has consented to be bound by a treaty *and* for which the treaty is in force (Article 2(1)(g)). At that point, and only at that point, is the state bound by the treaty (Article 26).[2] To consent to be bound is therefore the most significant act which a state can take in relation to a treaty. This chapter explains the various means by which consent can be expressed. The next chapter deals with entry into force. However, as will be explained, although two quite distinct steps are necessary to become a party (consent to be bound and entry into force) they can take place at the same time.

A state does not consent to be bound merely by adopting[3] or authenticating the text of a treaty, or by signing a Final Act; it must do something further. Article 11 lists the ways in which a state can express its consent:

- signature
- exchange of instruments constituting a treaty
- ratification, acceptance or approval
- accession
- any other agreed means.

Signature

It is quite common for consent to be expressed by signature. This is more likely for a treaty between two or only a few states, in which case the treaty will often also provide for entry into force on signature. This will,

---

[1] British Prime Minister Neville Chamberlain, 30 September 1938, on his return from Munich.
[2] See p. 93 below about the procedural provisions of a treaty which are binding before then.
[3] But see p. 90 below.

however, only be possible if the constitutions of the participants do not require that there be prior parliamentary approval, and there is no need for new legislation.[4] Article 12 provides that signature expresses consent to be bound when:

(a) the treaty so provides;
(b) it is otherwise established that the negotiating states were so agreed; or
(c) the intention of a state that signature should express its consent is apparent from the full powers of its representative or was expressed during the negotiations.

Usually these days either the treaty will specify how consent is to be expressed or it will be implicit from its terms. Therefore, when it is intended that signature is all that is necessary, this will normally be reflected in the entry into force clause. Typically this will provide that the treaty 'shall enter into force on the date of signature'. This formula has the advantage that it also effectively prevents a party from later claiming that the treaty is not in force because it has not been ratified. In 1990, Iraq claimed this in respect of the boundary treaty with Kuwait of 4 October 1963, even though the treaty did not provide for ratification and had been registered, by Kuwait, with the United Nations soon after it had been signed. The Security Council did not agree with Iraq.[5] In the past when a treaty provided for signature, but was silent as to how consent was to be expressed, there was sometimes doubt whether ratification was necessary. The Convention does not resolve the matter, but it is of little or no practical importance today. It has long been the practice of states whenever they intend a treaty to enter into force by a procedure involving more than just signature to provide evidence of that intention, and usually by an express provision in the treaty itself. Furthermore, when a treaty provides for ratification it is presumed that a state has not become bound by its conduct unless that is clearly its intention.[6] If there is no indication, express or implied, of the need for ratification the treaty will be presumed to enter into force on signature.[7]

Unless the treaty otherwise provides, a state is free to express its consent to be bound by signature even if other states require that their signature be ratified, but this is exceptional.

[4] See pp. 143–4 below.
[5] Resolution 687 (1991): see the sixth preambular paragraph, and para. 2.
[6] *North Sea Continental Shelf* cases, *ICJ Reports* (1969), p. 25, para. 28.
[7] Sinclair, pp. 39–41.

'Open for signature'

Many multilateral treaties, especially those concluded within the United Nations, or at a conference convened by the United Nations, will provide that they will be 'open for signature' until a specified date, after which signature will no longer be possible. Thereafter a state may only accede (see, for example Articles 81 and 83 of the Vienna Convention itself). Some treaties, such as the four Geneva Conventions of 1949, are open for signature indefinitely.[8]

Signature ad referendum

It can happen that a state which had been willing for signature alone to bring a treaty into force discovers at a late stage that it is not yet ready for entry into force. This problem can be solved by inserting a provision postponing entry into force. But this may not be suitable in all cases; if a signing ceremony has been fixed it could be awkward to postpone it. It might also be difficult technically to amend the signature copies of the treaty, particularly if this has to be done at short notice and they are in more than one language. The solution is for the representative concerned to sign, but add after his signature 'ad referendum', or words to that effect. If later confirmed, the signature will constitute full signature of the treaty (Article 12(2)(b)).

Confirmation can take any form, but is best done by diplomatic note or letter, not orally. Some states sign *ad referendum* to indicate that the treaty has to be referred for parliamentary approval before it can be ratified. But if the treaty provides that signature is subject to ratification, it is unnecessary to sign *ad referendum*.

The Convention leaves open the question of the effective date of a signature *ad referendum*. In principle, the signature should be effective from the date of signature, not confirmation: unlike ratification, confirmation is of the signature, not of the treaty. But it is open to the negotiating states to agree to a later date. Whether the date is important will depend on the nature and content of the treaty.

Place of signature

A treaty, whether in the form of a single instrument or an exchange of instruments, is almost always signed in the same place and at the same

---

[8] 75 UNTS 3 (Nos. 970–3); UKTS (1958) 39.

time. A bilateral treaty can be signed in a third state. This does not necessarily need that state's consent, but it should be informed as a matter of
courtesy. However, it can be signed in different places and at different
times if this is necessary for reasons of convenience, protocol or politics. A
multilateral treaty between only a few states will sometimes be signed by
one of them and then circulated to the others for their signature. Some
exchanges of notes may be 'true' exchanges in that they are exchanged like
normal correspondence, though most are exchanged simultaneously.
Original copies of a treaty between India and Pakistan were, for political
reasons, signed at the same time in their two capitals.[9] A defence MOU was
once signed in the following way. Each minister signed one original in his
capital and sent it to the other minister. They then telephoned each other
to say that they were ready to sign the original each had received from the
other. Each then did so, dating and retaining that original. Nor is there any
reason why a treaty should not be signed simultaneously in different
places with the signing being observed by the participants on a video-tele-
vision link.[10] This would require at least two originals.

Doubt about signature

When a treaty is signed, but there is doubt about the authority of a representative to sign, the matter can be cured by ratification even if the treaty
does not provide for it.

Initialling

Initialling the text of a treaty will constitute signature if the negotiating
states have so agreed (Article 12(2)(a)). Although a treaty can be constituted by an exchange of third-person diplomatic notes (which are initialled but not signed),[11] this is not common practice, and is to be
discouraged for other forms of treaty since initialling is more commonly
used as the means by which a text is adopted or authenticated.[12] If a state is
ready to be bound without ratification, there should be no reason – except
perhaps political – why the treaty should be initialled rather than be

---

[9] M. Tabory, 'Registration of the Egypt–Israel Peace Treaty', ICLQ (1983), p. 996, note 46.
[10] See p. 16 above on 'cyber' signings.
[11] See the China–UK Exchange of Notes on the Establishment of Consulates-General 1996
(UKTS (1996) 100).   [12] See pp. 66–72 above.

signed. In order to avoid misunderstandings, consent to be bound should therefore not be expressed by initialling unless the negotiating states are clearly agreed that this will be the legal effect (see the discussion of the Dayton Agreement below). But if initialling is acceptable, it is obviously preferable for each state to initial; a mixture of initials and signatures could easily lead to confusion as to the effect of initialling. When initialling for the purposes only of adoption or authentication, it is therefore important that the initials are *not* placed in the signature block (the place under the testimonium where the representatives sign), but rather in the lower corners of each page.[13]

The Dayton Agreement

Like so much about the General Framework Agreement for Peace in Bosnia and Herzegovina 1995,[14] the arrangements for expressing consent to be bound and entry into force were unique. The text was adopted on 21 November 1995 near Dayton, Ohio. Adoption was effected by the *signature* of an *Agreement on Initialling* by the three states, Bosnia and Herzegovina, Croatia and the Federal Republic of Yugoslavia (i.e., Serbia and Montenegro). This provided that (1) by *initialling* each signature block of the Dayton Agreement and its annexed Agreements the parties *expressed their consent to be bound* by them; (2) that the parties committed themselves to *signature* of the Dayton Agreement and its annexed Agreements in Paris, 'in their present form . . . thus establishing their *entry into force*'; and (3) that the *Agreement on Initialling* shall enter into force *on signature*. Thus the initialling of the Dayton Agreement and signature of the Agreement on Initialling together amounted to consent to be bound by the treaty. Signature in Paris on 14 December 1995 was, apart from political considerations, only for the purpose of bringing the Dayton Agreement into force. The paramount need was to ensure that the three states had no chance for second thoughts on the road between Dayton and Paris.

Witnessing

Sometimes the signature of a treaty between two or only a few states will, because of its political importance, be signed, as witnesses, by the heads of

---

[13] See p. 352 below.   [14] ILM (1996), p. 75.

state or government or foreign ministers of third states. The practice is not new. There are examples from as long ago as the Middle Ages, and no doubt before, of senior officials witnessing the signatures of heads of state. The signature of a witness, however distinguished or powerful, has no legal significance – it will, in itself, not make the state of the witness a guarantor of the performance of the treaty. It is no more than a reflection of the involvement of those states in the negotiations, or in promoting them, and an expression of their concern that the treaty should be a success. The Camp David Accords 1979[15] and the Dayton Agreement are perhaps the prime examples. The latter was witnessed in Paris by the Presidents of France and the United States, the heads of government of Germany, Russia and the United Kingdom and the representative of the European Union, each adding their signatures after those of the parties. The Israel–Jordan Treaty of Peace 1994 was witnessed by President Clinton.[16]

Exchange of instruments

It is common for treaties to be constituted by an exchange of instruments. It is the *act of exchange* which constitutes consent to be bound if the instruments provide that it shall have that effect, or if it is otherwise established that the states have so agreed (Article 13). Quite often the notes will provide that the agreement constituted by the exchange of notes will not enter into force until each has informed the other that its constitutional formalities (or such like) have been completed. This is a kind of ratification. The exchange usually takes the form of an exchange of notes (or sometimes an exchange of letters; the terminology is not legally significant). About one-third of the treaties registered each year with the United Nations are in this form. Although the exchange of notes began life as an informal means of concluding a treaty, it is now used at all levels and for any subject. Although the notes are often signed by ambassadors or other officials, they can be signed by ministers, even by heads of state or government. They can be on matters of national importance or the mundane.[17] Although they are often self-standing, they can be supplementary to another treaty. They are frequently used to amend a treaty. In the vast majority of cases the exchange is between two states. Although it can

---

[15] Tabory, 'Registration' (see note 9 above), p. 997.   [16] ILM (1995), p. 43.
[17] Such as the transfer of a hut in Antarctica (UKTS (1998) 16); see Appendix E.

be between more than two, this can cause technical problems which may outweigh the advantages of the form unless there are good political reasons.[18]

See pages 355–8 below on the form, wording and procedure for exchanges of notes.

Ratification

Ratification is defined by the Convention as 'the international act so named whereby a State establishes on the international plane its consent to be bound by a treaty' (Article 2 (1)(b)), although, as already explained, it is not the only way in which a state can express its consent to be bound. The most common misconception about ratification is that it is a constitutional process. But, as the definition makes abundantly clear, it is an 'international' act carried out on the 'international' plane. Although parliamentary approval of a treaty may well be required – and be referred to, misleadingly, as 'ratification' – that is a quite different process. Ratification consists of (1) the execution of an *instrument of ratification* by the executive and (2) either its exchange for the instrument of ratification of the other state (bilateral treaty) or its lodging with the depositary (multilateral treaty).

The normal reason for requiring ratification is that following adoption and signature of a treaty one or more of the negotiating states will need time before it can give its consent to be bound. There can be various reasons. First, the treaty may require legislation. This should be done before the treaty enters into force for the state: otherwise it risks being in breach of its treaty obligations.[19] Sometimes a state will ratify before the necessary legislation has been enacted. This may be done so that it can say that it has been one of the first to ratify, and thereby gain kudos[20] at home and abroad. Although the stratagem may also have the beneficial effect of encouraging other states to ratify early, it is inherently risky since the treaty might enter into force before the state has enacted the legislation. Secondly, even if no legislation is needed, the constitution may require parliamentary approval of the treaty, or some other procedure, like publication, before the state can ratify. Thirdly, even if no legislative or other

---

[18] For example, the double exchange of notes between Saudi Arabia and Qatar and Bahrain, see pp. 18–19 above. See also the multiple exchanges of notes mentioned in note 24, p. 19 above.
[19] See p. 144 below.   [20] Brownie points.

constitutional process has to be gone through, the state may need time to consider the implications of the treaty. That a state has taken part – even an active part – in the negotiations does not necessarily mean that it is enthusiastic about the subject or the text which was finally agreed. The breathing space provided by the ratification process allows time for reflection. Although bilateral treaties frequently provide for ratification, the need for it is generally greater for multilateral treaties.

These days even less formal instruments, such as exchanges of notes, can have similar, though simpler, ratification provisions.[21]

Most bilateral treaties now provide either that they shall be subject to ratification, or dispense with it by providing that they shall enter into force on signature, upon a specified date or event, or, rarely, on a date to be agreed.

Article 14(1) of the Convention provides that the consent of a state to be bound by a treaty is expressed by ratification when:

(a) the treaty so provides. This is the norm when ratification is required, and usually follows signature, though an express provision for signature is not always included;[22]

(b) it is otherwise established that the negotiating states were agreed that ratification should be required. This may be evidenced by a collateral agreement or in the *travaux*. Today that would be unusual: if a treaty is silent on the question of ratification it is presumed that it is not needed;

(c) the representative of the state has signed the treaty 'subject to ratification'. This is a unilateral act, and occasionally is expressly provided for in the treaty. Where the treaty provides that it will enter into force on signature or at a specified time, a signature expressed to be subject to ratification amounts to a conditional signature. However, unlike a signature *ad referendum*[23] the consent of the state to be bound will operate only as from the date of ratification. But in the interim the signature will have various legal effects;[24] or

(d) the intention of the state to sign subject to ratification appears from the full powers of its representative or was expressed during the negotiations.

If the treaty provides expressly that signature must be followed by ratification, it is not necessary for a representative to specify that his signature is subject to ratification.

It is another common misconception that once a treaty has been ratified it is then legally binding on the ratifying state. The situation is quite

---

[21] See p. 134, para(8) below.   [22] See p. 24 above.   [23] See p. 77 above.   [24] See p. 93 below.

different from the coming into force of legislation. Expressing consent to be bound does not, in itself, make the treaty binding on the state. *The treaty has to enter into force for that state.* When that happens the state becomes a 'party' to the treaty (Article 2(1)(g)). Whether, and when, ratification will bring the treaty into force for the state will depend on the provisions of the treaty.[25]

No obligation to ratify

Signature of a treaty imposes no obligation to ratify although, as already mentioned, a state should refrain from signature if it has little intention of ratifying.

Period for ratification

It is not usual to set a deadline for ratification, and some multilateral treaties are ratified (or acceded to) many decades later. The United States did not ratify the Genocide Convention 1948[26] until forty years later. Following the break-up of the Soviet Union, the Baltic states (not regarding themselves as successor states)[27] acceded to many treaties, including some nearly fifty years old. Libya and the United Kingdom acceded to the Hague Convention on the Pacific Settlement of Disputes 1907 some sixty-five and eighty years later, respectively.[28]

Ratification of part of a treaty

A state may consent to be bound by part of a treaty, provided this is permitted by the treaty or the other contracting states agree (Article 17(1)). Some multilateral treaties provide that on ratification a state is required to choose between certain options, in which case the choice must be made then if the ratification is to be effective (Article 17(2)). The Conventional Weapons Convention 1980 has three Protocols,[29] and requires that on depositing an instrument of ratification a state must notify its consent to be bound by at least two of them. If this is not done the instrument will not

---

[25] See pp. 131–5 below.   [26] 78 UNTS 277.   [27] See p. 314 below.
[28] 205 CTS 233; UKTS (1986) 66. The jurisdiction of the ICJ in the *Lockerbie* case is *not* founded on the Hague Conventions: see ILM (1998), p. 587.
[29] 1342 UNTS 137 (No. 22495); ILM (1980), p. 1523; UKTS (1996) 105.

be effective. The notification should be included in, or accompany, the instrument. This case should be distinguished from provisions which give a state an option which it is free to exercise or to decline. These often relate to means of settling disputes arising under the treaty.[30]

Exchange or deposit of instruments of ratification

One further step has to be taken. Article 16 (which also applies to 'acceptance' and 'approval': see below) provides that, unless the treaty provides otherwise, the consent of a state to be bound is established upon one of the following.

(1) The *exchange* of instruments of ratification between the contracting states. This is normal only for bilateral treaties. Unless the states want to emphasise the importance of the occasion, no ceremony is necessary, the exchange taking place in one of the foreign ministries and at whatever level is felt appropriate. Unless the treaty is of high political importance, the exchange would usually be effected by the head of the treaty department of the foreign ministry and a member of staff of the other state's embassy. Full powers are not needed. Although the exchange does not have to be simultaneous, this is almost invariably the practice. If it is not simultaneous the effective date of the exchange will be the date on which the later of the two instruments is received. If, as is usually the case, the treaty was signed in one of the states, it is the custom for the exchange to take place in the other state. The host state for the exchange should produce two originals of a Certificate of Exchange (sometimes called a *Procès-verbal* or Protocol)[31] (see Appendix M). The text of the Certificate, including any foreign language text, should be agreed in advance. The Certificate is signed when the instruments are exchanged, the representative of the other state taking away the original Certificate in which his state is given 'precedence'.[32] The Certificate is not published.

(2) The *deposit* of an instrument of ratification with the depositary of the treaty. This is the normal practice for multilateral treaties.

(3) The *notification* of the instrument of ratification to the other contracting state or states or to the depositary, if so agreed. This is a simplified form of exchange or deposit, but is best avoided in the interests of certainty and simplicity. It is hardly, if ever, now done.

Consent to be bound is effective from the date of exchange, deposit or receipt of notification. That date is the date of ratification, no other; and

---

[30] See p. 295, para. (2) below.   [31] Not to be confused with a treaty named 'Protocol'.
[32] See pp. 353–4 below.

certainly *not* the date on which any parliamentary approval was given. Whether, and when, the treaty then enters into force for the ratifying state will depend on other factors (see Chapter 9).

Conditional ratification?

Ratification must be unconditional; it cannot be made dependent on the receipt or deposit of other instruments of ratification, unless the treaty provides for this.[33] This does not, however, prevent (valid) reservations being attached to the ratification, or even the withdrawal of the instrument before entry into force.[34]

Instrument of ratification

Who can sign?

An instrument of ratification has to be signed on behalf of the state. The international practice is for this to be done as for full powers, that is, by the head of state, head of government or foreign minister ('the Big Three'), depending on the constitution and practice of each state. If anyone else signs, full powers authorising that person to do so will have to be produced. An instrument signed by a deputy- or vice-minister for foreign affairs will not be acceptable without full powers, unless it is clear that the minister is in charge of the foreign ministry *ad interim* or is acting foreign minister. Similarly, an instrument signed by another minister, including another cabinet minister, is not acceptable, even if the subject matter lies within his responsibility, unless the instrument is accompanied by a declaration (in effect full powers), signed by one of the Big Three, that under the law of the state the minister is authorised to bind the state in respect of the treaty.[35] So it is much simpler for one of the Big Three to sign.

Form and content of an instrument of ratification

The form and content of an instrument of ratification is not laid down by the Convention. Since, however, Article 2(1)(b) defines ratification as 'the

---

[33] *Satow*, para. 32.10.   [34] See p. 95 below.
[35] *UN Depositary Practice*, paras. 122–3, and Annex XV thereto.

international act so named whereby a State establishes on the international plane its consent to be bound by a treaty', the instrument must give clear and unambiguous expression to that intention. It is not enough to say that 'the necessary steps for the purpose of ratification have been taken'. The instrument must (1) identify the treaty by its title and the date when and place where it was concluded; (2) give the name and title of the person signing the instrument of ratification; and (3) state when and where the instrument was issued. The instrument can be in the form of a letter. An unsigned instrument is not acceptable, even if it bears the seal of one of the Big Three, since it is important to ensure that the act of ratification has been approved at the proper level. However, in exceptional circumstances the practice of the UN Secretary-General is to accept a letter from a permanent representative to the United Nations, accompanied by a fax of the signed instrument, confirming that the original is 'in the post'.[36] But if the instrument should not be received within a few days, the Secretary-General may refuse to treat the state as having ratified.

There is no rule as to the language in which the instrument must be drawn, but it is obviously sensible to use an official language of the depositary. But even if the instrument is not in any of these languages, it will still be acceptable. However, the depositary will not be able to acknowledge receipt until he has had the text translated to see exactly what it is and what it contains.

Appendix L gives as an example an instrument of ratification with the simplified wording now used by the British Foreign Secretary. It is no longer normal practice to attach a copy of the treaty to the instrument.

Occasionally a state will misdescribe the instrument: a state which has signed may deposit an instrument of 'accession'; a state which did not sign may deposit an instrument of 'ratification'. The depositary will then seek confirmation that the instrument should be treated as one of ratification or accession, as the case may be.

To be valid an instrument must be deposited within the time limit (if any) prescribed by the treaty.

Place of deposit of instruments

Instruments should be deposited at the seat of government of the depositary state or, if the depositary is an international organisation, at its

---

[36] Cf. the similar practice as to full powers at p. 63–4 above.

headquarters. A ceremony is only held if the event is important politically. Otherwise the instrument is simply delivered to the depositary. This can be done by post. However, given the importance of the instrument, and the trouble that has been taken over it, it is prudent to deliver it by hand. Instruments have been known to be mislaid in even the best organised of foreign ministries.

Acknowledgment and date of deposit

The depositary will send the ratifying state a formal acknowledgment of receipt of the instrument and notify the other parties and states entitled to become parties. Provided the instrument is valid, and meets all the necessary conditions for effectiveness, the date of deposit will be given as the date the instrument is actually received by the depositary, except in the various exceptional circumstances mentioned above.

Acceptance or approval

Consent to be bound can be expressed by 'acceptance' or 'approval' under conditions similar to those which apply to ratification (Article 14(2)). There is no substantive difference between signature subject to acceptance or approval and signature subject to ratification. It is now common for multilateral treaties (though not the Convention itself) to provide that they shall be 'subject to ratification, acceptance or approval'.

The use of acceptance or approval was developed in order to enable some states to avoid constitutional requirements to obtain parliamentary authority to ratify, particularly when the parliamentary process was described as 'ratification', and no clear distinction was drawn by the parliament or the constitution between that process and ratification on the international plane.[37]

The rules applicable to ratification apply equally to acceptance or approval. Unless the treaty provides otherwise, acceptance or approval have the same legal effect as ratification. Expressing consent to be bound by acceptance or approval, but without prior signature, is analogous to accession (see below), and for some treaties it is the only way to express consent. Treaties adopted within the Food and Agricultural Organisation (FAO) do not include provision for signature, consent being expressed

---

[37] See p. 81 above and Article 2(2).

by an instrument of acceptance, though this is now an outdated practice.[38]

Accession

Article 15 provides that accession is a means by which a state can consent to be bound by a treaty if:

(a) the treaty so provides;
(b) it is otherwise established that the negotiating states were agreed that consent could be so expressed; or
(c) all the parties have subsequently agreed that a state may express its consent by such means.[39]

Accession is primarily the means for a state to become a party if, for whatever reason, it is unable to sign the treaty. This may be because, as in Article 81 of the Convention itself, the treaty restricts signature to certain states, or because there is a deadline for signature and it has passed. Previously, for a few treaties it was the only means of becoming a party.[40]

No state has a right to accede unless the treaty so provides or the parties agree. In practice accession is mainly relevant to multilateral treaties. Today multilateral treaties which are subject to ratification – which is most of them – will almost always include an accession clause, and the right to accede will usually be exercisable even before the entry into force of the treaty. This is commonly done by making entry into force conditional on the deposit of a certain number of instruments of ratification (or acceptance or approval) or accession. Article 83 of the Convention provides that it:

> shall enter into force on the thirtieth day following the date of deposit of the thirty-fifth instrument of ratification or accession.

If, however, the treaty provides that a state may accede only after a certain date or event (e.g., entry into force of the treaty), but an instrument of accession is received before then, the depositary will inform the state that the instrument will be held until that date has arrived or the event has happened. Until then the instrument will not be counted for the purposes of calculating when the conditions for entry into force have been met.

---

[38] See Article X of the Compliance Agreement adopted by the FAO Conference in 1993 (ILM (1994), p. 968).
[39] That is, following entry into force: see the definition of 'party' (Article 2(1)(g)).
[40] *Satow*, paras. 32. 22 and 32.23.

Pre-conditions for accession

As with the right to sign, the right to accede may be restricted to a specified category or categories of states, and may be made subject to conditions or consent. The conditions may be matters of fact, for example, that the state is already a party to a specific treaty. Article 22 of the 1991 Environmental Protocol to the Antarctic Treaty[41] provides that, after the deadline for signature, the Protocol is open for accession by any state which is party to the Antarctic Treaty. The conditions may require the parties to determine collectively that they are satisfied that the state has met the conditions. The Convention on the Conservation of Antarctic Marine Living Resources 1980 (CCAMLR) is 'open for accession by any State interested in research or harvesting activities in relation to the marine living resources to which [the] Convention applies'.[42] The parties have interpreted this as requiring them to reach a collective determination whether the applicant state is truly interested in such activities. In practice the CCAMLR Secretariat circulates a note about the applicant state and if no party objects the application is deemed accepted.

The Framework Convention for the Protection of National Minorities provides in Article 29(1) that after its entry into force 'the Committee of Ministers of the Council of Europe may *invite* to accede to the Convention . . . any non-member State of the Council of Europe'.[43] Even when the accession clause provides for invitations to accede, it is sometimes necessary to conclude a treaty (usually called a protocol) to formalise the accession and make any consequential modifications to the principal treaty. This will often be needed if the treaty concerns a collaborative project.[44]

There are instances of the parties to a bilateral treaty consenting to a third state acceding to it, so making it multilateral. The Franco-German Convention on the Construction and Operation of a Very High Flux Reactor 1967 provides that:

> The present Convention shall be open to accession by third States. Any accession shall require the consent of the signatory Governments. The conditions

---

[41] ILM (1991), p. 1460; UKTS (1996) 6.
[42] Article XXIX (402 UNTS 71; ILM (1980), p. 837; UKTS (1982) 48; TIAS 10240).
[43] ILM (1995), p. 353; UKTS (1998) 42.
[44] The 1996 Protocol Additional to the 1995 Agreement between Estonia, Finland and Sweden regarding the M/S *Estonia* in effect amended that Agreement to allow other states to accede to it (UKTS (1999) 74).

of accession shall be the subject of an agreement between the signatory
Governments and the Government of the acceding State.[45]

The France–United Kingdom European Air Group Agreement 1998 provides for other European states to accede to it by means of *ad hoc* protocols.[46] When a treaty has been amended or supplemented by later treaties,
and it is necessary or desirable that an acceding state should be bound also
by those treaties, when inviting a state to accede the parties will require as
a condition for accession that the state consents to be bound by the later
treaties as well. This is most easily done by a declaration in the instrument
of accession that accession to the principal treaty constitutes accession to
the other treaties also. The treaties should be listed. It is even better if the
accession clause in the principal treaty includes such a condition.

Accession 'subject to ratification' does not amount to accession, but is
equivalent to signature subject to ratification. It is now rarely found, and is
probably due to a misunderstanding of the nature of accession.

The rules on deposit of instruments of ratification (or acceptance or
approval) apply also to instruments of accession; and, unless the treaty
provides otherwise, accession has the same effect as ratification.[47]

Any other agreed means

Article 11 is a good example of the inherent flexibility of the law of treaties,
as reflected in many parts of the Convention,[48] in that it provides that the
consent of a state to be bound may be expressed by any other agreed means.
The agreement does not have to be express: it is enough for it to be implicit
in the text of the treaty or otherwise established, for example by conduct.
Thus it is possible for a treaty to be adopted, without signature[49] or any other
procedure, and enter into force *instantly* for all the adopting states.
The treaty which established the Preparatory Commission of the
Comprehensive Nuclear-Test-Ban Treaty 1996 (CTBT) was adopted by a
resolution of the states which had signed the CTBT and was effective, at least
in international law, immediately without any further act by those states.

A most ingenious device is the 'simplified procedure' of Article 5 of the

---

[45] 821 UNTS 345 (No. 11764); UKTS (1976) 31.   [46] UKTS (1999) 10. See Article 35.
[47] Unless otherwise indicated, in this book the terms 'ratification' and 'consent to be bound' are
used to cover also approval, acceptance or accession.   [48] See note 2, p. 3 above.
[49] As to the lack of need for signature, see p. 24 above.

1994 Agreement relating to the Implementation of Part XI of the UN Convention on the Law of the Sea 1982.[50] The purpose of the Agreement, though not expressed as such, is to amend Part XI in such a way as to enable industrialised states to become parties. Because sixty-four states had ratified the Convention by the date of adoption of the Agreement, and the Convention would therefore enter into force four months later, there was an urgent need politically for a means by which the contracting states to the Convention could establish their consent to be bound by the Agreement in a low-key manner. For some there could have been domestic political problems if they had had to seek the approval of their parliaments to ratify the Agreement. It was therefore agreed that if a contracting state to the Convention merely signed the Agreement it would be considered to have established its consent to be bound unless it notified the depositary, within twelve months of the adoption of the Agreement, that it would not avail itself of this simplified procedure.[51]

'Signatory', 'party' and 'adherence'

In the media – and all too often in foreign ministries – it is said that a state is a 'signatory' of a treaty, with the implication that it is a party. As will have been evident from this chapter, there are several ways in which consent to be bound can be expressed; signature is only one and is often subject to ratification. And even when consent has been given, it does not mean that the treaty has entered into force, which would then make the state a 'party'. 'Signatory' is therefore a *loose and misleading term, and should be avoided* except when it is clear from the context in which it is used that it refers only to the fact that a state has signed, *and nothing more.* To avoid misunderstandings, if one wants to say merely that a state has signed, it is still preferable to say just that, adding, if appropriate, that it is subject to ratification. If a state has ratified, one should say exactly that. When a treaty is in force for a state, including when the treaty enters into force on signature, one should *always* describe it as a 'party'. One may also use a generic term to express the fact that a state has consented to be bound by saying, at least in English, that it has 'adhered' to a treaty.[52] This should

---

[50] ILM (1994), p. 1313; UN Reg. No. 31364.
[51] See D. Anderson, 'Further Efforts to Ensure Universal Participation in the UNCLOS', ICLQ (1994), pp. 886–93. See also p. 140 below and pp. 222–3 below.
[52] Note that the French for accession is 'adhésion'.

not be confused with the, now archaic, provisions in treaties for adhesion or adherence, which have now been replaced by accession clauses.[53]

The 'all states' and 'Vienna' formulas

During the Cold War problems arose over the application of treaty provisions under which 'all states' or 'any state' were entitled to become parties. At the time there were some entities over which there were disputes as to whether they were states, for example, the German Democratic Republic, North Korea and North Vietnam. To avoid differences over whether they had the necessary capacity to become party to a particular treaty, the so-called 'Vienna formula' was inserted into new treaties. Under it a disputed entity was entitled to become a party if it was a member of at least one of a number of specified international organisations. When this was first used is not clear (at least to the present author), but it is to be found in a simple form in the 1956 Statute of the International Atomic Energy Agency (IAEA).[54] Article 81 of the Vienna Convention is a typical example of the later, more elaborate form:

> The present Convention shall be open for signature by all States Members of the United Nations *or* of any of the specialised agencies *or* of the International Atomic Energy Agency *or* parties to the Statute of the International Court of Justice, *or* by any other State invited by the General Assembly of the United Nations to become a party.

There has been no need for such a formula since 1973. When in that year the Internationally Protected Persons Convention was adopted, the UN General Assembly issued a general statement that the Secretary-General, in discharging his functions as depositary of a treaty with an 'all states' clause, would follow the practice of the General Assembly and, whenever advisable, would request the opinion of the Assembly before receiving a signature or an instrument of ratification or accession.[55] Many older treaties retain the formula.[56] In most cases this will, as in the past, cause no problem unless there is uncertainty about the status of an entity. For

---

[53] See O'Connell, p. 229.   [54] 276 UNTS 3 (No. 3988); UKTS (1958) 19. See Article XXI.A.
[55] See the commentary on the Convention by M. Wood in ICLQ (1974), p. 791 at pp. 816–17; and UN Juridical YBs 1974, p. 157, and 1976, p. 186.
[56] For some earlier UN treaties General Assembly resolutions have opened up participation to 'all states'.

example, although it is clearly a state, there is serious doubt whether the Federal Republic of Yugoslavia can become party to treaties containing the formula, given its present equivocal position in the United Nations family of organisations.[57] At least one quite recent environmental treaty has used the Vienna formula, but this would seem to have simply been an unfortunate mistake.[58]

'All states' clauses should therefore now be used for treaties which are intended to have universal application.[59] Nevertheless, the depositary of a multilateral treaty may sometimes receive an instrument of ratification from an entity about which there is doubt or controversy as to whether it is a state.[60]

Rights and obligations prior to entry into force

In the period prior to the entry into force of a treaty, the acts of adopting, signing and consenting to be bound will create certain rights and obligations for the negotiating states, and for any depositary. The most obvious relate to those matters which have to be attended to so that the treaty can enter into force. As from the moment the text is adopted the provisions on depositary functions, authentication, consent to be bound, reservations, and other matters arising necessarily before entry into force, will apply (Article 24(4)). Other rights and obligations will arise during the interim period if the Convention or the treaty in question so provides.

Obligation not to defeat the object and purpose of a treaty prior to its entry into force

Article 18 requires a state 'to refrain from acts which would defeat the object and purpose of a treaty' before its entry into force for that state. When the treaty is subject to ratification, acceptance or approval, this obligation lasts until the state has made clear its intention not to become a party.[61] When a state has expressed its consent to be bound, the obligation

---

[57] See p. 316 below.
[58] UN Framework Convention on Climate Change 1992 (ILM (1992), p. 851; UKTS (1995) 28; UN Reg. No. 30822).
[59] See Articles XVIII and XX of the Chemical Weapons Convention 1993 (ILM (1993) p. 804; UKTS (1997) 45; UN Reg. No. 33757).   [60] See p. 265 below.
[61] In 1987, the United States announced that it would not ratify the Additional Protocol to the Geneva Conventions: see AJIL (1987), p. 910.

continues pending entry into force of the treaty, provided this event is 'not unduly delayed'. There is not only uncertainty as to whether the provision reflects customary law,[62] but also the extent of the obligation. What is certain is that one can determine whether the provision applies only by examining the treaty in question in the light of all the circumstances. There is virtually no practice in the application of the provision, but, given the manner in which it is formulated, the discussions in the International Law Commission[63] and the views of writers,[64] it is possible to formulate the following propositions.

A state is not required to comply in any *general* sense with a treaty or its object and purpose before it enters into force. It is sometimes argued that a state which has not yet ratified a treaty must, in accordance with Article 18, nevertheless comply with it, or, at least, do nothing inconsistent with its provisions. The argument is clearly wrong, since the act of ratification would then have no purpose because the obligation to perform the treaty would not then be dependent on ratification. The obligation in Article 18 is only to 'refrain' (a relatively weak term) from acts which would 'defeat' (a strong term) the object and purpose of the treaty. The signatory state must therefore not do anything which would affect its *ability* fully to comply with the treaty once it has entered into force. It follows that it does not have to abstain from all acts which will be prohibited after entry into force. But the state may not do an act which would (not merely might) invalidate the basic purpose of the treaty. Thus, if the treaty obligations are premised on the *status quo* at the time of signature, doing something before entry into force which alters the *status quo* in a way which would prevent the state from performing the treaty would be a breach of the article. The test is objective, and it is not necessary to prove bad faith. In the following examples there would probably be a breach of the obligation:

(1) The treaty provides for the return of objects, which are then destroyed by the possessor state before ratification.

---

[62] See Sinclair, pp. 19 and 43.
[63] See in particular the *Yearbook of the International Law Commission* (1965), Part I, pp. 87–99 and 262–3 and Part II, pp. 43–5.
[64] See, for example, Rogoff, 'The International Legal Obligations of Signatories to an Unratified Treaty', *Maine Law Review* (1980), pp. 263–99; McDade, 'The Interim Obligation between Signature and Ratification', NILR (1985), pp. 5–47; and J. Klabbers, 'Protection of Legitimate Expectations in EC Law', *Kansainvälistä* (1997), pp. 732–42.

(2) The treaty provides for territory to be ceded. Before ratification the ceding state transfers part of the territory to a third state.

(3) A number of states sign the treaty, each undertaking to reduce its existing armed forces by one-third. Entry into force has not been unduly delayed. After ratifying the treaty a state then announces that it has embarked on a long-term programme to double its forces.[65] The position would be different if the state had signed subject to ratification: its announcement would then amount in effect to an expression of its intention not to become a party.

These are fairly obvious examples. In the apparently only reported decision, it was decided by a Greco-Turkish Mixed Arbitral Tribunal in 1928 that a Turkish seizure of Greek property before the entry into force for Turkey of the Treaty of Lausanne was invalid, since if the treaty had then been in force it would have been a material breach.[66] This view is supported by the *travaux* of Article 18.[67]

Withdrawal of consent to be bound before entry into force

A question that sometimes (though very rarely) arises is whether a state which has consented to be bound may nevertheless withdraw its consent before the treaty enters into force. The answer does not depend on whether the treaty is bilateral or multilateral; though if a state has expressed its consent to be bound by signature alone it is not easy to see how this could be 'withdrawn'. What little authority there is is conflicting and there is hardly any state practice.[68] But, in principle, there would seem to be no reason why it cannot be done given certain circumstances. The consent is consent to be bound once the treaty has entered into force, not before. At the Vienna Conference one delegate referred to the 'sovereign right of a State to withdraw from the treaty at any time before it finally became binding'.[69] No delegate challenged this assertion. Also relevant is Article 68, which provides that a notification or instrument regarding invalidity, withdrawal etc., may be revoked at any time before it takes effect. The International Law Commission felt that the right to revoke was implicit given that the notification or instrument would not take effect

---

[65] See also O'Connell, pp. 222–4.   [66] 4 ILR 395; McDade, 'Interim Obligation', p. 14.

[67] McDade, 'Interim Obligation', pp. 24–5.

[68] Elias, *The Modern Law of Treaties* (1974), pp. 38–9; and the article by S. Rosenne in the *Max Planck Encyclopaedia of Public International Law* (1984), vol. 7, p. 467 (first column).

[69] *Official Records*, 19th Meeting, p. 100. The delegate was from the Ukraine SSR and at the time (1968) was in effect speaking for the Soviet Union.

until a certain date.[70] In 1952 Greece withdrew an instrument of acceptance deposited in 1950. After the treaty had later entered into force, Greece 'reconfirmed' its acceptance. In 1958 Spain withdrew an instrument of accession two months after it had been deposited, but before the treaty had entered into force. At the same time it deposited a new instrument containing a reservation. In both cases the UN Secretary-General notified the other states concerned. No objection was made.[71] In view of these cases, it is now the practice of the Secretary-General to regard withdrawal of consent before the entry into force of a treaty as permissible, on the understanding that until entry into force states are not definitively bound.[72]

The obligation under Article 18 does not prohibit a state from withdrawing an instrument. The obligation under the article is to refrain from *acts* which would defeat the object and purpose of the treaty before its entry into force for the state. It relates therefore to the *substance* of the treaty, rather than the procedure by which the state consents to be bound or by which the treaty enters into force. Mere withdrawal of an instrument will not, in itself, be a breach of the obligation in Article 18, since it must have the effect of defeating the object and purpose of the treaty.

But, even if there are no legal consequences of withdrawal, it could be damaging politically. The deposit of an instrument of ratification is a solemn act. Even if a new government coming to power does not like the treaty, that would not be a good reason to withdraw consent. The consent given by the previous government was given on behalf of the state, which continues in being despite the change of government. In giving consent to be bound a government engages the honour not just of itself but of its state.

Development of treaties

It is convenient to deal with this topic here. As we shall see, the inclusion of a built-in, compulsory amendment procedure enables a treaty to be adjusted more easily to meet changing needs.[73] This is especially so for procedures by which detailed, technical annexes can be amended by tacit agreement. But, in addition to a need for amendments to be made simply

---

[70] ILC Commentary, p. 264.   [71] See also p. 130 below.
[72] *UN Depositary Practice*, paras. 157–8.   [73] See pp. 215–18 below.

and quickly, there is sometimes a need for provisions by which a *legal regime* created by the treaty can develop. The procedures which have been devised are in no way outside the ambit of the Convention, its rules being broad and flexible enough to allow for many different types of regime.[74] This can be done in three main ways:

(1) framework treaties;
(2) legally binding measures adopted by organs of international organisations; and
(3) jurisprudence of tribunals established by the treaty.

A treaty may also develop in other ways which do not involve the creation of legal rights and obligations, such as by the adoption of guidelines and codes of conduct, but this is outside the scope of this book.

Framework treaties

The term 'framework treaty' is a relatively recent invention. It describes a multilateral treaty which is no different in its *legal* effect from other treaties. The term is no more than a description of a type of treaty which provides a framework for later, and more detailed, treaties (usually called protocols), or national legislation, which elaborate the principles declared in the framework treaty. The term is used particularly in connection with environmental treaties.[75]

Measures

It is not unusual when establishing an international organisation for the constituent instrument (i.e., the constitution) to give one of its organs the power to impose on the member states legally binding measures by which the object and purpose of the organisation can be more effectively achieved. The UN Charter is the most obvious example. If, under Chapter VII of the Charter, the Security Council determines that there is a threat to international peace and security it can impose measures to maintain or restore international peace and security. These can be a demand that an

---

[74] For a (debatable) analysis of contemporary procedures, see M. Fitzmaurice, 'Modifications to the Principles of Consent in Relation to Certain Treaty Obligations', *Austrian Review of International and European Law* (1997), p. 275.
[75] See Birnie and Boyle, *International Law and the Environment* (1992), pp. 13 and 27.

aggressor state leave territory it has occupied, the imposition of economic and other sanctions, the authorisation for the use of force or even the establishment of international criminal tribunals. Under Articles 25 and 48 of the Charter all Members of the United Nations have a legal obligation to carry out the measures. Although the measures apply only to particular situations (e.g., Bosnia), nevertheless by its actions over a period, and especially since the invasion of Kuwait in 1990, the Security Council has created important precedents. As a result, the parameters within which the Council may take measures have been more clearly defined.[76]

The Antarctic Treaty 1959 is short in length and short on detail.[77] There was therefore a need for it to include a dynamic element. Article IX provides for those parties which conduct substantial scientific research activity in Antarctica (the so-called Consultative Parties), by unanimity, to recommend to their governments measures in furtherance of the principles and objectives of the Treaty. Between 1961 and 1995 they recommended some 209 measures on a variety of subjects, including protection of fauna and flora, historic sites and specially protected areas; air safety; telecommunications; tourism; minerals exploration and disposal of nuclear waste. Article IX(4) provides that the measures 'shall become effective' when they have been formally 'approved' by the governments of all the Consultative Parties. The legal effect of this has been questioned since Article IX does not expressly provide that the measures once approved shall be legally binding.[78] But the long-established practice of the Consultative Parties shows that they regard measures which have been duly approved by all of them to be legally binding, at least in so far as their nature and content is capable of creating legal obligations.[79] Under Article IX(6) of its sister treaty, the Convention on the Conservation of Antarctic Marine Living Resources 1980 (CCAMLR), it is expressly provided that measures adopted by the CCAMLR Commission, again by unanimity, become binding on those parties which are members of the Commission 180 days after they have been notified to them, except that a member can opt out by making an objection within ninety days.[80]

---

[76] See R. Higgins, *Problems and Processes* (1994), pp. 169–85; and Bailey and Daws, *The Procedure of the UN Security Council* (1998), especially pp. 363–77.

[77] 402 UNTS 71 (No. 5778); UKTS (1961) 97.

[78] See A. Watts, *International Law and the Antarctic Treaty* (1992), pp. 24–32. For examples of measures, see ILM (1996), p. 1165.   [79] See pp. 192–3 below.

[80] 402 UNTS 71; ILM (1980), p. 837; UKTS (1982) 48; TIAS 10240.

Articles 37, 38 and 54(1) of the Convention on International Civil Aviation 1944 (Chicago Convention) empower the Council of the International Civil Aviation Organisation (ICAO) to adopt, by a simple majority of its members, international standards for air navigation. If a Member State cannot, for whatever reason, apply a particular standard, it must notify the Council. The standards are regarded as legally binding on all Member States, except in so far as a Member State has notified the Council otherwise.[81]

Regulations and directives made by the Council of Ministers under the constituent instruments of the European Community, as well as decisions on a common position or joint action, taken by the Council of Ministers in furtherance of the Common Foreign and Security Policy under the Maastricht Treaty on European Union, are binding on all the Member States and are not subject to confirmation or any procedure similar to ratification.[82]

Chapter VII decisions of the Security Council, measures under the Antarctic Treaty and CCAMLR, ICAO standards and EC and EU decisions, although binding in international law, may of course still need to be implemented in domestic law.

International tribunals

As part of a treaty regime states may establish an international court or tribunal to help further the object and purpose of the treaty. This has certainly been the task of the European Court of Human Rights, which has translated the general human rights principles of the European Convention on Human Rights into a highly developed body of jurisprudence. The Court of Justice of the European Communities has performed a similar role. Both courts – like domestic courts the world over – have developed the regimes created by their governing treaties in ways which had not been expected.[83]

---

[81] 15 UNTS 295 (No. 102); UKTS (1953) 8. See N. Matte, *Treatise on Air-Aeronautical Law* (1981), pp. 184–5

[82] MacLeod, Hendry and Hyett, *The External Relations of the European Communities* (1996), pp. 416–18.   [83] See, for example, the *Belilos* case, at p. 118 below.

8

Reservations

The subject of reservations to multilateral treaties is one of unusual –
in fact baffling – complexity.

a matter of considerable obscurity in the realm of
juristic speculation.

These views expressed by the eminent international lawyers, Hersch
Lauterpacht and O'Connell in 1953 and 1970 respectively, are even truer
today.[1] One might be forgiven for thinking that the last word had been said
in Articles 19–23, but, as is apparent from the vast amount which has been
written on the subject since the Vienna Convention was concluded,[2] a spir-
ited debate has developed on how the articles should be applied. Although
much of the discussion has centred on competing doctrines, it would be
wrong to think that the problems are just theoretical. Since the Second
World War, and especially during the last quarter of the twentieth century,
there was an enormous increase in the number and complexity of multilateral treaties on all subjects, and in the numbers of states adhering to them.
In 1945 the United Nations had fifty-one Members; by 1999 it had 187.[3]
There are only about three states which are not Members. In the twenty
years from 1975 to 1995 just one state, the United Kingdom, became a party
to some 330 multilateral treaties, and made reservations to forty-five of
them. Every week foreign ministries will be notified of new reservations.
They will have to consider whether they are acceptable and, if not, what to
do about them. Officials, including legal advisers, will be hampered by the
uncertainties which surround – or are thought to surround – the subject,
and which also cause problems for depositaries.

---

[1] ILC Yearbook 1953, vol. II (A/CN.4/63), p. 124; O'Connell, p. 230.
[2] See the (non-exhaustive) bibliography in UN Doc. A/CN.4/478 Rev.1, and the numerous references in W. Schabas, 'Reservations to Human Rights Treaties: Time for Innovation and
Reform', Canadian YBIL (1994), pp. 39–81.
[3] If one excludes the Federal Republic of Yugoslavia: see p. 316 below.

Following difficulties experienced by states in operating the regime laid down by the Convention, in 1993 the subject of reservations was referred to the International Law Commission for re-examination, and in 1994 Professor Alain Pellet was appointed as its Special Rapporteur.[4] The work is, understandably, very far from finished, and the ultimate outcome uncertain. This chapter will therefore not venture to anticipate what the Commission may propose.

The subject cannot be explained effectively without a close study of the contemporary practice of states. Decisions of international courts and tribunals are not a sufficient guide, since questions of reservations come before them infrequently.[5] This chapter will explain, as far as possible in practical terms, the role played by reservations, the application of the rules in the Convention, some outstanding issues and ways in which problems can be managed even now.

A state may seek to adjust the way in which a treaty will apply to it by means of interpretative declarations or reservations.

Interpretative declarations

Interpretative declarations are as widely used as reservations.[6] They are not a recent invention. The first may have been made by the United Kingdom in respect of an instrument adopted at the Congress of Vienna in 1815.[7] During the course of the negotiation of a multilateral treaty there will often be differences of view as to the meaning of a particular provision. If these cannot be resolved a delegation may make a formal statement expressing the interpretation favoured by its government. If a summary record is made of the proceedings, the statement should appear in it. It then becomes part of the negotiating history (*travaux*). But whether or not a record is kept, a state may feel it necessary or desirable to repeat its

---

[4] See the 1997 and 1998 ILC Reports (UN Docs. A/52/10, paras. 44–157 and A/53/10, paras. 469–540), and the first three meticulous reports of the ILC's Special Rapporteur (A/CN.4/470 and Corrs. 1 and 2; A/CN.4/477 and Add. 1; and A/CN.4/491 and Adds. 1–6). See also F. Horn, *Reservations and Interpretative Declarations to Multilateral Treaties* (1988). Although out of date, O'Connell, pp. 229–39, analyses the principal problems.

[5] For an instructive exception, see the France–UK Continental Shelf Arbitration 1977–8 (54 ILR 6) and the detailed discussion of it by Sinclair, at pp. 70–7.

[6] See, generally, UN Doc. A/CN.4/491/Add.4 (Third Pellet Report) and the 1998 Report of the International Law Commission, UN Doc. A/53/10, paras. 478–9, and note 177, and paras. 505–19.   [7] 64 CTS 454.

interpretation, usually at the time of signature or ratification. Pellet defines an interpretative declaration as:

> a unilateral declaration, however phrased or named, made by a State or by an international organisation whereby that State or that organisation purports to clarify the meaning or scope attributed by the declarant to the treaty or to certain of its provisions.[8]

Of course if a difficulty becomes apparent only after the treaty has been concluded, a declaration may be made even if the matter had not been raised before. The purpose of an interpretative declaration is very often to establish an interpretation of the treaty which is consistent with the domestic law of the state concerned. When ratifying the International Covenant on Civil and Political Rights, Austria declared that it 'understood' that Article 26 (non-discrimination) did not exclude different treatment for Austrian nationals and for aliens.[9] When ratifying the Rights of the Child Convention 1989, the United Kingdom made several declarations, one of which interpreted the references to 'parents' to mean:

> only those persons who, as a matter of national law, are treated as parents. This includes cases where the law regards a child as having only one parent, for example, where a child has been adopted by one person only, and in certain cases where a child is conceived other than as a result of sexual intercourse by the woman who gives birth to it [e.g. by in vitro fertilisation by donor] and she is treated as the only parent.[10]

This was designed to reflect UK domestic legislation, but was also a desirable elaboration of the term.[11]

An interpretative declaration will become an element in the interpretation of the treaty, and, provided it is not a disguised reservation (see below), the rules on interpretation in Articles 31 and 32 will apply to it. If other parties do not make conflicting declarations or indicate their disagreement, they may, depending on the circumstances, be regarded as having tacitly accepted it. When acceding to the Vienna Convention Syria declared that in Article 52 (coercion) the reference to 'force' included economic and political coercion. Other parties formally rejected this.[12]

---

[8] UN Doc. A/CN.4/491/Add.4, para. 361.
[9] See UN Multilateral Treaties, Chapter IV.4. For the Covenant, see note 27 below.
[10] See UN Multilateral Treaties, Chapter IV.11.
[11] Human Fertilisation and Embryology Act 1990, sections 27–9. For details of UK practice in making interpretative declarations, see BYIL (1997), pp. 482–5.
[12] UN Multilateral Treaties, Chapter XXIII.1.

However, the vast majority of interpretative declarations do not produce any response.[13]

It is possible for a party to make an interpretative declaration with regard to a *bilateral* treaty, although agreed declarations are more common.[14] Provided unilateral declarations do not attempt to modify the treaty, they raise no problem of principle. Although the content of some have been challenged, the right to make them has not. A declaration which is no more than a statement of general policy, or informs the other party as to how the declarant state will implement the treaty, should pose no problem. The United States has been the most active. In the period 1975 to 1995 it attached interpretative declarations to instruments of ratification of twenty-eight bilateral treaties.[15] US practice is to give the other state the text of the declaration before the exchange of instruments of ratification. This gives both parties an opportunity to agree on how to deal with the matter. In 1986 the US instrument of ratification of the UK–US Mutual Legal Assistance Treaty concerning the Cayman Islands included certain unilateral 'understandings'. The UK instrument of ratification was accompanied by an interpretative statement to the effect that the United Kingdom regarded the US understandings as not modifying the US obligations under the Treaty. This procedure had been agreed in advance.[16] There do not appear to be any cases where the content of a genuine interpretative declaration has been objected to, and there is no need for the other state to accept it expressly. But if no objection is made the declaration may be taken into account in interpreting the treaty (Article 31(2)).

Political declarations

When signing or ratifying a multilateral treaty, a state may make a declaration which is not intended to have any legal effect, or at least not in respect of the treaty itself. A declaration may be as to the general policy of the state towards the subject matter of the treaty, or a disclaimer that ratification does not signify recognition of a particular party as a state.

---

[13] As to other declarations made on ratification of the Convention, see Sinclair, pp. 63–8.
[14] See generally UN Doc. A/CN.4/491/Add.4, paras. 494–521.
[15] See also Whiteman, vol. 14, pp. 164–70.
[16] UKTS (1990) 82; UN Reg. No. 28332; UN Doc. A/CN.4/491/Add.4, paras. 505–6.

Disguised reservations

In many cases a declaration will be in terms which leave no doubt that it is intended to be a reservation, being either headed 'reservation' or prefaced by words such as 'the Government of Freedonia reserves . . .'[17] In other cases a state may make a declaration which is in fact an attempt (as in the definition of reservation) 'to exclude or to modify the legal effect of certain provisions of the treaty in their application to that State'. Nor is it uncommon for what is in fact a reservation to be described as an 'understanding', 'explanation' or 'observation'. If a state makes its acceptance of certain provisions on the 'understanding' that they are to be interpreted in a particular way, that may, depending on the circumstances, amount to a reservation.[18] The situation is complicated by the fact that these terms are used also for genuine interpretative declarations. Disguising a reservation may be done because the treaty prohibits reservations, or because it may be more acceptable politically for a state not to appear to be attaching conditions to its participation in a treaty. But, as the definition of reservation makes clear, it does not matter how the declaration is phrased or what name is given to it, one must look at the substance.[19]

Bulgaria's ratification of the Customs Convention on the International Transport of Goods under Cover of TIR Carnets 1975 (TIR Convention) was accompanied by a 'declaration' denying the right of economic unions to become parties to the Convention. The Member States of the European Economic Community, and the Community itself, responded by pointing out that the TIR Convention allowed for such participation; that the declaration had the appearance of a reservation; and that the Convention prohibited reservations except to the dispute settlement article.[20] On ratifying the Seabed Arms Control Treaty 1971,[21] Yugoslavia made a declaration to the effect that if a party wished to exercise inspection rights under the Treaty above the continental shelf of another party it had to give it advance

---

[17] See, for example, the numerous declarations made by parties to the International Covenant on Civil and Political Rights in *UN Multilateral Treaties*, Chapter IV.4. But see p. 167 below on territorial extension.

[18] Pellet does not regard a 'conditional interpretative declaration', as a reservation: UN Doc. A/CN.4/491/Add.4, paras. 314–99.

[19] See the 'understandings', 'interpretations', 'views', 'declarations', etc. made by the United Kingdom on ratification in 1998 of Additional Protocol I to the Geneva Conventions (UKTS (1999) 29, pp. 74–6).

[20] See *UN Multilateral Treaties*, Chapter X.A-16. The Convention is in 1079 UNTS 89 (No. 16510). For other examples of UK responses to declarations, see BYIL (1997), pp. 485–6.

[21] 955 UNTS 115 (No. 13678); ILM (1971), p. 145; UKTS (1973) 13.

notice. The United Kingdom responded that it could not accept this as a valid interpretation and that, in so far as it was intended to be a reservation, the United Kingdom formally objected to it on the ground that it was incompatible with the object and purpose of the Treaty.[22] The UN Convention on the Law of the Sea 1982 prohibits reservations except where expressly permitted, but allows a state to make interpretative 'declarations or statements', provided these do not 'purport to exclude or modify the legal effect of the provisions of this Convention in their application to that State'.[23] Many have been made, and many objected to as being reservations.[24] On ratification of the Chemical Weapons Convention 1993[25] the United States stated that, for the purposes of the Annex on Implementation and Verification, it would be a 'condition' that no sample collected by an inspection team could be removed from the United States for analysis. The Annex does not envisage any such restriction. Thus, although not labelled 'reservation', the statement, and in particular the use of the term 'condition', clearly went beyond interpretation, and amounted to a reservation.

Reservations[26]

Article 2(1)(d) defines a reservation as:

> a unilateral statement, however phrased or named, made by a State, when signing, ratifying, accepting, approving or acceding to a treaty, whereby it purports to exclude or to modify the legal effect of certain provisions of the treaty in their application to that State.

Although a reservation is 'unilateral' in the sense that it has not been agreed by the negotiating states, two or more states can agree to make the same reservation. Reservations must be distinguished from 'derogations'. The latter are statements authorised by a treaty by which a party is able to exclude certain provisions in their application to it during a particular period, such as a public emergency.[27]

---

[22] See UKTS (1975) 125, pp. 9–11.

[23] Articles 309 and 310 (ILM (1982) p. 1261; UN Reg. No. 31363).

[24] See *UN Multilateral Treaties*, Chapter XXI.6. For the UK objections, see BYIL (1997), pp. 494–5.   [25] ILM (1993), p. 804; UKTS (1997) 45; UN Reg. No. 33757.

[26] See generally UN Doc. A/CN/.4/491/Add.5, paras. 422–5 and 446–93.

[27] Article 4(3) of the International Covenant on Civil and Political Rights 1966 (999 UNTS 171 (No. 14668); ILM (1967), p. 368; UKTS (1977) 6); and Article 15 of the European Convention on Human Rights (213 UNTS 221 (No. 2889); UKTS (1953) 71).

Bilateral treaties

The Convention does not generally distinguish between bilateral and multilateral treaties, even for reservations. One has therefore to look to basic principles and state practice when examining the question of reservations and interpretative declarations made in connection with bilateral treaties. Although the Convention does not say so, a 'reservation', as that term is defined in Article 2(1)(d), cannot be made to a bilateral treaty. Since there are only two possible parties, a bilateral treaty is more like a contract, *all* the terms of which must be agreed before it can bind the parties. Making a 'reservation' to a bilateral treaty amounts therefore to a request for a modification to the treaty, usually in favour of the requesting state. The treaty cannot therefore be binding unless and until the other state accepts. The reservations regime of the Convention is therefore inapplicable.

Nevertheless, the United States has a long history of making its ratification of bilateral treaties conditional on modifications being made. This is due to the power given to the Senate by the Constitution.[28] Because the President needs Senate approval ('Advice and Consent') before he can ratify certain treaties,[29] the Senate will sometimes give its approval only on condition that the President obtains a modification. This is often misleadingly described by the Senate as a 'reservation'. It has happened over 100 times in the last 200 years, and at least thirteen times between 1975 and 1985,[30] with nine of the thirteen treaties being double taxation agreements. Although, in theory, the acceptance of the other state could be tacit, this does not seem to happen. The US Senate approved the UK–US Supplementary Extradition Treaty 1985 on condition that certain amendments were made. The US Government informed the UK Government of this and it was decided to amend the treaty by an exchange of notes. The US note recorded the Senate's condition and attached the articles of the Treaty as they would read if amended. The note explained that the President could not execute the instrument of ratification unless the amendments were made, and asked if they would be acceptable to the UK Government. The UK note confirmed that they were acceptable and instruments of

---

[28] See pp. 108–9 below on the Senate's attitude to 'no reservations' articles in multilateral treaties.

[29] See pp. 157–8 below.

[30] It is unclear whether 'reservations' have been made since. A 'proviso' attached to Senate approval of a bilateral treaty has effect, if any, only in US domestic law, and is therefore *not* included in the instrument of ratification: see AJIL (1997), pp. 90–1.

ratification were exchanged in December 1986.[31] Other states do not make their acceptance of bilateral treaties conditional, except for treaties with the United States, and then generally in response to a US 'reservation'.

If a parliament refuses to approve a bilateral treaty or to pass implementing legislation, the correct course is for the government to seek to renegotiate the treaty, or at least part of it.

Multilateral treaties

The need to make reservations stems from the nature of the multilateral treaty-making process. A commercial contract is usually between two, or at least a limited number of, parties. In contrast, even when states are part of the same continent, they have their own domestic legal systems, varying national policies and, often, different languages. The problems these pose for the successful negotiation of even a regional treaty are multiplied when the treaty is intended to have general application, as do most treaties adopted in the United Nations or the specialised agencies. In the United Nations multilateral treaties are negotiated by up to 190 states, if one includes observer states. Reaching agreement on a text requires compromises to accommodate all their differing interests and concerns. Now that most multilateral treaties are adopted by consensus, inevitably some, if not most, of the negotiating states will be dissatisfied with at least some aspect of the resulting text. But a state may, for political reasons, be reluctant to stand in the way of reaching consensus, and may even sign a treaty despite its unhappiness at the result.[32] If it is greatly dissatisfied it will have the option of not becoming a party. If this would be difficult politically, a state may seek to adjust certain provisions *in their application only to it* so as to make it possible for it to become a party. Sometimes a parliament will require such adjustments as a condition of its consent to ratification. We shall see later some of the problems which this can cause.

But one should not exaggerate the problem. Except perhaps for some human rights treaties, reservations are generally not so numerous or so extensive as to jeopardise the effectiveness of a treaty, though in some cases this may be because states which have real difficulty simply decide not become parties. Despite what has been written on the subject, most reservations can be dealt with perfectly well by application of the provisions in Articles 19–23.

---

[31] Cmnd 9915 and UKTS (1988) 6; TIAS 12050.   [32] See p. 67 above on consensus.

Reservations generally *not* prohibited

There is nothing inherently wicked or even undesirable in formulating a reservation to a multilateral treaty. It would be quite wrong to think that the world is divided into reserving states and objecting states. As with diplomatic relations – where every state is both a sending state and a receiving state – many states make reservations and object to reservations. In fact, reservations are generally not objected to. In many, if not most, cases the purpose of the reservation is merely to adjust the reserving state's obligations under the treaty to conform to its domestic law where, for political, cultural or social reasons, it is not feasible or desirable to change the law. Many states have made reservations to the Rights of the Child Convention 1989. The United Kingdom made several detailed ones, some of which were made only in respect of its overseas territories.[33] There have been no objections. These realities need to be emphasised since they are sometimes obscured by the great debate about the legal effect of prohibited reservations and objections to them, which we will come to later.[34]

Article 19 states the basic rule that a state *may* formulate a reservation *unless*:

(a) the reservation is prohibited by the treaty;

(b) the treaty provides that only specified reservations, which do not include the reservation in question, may be made; or

(c) in cases not falling under subparagraphs (a) and (b), the reservation is incompatible with the object and purpose of the treaty ['the compatibility test'].

Although only paragraph (a) expressly uses the term 'prohibited', we will use it when also referring to paragraphs (b) and (c) since they also deal with prohibited reservations. We will examine each paragraph in turn.

Exception (a): the reservation is prohibited by the treaty

It is increasingly common for treaties, particularly on human rights or those which result from a 'package deal', such as the UN Convention on the Law of the Sea 1982 and the Statute of the International Criminal Court 1998, to provide expressly that reservations are not permitted. This can cause problems, in particular for the United States, given the way the

---

[33] See *UN Multilateral Treaties*, Chapter IV.11.   [34] See p. 116 below.

Senate jealously guards its power to refuse or give conditional approval to those treaties which have to be submitted to it.[35] When approving the ratification of the Straddling Stocks Agreement 1995 the Senate criticised the 'no reservations' clause in Article 42 because it had:

> the effect of inhibiting the Senate from exercising its constitutional duty to give advice and consent to a treaty, and the Senate's approval of this treaty should not be construed as a precedent for acquiescence to future treaties containing such a provision.[36]

The Constitution of the International Labour Organisation prohibits the making of reservations to the ILO Conventions.[37] This is because of the unique, trilateral negotiating structure of ILO: trade unions, employers' associations and governments. As indicated above, there may, however, be some scope for (genuine) interpretative statements.

Exception (b): the treaty provides that only specified reservations may be made

In the course of the negotiation of a treaty it may become evident that it will not be possible to reach consensus unless certain states are given the possibility of opting out of one or more provisions. Although the treaty could be silent on the question of reservations (and many are), this may be unsatisfactory since it leaves uncertain which reservations will be permissible, since that will depend on whether they satisfy the compatibility test in exception (c). It is therefore prudent to specify the matters on which reservations are permitted. Examples include the following.

(1) A contracting state may exclude certain specific subjects from the scope of the treaty. The Revised General Act for the Pacific Settlement of International Disputes 1949 lists the types of disputes (e.g., territorial) which a state can, by a reservation, exclude from the settlement procedures of the Act as it would apply to that state.[38] Article 2 of the Second Optional Protocol 1989 to the International Covenant on Civil and Political Rights permits a reservation to be made to allow for capital punishment in the case of serious military offences in wartime.[39] Of the present thirty-one parties three have made that reservation.[40]

---

[35] See pp. 157–8 below.   [36] AJIL (1996) p. 647.
[37] 15 UNTS 35; UKTS (1948) 47; UKTS (1961) 59; and UKTS (1975) 110. For the 1986 amendments, see Italian YBIL (1986–7), pp. 216–50.
[38] 71 UNTS 101 (No. 912). See also *UN Multilateral Treaties*, Chapter II.1.
[39] ILM (1990), p. 1465; UN Reg. No. 14668.   [40] *UN Multilateral Treaties*, Chapter IV.12.

(2) A reservation may be made in respect of one or more specified articles, such as an article providing for the submission of disputes about the interpretation or application of the treaty to the International Court of Justice or other settlement mechanism. The TIR Convention 1975 prohibits all reservations except to the article on dispute settlement.[41]

(3) An agreement may provide that reservations may be made only in respect of certain rights and obligations. The Convention on the Recognition and Enforcement of Decisions relating to Maintenance Obligations 1973 prohibits reservations, except for some which are specified with great precision.[42]

A provision that reservations may be made to articles *other than* certain specified articles means that a reservation to an article which is not so specified will be subject to the compatibility test. Article 29(1) of the Council of Europe Convention on Nationality 1997 states this expressly in providing that, with the exception of certain chapters, reservations may be made to the rest of the Convention so long as they are compatible with its object and purpose.[43]

Whether a reservation is permissible under exceptions (a) or (b) will depend on interpretation of the treaty.

Exceptions (a) and (b) do not apply, and the reservation is incompatible with the object and purpose of the treaty (compatibility test)

Whereas it is relatively easy to determine whether a reservation is expressly or impliedly prohibited under exceptions (a) or (b), when a treaty is silent on the matter of reservations it can be extremely difficult to assess whether a reservation passes the compatibility test in exception (c).[44] Many differing views have been expressed as to how the test should be applied, especially to human rights treaties,[45] but the practice of states is patchy and uncertain. A reservation to the UN Torture Convention which sought to exclude from it torture of suspected (or even convicted) terrorists would be a clear case of incompatibility. In the case of that treaty, in 1988 Chile made a reservation designed to permit an alleged torturer to plead the defence of 'superior orders', a defence expressly precluded by the treaty. After several objections that the reservation was

---

[41] See note 20 above.   [42] 1021 UNTS 209; UKTS (1980) 49 (Articles 26 and 34).

[43] ILM (1998), p. 44.

[44] There is a *considerable* literature. See, for example, Schabas, 'Reservations to Human Rights Treaties', (note 2 above) pp. 39–81; L. Lijnzaad, *Reservations to UN Human Rights Treaties* (1995); and R. Higgins, 'Human Rights: Some Questions of Integrity', *Modern Law Review* (1989), p. 1.

[45] See pp. 119–23 below.

incompatible, it was withdrawn.[46] In 1980 Burundi made a reservation to the Convention on the Prevention and Punishment of Crimes against Internationally Protected Persons 1973, in which it purported to exclude from its scope alleged offenders who were members of national liberation movements. Four parties objected that the reservation was incompatible with the object and purpose of the treaty, three of them saying that until it was withdrawn they would be unable to consider Burundi as having validly acceded. The reservation was withdrawn.[47] A reservation made by the United States on its ratification in 1992 of the International Covenant on Civil and Political Rights 1966 reserved the right to execute convicted persons (other than pregnant women) even if they were under 18 years of age when they committed the crime. Eleven European States objected that the reservation was incompatible with the object and purpose of the Covenant in that it amounted to a general derogation[48] from the prohibition in the Covenant on the execution of minors, and that the Covenant does not permit general derogations from that prohibition.[49] This was, however, quite surprising since some of the objecting states had themselves made reservations to other articles of the Covenant from which derogation is not permitted.[50] The Human Rights Committee has since expressed the view that a reservation to a non-derogable article would not necessarily fail the compatibility test, but that there would be a heavy onus on the reserving state to justify the reservation.[51] However objectionable it may be to some states, it is therefore not clear that the US reservation fails the test.

Today, as treaties become longer and more complex, identifying the object and purpose of a treaty such as the UN Convention on the Law of the Sea 1982[52] is virtually impossible given its 320 articles and nine annexes, unless for this purpose it is permissible to break down the treaty into various subjects, such as high seas, straits, continental shelf etc. Applying the compatibility test to a human rights treaty such as the Covenant, which covers a wide range of subjects, is especially difficult.[53]

---

[46] 465 UNTS 85 (No. 24841); ILM (1984), p. 1027; UKTS (1991) 107. See *UN Multilateral Treaties*, Chapter IV.9, footnotes to entry for Chile.

[47] 1035 UNTS 167 (No. 15410); UKTS (1980) 3. For the text of the reservation and the objections, see *UN Multilateral Treaties*, Chapter XVIII.7. [48] See p. 105 above. [49] See Chapter IV.4.

[50] Schabas 'Reservations to Human Rights Treaties', (note 2 above) at pp. 49–53.

[51] General Comment No. 24 (ILM (1995), p. 839).

[52] ILM (1982), p. 1261; UN Reg. No. 31363; UKTS (1999).

[53] See J. Klabbers, 'Some Problems Regarding the Object and Purpose of Treaties', Finnish YBIL (1997), pp. 138–60.

Since the Vienna Convention on the Law of Treaties is itself a treaty, one can make reservations to it; but as its final clauses do not include a reservations article, a reservation has to pass the compatibility test. Many reservations have been made.[54] In 1997 Guatemala made certain reservations which called into question important and well-established rules of customary international law which the Convention codified. In particular, it said that the rule in Article 27 (internal law may not be invoked as justification for failure to perform a treaty) would not apply with respect to the Guatemalan Constitution. Since the rule is so fundamental to the law of treaties, the reservation plainly failed the compatibility test and some states lodged objections to it. The situation would of course be different if the principle in Article 27 were to be invoked as the ground for an objection to a so-called 'constitutional' reservation.[55]

Acceptance of, and objection to, reservations

A point which is generally overlooked is that, even when a reservation is not prohibited under Article 19(a), (b) or (c), that does not mean that other contracting states cannot object to it. By formulating a reservation the reserving state is consenting to be bound subject to a condition laid down by it. It makes an offer which is subject to acceptance by the other contracting states. It will, therefore, not be legally effective in relation to another contracting state unless that state has accepted it either expressly or by necessary implication. The only exceptions are when a reservation has been expressly authorised by the treaty (Article 20(1)). But, in practice, most objections seem to be made on the ground that the reservation is prohibited, and usually because either it fails the compatibility test or its effect would be contrary to general international law, for example an excessive assertion of extraterritorial jurisdiction. But we will first look at Article 20(2) and (3).

Plurilateral treaties

The term 'plurilateral' is probably only used in international law, and then mainly in respect of reservations to treaties. It describes a treaty negotiated between a limited number of states with a particular interest in the subject matter. Article 20(2) provides that if it appears from the object and

---

[54] See *UN Multilateral Treaties*, Chapter XXIII.1.   [55] See p. 120 (note 73) below.

purpose of the treaty that the application of it in its entirety, and between all the parties, is an essential condition for the consent of each of them to be bound by it, any reservation will require the acceptance of all the parties. Examples might include the Constantinople Convention 1888,[56] which provides for freedom of navigation through the Suez Canal for all states, but was negotiated by only nine states, and the Antarctic Treaty 1959[57] which had fifteen negotiating states. Both treaties created special regimes, for which the integrity of the treaty is vital. In the latter case, the possibility of reservations concerning claims and counter-claims to sovereignty in parts of Antarctica was avoided by a saving provision, Article IV, protecting the differing legal positions.

Constituent instrument of an international organisation

Where a treaty forms the constitution of an international organisation it is also essential to preserve its integrity. Article 20(3) provides that a reservation to such a treaty will require the acceptance of the competent organ of the organisation – usually an assembly of the members – unless the constituent instrument otherwise provides. The Treaty of Rome 1957, and other constituent treaties of the European Communities, are accompanied by national declarations, agreed in advance, which adjust the detailed application of each instrument to the particular circumstances of individual Member States.

All other cases

We will examine first the rules of the Convention on acceptance of, and objection to, reservations, and then some issues which have been raised about them. But, first, some history.[58]

The law before the Convention

Before 1951 generally the rule was unanimity. Just as the adoption of a treaty used always to require the agreement of all the negotiating states,[59] so a reservation was only effective if it had been accepted by all, expressly or tacitly, and usually before signature. In 1951 the UN General Assembly

---

[56] 171 CTS 241.   [57] 402 UNTS 71 (No. 5778); UKTS (1961) 97.
[58] For a more detailed, yet concise, account see Sinclair, pp. 54–63.   [59] See p. 66 above.

asked the International Court of Justice for an advisory opinion about certain reservations which had been made to the Genocide Convention 1948. The opinion, reached by only seven votes to five, resulted in the following guidance:

(1) If a reservation has been *objected to by one or more parties, but not by others*, the reserving state will be a party, *provided the reservation is compatible with the object and purpose.*

(2) If a party objects to a reservation because it considers it incompatible with the object and purpose, that party may consider the reserving state as not a party.

(3) If a party accepts a reservation as being compatible with the object and purpose, it may consider the reserving state as a party.[60]

In 1952 the UN General Assembly asked the Secretary-General to conform his practice to the advisory opinion, so that when as depositary he received reservations or objections in respect of new multilateral treaties concluded under UN auspices he would not consider their legal effect, but communicate them to all states concerned, leaving it to each to draw its own conclusions.

At first the compatibility test was criticised as being subjective and unworkable, and that points (2) and (3) above would lead to fragmentation of multilateral treaties. But, during the period 1951–62, when the International Law Commission was studying reservations as part of its work on the law of treaties, the process of decolonisation quickened and it became clear that the much greater number of potential parties to multilateral treaties made adherence to the unanimity principle impractical, and a more flexible system developed. The basic approach taken by the Court, and followed by the General Assembly, found favour with the International Law Commission, which recognised that the difficulty with the compatibility test lay not so much in the test itself, but in the process by which it is applied.

The rules of the Convention

Article 20(4) sets out the residual rules to be applied when one is not dealing with an expressly authorised reservation, a plurilateral treaty or the constituent instrument of an international organisation. The rules were intended to be a flexible means of accommodating the different needs of the reserving state and the other contracting states:

[60] *ICJ Reports* (1951), p. 15

(a) *acceptance* by another contracting State of a reservation constitutes the reserving State a party to the treaty *in relation to that other State* if or when the treaty is in force for those States;

(b) an *objection* by another contracting State to a reservation does not preclude the entry into force of the treaty as between the objecting and reserving States *unless a contrary intention is* definitely *expressed by the objecting State*;

(c) an act expressing a State's consent to be bound by the treaty and containing a reservation is effective as soon as *at least one other contracting State has accepted the reservation.*

It is rare for a contrary intention (paragraph b) to be 'definitely' (i.e., explicitly) expressed. The most noteworthy example may be the general objection by the Netherlands to the reservations to the Genocide Convention made by communist countries, some developing countries and the United States in which they refused to accept the jurisdiction of the International Court of Justice over disputes between the parties. The Netherlands stated that it did 'not deem any state which has made or which will make such reservation a party to the Convention'.[61] But, as we shall see, in many cases an objecting state will say expressly that it will nevertheless regard the treaty as in force between it and the reserving state.

Article 20(5) provides that acceptance of a reservation can be *tacit*. The combined effect of that provision and paragraph (c) is that the reserving state will become a contracting state unless *all* the other contracting states (1) object to the reservation *and* (2) explicitly object to the reserving state becoming a contracting state. This is most unlikely ever to happen. Under the International Law Commission's draft articles a mere objection to the reservation would have precluded the treaty entering into force between the reserving and objecting states. Instead of this the Convention puts the onus on the objecting state both to express its objection and, if it does not want the treaty to enter into force between it and the reserving state, to say so explicitly. In putting this responsibility on the objecting state, the Vienna Conference did not take sufficiently into account the actual practice of states. It would be wrong to think that every foreign ministry agonises over every reservation notified to it. Even in the best managed ministries reservations are not always given the attention they deserve. There are many other matters to attend to and reservations may not be seen as a priority. If one studies any list of reservations it is surprising how few states object even though a clearly

[61] See *UN Multilateral Treaties*, Chapter IV.1.

objectionable reservation has been made. As O'Connell said in 1970, 'the almost universal failure of states to object to reservations, whether implicitly permitted or not, is the basic reason for the juristic bewilderment that has confounded this subject'.[62] Even more striking is the absence of express acceptances. It must therefore be questionable if the provision for tacit acceptance in Article 20(5) represented customary international law.

It is thus possible that not every party to a multilateral treaty will be bound by the treaty to every other party. A reserving state, Utopia, may be a party to a treaty in relation to Ruritania (which raised no objection), but not Freedonia (which did, and said expressly that it precluded the treaty entering into force between it and Utopia), although Ruritania and Freedonia may themselves be mutually bound. However, although such a result is not surprising if the reservation is permissible, as we shall also see, there is good reason to believe that the scheme of Article 20(4) and (5) does *not* apply when the reservation is prohibited, including when it has been objected to, by only one contracting state, on the ground that it fails the compatibility test.

The legal effects of reservations and objections to reservations

Article 21(1) sets out the rules governing the legal effects of a reservation which has been established[63] with regard to another party, that is to say a reservation which is legally effective in relation to another party, being not prohibited under Article 19(a), (b) or (c) or objected to by the other party. Such a reservation:

(a) modifies for the reserving State *in its relations with that other party* the provisions of the treaty to which the reservation relates to the extent of the reservation; and

(b) modifies those provisions to the same extent for *that other party* in its relations with the reserving State.

But, the reservation does not modify the provisions of the treaty for the other parties to the treaty as between themselves (Article 21(2)).

There is nothing exceptional in these rules, which reflect the consensual nature of the relations between the parties – each is only bound to the

---

[62] O'Connell, p. 235.
[63] That is, in accordance with the requirements of Articles 19, 20 and 23 (see below).

extent to which it has agreed to be bound – so that if a party has made an effective reservation it will operate reciprocally between it and any other party which has not objected to it, modifying the treaty to the extent of the reservation for them both in their mutual relations. But as between the other parties the treaty is unaffected.

Article 21(3) provides that when an objecting state has not opposed the entry into force of the treaty between itself and the reserving state, the *provisions* to which the reservation relates do not apply as between the two states to the extent of the reservation. This deals with the situation where an objecting state does not indicate 'definitely' that the reservation will preclude the entry into force of the treaty as between the two states (Article 20(4)(b)).[64]

Some unresolved issues

The main unresolved issue is whether the regime constructed by Articles 20 and 21 applies to *all* reservations. Certainly it works satisfactorily with respect to permissible reservations. But if one attempts to apply it to reservations prohibited under Article 19(a), (b) or (c), problems arise. Nevertheless there is a view that there is nothing in the scheme which precludes its application to a prohibited reservation; provided it has been accepted under Article 20(4) – which, under Article 20(5), can be done, and usually is done, tacitly – the reserving state will become a party in relation to those states which do not object. The argument must necessarily seek to draw a distinction between reservations prohibited by Article 19(a) and (b) and those prohibited by Article 19(c), on the basis that the question whether a reservation passes the compatibility test is a matter for each contracting state. But Article 19 makes no such distinction. It authorises the formulation of reservations subject to three exceptions. It is most unlikely that Articles 20 and 21 were intended to apply to reservations which Article 19 says may not be made. It is not argued that if a *treaty* prohibits the making of reservations, or allows only specified ones, a contracting state could nevertheless accept (perhaps even tacitly) a reservation prohibited by the treaty. The rules in Article 21 on the legal effects of reservations refer to reservations 'established' in accordance with Articles 19,

---

[64] See the detailed discussion on this point in the award in the 1977 *Anglo-French Continental Shelf* arbitration in Sinclair, pp. 76–7.

20 and 23, and it is hard to see how one could validly establish a reservation when it is prohibited by Article 19.

When a treaty is silent about reservations the determination whether a reservation passes the compatibility test is not easy, but there is no reason in principle why the reservation should be treated any differently to the other classes of prohibited reservations. In the advisory opinion the Court maintained that, if a reservation has been objected to by some but not others, the reserving state can be regarded as a party '*if* the reservation is compatible with the object and purpose of the [Genocide] Convention; otherwise, that state cannot be regarded as being a party to the Convention'. The compatibility test should be applied objectively, even if in most cases it has to be applied by states rather than by a court – a situation which is quite normal in international law. And if a reservation has been objected to by even one contracting state for failing the test, the reserving state has an obligation to consider the objection in good faith. If the two states (there may of course be more) cannot agree, the question then becomes a matter of concern to the other contracting states, whether or not they have objected.

There is a related question: if a state has made a prohibited reservation, is it then bound by the treaty but without the benefit of the reservation? The Convention does not provide an explicit answer. In some cases the government of the reserving state will have obtained parliamentary approval for ratification only on condition that the reservation is made. In the *Belilos* case in 1988, the European Court of Human Rights held that a declaration by Switzerland on ratifying the European Convention on Human Rights (ECHR) was an invalid reservation, but that it could be disregarded, Switzerland remaining bound by the ECHR in full.[65] Although Switzerland had the option of withdrawing from the ECHR, it did not; and no doubt for good political reasons. The Court came to a similar decision in 1995 in the *Loizidou* (*Preliminary Objections*) case, holding that Turkey was bound by its acceptances of the right of individual petition and of the jurisdiction of the Court, but without the invalid reservations attached to those acceptances.[66] This decision and *Belilos* need, however, to be seen in the light of the particular circumstances. The issue arose within a regional system dedicated to adherence to common social and political values. As the Court said in *Loizidou*, the ECHR has a special character and must be

---

[65] ECHR Pubs. Series A, vol. 132 (1988); S. Marks, 'Reservations Unhinged: The Belilos Case Before the European Court of Human Rights', ICLQ (1990), p. 300.
[66] ECHR Pubs. Series A, vol. 310 (1995).

interpreted in the light of contemporary conditions, its enforcement machinery and its object and purpose. Also, although the Court applied the rules on interpretation in Articles 31 and 32, it did not refer to the Convention's rules on reservations. It made much of the point that when Turkey made its reservations it was well aware of *Belilos* and therefore knew the risk it ran in making invalid reservations.

The objections to the reservations made in 1998 by Guatemala to the Convention itself[67] show a divergence of views by states on the question of whether a *prohibited* reservation can be disregarded. Austria and Germany said that their objections did not preclude the entry into force of the Convention between them and Guatemala, so leaving ambiguous the effect of the reservation on Guatemala's obligations under the Convention. The United Kingdom did not say what effect its objection would have. In contrast, Denmark, Finland and Sweden each said that, although their objections did not preclude the entry into force of the Convention between them and Guatemala, it would be 'without Guatemala benefiting from these reservations'. This approach went further than *Belilos*, in that there were no special circumstances as in *Belilos*, and ignored the plain fact that the reserving state had made it clear that it was willing to be bound only subject to a condition.[68] The better view, therefore, is that if one or more contracting states have objected to the reservation as being prohibited, the reserving state must decide whether or not it is prepared to be a party without the reservation; and until it has made its position clear it cannot be regarded as a party. There is an express provision to this effect in the AETR II Agreement 1970.[69] This may be the way the International Law Commission is now thinking.[70]

Reservations to human rights treaties[71]

In the case of a human rights treaty there may be weighty political reasons why a state is reluctant to object to the entry into force of the treaty between it and a reserving state, even when it has objected to reservation on the ground that it fails the compatibility test. Such treaties became enormously important in the second half of the twentieth century. They

---

[67] See p. 112 above.
[68] See also the objection by Denmark to reservations by Yemen to CERD (*UN Multilateral Treaties*, Chapter IV.2).   [69] See pp. 124–5 below.   [70] See p. 123 below.
[71] There is a *huge* literature. For a recent survey of the subject see J. Gardner (ed.), *Human Rights as General Norms and a State's Right to Opt Out* (1997).

have created not only a network of mutual bilateral undertakings for the parties, but also norms of behaviour for the parties in their treatment of persons for whom they are responsible, including aliens. It is understandable that most objecting states are reluctant to take the position that the treaty will not be in force between it and the reserving state unless and until the reservation is withdrawn. As fellow parties, they may feel better able to persuade the reserving state to bring its laws and practices into line with the treaty, and withdraw the reservation. In fact, when faced with a questionable reservation most parties to human rights treaties remain silent. And those that do express views formally, frequently take differing positions. This is illustrated by the variety of responses by some western European states to the following general reservation made by the United States in 1988 to the Genocide Convention:

> nothing in the Convention requires or authorises legislation or other action by the United States of America prohibited by the Constitution of the United States as interpreted by the United States.

That such a 'constitutional reservation' should be made was not surprising. For some years the United States Senate had authorised the President to ratify human rights treaties only if he made it clear that the United States Constitution will prevail over them.[72] Denmark, Finland, Greece, Ireland, Norway and Sweden objected that the reservation was contrary to the general rule that a party may not invoke its internal law as justification for failure to perform a treaty (Article 27), but, apart from Sweden, they did not specify the legal effect of their objection.[73] Sweden said its objection 'does not constitute an obstacle to the entry into force of the Convention between Sweden and the United States' (such a statement being regularly found in objections to human rights treaties and illustrating the political dilemma of the objecting state). Italy and the United Kingdom objected that the reservation 'creates uncertainty as to the extent of the obligations which the Government of the United States is prepared to assume with regard to the Convention'. Neither said what were the legal consequences. The Netherlands objected on both of the two last grounds, but did not specify any legal consequences. In contrast, Spain did not object, but inter-

---

[72] See pp. 108–9 above.

[73] Article 27 is not in the part of the Convention which deals with reservations and should not therefore be relied upon to found an objection to a reservation; it is usually because the internal law of the state is incompatible with the treaty that a reservation is made. Article 27 applies only once the reserving state's obligations under the treaty have been determined: see Schabas 'Reservations to Human Rights Treaties', (note 2 above), p. 59.

preted the reservation to mean that legislation or other action by the United States would continue to be in accordance with the Convention. This had more of the Nelson touch.[74] There was also inconsistency in the responses by such states when a similar constitutional reservation was made by the United States with respect to the Torture Convention.[75]

When other states have made constitutional reservations, the responses have also been inconsistent. The attitude of the United States to constitutional reservations made by other states is intriguing. In response to a reservation by Colombia to the Vienna Drugs Convention 1988, in which Colombia said that it would be contrary to its constitution for it to extradite its own nationals, the United States objected that the statement 'purports to subordinate Colombia's obligations under the Convention to its Constitution'.

Since constitutional reservations make it difficult, if not impossible, to determine their effect on the reserving state's obligations, the United Kingdom has adopted a temporising, non-committal approach. In response to four constitutional reservations made in 1990 by the Republic of Korea to the International Covenant on Civil and Political Rights, the United Kingdom stated that it was:

> not however able to take a position on these purported reservations in the absence of a sufficient indication of their intended effect, in accordance with the terms of the Vienna Convention on the Law of Treaties and the practice of the parties to the Covenant. Pending receipt of such indication, the Government of the United Kingdom reserve their rights under the Covenant in their entirety.[76]

The effect of this statement is to suspend the time limit for making objections, whatever that might be,[77] until the reserving state has made clear the effect of the reservation. Of course, one hopes that the reservation will be withdrawn or at least made specific. Within two years Korea had withdrawn two of the reservations.[78]

Another similar, and particularly troublesome, general reservation is one which seeks to subordinate a human rights treaty to the domestic law of the reserving state, in particular to Islamic laws. For example, when ratifying the Rights of the Child Convention 1989, Iran reserved the right 'not to apply any provisions or articles of the Convention that are

---

[74] A masterly or sympathetic approach to a problem (OED).
[75] *UN Multilateral Treaties*, Chapter IV.9.   [76] *UN Multilateral Treaties*, Chapter IV.4.
[77] See p. 127 below.   [78] *UN Multilateral Treaties*, Chapter IV.4.

incompatible with Islamic laws'. This and similar reservations to that Convention by other Islamic states were objected to in 1991 by some western European states, generally on the ground that the reservations cast doubt on the commitment of the reserving state to the object and purpose of the Convention, but in each case the objecting state said that the objection did not preclude the entry into force of the Convention between it and the reserving state.[79] However, such objections can lead to a withdrawal or modification of the reservation.[80] In 1995 Malaysia attached reservations to its accession to the Convention on the Elimination of all Forms of Discrimination Against Women 1979 (CEDAW), which were to the effect that certain of its provisions would not apply if they conflicted with *Sharia'* law or the Malaysian Constitution. Following some objections, the reservations were withdrawn in 1998.[81]

But it would be wrong to see human rights treaties as a special case, and the International Law Commission seems disinclined to do so. The problem of the legal effect of objections is the same for all multilateral treaties, it is just that the problem occurs more often, and more acutely, with human rights treaties because they have to reconcile not just different national policies, but different religious and social systems. Moreover, the phenomenon of constitutional and domestic law reservations does not seem to have existed when the Convention was adopted in 1969, due no doubt to the fact that the era of modern universal human rights treaties only really began in 1966 with the two International Covenants.

Treaty-monitoring bodies

The problem of determining whether a reservation is permissible, and in particular whether it passes the compatibility test, is further compounded by the absence in most cases of a standing tribunal or other organ with competence to decide such matters. Regional human rights treaties, such as the European Convention on Human Rights and the American Convention on Human Rights,[82] each have a standing court. Most modern universal human rights treaties establish no more than a committee of (albeit distinguished) independent experts to monitor the way in which the parties carry out their obligations. The best known is the Human Rights Committee established by the International Covenant on Civil and

---

[79] *Ibid.*, Chapter IV.11.   [80] *Ibid.*, Chapter IV.8, note 14, and Chapter IV.11, note 4.
[81] *Ibid.*, Chapter IV.8.   [82] ILM (1970), p. 673; UKTS (1980) 58.

Political Rights 1966.[83] Consisting of eighteen members, its role is to scrutinise and comment on periodic reports by the parties on their implementation of the Covenant; to consider complaints from parties about alleged violations by other parties; and to examine communications (petitions) from individuals alleging violations, provided the party said to be at fault has recognised the competence of the Committee for this purpose. The Committee is not empowered to give decisions binding on the parties. Nevertheless, in 1994 in its General Comment No. 24 the Committee, in the course of expressing views on the problems of reservations, said that it must necessarily take a view as to the status and effect of a reservation if this is needed in order to carry out its functions under the Covenant, in particular considering reports from parties. The Committee gave the impression that it could in such circumstances make an authoritative determination. This view of the Committee has been severely criticised since it was not given the power to pronounce on general questions of international law. Nor can it be equated to an international court or tribunal, which reaches decisions binding on the parties only after hearing full legal argument.[84]

The International Law Commission study

The International Law Commission has since 1993 had on its agenda 'Reservations to Treaties'.[85] The state of uncertainty about the subject is well illustrated by the first report of the Special Rapporteur of the Commission, Professor Pellet, in which he listed no less than fifteen main unresolved questions, and seventeen of a lesser order.[86] In 1997, the Commission, having discussed the report, adopted, though not without some hesitation, some 'preliminary conclusions'.[87] The most relevant for present purposes were:

(1) Articles 19–23 govern the regime of reservations to treaties.
(2) Compatibility with the object and purpose is the most important criterion for determining the admissibility of reservations.
(3) The regime of the Convention applies equally to normative (i.e., law-making) treaties, including human rights treaties.

---

[83] 999 UNTS 171 (No. 14668); ILM (1967), p. 368; UKTS (1977) 6. The Committee should not be confused with the UN Commission on Human Rights established by ECOSOC in 1946.
[84] See ILM (1995), p. 839. The text, and the observations of France, the United Kingdom and the United States, are in Gardner, *Human Rights*, (note 71 above), pp. 185–207.
[85] See note 4 above. [86] UN Doc. A/CN.4/470, paras. 124–5 and 148–9.
[87] UN Doc. A/52/10, paras. 44–157, at para. 157 (and the references in note 4 above).

(4) If a reservation is inadmissible it is the *reserving* state that has the responsibility to take action (e.g., by withdrawing or modifying the reservation, or foregoing becoming party).

(5) Where a human rights treaty establishes a monitoring body, unless the treaty provides otherwise the body is competent only to comment on and make recommendations as to the admissibility of reservations (in other words, it did not agree with the Human Rights Committee).[88]

These points are useful, but leave many questions unanswered, in particular how the admissibility of a reservation is to be determined. The Commission does not intend to propose amendments to the Convention, but to prepare a draft 'Guide to Practice'. Its purpose would be to remedy the ambiguities and clarify the obscurities in the Convention and state practice, and include model clauses which might be used in new treaties.

In 1997 the Sixth (Legal) Committee of the UN General Assembly discussed that year's report of the International Law Commission. There were forty-seven speakers – evidence of the importance attached to the subject. Almost all reaffirmed that the Convention regime applied to all treaties, and disagreed in varying degrees with the view that treaty-monitoring bodies were competent to make authoritative determinations. The idea of formulating a Guide to Practice was generally welcomed. The General Assembly 'took note' of the report's preliminary conclusions. At its 1998 and 1999 sessions the Commission provisionally adopted some draft guidelines limited to certain aspects of reservations,[89] but the Sixth Committee did not hold a substantive debate on the topic. The work of the Commission is likely to take many years to complete, the most difficult problems having not yet been addressed.

Some ways of minimising the problem of reservations

The problems of reservations may be lessened, or even avoided, if provision is made in each new treaty, but this is not new. The European Agreement concerning the Work of Crews of Vehicles Engaged in International Road Transport 1970 (AETR II Agreement) provides that:

> If . . . a State enters a [non-authorised] reservation . . . the Secretary-General of the United Nations shall communicate the reservation to [the contracting states]. The reservation shall be deemed to be accepted if *none* of the said States has, within six months after such communication, expressed its oppo-

---

[88] See p. 123 above.   [89] UN Doc. A/53/10, para. 540. See also A/54/10, para. 470.

sition to acceptance of the reservation. *Otherwise, the reservation shall not be admitted, and, if the State which entered the reservation does not withdraw it the deposit of that State's instrument of ratification or accession shall be without effect.*[90]

The Convention on Psychotropic Substances 1971 authorises certain reservations to be made and provides that:

A State which desires to become a party but wishes to be authorised to make [non-authorised] reservations . . . may inform the Secretary-General of such intention. Unless by the end of twelve months after the date of the Secretary-General's communication of the reservation concerned, this reservation has been objected to by one third of the [contracting states] . . . it shall be deemed to be permitted, it being understood, however, that States which have objected to the reservation need not assume towards the reserving State any legal obligation under this Convention which is affected by the reservation.[91]

A more recent formulation is found in the FAO Compliance Agreement 1993:

Acceptance of this Agreement may be made subject to reservations which shall become effective only upon *unanimous* acceptance by all parties to this Agreement. The Director-General [of the FAO] shall notify forthwith all parties of any reservation. Parties not having replied within three months from the date of notification shall be deemed to have accepted the reservation. Failing such [i.e., unanimous] acceptance, the State or regional economic organisation making the reservation *shall not become a party to this Agreement.*[92]

Of course in this case the reserving state could withdraw the reservation before the end of the three months or deposit a fresh acceptance without the reservation.

Another approach is to permit reservations only in respect of the annexes to a treaty, or certain of them. This is a relatively recent development, and is to be found particularly in arms control treaties. Article XXII of the Chemical Weapons Convention 1993 (CWC) prohibits reservations to the CWC itself, but allows them to be made in respect of its Annexes, provided the reservations are compatible with the object and purpose of the CWC.[93] The Comprehensive-Nuclear Test-Ban Treaty 1996 prohibits

---

[90] 993 UNTS 143 (No. 14533) (Article 21(2)).
[91] 1019 UNTS 175 (No. 14956); ILM (1971), p. 261; UKTS (1993) 51 (Article 32(3)).
[92] ILM (1994), p. 968.   [93] ILM (1993), p. 804; UKTS (1997) 45; UN Reg. No. 33757.

reservations to the Treaty and its Annexes, but allows them to the Protocol to the Treaty and the Annexes to the Protocol, provided they are not incompatible with the object and purpose of the Treaty.[94] In both treaties, the attachments contain very detailed provisions which may need certain adjustment in their application to some contracting states.

Procedure

The procedural provisions in Article 23 are important, since the *chapeau* to Article 21(1) makes it clear that to have legal effect a reservation must be established in accordance with not only Articles 19 and 20, but also with Article 23. Some of the procedures may not reflect customary international law, especially the time limit in Article 20(5) and which the UN Secretary-General does not apply.[95]

Reservations

The *chapeau* to Article 19 provides that a reservation may be formulated when signing, ratifying, accepting, approving or acceding to a treaty, but does not prohibit a reservation being made at another time if this is provided for in the treaty.[96] A statement made during the negotiation of the treaty or on its adoption, even if recorded formally, must be made again if it is to be effective as a reservation. If it is made on signature of a treaty which is subject to ratification, to be effective it must be formally confirmed by the reserving state when expressing its consent to be bound, the reservation then being considered to have been made on the date of confirmation (Article 23(2)). This latter provision is important for the purposes of calculating the start of the twelve-month period specified in Article 20(5). A different rule can apply to the constituent instruments of an international organisation (Article 5). Reservations to amendments to the ITU constituent treaties can be made only at the time of adoption.[97]

A reservation or an express acceptance of a reservation must be made in writing and communicated (in practice, by the depositary) to the contracting states and other states entitled to become parties to the treaty (Article 23(1)).

---

[94] ILM (1996), p. 1443.   [95] See p. 127 below.
[96] See Professor Pellet's 3rd Report (UN Doc. A/CN.4/491/Add.3, paras. 135–43).
[97] See Article 32, paragraph 16 (446) of the ITU Convention of 1992 (UKTS (1996) 24, at p. 63).

The practical effect is that in most cases the reservation must either be included in the instrument of ratification or accompany it, in which case it must be referred to in the instrument. Typically the substance of the reservation will be contained in a note or letter from a diplomatic representative of the reserving state. A reservation made on signature should in principle be written under or next to the signature. But, unless the text is very short, it is usual to give the text formally to the depositary at the time of signature. It is then deemed to accompany the signature. It is therefore advisable to put the text in a first- or third-person diplomatic note.

Objections to reservations

To be effective an objection to a reservation cannot be made until the objector is a contracting state (i.e., has consented to be bound by the treaty), but it can then object to any reservations, past or future. The objection must be made in writing and communicated (in practice by the depositary) to the other contracting states and other states entitled to become parties to the treaty (Article 23(1)). If objection is made to a reservation made on signature subject to ratification, and before the reservation has been confirmed on ratification, the objection does not have to be confirmed (Article 23(3)). No reasons for an objection have to be given, though they often are. Even if the basis for the objection is pure policy, it will have the same effect as an objection on legal grounds. An objection can also be expressed in general terms so as to apply also to other reservations made in the same terms in the future.[98]

Article 20(5) provides that, except when objecting to a reservation to the constituent instrument of an international organisation, or where the treaty otherwise provides, a reservation is considered to have been accepted by a state if it has raised no objection within twelve months after it was notified of the reservation, or by the date it expressed its consent to be bound by the treaty, whichever is later. This provision does not apply to the Convention itself because of its non-retroactivity clause (Article 4). Moreover, it has not been established that the rule reflects customary international law, and the practice of the UN Secretary-General is not to refuse objections received after the twelve-month period.[99] Therefore Article 20(5), as such, will not apply unless both the reserving

---

[98] See p. 115 above on the objection by the Netherlands to a common reservation to the Genocide Convention.   [99] *UN Depositary Practice*, paras. 212–14.

and objecting states are parties to the Convention and the rule against retroactivity (Article 4) does not apply to the treaty in question. And even where the provision does apply, if the effect of the reservation is not clear, the period will not start to run until the effect has been clarified.[100]

Withdrawal of reservations and of objections to reservations

Reservations are from time to time withdrawn. Sometimes this is done in response to objections from other contracting states; sometimes because conditions have changed. With the end of the Cold War, several former East-bloc states withdrew their reservations to dispute settlement clauses, such as Article 66 of the Convention itself.[101] Since a reservation can be withdrawn, it may in certain circumstances be possible to modify or even replace a reservation, provided the result is to limit its effect. Some treaties make express provision for this.[102]

Withdrawal of a reservation, or an objection, is regulated by Articles 22 and 23(4). Withdrawal must be done in writing, usually to the depositary, who will notify the contracting states. Unless the treaty provides otherwise, withdrawal of a reservation or an objection can be done at any time, and the consent of a state which has accepted a reservation is not necessary for its withdrawal (and would be impractical given that most acceptances are tacit). Unless the treaty otherwise provides, or it is otherwise agreed, the withdrawal of a reservation becomes operative in relation to another contracting state when it has been notified of it. Withdrawal of an objection only becomes operative when notice of it has been received by the reserving state.

Functions of the depositary in relation to reservations

Treaties with provisions on reservations

If a treaty contains provisions as to reservations, the depositary will normally be guided by them when considering whether to accept a signature or an instrument accompanied by a reservation. If the treaty *expressly* forbids all reservations or reservations to specific articles, or *expressly* authorises reservations to specific articles only, the depositary must apply those provi-

---

[100] See p. 121 above.   [101] See *UN Multilateral Treaties*, footnotes to Chapter XXIII.1.
[102] See Article 13(2) of the European Convention on the Suppression of Terrorism 1957 (1137 UNTS 93; UKTS (1978) 93).

sions. Except for those cases where there is a question whether the reserva-tion is compatible with the object and purpose of the treaty, if in the opinion of the depositary a reservation is prohibited, the depositary should query it with the reserving state. Alternatively, the depositary can circulate the statement to the interested states, leaving it to them to decide if it amounts to a reservation. Article 309 of the United Nations Convention on the Law of the Sea 1982 prohibits reservations. On ratifying the Convention the Philippines expressed various 'understandings'. The UN Secretary-General, as depositary, circulated the understandings and received a number of objections that the understandings were reservations.[103]

Treaties silent as to reservations

Since December 1959, the UN Secretary-General, when acting as deposi-tary of a treaty which is silent as to reservations (in respect of which it is therefore permissible to make reservations provided they satisfy the com-patibility test), restricts himself to communicating to the states concerned the texts of reservations, and later any objections to them, but without commenting on the legal effect of either.[104] It is also the practice of the UN Secretary-General to ignore the possibility that a reservation which might be invalid might render void the consent of the reserving state to be bound; and in calculating whether the necessary minimum number of instruments have been deposited for the treaty to enter into force, he takes no account of the possible effect of a possibly invalid reservation.[105]

Reservations made after deposit of the instrument of ratification

Although the Convention does not authorise the making of reservations later than when a state consents to be bound, if the UN Secretary-General subsequently receives a reservation he will sometimes circulate the text with a note that, unless he receives an objection within ninety days, the res-ervation will be deemed to have been accepted. This is only done when the reservation is specifically authorised by the treaty or is the same as one already made by another state. The same approach is also adopted when a state wishes to modify a reservation, which may be done when a state wishes to restrict the scope of a reservation, and is therefore not objection-able. In such a case the Secretary-General will circulate the text. If no

---

[103] *UN Depositary Practice*, paras. 194–6.   [104] *Ibid.*, paras. 173–81   [105] *Ibid.*, paras. 184–8.

objection has been received within ninety days he treats this as tacit acceptance of the modified reservation. Although the ninety-day period has not
been questioned, it has no basis in the Convention. A revision which would
change the character or scope of the original would not be permissible.[106]

Can a reservation be made on reaccession?

Trinidad and Tobago acceded to the (First) Optional Protocol to the
International Covenant on Civil and Political Rights in 1980.[107] In June
1998 it withdrew from the Protocol and immediately reacceded to it, but
this time with a reservation which excluded the competence of the Human
Rights Committee to receive and consider communications (petitions)
from 'Death Row' prisoners.[108] There must be a question whether the stratagem was effective for this purpose. Although there is nothing in the
Protocol to prevent a party from withdrawing and then reacceding, can a
party reaccede solely for the purpose of making a reservation which it did
not make originally, and which it was then too late to make? In any event,
even if the reservation is not prohibited, another party would be entitled to
object to it and to state 'definitely' that the objection precludes the entry
into force of the Protocol as between that party and Trinidad and Tobago.
Even if the reservation is effective, that will not affect the obligations of
Trinidad and Tobago under the Covenant itself; when considering the periodic reports by Trinidad and Tobago, the Human Rights Committee will be
able to question it about its policies and practices on capital punishment.

Objections

When the UN Secretary-General receives an objection to a reservation,
but it does not specify whether it precludes the entry into force of the
treaty between the objecting and reserving states, he does not, despite
the presumption in Article 20(4)(b), pronounce upon the legal effect of
the objection as between the states concerned. Nor does he refuse an
objection received after the twelve-month deadline provided for by Article
20(5), though when circulating the text he describes it as a 'communication'.

---

[106] *Ibid.*, paras. 204–6   [107] 999 UNTS 171 (No. 14668).
[108] A similar procedure was followed by Guyana in 1999.

9

Entry into force

> The treaty becomes international law after 40 countries have ratified it.[1]

This is a common misconception. When a treaty has entered into force, it is in force *only* for those states which have consented to be bound by it. A treaty is therefore not like national legislation which, once in force, is in force for all to whom it is directed. A treaty is much closer in character to a contract. For the position of third states, see Chapter 14.

Each of the states for which a treaty is in force is a 'party' (Article 2(1)(g)). Thereafter it should never be referred to by the – uninformative and misleading – term 'signatory'.[2] But it must also be remembered that when a state expresses its consent to be bound it does not necessarily mean that the treaty will enter into force for it at that time: that will depend on whether the treaty is already in force (for the states which have already consented to be bound) or whether further consents are needed to bring it into force. A state's consent may of course have the effect of bringing the treaty into force if it is the last one needed to do that.

However, this does not mean that a treaty will have no legal effects before it enters into force. Certain of its provisions have to apply from the moment it is adopted, such as those on authentication of the text, right to participate, entry into force and depositary functions (Article 24(4)).

Express provisions

A treaty enters into force in such manner and on such date as provided for in the treaty or as the negotiating states may agree (Article 24(1)). There are various ways:

(1) On a date specified in the treaty. The parties are free to specify a date later than that of signature, or even for the treaty to operate retrospectively. Because of

---

[1] *The Times*, 26 June 1998, on the Landmines Convention.   [2] See p. 91 above.

the difficulties in getting multilateral treaties ratified, it is unusual for them to specify a date for entry into force. Inserting a specific date may serve a political purpose by encouraging states – or, perhaps more to the point, their parliaments – to meet the deadline. Such a provision is therefore usually subject to a proviso. Article 16 of the Montreal Protocol on Substances that Deplete the Ozone Layer 1987 provided that it would enter into force on 1 January 1989, but only if by then it had been ratified by eleven states or regional economic integration organisations, and certain other conditions had been satisfied.[3]

(2) On signature *only* by all the negotiating states. This is common for bilateral treaties which do not have to be approved by parliaments (see Appendix B), and is sometimes found in treaties between a few states (plurilateral treaties) even when the subject is of major importance, such as the Dayton Agreement 1995[4] or the London Agreement 1945, which established the Nuremberg Tribunal.[5]

(3) On ratification by both (or all) signatory states. If a multilateral treaty requires ratification by all the negotiating states, entry into force may be expressed to be on, or at a specific time after, the deposit of the last instrument of ratification. Article 45(1) of the Europol Convention 1995 provides that:

> This Convention shall enter into force on the first day of the month following the expiry of a three-month period after the notification [that it has completed its constitutional requirements] by the Member State which, being a member of the European Union *on the date of adoption by the Council of the Act drawing up this Convention*, is the last to fulfill that formality.[6]

This apparently elaborate formula is essential. First, it ensures that the treaty cannot enter into force until all EU Member States have consented to be bound. Secondly, it has the effect of excluding from that calculation any *new* Member States. Since the treaty gives them the right to accede at any time, without the emphasised words the entry into force of the treaty could be delayed for many years if new states join the EU before all the Member States at the time of the adoption of the treaty have consented to be bound. Thirdly, without the special formula, the treaty might not enter into force at all if not all new Member States were to accede. Some non-EU treaties fall into this trap.[7] The alternative is for the treaty to prohibit accessions by new Member

[3] 1522 UNTS 3 (No. 26369); ILM (1987), p. 1550. See also the Maastricht Treaty 1992, Title VII, Article R (UKTS (1994) 12).   [4] ILM (1996), p. 75. See p. 79 above.
[5] 82 UNTS 279.   [6] (UK) European Communities Series No. 13 (1995), Cm 3050.
[7] Cf. Article 4 of Protocol No. 11 to the European Convention on Human Rights (ILM (1994), p. 960). Similar problems can occur with amendments: see p. 218 below.

States until the treaty is in force, or not to count their accession for the purpose of entry into force. But the former may not be feasible politically.

(4) Conditional on the signature (or, more usually, ratification) of certain states specified by number, name or category. The Nuclear Non-Proliferation Treaty 1968 provided for entry into force after ratification by forty signatory states, including ratification by the three depositary states, the Soviet Union, the United Kingdom and the United States.[8] The entry into force of the 1984 Protocol to the Convention on Long-Range Transboundary Air Pollution (EMEP) required ratification by nineteen states and organisations within the geographical scope of the Protocol which, being Europe, meant that the instruments deposited by Canada and the United States before the entry into force of the Protocol did not count for that purpose.[9] The Comprehensive Nuclear-Test-Ban Treaty 1996 cannot enter into force until the forty-four states named in Annex 2 to the Treaty have ratified.[10]

(5) On signature (or, more usually, ratification) by a minimum number of the negotiating states (see, for example, Article 84(1) of the Vienna Convention itself). The minimum number for a multilateral treaty is two. The four Geneva Conventions of 1949, their Additional Protocols of 1977,[11] and other treaties on international humanitarian law, require only two ratifications to enter into force. In those cases, although the treaty will at first bind only the two states, this reflects the nature of such treaties, the purpose of which is to protect military personnel of the parties to a conflict and civilians. A humanitarian law treaty therefore creates, in effect, a network of 'bilateral treaties' between the parties. But for most multilateral treaties the number for entry into force is larger, often much more than the thirty-five needed to bring the Vienna Convention into force. The UN Convention on the Law of the Sea 1982 (UNCLOS) needed sixty ratifications, as does the Statute of the International Criminal Court 1998.[12] A large number is usually chosen to ensure that the treaty receives a broad measure of acceptance before it enters into force. This will be important if it requires parties to make significant financial contributions to a new international organisation. In the case of UNCLOS, this aim was not realised because the industrialised states did not ratify until after entry into force, and then only after UNCLOS had been effectively amended by the 1994 Implementation Agreement.[13] The 1984

---

[8] 729 UNTS 161 (No. 10485); ILM (1968), p. 809; UKTS (1970) 88; TIAS 6839. For the reason why there are three depositaries, see p. 263 below.

[9] ILM (1988), p. 701; UKTS (1988) 75: see Article 10(1)(a). See also Article 6 of the UNCLOS Implementation Agreement 1994 (ILM (1994), p. 1313; UKTS (1999) 82.

[10] ILM (1996), p. 1443. They include India, Pakistan and the United States.

[11] 75 UNTS 3 (No. 17512); ILM (1977), p. 1391; UKTS (1999) 29 and 30.

[12] ILM (1998), p. 1002.   [13] ILM (1994), p. 1313; UKTS (1999) 82. See pp. 90–1 above.

Protocol amending the Chicago Convention required 102 ratifications, and, not surprisingly, did not enter into force until 1998.[14] Certain treaties to which international organisations are parties, in particular regional economic integration organisations, such as the European Community, provide that, in addition to its Member States, the organisation can become a party in its own right, except that its instrument of ratification shall not be counted in addition to those deposited by its Member States.[15]

(6) As in 4 or 5 above, but the minimum number of states or organisations must also fulfil other conditions. These are often financial or economic, and designed to ensure that the treaty does not enter into force until the states which have a significant interest in the subject matter have ratified or, as in the case of commodity agreements, there is a balance between producing and consuming states. Article 10(1)(b) of the EMEP (see (4) above) imposed a further condition for entry into force: that the aggregate of the UN assessment rates for the European states which ratify had to exceed 40 per cent. The Montreal Protocol on Substances that Deplete the Ozone Layer 1987 had a similar provision, entry into force being dependent on eleven ratifications 'representing at least two-thirds of the 1986 estimated global consumption of the controlled substances [i.e., CFCs]'.[16] Since the Protocol did not define 'estimated global consumption', the UN Secretary-General, as depositary, notified the entry into force of the Protocol only after having obtained confirmation, in the form of data provided by the states concerned, that the necessary conditions for entry into force had been met.[17]

(7) On the exchange of instruments of ratification (bilateral treaty).

(8) On notification by each signatory state to the other (or others) of the completion of its constitutional requirements. This formula can be used even if the other state (or some of the other states) does not have to satisfy any such requirements, in which case the notification would be a mere formality. The notification is usually by third-person diplomatic note. Again, this is more common for bilateral treaties or multilateral treaties which are between only a few states.

(9) In the case of a treaty constituted by an exchange of notes, on the date of the reply note, though a further stage (such as in 8 above) is frequently added.

---

[14] ILM (1984), p. 705.

[15] See Article 305(1)(f) of, and Article 8 of Annex IX to, UNCLOS (ILM (1982), p. 1261; UKTS (1999) 81; and Article XI(2) of the FAO Compliance Agreement 1993 (ILM (1994), p. 968). Nor can the organisation and its member states usually have more votes in aggregate than the total votes of the member states (see p. 55, note 39, above).

[16] 1522 UNTS 3 (No. 26369); ILM (1987), p. 1550; UKTS (1990) 19. The deadline was met.

[17] See also Article 15 of the Bribery Convention 1997 (ILM (1998), p. 1). See further examples in UN Depositary Practice, paras. 226–32.

(10) As in 9 above, but on a date earlier or later than that of the reply note.

(11) On a date to be agreed. The 1998 Netherlands–United Kingdom Agreement on a Scottish Trial in the Netherlands (for those accused of the Lockerbie bombing) provides that it shall enter force on a date to be agreed.[18]

No provision or agreement on entry into force

If the treaty has no express provision on entry into force, and there is no agreement about it between the negotiating states, the treaty will enter into force as soon as all those states have consented to be bound (Article 24(2)). The Iraq–United Nations Memorandum of Understanding 1998 (actually a treaty) had no provision for ratification or entry into force.[19] The agreement may be implicit. No provisions were needed in the 1995 treaty between Norway and the United Kingdom concerning the disposal of the 'Brent Spar' offshore installation since it contains only assurances by the United Kingdom about the eventual disposal of the installation.[20]

Date of entry into force

In the case of *multilateral* treaties it is usual to provide that the *date* of entry into force will be a specified number of days, weeks or months following the deposit of the last instrument of ratification which is needed to bring the treaty into force (see, for example, Article 84(1) of the Vienna Convention itself). The period may be of any length, but the normal range is from thirty days to twelve months. This breathing space gives the depositary time to notify the contracting states of the forthcoming entry into force. In addition, contracting states may need time to bring into effect implementing legislation which they have previously enacted (or even to enact it). It also allows time for other necessary preparations.

One must be careful in calculating the date of entry into force. If the period is thirty days following deposit of the last necessary instrument, the time runs from the day *after* the date of deposit. If that date is 14 January the treaty will enter into force on 13 February. If the period is one month, it will run from the date of deposit. If that is 14 January, the treaty will

---

[18] ILM (1999), p. 926; UKTS (1999)) 43; UN Doc. S/1995/795. It entered into force on 8 January 1999. See also p. 148 below.   [19] ILM (1998), p. 501.
[20] UKTS (1995) 65. For the 1998 Brent Spar Treaty, see UKTS (1998) 46.

enter into force on 14 February, the same date one month later. When there is no corresponding date (e.g., no '30' February or '31' April), the treaty will enter into force on the last day of the next month, that being the nearest corresponding day.[21]

Another formula provides that the treaty shall enter into force 'on the first day of the second [or third] month' following the deposit of the last instrument of ratification needed for entry into force. The Council of Europe Framework Convention for the Protection of National Minorities 1995 provides that it:

> shall enter into force on the first day of the month following the expiration of a period of three months after the date on which twelve Member States of the Council of Europe have expressed their consent to be bound.[22]

This apparently convoluted way of saying that the treaty will enter into force after three *complete calendar* months have passed, nevertheless has the merit of certainty, leaving no doubt as to precisely when the treaty will enter into force.

In the case of a *bilateral* treaty, it is good practice to confirm the date in the Certificate of Exchange of Instruments of Ratification.[23] Once instruments have been exchanged, it is not usual to provide for any further delay before entry into force.

Ratification after the treaty has entered into force

When a state gives its consent to be bound following the entry into force of the treaty, it will enter into force for that state on the date of deposit of the instrument expressing consent, unless the treaty otherwise provides (Article 24(3)). A multilateral treaty will usually provide that it will enter into force for such a state after a specified period has elapsed following deposit. This is often the same period as for the original entry into force of the treaty, and gives time for the depositary to notify the existing parties. Particular care must be taken in drafting the clause; and there is a surprising range of them. One should try to avoid a formula such as:

> The present Convention shall enter into force three months after the date on which [twenty] states have deposited their instruments of ratification. For

---

[21] *UN Depositary Practice*, para. 236.   [22] ILM (1995), p. 353; UKTS (1998) 42.
[23] See p. 84 above and Appendix M.

each state which *thereafter* [or *subsequently*] ratifies, the present Convention shall come into force three months after deposit of its instrument of ratification.

In this example it is not clear if 'thereafter' (or 'subsequently') refers to (a) the date of fulfilment of the *conditions* for entry into force (i.e., the date when the minimum number of instruments have been received), or (b) the *actual date* of entry into force, which is usually later. It has been the consistent practice of the UN Secretary-General, when acting as depositary, to interpret such terms in accordance with alternative (a), and most treaties now adopt the formula in Article 84(2) of the Vienna Convention:[24]

(1) The present Convention shall enter into force on the thirtieth day following the date of deposit of the thirty-fifth instrument of ratification or accession.

(2) For each State ratifying or acceding to the Convention *after the deposit of the thirty-fifth instrument of ratification or accession*, the Convention shall enter into force on the thirtieth day after deposit by such State of its instrument of ratification or accession.

Similar problems arise with denunciation clauses.[25]

Who determines the date of entry into force?

In the case of a multilateral treaty, the date on which it will enter into force is normally determined by the depositary, who will notify the parties and other states concerned by a formal note. If there are doubts whether the conditions for entry into force have been met, the depositary may have to consult the interested states.

Time of entry into force

On rare occasions it will even be necessary to determine precisely the time on a given day that the treaty will have entered into force.[26] This may have to be resolved by an interpretation of the treaty, but when such a question can be foreseen it is preferable to cover the point in the treaty. This is especially so when the parties inhabit different time zones. Similar, and very practical, problems can arise with termination clauses.[27]

---

[24] *UN Depositary Practice*, paras. 244–5.   [25] See pp. 229–30 below.   [26] McNair, pp. 198–9.
[27] See pp. 225–6 below.

Date from which the treaty speaks

When drafting a treaty which, for example, provides for the transfer of rights, it is important to make clear if the rights are those existing at the date of adoption, signature or entry into force, or at some other date.[28]

Effect of withdrawal of an instrument or extinction of a state

In calculating whether the minimum number of instruments of ratification needed to bring a treaty into force have been deposited, the depositary will discount any which have been withdrawn. But if the instrument is withdrawn *after* deposit of the last instrument needed to bring the treaty into force, it appears to have been the practice of the UN Secretary-General not to regard the withdrawal as affecting satisfaction of the conditions for entry into force. Thus, if, say, forty ratifications are needed for entry into force, the conditions would be satisfied even if one of the forty is withdrawn *before* entry into force.[29] This may, however, be too literal an approach, and consequently not a correct application of the essential premise that all conditions for entry into force must have been satisfied. One of the conditions, albeit implicit, must surely be that on entry into force there will still be the minimum number of parties, i.e. 40, not 39.

The same considerations apply if a ratifying state ceases to exist.

Reservations attached to instruments

The depositary does not necessarily have to disregard any ratification containing reservations to which other contracting states may have objected. In the case of the Vienna Convention itself, several of the first thirty-five instruments of ratification needed for it to enter into force contained reservations to which objections had been lodged. The UN Secretary-General, as depositary, consulted the contracting states, stating his assumption that, for the purpose of calculating the date of entry into force, account should be taken of all thirty-five instruments. No one objected.[30]

---

[28] McNair, pp. 204–5.   [29] *UN Depositary Practice*, para. 159.   [30] Sinclair, p. 45.

Provisional application

The subject of Article 25 is sometimes loosely described as provisional 'entry into force'. This may be because the draft article prepared by the International Law Commission so described it, but, as Article 25 makes clear, it is concerned only with the *application* of a treaty on a provisional basis. To speak of provisional entry into force is confusing, and could mislead one into believing that the treaty is already in force, albeit on some kind of conditional basis.

A treaty is applied provisionally pending its entry into force if it so provides or if the negotiating states have in some other manner so agreed. When the treaty has a provisional application clause, the obligation of a state to apply the treaty provisionally is created by its participation in the adoption of the treaty. If there is no clause, the obligation arises if the state supports provisional application, usually by voting for a resolution to that effect. A state which does not so vote, or does not join a consensus, will be under no such obligation. And, should a treaty clause or a resolution be expressed to apply only to signatory states, it will not apply to a negotiating state until it has signed. Even after entry into force, provisional application may continue among those states which have not by then ratified.[31] The date from which a treaty is to be applied provisionally can be the date of adoption or signature or whatever the negotiating states can agree on. The most famous, but hugely untypical, example of provisional application is the General Agreement on Tariffs and Trade 1947 (GATT), which has been applied provisionally for decades by a Protocol of Provisional Application.[32]

Unless the treaty provides, or the negotiating states have agreed otherwise, provisional application is terminated with respect to a state if it notifies to the other states between which it is being applied provisionally its intention not to become a party to the treaty (Article 25(2)).

At the time the Convention was adopted, provisional application clauses were relatively rare.[33] The growing need for them has been caused by a combination of the need to bring treaties into force early when they

[31] *Ibid.*, pp. 46–7.
[32] 55 UNTS 171 (No. 814 ((b)) and 55 UNTS 308 (No. 814 I(c)). And see *UN Multilateral Treaties*, Chapter X.1.
[33] See Blix and Emerson, pp. 84–6; and R. Lefeber, 'The Provisional Application of Treaties', in Klabbers and Lefeber (eds.), *Essays on the Law of Treaties* (1998), p. 82.

are subject to ratification, and the problem of achieving that objective. This is especially difficult for treaties adopted within the United Nations or the specialised agencies since they require a substantial number of ratifications for entry into force. The Vienna Convention itself required the relatively small number of thirty-five, but, as we have seen, the 1984 Protocol amending the Chicago Convention needed 102.[34] Nevertheless, provisional application clauses are not generally favoured, since many states still have to obtain parliamentary consent to provisional application.[35]

The period of provisional application can be limited. The OSCE Open Skies Treaty 1992 provides that certain of its provisions shall be provisionally applied, and that:

> This provisional application shall be effective for a period of 12 months from the date when this Treaty is opened for signature. In the event that this Treaty does not enter into force before the period of provisional application expires, that period may be extended if all the signatory States so decide. The period of provisional application shall in any event terminate when this Treaty enters into force. However, the States Parties may then decide to extend the period of provisional application in respect of signatory States that have not ratified this Treaty.[36]

Other parts of the Treaty were in fact provisionally applied from July 1990, and the whole Treaty was provisionally applied from 1992 until its entry into force.

Article 7 of the 1994 Agreement relating to the Implementation of Part XI of the UN Convention on the Law of the Sea 1982 (Implementation Agreement) is unusual in that it provided that if the Agreement had not entered into force by 16 November 1994 (which it did not) it would be applied provisionally by states which had agreed to its adoption, or had signed it, *unless they notified the depositary otherwise*. In other words, it amounted to *implied* consent to provisional application, but with an opt-out.[37] Out of seventy-nine signatories of the Agreement, seventeen opted out.

---

[34] See also Article 45 of the European Energy Charter 1994 (ILM (1995), p. 373).

[35] See Lefeber, 'Provisional Application', (note 33 above), pp. 89–90.

[36] See Article XVIII, Section 1, in A. Bloed, *The Conference on Security and Co-operation in Europe* (1993), p. 1306.

[37] ILM (1994), p. 1313; UKTS (1999) 82. See D. Anderson, 'Legal Implications of the Entry into Force of the UN Convention on the Law of the Sea', ICLQ (1995), pp. 313–26; and pp. 90–1 above and pp. 222–3 below.

One alternative is to provide in the Final Act that:

> The Meeting agreed that it was desirable to ensure the effective implementation at an early date of the provisions of the Protocol. Pending entry into force of the Protocol it was agreed that it was desirable for all Contracting Parties to the Antarctic Treaty to apply Annexes I–IV, *in accordance with their legal systems and to the extent practicable*, and to take individually such steps to enable it to occur as soon as possible.

The treaty in question, the 1991 Protocol on Environmental Protection to the Antarctic Treaty,[38] required ratification by all twenty-six negotiating states to enter into force. Because of this, and the complexities of the implementing legislation, entry into force was delayed for six years. Practical implementation during the period before entry into force was patchy at best. But this would have been so with or without the exhortation in the Final Act. The inclusion of the phrase 'in accordance with their legal systems and to the extent practicable', or something similar, is found in most provisional application clauses, such as that in the Implementation Agreement.

Preparatory commissions

A further approach, which is increasingly being employed once a treaty has been adopted, is to establish a preparatory commission or 'prepcom'. This is usually a body composed of all the negotiating or signatory states and entrusted with the task of making the necessary arrangements for when the treaty enters into force. For example, although a monitoring body established by the treaty will not be able to meet formally until the treaty has entered into force, it is desirable that its draft rules of procedure should be prepared, secretariat staff engaged, premises found and, perhaps most important of all, financial arrangements settled. The need for a prepcom is particularly acute when the treaty establishes an international organisation, which needs to be able to begin work as soon as the treaty enters into force. The prepcom for the GATT was the Interim Commission for the International Trade Organisation (ICITO), which was established by a resolution of the UN Conference on Trade and Development and Employment 1947–8.[39] A prepcom was established for

---

[38] ILM (1991), p. 1460; UKTS (1999) 6.   [39] Cmd 7375.

the UN Convention on the Law of the Sea 1982 and met for many years. The 1998 Conference on the Establishment of an International Criminal Court adopted a resolution establishing a prepcom for the Court. Its tasks include drafting rules of procedure, a headquarters agreement, financial regulations, privileges and immunities and a budget for the first financial year.[40] This prepcom follows a pattern set by the United Nations itself in 1945,[41] and is no more than a committee. In contrast, the Comprehensive Nuclear Test-Ban Treaty 1996 (CTBT) provides for an elaborate verification and monitoring regime, involving the establishment of numerous monitoring stations throughout the world.[42] This requires not only their construction, but the drafting and negotiation of bilateral agreements, with provisions for privileges and immunities. For this purpose, later in 1996 a meeting of the signatory states adopted a resolution which approved a supplementary treaty (named simply 'Text'). This established a prepcom composed of representatives of all signatory states, but which has legal personality and a Provisional Technical Secretariat to serve it, and imposed various financial obligations on the signatory states pending entry into force of the CTBT.[43]

Retroactive effect of a treaty

A treaty will not have retroactive effect so as to bind a party with respect to any act or fact which took place, or any situation which ceased to exist, before its entry into force for that party, unless this is provided for in the treaty (Article 28). A treaty can, of course, apply to a pre-existing act, fact or situation which continues after entry into force. An international court or tribunal may have under the jurisdictional clause of a treaty jurisdiction over matters occurring before entry into force of the treaty.

---

[40] ILM (1998), p. 1002; UN Doc. A/CONF.183/C.1/L.76/Add. 14.
[41] See Goodrich and Hambro, *Charter of the United Nations* (3rd edn, 1969), pp. 8–9.
[42] ILM (1996), p. 1443.   [43] CTBT/MSS/RES/1; UKTS (1999) 46. See also p. 22 above.

10

Treaties and domestic law

Treaties are made to be performed.[1]

It should not be assumed that once a treaty has entered into force for a state it is then in force *in* that state; in other words, that it has become part of its law. The point is of particular importance for treaties which accord rights to individuals, such as human rights treaties, where the rights conferred are intended to be exercised by individuals (and sometimes corporations). International law and domestic law (the law in force within a state; sometimes termed 'municipal', 'internal' or 'national' law) operate on different planes. International law is concerned with the rights and obligations of states and other international legal persons, such as international organisations. When a treaty provides for rights or obligations to be conferred on persons, they can be given effect *only* if they are made part of the domestic law of the parties and with provisions in that law for enforcement. An example is the immunities and privileges granted to diplomatic missions and their staff by the Vienna Convention on Diplomatic Relations 1961.[2] A diplomat's immunity under that Convention can only be fully effective if the domestic law of the receiving state accords him immunity from its jurisdiction.

Whether rights and obligations created by a treaty need to be enforceable in domestic law, and, if so, whether in fact they are, is a matter of concern to both the public international lawyer and the domestic lawyer. If the international lawyer works in a foreign ministry he, and his diplomat colleagues, will be concerned to know what, if any, effect a treaty under negotiation will need to have in his domestic law; and whether legislation will be necessary in order to implement the treaty. When another ministry is conducting the negotiations its officials will have the same concerns. All

---

[1] P. Reuter, *Introduction to the Law of Treaties* (2nd English edn, 1995), para. 44.
[2] 500 UNTS 95 (No. 7310); UKTS (1965) 19. See the (UK) Diplomatic Privileges Act 1964.

those concerned with negotiations need to assure themselves that if their state should become a party there will be no domestic legal obstacle to its full implementation, since that could have consequences, both international and domestic.

Duty to perform treaties

Article 26 contains the fundamental principle of the law of treaties: *pacta sunt servanda*:

> Every treaty in force is binding upon the parties to it and must be performed in good faith.

It is followed in Article 27 by its corollary: a party may not invoke the provisions of its internal law as justification for its failure to perform a treaty.[3] Thus, if a new law or modification to existing law, is needed in order to carry out the obligations which will be laid upon it by the treaty, a negotiating state should ensure that this is done at least by the time the treaty enters into force for it. If this is not done, not only will the state risk being in breach of its treaty obligations, but it will be liable in international law to another party if as a result that party, or its nationals, is later damaged. Although it may be tempting, a state cannot plead that it is waiting for its parliament to legislate.

Even if the treaty does not enter into force for the state at the time it consents to be bound,[4] the date of entry into force may come earlier than expected. It is therefore desirable that any necessary legislation is made *before* the state gives its consent, though the actual coming into force of the legislation can certainly be postponed until the entry into force of the treaty.

The Commonwealth Secretariat publishes 'accession kits'. These explain in a practical manner how a state can legislate to implement certain important multilateral treaties, such as the Chemical Weapons Convention 1993. The kits include illustrative model legislation and explanatory memoranda on the incorporation of the treaty into domestic law. Although designed with Commonwealth states in mind, they may well be of value to others.[5]

---

[3] For this purpose, internal law includes, for example, EC law. See p. 120 above regarding objections to a reservation on the ground that it is incompatible with Article 27.

[4] See pp. 82–3 above.

[5] Commonwealth Secretariat, Legal and Constitutional Affairs Division, Marlborough House, Pall Mall, London SW1Y 5HX; tel. ++ 44(0)20 7747 6420 (fax 7839 3302).

A state cannot plead a change of government to excuse failure to implement a treaty. Since the treaty is entered into on behalf of the *state*, the new government must also perform the treaty. Nor is it easy to plead that a treaty is invalid because its consent to be bound was expressed in violation of its law.[6]

Constitutional provisions

Some treaties, such as treaties of alliance (or for that matter, the Vienna Convention itself), do not need to have effect in the domestic law of the parties. But, given the subject matter of treaties today, many need to be given some effect in domestic law. It may, for example, be necessary to create new criminal offences. How this is done depends on the constitution of each state. Although no two constitutions are identical, there are two general approaches: 'dualism' and 'monism'. It must be stressed, however, that both are doctrines developed by scholars in an attempt to explain the different approaches taken by states. Although monism is often presented as the opposite of dualism, this is misleading. If one examines even a small selection of constitutions it soon becomes apparent that many contain both dualist and monist elements. In this matter the constitutional practices of states make up a spectrum. At one end is found the United Kingdom, which has perhaps the purist form of dualism. At the other end might be said to be Switzerland, which has perhaps the most developed form of monism. In between these two extremes there are many variations.[7] But, as with other aspects of domestic legal systems, despite apparently very different laws and procedures the end result is often surprisingly similar, differences in language and custom masking essential similarities. It is necessary, however, to be familiar with the different approaches, since constitutional constraints on one of the negotiating states may affect the way final clauses are drawn, especially in respect of ratification, entry into force and provisional application, or may even suggest that an MOU may be preferable to a treaty.

---

[6] See p. 252 below.
[7] See the useful summary of the constitutions of several states in Monroe Leigh (ed.), *National Treaty Law and Practice* (1995). Blaustein, *Constitutions of the World* (G. H. Flanz ed., loose-leaf) is an invaluable source for the texts of constitutions. See also Reisenfeld and Abbott, *Parliamentary Participation in the Making and Operation of Treaties: A Comparative Study* (1993).

A brief description of the monist approach will be given, with some examples. This will be followed by an explanation of the dualist approach. The constitutional practice of the United Kingdom will be dealt with in some detail. Not only is it the prime example of dualism, but it has been followed in almost all other Commonwealth states, which amount to nearly a third of all states. This section will end with a description of how treaties are dealt with in the United States Constitution, which combines both approaches, and needs to be understood given the importance of the United States for treaty-making.

Monism

The essence of the monist approach is that a treaty may, without legislation, become part of domestic law once it has been concluded in accordance with the constitution and has entered into force for the state. However, as we shall see, in many cases legislation will also be needed. When legislation is not needed such treaties are commonly described as 'self-executing'. Although there are many variations in how the monist approach is expressed in constitutions, three main features are common to most. First, although the constitution requires the treaty to have first been approved by parliament, there are exceptions for certain types of treaties or certain circumstances. Secondly, a distinction is made between treaties according to their nature or subject matter, some being regarded as being self-executing, others requiring legislation before they can have full effect in domestic law. Thirdly, a self-executing treaty may constitute supreme law and override any inconsistent domestic legislation, whether existing or future, though in some states where parliament is supreme later legislation can override a self-executing treaty.

France[8]

In France, the executive has sole responsibility for concluding treaties. But, in view of the supremacy of treaties under the constitution, the National Assembly and the Senate should authorise ratification if the treaty concerns peace, trade, an international organisation which has the power to restrict the exercise of French sovereignty, expenditure not budgeted for,

---

[8] Monroe Leigh (note 7 above), pp. 1–41.

individual status or territory, or if the treaty would modify existing legislation or have new legislative effect. Although authorisation is given in the form of a statute (*loi*), it has no normative effect. And, if the executive ratifies a treaty without obtaining the approval of parliament when it should have, the only sanction is political. Although there are now more matters for which authorisation should be sought, the executive has complete discretion as to whether to seek it. The *Conseil Constitutionnel* has authority to pronounce on whether a treaty conforms to the Constitution, but only if the President, Prime Minister, President of the Senate, President of the National Assembly or sixty members of either of the latter two bodies ask the *Conseil*. Those treaties which may affect the rights and duties of individuals must be published in the *Journal Officiel*. They then prevail over existing or later legislation. Until so published a treaty cannot be applied by the courts, but once published the courts will apply it from the date it entered into force for France. If the terms of a treaty are not clear, a court will not apply them; similarly, if the terms are not capable of being applied as domestic law without new legislation (i.e., are not self-executing), such as those of the Convention on the Rights of the Child 1989.[9]

Germany[10]

Under the German Constitution (Basic Law) the conclusion of treaties is the responsibility of the executive, though the Foreign Relations Committee of Parliament is informed when a treaty is concluded. Only a limited number of categories of treaties need the consent of Parliament before they can be ratified, namely, normative treaties, the implementation of which needs legislation, and treaties affecting federal legislation or of high political importance. Even in those cases Parliament cannot amend the treaty, impose conditions or require reservations to be made. Its approval is given by a law. Whether a treaty needs the consent of Parliament is ultimately a matter for the Constitutional Court, but if the Foreign Relations Committee considers that the consent of Parliament is needed, in practice it will be sought. The law approving ratification of the treaty has the effect also of making the treaty part of German law with effect from the day the treaty enters into force for Germany. If the treaty would affect existing laws or require new legislation, a separate law has to be enacted.

---

[9] ILM (1989), p. 1448; UKTS (1992) 44; UN Reg. No. 27531.   [10] Monroe Leigh, pp. 43–77.

As regards international agreements made by the *Länder*, see page 49 above.

The Netherlands

The basic constitutional rule is that all treaties need the approval of Parliament, unless they are exempted by an Act of Parliament. An Act of 1994 lays down which treaties must be submitted to Parliament for approval (which can be express or tacit) and requires the foreign minister to submit to Parliament periodically a list of all treaties then under negotiation, unless the negotiations are confidential.[11] A treaty which would conflict with the Constitution must be submitted for express approval. No approval is required if the treaty is only to implement an already approved treaty; is for no more than a year and involves no substantial obligations (extension of the period being possible);[12] is to extend a treaty; is to amend an annex; or, in exceptional circumstances, if it is in the interests of the state that it should remain secret or confidential. This last exception is surprising in view of Article 102 of the United Nations Charter.[13] If a treaty is capable of binding on all persons without need for legislation it prevails over existing or future legislation.

Poland

Under Article 91 of the Polish Constitution of 1997 a treaty, once it has been ratified and promulgated in the official gazette and entered into force for Poland, constitutes part of the domestic legal order and applies directly, unless its application depends on the enactment of a law. If a treaty is ratified following the grant of consent by Parliament, it has precedence over laws inconsistent with it.

Russia

In 1995 Russia adopted a new Federal Law on International Treaties.[14] The Law goes into considerable detail about the respective roles of the execu-

---

[11] J. Klabbers, 'The New Dutch Law on the Approval of Treaties', ICLQ (1995), pp. 629–43.

[12] For an example, see p. 135, para. (11), above about the Netherlands–United Kingdom Agreement on a Scottish Trial in the Netherlands.   [13] See p. 275 below.

[14] ILM (1995), p. 1373; and generally Mullerson, Fitzmaurice and Andenas (eds.), *Constitutional Reform and International Law in Central and Eastern Europe* (1998), pp. 259–78 and 295–317 (text of the Law).

tive and the legislature, and various other organs and agencies of the state. This is due to the complex constitutional structure of the Russian Federation. The Law closely follows the Vienna Convention, its main interest for present purposes being in the procedures for approval of treaties, and their place in domestic law. The conclusion of treaties is the exclusive responsibility of the executive, but certain categories are required to be made subject to ratification, which in turn requires the approval of Parliament (the State Duma and the Federal Assembly) by means of a federal law. These include treaties which will need new laws or changes to existing laws, and treaties concerning human rights, territorial demarcation, defence and international security, and participation in international organisations if this would involve transfer of powers of the Russian Federation or if decisions of the organs of the organisation would be binding on the Federation. Provided the treaty has not entered into force for Russia, the Constitutional Court has the power to pronounce on whether it conforms to the Constitution. Treaties are an integral part of the legal system, and prevail over inconsistent domestic law. A treaty has direct effect if it is in force for Russia, has been published there officially and does not require legislation in order to implement it.

Switzerland

Under the Swiss Constitution treaty-making power is vested in the Confederation. The Federal Council (i.e., the executive) is thus entitled to conclude treaties even on matters within the competence of the constituent units of the Confederation (the cantons).[15] Although the Constitution provides for the Federal Assembly to approve treaties, in constitutional practice about 60 per cent are not specifically approved by the Federal Assembly. The Federal Council may conclude such 'executive treaties'[16] provided the Federal Assembly has authorised them beforehand, either expressly or implicitly, or if they concern a matter of minor importance which does not primarily affect individuals. In other cases, if the matter is urgent, the Federal Council may apply a treaty provisionally, but cannot ratify it without the approval of the Federal Assembly.

In practice the Federal Council has a large measure of discretion as to

---

[15] See p. 49 above on treaty-making by the cantons.
[16] See p. 158 below on US executive agreements.

whether to submit a treaty for approval. When it does so it has to be done between signature and ratification. The treaty will be accompanied by the text of any reservations which the Federal Council proposes to make. The Federal Assembly may reformulate them or add new ones. A treaty approved by the Federal Assembly which is of indefinite duration and not capable of being denounced, which provides for participation in an international organisation or concerns multilateral law-making must be submitted to a referendum of all Swiss citizens if 50,000 citizens or eight cantons so demand. Other treaties are submitted to a referendum if both Houses of the Federal Parliament (the Federal Assembly and the Council of States) so decide. Since 1977 adherence to a collective security treaty or to a treaty establishing a supranational body must be submitted to a referendum of Swiss citizens and the cantons. A majority of citizens and the cantons (notably Geneva) voted in 1986 against joining the United Nations, and in 1992 against participation in the European Economic Area.

Once a treaty enters into force for Switzerland, it becomes part of Swiss law; there is no need for it to be formally incorporated. This is so whether or not the Federal Assembly has specifically approved the treaty. Treaties prevail over inconsistent law, existing or future. However, Parliament can enact a law which is inconsistent with a treaty to which Switzerland is bound, provided this is done deliberately, though there is a growing tendency in the jurisprudence of the Federal Tribunal (Supreme Court) in favour of recognising the primacy of treaties. Once it has become part of the law, it can be invoked before domestic courts, provided it is self-executing. For this purpose the treaty must be precise enough for the courts to apply it. Whether a treaty is self-executing will also depend on its nature and purpose.

Dualism

Under the dualist approach, the constitution of the state accords no special status to treaties; the rights and obligations created by them have no effect in domestic law *unless legislation is in force to give effect to them*. When the legislation is specifically made for this purpose, the rights and obligations are then said to be 'incorporated' into domestic law. This approach reflects, on the one hand, the constitutional power of the executive generally to bind itself to a treaty without the prior consent of the legislature and, on the other hand, the supreme power of the legislature under the constitution to make laws. In the United Kingdom, this division of powers was a product of the seventeenth-century constitutional struggle between the King of England and Parliament. This resulted in the power to legislate being almost completely vested in Parliament, yet with the Crown retaining in common law certain 'royal prerogatives' (the right to act without the consent of Parliament), which included the conduct of foreign relations and the making of treaties.[17] This division of powers was inherited by most former colonies of the United Kingdom, the United States being the principal exception.

With dualism the provisions of a treaty which have been incorporated into domestic law *have the status only of domestic law*, and can be amended or repealed by later legislation. If such action were to result in breach of the treaty, there would be no remedy in domestic law since there would have been no violation of it. The attraction of this approach is much greater certainty as to the effect which the treaty has (or has not) in domestic law. Nevertheless, in certain limited circumstances, the courts will have regard to unincorporated treaties.[18]

United Kingdom constitutional practice

The various methods by which treaty provisions may be incorporated into domestic law may be better understood by an explanation of the constitutional practice of the United Kingdom.[19] The treaty-making power of the Crown is exercised by the Secretary of State for Foreign and Commonwealth Affairs (foreign minister). Although there is no requirement for Parliament to consent to the Crown entering into a treaty, under a constitutional practice (known as the Ponsonby Rule) a treaty which is subject to ratification or analogous procedure is laid before Parliament, with a short explanatory memorandum, for twenty-one days while Parliament is sitting. This is so that Parliament can be informed of the treaty. It may debate it if it wishes, but this seldom happens unless an Act

---

[17] See O'Connell, pp. 216–17; Wade and Bradley, *Constitutional and Administrative Law* (10th edn, 1985), p. 245.

[18] See R. Gardiner, 'Treaty Interpretation in the English Courts since Fothergill v. Monarch Airlines', ICLQ (1995), p. 620.

[19] See the detailed account by Sinclair and Dickson of United Kingdom treaty law and practice in Monroe Leigh (note 7 above), pp. 223–60; *Oppenheim*, pp. 56–63; and BYIL (1992), p. 704.

of Parliament is needed or the treaty is of major political importance, in which case the Government would normally arrange for a debate anyway.

Under the constitution no provisions of a treaty can have effect in domestic law unless legislation has so provided. Legislation can take three main forms:

(1) An Act of Parliament for the purpose of incorporating the treaty into the law of the United Kingdom. The text of the whole or part of[20] the treaty may be scheduled to the Act, which will provide that those provisions of the treaty set out in the schedule 'shall have the force of law in the United Kingdom'. But, even when treaty provisions are scheduled to an Act, they will not necessarily become part of the law. The Geneva Conventions Act 1957, as amended by the Geneva Conventions (Amendment) Act 1995, has annexed to it the (complete) text of the four Geneva Conventions of 1949 and the two Additional Protocols of 1977, but the Act does not provide that their provisions shall have the force of law in the United Kingdom.[21] The main purpose of the Act is to enable 'grave breaches' of the Conventions to be prosecuted, and to protect the Red Cross emblem. Scheduling the texts therefore enables those provisions to be seen in context. The other provisions of the Conventions are implemented by administrative means, including disciplinary regulations of the armed forces. The 1995 Act provides that, if the United Kingdom makes any reservations or declarations when ratifying either Additional Protocol, an Order in Council may certify that they had been made and that the scheduled Protocol shall be interpreted subject to and in accordance with such reservations and declarations.[22] When there is no authentic English text of the treaty the practice now is to attach the original foreign language text, with an English translation.[23] Alternatively, none of the treaty is scheduled. Instead the Act makes such changes to the law as are necessary to give effect to the treaty.[24] The Act may, for example, simply authorise expenditure required by the treaty. In such cases it may or may not declare that its purpose is to give effect to the treaty. This can have implications for the interpretation of the legislation (see below).

---

[20] Compare the Diplomatic Privileges Act 1964 (part of the treaty) with the Consular Relations Act 1968 (whole of the treaty).

[21] See *Cheng* v. *Conn, Inspector of Taxes* [1968] 1 All ER 779; and Rowe and Meyer, 'The Geneva Conventions (Amendment) Act 1995: A Generally Minimalist Approach', ICLQ (1996), pp. 476–84.   [22] Section 4(7). An Order was made: SI 1998 No. 1754.

[23] Carriage by Air Act 1961 and Carriage by Air (Supplementary Provisions) Act 1961. Both implement treaties modifying the Warsaw Convention 1929, and have French as the only authentic text.

[24] See the State Immunity Act 1978, which mainly implements the European Convention on State Immunity 1972 (ILM (1972), p. 470; UKTS (1979) 74).

(2) An Act of Parliament conferring all the powers necessary to carry out obligations under *future* treaties. For example, bilateral air services agreements can
be concluded without the need each time for fresh legislation since existing
legislation, both primary and secondary, is sufficient to implement the agreements.

(3) An Act of Parliament which provides a framework within which secondary
legislation can be made to give effect to a certain category of treaty, often bilateral. The Act can either:

(a) authorise the Crown to make *secondary legislation making the treaties
part of domestic law.* This is usually done by an Order made by 'the
Queen in Council' (Order in Council) to which the text of the treaty is
attached. Such legislation is frequently made for bilateral double taxation conventions,[25] extradition treaties[26] and social security conventions;[27]

(b) authorise the Crown to make *secondary legislation to implement obligations imposed by certain categories of treaty.* The treaty is not attached
to the secondary legislation. Instead its provisions are translated into
the language of the Act, and if necessary elaborated. Typical of this
method is the International Organisations Act 1968, under which
Orders in Council are made to give effect to treaties conferring privileges and immunities on international organisations and tribunals,
and persons connected with them.[28] The Orders have to be approved,
in draft, by both Houses of Parliament. This requires a short debate in
each House. Orders on other matters, particularly if, unlike diplomatic immunity, they do not have the effect of restricting the rights of
the ordinary citizen, are generally not subject to that procedure, but
are sometimes subject to annulment (cancellation) by Parliament
after they have been made. The United Nations Act 1946 empowers the
Crown to make such provision in Orders in Council as are 'necessary
or expedient' to enable measures adopted by the United Nations
Security Council to be effectively applied. The power is used extensively to implement measures adopted by the Security Council under
Chapter VII of the UN Charter, which can include economic and other
sanctions, the establishment of *ad hoc* international criminal tribunals, and privileges and immunities. In 1998 an Order was made to

---

[25] Income and Corporation Taxes Act 1988, section 788(10); SI 1991 No. 2876 (Czechoslovakia).
[26] Extradition Act 1989, section 4; SI 1990 No. 1507 (giving effect to the European Convention on
Extradition 1957, including reservations and declarations made by the parties).
[27] Social Security Act 1975, section 143; SI 1991 No. 767 (Norway).
[28] See the Tribunal for the Law of the Sea (Immunities and Privileges) Order 1996 (SI 1996 No.
272).

enable a Scottish court to hold a trial in the Netherlands of the two Libyans accused of the sabotage of flight PA 103 at Lockerbie in 1988.[29] Although the Orders are laid before Parliament, they are not subject to its approval, and so can be made and brought into effect quickly, if necessary on the day they are made. This is important for the effectiveness of a sanctions regime. The Orders cannot be revoked except by another Order or by Act of Parliament.

Since treaties are not supreme law in the United Kingdom, even if they have been incorporated, Parliament, being supreme, can enact legislation which is inconsistent with treaty obligations. There have been instances of United Kingdom legislation being held by the European Court of Human Rights to be in breach of the European Convention on Human Rights (ECHR). Parliament has in such cases passed new or amending legislation. It has no *constitutional* duty to do so, but under Article 46(1) of the ECHR, as amended, the United Kingdom has an obligation in international law to comply with judgments in cases to which it is a party. Provisions of the ECHR have now been incorporated into the law of the United Kingdom by the Human Rights Act 1998.[30] The Act requires courts and public bodies to apply existing and future legislation as far as possible in a way compatible with the ECHR. If a court determines that a provision is incompatible with a right under the ECHR, it may make a 'declaration of incompatibility'. An order can then be made to remove the incompatibility, including one which has been so determined by the European Court of Human Rights. The order can override earlier primary legislation. Section 19 of the Act requires a draft Act of Parliament to be accompanied by a statement that it is compatible with rights under the ECHR.

Scotland and Northern Ireland[31]

Under the Scotland Act 1998 the Scottish Administration has competence for carrying out the United Kingdom's treaty obligations on matters which have been devolved to Scotland. Although the power to legislate to implement international obligations on any subject has been retained by the United Kingdom Parliament, whether it or the Scottish Parliament should

---

[29] The High Court of Justiciary (Proceedings in the Netherlands) (United Nations) Order 1998 (SI 1998 No. 2251), implementing Security Council Resolution 1192 (1998). See also UN Doc. S/1998/795, which includes the draft of the Order and the Netherlands–UK Agreement.

[30] ILM (1999), p. 464.   [31] See also p. 51 above.

enact implementing legislation for Scotland will be a matter for consultation in each case between the United Kingdom Government and the Scottish Administration and Scottish Parliament. For this purpose the United Kingdom Parliament will not, without the consent of the Scottish Parliament, legislate on a matter which has been wholly devolved to Scotland. Guidelines, in the form of a 'concordat', have been drawn up by the Foreign and Commonwealth Office and the Scottish Administration.

The situation with respect to Northern Ireland under the Northern Ireland Act 1998 is similar, and subject to arrangements with the Northern Ireland Administration.

Interpretation and application of treaties by United Kingdom courts

Generally judges in the United Kingdom have, at least in the past, not been at their happiest when confronted by a treaty. Admittedly, they are not helped by the strict separation of treaties from domestic law inherent in the dualist approach. The courts have, however, developed certain principles which alleviate some of the strictness of dualism:[32]

(1) If the language of legislation implementing a treaty is unambiguous, the courts will not look behind the legislation at the treaty.

(2) If the language is ambiguous, the court will look at the treaty, if necessary all of it. It will do this even if the legislation does not mention the treaty.

(3) Ambiguous legislation will be interpreted in the way which is most consistent with the international obligations of the United Kingdom, including unincorporated treaties (such as the European Convention on Human Rights even before it was incorporated).

(4) In so far as a treaty has been incorporated by attaching all or part of it to legislation, the courts should interpret it according to the rules of international law, in particular Articles 31–33 of the Vienna Convention (even though the Convention has not been incorporated).[33] They do not always do so, but they are getting better.[34]

---

[32] R. Higgins on United Kingdom practice in Jacobs and Roberts (eds.), *The Effect of Treaties in Domestic Law* (1987), pp. 123–39; *Oppenheim*, pp. 60–3; I. Sinclair, 'The Principles of Treaty Interpretation and their Application by the English Courts', ICLQ (1963), pp. 508–51.

[33] *R. v. Lambeth Justices ex parte Yusufu* [1985] *Times Law Reports* 114; *Sidhu v. British Airways* [1997] 1 All ER 193 at 201–12.

[34] See Gardiner, 'Treaty Interpretation' (note 18 above); *Oppenheim*, p. 1269, note 2 (significantly, perhaps the longest footnote in that noteworthy work); and C. Kuner, 'The Interpretation of Multilingual Treaties', ICLQ (1991), p. 953, at pp. 960–1.

EC law and the United Kingdom

Because the United Kingdom is dualist, EC law is enforceable in the United Kingdom only because United Kingdom legislation so provides.[35] But when applying EC law, the UK courts must construe it as EC law, not as United Kingdom law, and follow decisions of the European Court of Justice. However, because decisions taken under either the Common Foreign and Security Policy (CFSP) or Justice and Home Affairs (JHA), or 'EU law', are not required to have direct effect in the domestic law of the Member States, they are not enforceable in the United Kingdom without legislation.

Other Commonwealth states

Naturally those Commonwealth states which had been under the sovereignty of the United Kingdom, which is almost all of the other fifty-three Members, acquired constitutions which embodied the dualist approach. Even when the constitutions have been changed, most still follow the same approach. In 1989 Antigua and Barbuda enacted a Ratification of Treaties Act. Although this requires that treaties regarding the international status of the state, its security or sovereignty or membership of an international organisation, be authorised or approved by the legislature, it provides that '[no] provision of a treaty shall become, or be enforceable as, part of the law of Antigua and Barbuda except by or under an Act of Parliament'. The Act also expressly confirms the exclusive power of the Government to enter into all other treaties.

In contrast, the South African Constitution provides that ratification of certain treaties needs the agreement of Parliament. The treaty then forms part of the law of South Africa if self-executing and is not inconsistent with the Constitution or an Act.[36] Applying this test may not be easy. In many cases implementing legislation will be necessary.

Is one approach better?

One can argue long about the relative merits of the monist and dualist approaches. The workings of dualist systems may from the above account seem to be more complicated. This may be because dualist procedure has

---

[35] See section 3(1) of the European Communities Act 1972.
[36] Article 231, in Blaustein and Flanz, *Constitutions of the World* (loose-leaf).

been described in greater detail. The value of dualism is greater certainty and precision. In a dualist system, whether a treaty is part of domestic law depends on whether legislation has been made to make it so: if no legislation has been made, it is not part of domestic law. This puts a burden on government to decide, before it ratifies, whether legislation will be needed. This requires a detailed examination of the treaty. Thus, the onus is on government and parliament, rather than the citizen or the courts, to determine how far the treaty is to be part of domestic law. Under a monist system it may be many years after the treaty entered into force for a state that such a determination is made by a court deciding, usually on an application by a citizen, whether a provision is self-executing. Of course the advantages of dualism will be lost if the government is not diligent in vetting treaties before ratification. But the author is not aware of any significant case in recent times where the United Kingdom did not enact the legislation necessary to carry out its treaty obligations. The case of the European Convention on Human Rights was rather special, the British Government in the 1950s having honestly, though some might even say chauvinistically, believed that the law of the United Kingdom already gave full effect to that Convention. They had not bargained for the activism of the European Court of Human Rights, or the changes in society in the last decades of the twentieth century.

United States

The way treaties are dealt with under the Constitution of the United States reflects both dualist and monist approaches, and has rightly been described as 'remarkably complex'.[37] Any non-American lawyer who has to deal with the status of a treaty in the law of the United States would be well advised to consult a good American law firm. Under Article II, section 2(2), of the Constitution the President may ratify a 'Treaty' only with the 'Advice and Consent' of the Senate signified by the affirmative vote of two-thirds of the members present. This is sometimes referred to,

---

[37] J. Jackson, in Jacobs and Roberts (eds.), *The Legal Effects of Treaties in Domestic Law* (1987), pp. 141–69 (which is the primary source for this section, regrettably it having proved not possible to obtain more authoritative comments). See also Reisenfeld and Abbott *Parliamentary Participation* (note 7 above), pp. 205–328. For a critical commentary on compliance by the United States with treaties, see D. Vogts, 'Taking Treaties Less Seriously', AJIL (1998), pp. 458–62.

misleadingly, as 'ratification',[38] since that act can be done only by the President. These days the Senate will often withhold its approval. Although the Constitution mentions only one type of international agreement ('a Treaty'), from its earliest days an alternative form has been employed by the United States Government in order to avoid the problems inherent in obtaining Senate approval. Such treaties are termed 'executive agreements'. They do not have to be submitted to the Senate, but are regarded by both the Government of the United States and other states as treaties for the purposes of international law.[39] Unless otherwise indicated, a reference in the following pages to a 'treaty' includes an executive agreement; and a reference to a 'Treaty' (with a capital 'T') is to a treaty which requires the approval of the Senate.

Most treaties entered into by the United States have been, and still are, executive agreements, and which can be broken down into four categories:

(1) those authorised by a prior Act of Congress;
(2) those subsequently approved by Act of Congress;
(3) those entered into by the President in exercise of his executive power (a controversial and ill-defined area); and
(4) those authorised by a previous Treaty or executive agreement.

Under a federal statute, known as the 'Case Act',[40] all executive agreements have to be notified to Congress within sixty days of entry into force, and published annually.

'Self-executing' treaties

Under Article VI, section 2, of the Constitution all Treaties are the 'supreme law of the land'. This has been interpreted by the Supreme Court as applying also to executive agreements. The provision is often, and misleadingly, described as making treaties 'self-executing'. By this is meant that the treaty, once it has entered into force, is directly applicable as if it were an Act of Congress. Contrary to what is sometimes asserted, whether it is self-executing does not depend on whether it is a Treaty or an executive agree-

---

[38] See p. 81 above.
[39] The Mexican Law on Treaties draws a number of similar distinctions between 'treaty' and 'inter-institutional agreement' (ILM (1992), p. 393).
[40] Public Law 92-403, as amended by 1 USC 112b (ILM (1972), p. 1117 and ILM (1979), p. 82).

ment.[41] The concept has led inevitably to considerable confusion and uncertainty, since there is no sure method for determining whether a treaty is or is not self-executing. The matter has ultimately to be decided *in each case* by the courts. There is now considerable jurisprudence, but it is not easy even for American lawyers to advise whether a particular treaty, or part of it, is self-executing. The crucial factor is the intention of the parties. In some cases, the other party to a treaty may have to intervene in legal proceedings in the United States to protect its position. However, a treaty will not be self-executing if it clearly envisages implementing legislation. But that is the exception; usually it is necessary to consider various factors such as: language and purpose, the specific circumstances, the nature of the obligations and the implications of permitting a private right of action without the need for legislation.

Hierarchy of norms

If a treaty is self-executing it may come into conflict with US domestic law. Whenever possible the courts will seek to reconcile the two, but that is not always feasible. When this happens the residuary rules are:

(1) treaties prevail over common law;

(2) treaties prevail over state law;

(3) the Constitution prevails over *all* treaties. The rule may, in part, have led in recent years to the Senate requiring the President to attach a reservation when ratifying certain human rights treaties to the effect that:

> nothing in the Convention requires or authorises legislation or other action by the United States of America prohibited by the Constitution of the United States as interpreted by the United States [42]

(4) in the case of a conflict between a Treaty and an Act of Congress, the later in time prevails. However, there is still considerable uncertainty over whether a later executive agreement prevails. The judicial decisions do not give a clear guide, though it is probably fair to say that generally an executive agreement concluded in exercise only of the executive power of the President will not prevail over a prior Act of Congress.

---

[41] In some cases, the US has made a declaration that a treaty is 'non-self-executing'. See *UN Multilateral Treaties*, Chapter IV.2 (racial discrimination), 4 (ICCPR) and 9 (Torture); and D. Sloss, 'The Domestication of International Human Rights: Non-Self-Executing Declarations and Human Rights Treaties', *Yale Journal of International Law* (1999), p. 129.

[42] See p. 120 above.

Interpretation of treaties by US courts

When a court in the United States is called upon to interpret a treaty it tends to have regard less to the text and more to the intention of the parties. The object and purpose is looked at closely (in this a US court follows a similar approach to that which it adopts for the interpretation of legislation, where the 'legislative history' may be examined in depth). Where there is more than one reasonable interpretation, the one which is more favourable to private rights will be adopted. The courts do not follow the formal scheme of Articles 31 and 32 of the Convention (to which the United States is not yet a party). The court will give weight to an interpretation given by the Government in *amicus curiae* briefs[43] and, when applicable, to any understanding expressed by the Senate when giving its advice and consent.

Implementation by federal states

The performance of treaties by federal states can give rise to special problems.[44] Although Article 29 provides that, unless there is a different intention, a treaty is binding upon each party in respect of its entire territory,[45] it may be difficult in some federal states for the federal government to ensure that a treaty is fully implemented in all the constituent units. This may be because under a federal constitution certain powers, such as taxation and criminal justice, are often shared with the constituent units. If the units have to legislate there could be delays or even obstruction. The federal constitution may therefore provide for such matters to be vested exclusively in the federal government when powers have to be exercised in performance of a treaty obligation; or, under a monist-type constitution, a treaty once ratified may override inconsistent state law. It may be partly for this reason that human rights treaties are submitted to the US Senate, so that once they have eventually been approved by it, and have entered into force for the United States, they clearly prevail over state law.

Although, in principle, executive agreements also override state law, in practice it is not always easy for the Unites States Government to convince state governments and legislatures that they are obliged to comply with

---

[43] In the United States, a written statement filed with the court by someone who is not a party to the case, but has an interest in the outcome and wishes to influence the court.
[44] See also pp. 48–52 above and pp. 169–72 below.   [45] See p. 163 below.

them. This happens most frequently with provisions for exemption from taxes. The problem is not caused by the nature of the instrument requiring action by the states, but by the jealous guarding by the states of what they see as their rights. It is due to such problems that in the UK–US Air Services Agreement ('Bermuda 2') (which is an executive agreement) the obligation to exempt airlines from dues and taxes was limited to 'best efforts'.[46] However, the award in the UK–US Heathrow User Charges Arbitration 1988 to 1994 invested this formula, at least in respect of aircraft user charges, with rather more substance than perhaps either government had originally intended.[47]

---

[46] 1079 UNTS 21 (No. 16509); UKTS (1977) 76. See Article 8(5).
[47] 102 ILR 215 at pp. 290–5. See Article 10 of the Agreement.

11

Territorial application

It comes with the territory.[1]

Not every treaty has to be given legal effect in the territory of a party. A treaty of alliance may need no implementing legislation. Yet, some treaties apply to the activities of a party or its nationals outside its territory. A party to the Antarctic Treaty 1959,[2] which applies to the area south of 60° south latitude, is required to apply the Treaty to its nationals in that area. But even the Antarctic Treaty and its sister treaties, as well as many other treaties, have to have legal force also in the territory of the parties. The 1991 Protocol on Environmental Protection to the Antarctic Treaty[3] applies to the Antarctic Treaty area, but requires controls to be exercised in the territory of a party over the organisation of Antarctic expeditions. In fact, all treaties will require some *action* within the territory of the parties, though not always legislation.

'Territory' – though not defined in the Convention – embraces all the land, internal waters and territorial sea, and the airspace above them, over which a party has sovereignty. Unless it appears otherwise from the treaty, references to territory do not include the continental shelf or exclusive economic zone or fishery zones, over which a state has only sovereign rights. Territory thus comprises the metropolitan territory of a state and any other territory under its sovereignty. Non-metropolitan territories, which were previously referred to as 'dependent territories', or 'dependencies', are today generally called 'overseas territories'.[4] A non-authoritative list of overseas territories is in Appendix R.

In most cases a treaty will be silent as to its territorial scope. This is not usually a problem unless a party has overseas territories and the content of

---

[1] Arthur Miller, *Death of a Salesman* (1949), 'Requiem'.
[2] 402 UNTS 71 (No. 5778); UKTS (1961) 97. Some of the parties to the Treaty have territory within the area, but their sovereignty is not necessarily recognised by the other parties, or by non-parties.　[3] ILM (1991), p. 1461; UKTS (1999) 6.　[4] See *Oppenheim*, pp. 275–82.

the treaty is capable of applying to them. Then one will need to know if it will apply, particularly if legislation will to be needed to implement the treaty. The Vienna Convention does not attempt to provide an answer. Article 29 merely lays down a residual rule: a treaty is binding upon each party in respect of its entire territory, unless a different intention appears from the treaty or is otherwise established. That intention can be established in various ways.

Because of their very nature, treaties like the Charter of the United Nations have to apply to all the territory of the parties in order to be effective. Other treaties will, by their terms, identify explicitly or by necessary implication the territory of the parties to which they relate.[5] It is sometimes implicit in the terms of a treaty that it applies only to metropolitan territory. The Treaty between France and the United Kingdom about the Channel Tunnel can, for inescapable geographical reasons, apply only to the metropolitan territory of France and the United Kingdom.[6] On the other hand, a treaty may apply only to an overseas territory or territories. The express scope of the 1947 Agreement establishing the South Pacific Commission (now the Pacific Community) is such that it applies only to the parties' territories in the South Pacific.[7] The area of application of the Convention on the Conservation of Antarctic Marine Living Resources 1980 (CCAMLR) is defined in a way which covers sub-Antarctic territories of the parties.[8] The France–United Kingdom Agreement concerning the delimitation of the maritime areas between Guadeloupe and Montserrat naturally cannot apply to metropolitan territory.[9]

Territorial extension clauses

Bilateral treaties

Some bilateral treaties have provisions for extending them to overseas territories. They are typically found in treaties on matters such as double taxation, extradition, narcotic drugs, mutual legal assistance and investment protection. The South Africa–United Kingdom Investment Promotion

---

[5] See Article 27 of the European Convention on Extradition 1957 (359 UNTS 273 (No. 5146); UKTS (1991) 97).   [6] UKTS (1992) 15.

[7] 97 UNTS 227 (No. 1352); UKTS (1952) 21. See Article II.

[8] 402 UNTS 71; ILM (1980), p. 837; UKTS (1982) 48; TIAS 10240.   [9] UKTS (1997) 28.

and Protection Agreement 1994 provides that, in addition to the United Kingdom (i.e., Great Britain and Northern Ireland):

> At the time of ratification of this Agreement, or at any time thereafter, the provisions of this Agreement may be *extended to such territories for whose international relations the Government of the United Kingdom are*[10] *responsible* as may be agreed between the Contracting Parties in an Exchange of Notes.[11]

The emphasised words are wide enough to include territory over which a party does not have sovereignty, such as a protected state, though the United Kingdom no longer has any.

Multilateral treaties

Before the era of decolonisation it was common to include in multilateral treaties a provision such as Article XII of the Genocide Convention 1948:

> Any Contracting Party may at any time, by notification addressed to the Secretary-General of the United Nations, *extend* the application of the present Convention to all or any of *the territories for the conduct of whose foreign relations that Contracting Party is responsible.*[12]

Alternatively, some treaties had an article under which a state could exclude all or some of its territory from their scope.[13] But, from the 1960s both types of 'colonial clause' fell out of favour, especially for treaties negotiated within the United Nations or its specialised agencies. Newly independent states and those of the Soviet bloc saw them as acknowledgments of colonialism. Other means were therefore established by which states could extend treaties to their overseas territories (see below), and, since the objection to territorial extension clauses was essentially political, other states acquiesced in this. Now that the Cold War has ended, and overseas territories which wished to have their independence have now achieved it, the clauses ought now to be more acceptable. The Convention on Temporary Admission [of goods] 1990, adopted under the auspices of the Customs Co-operation Council, provides that:

---

[10] The Government of the United Kingdom is referred to in the plural since, in strict constitutional theory, it consists of a group of ministers advising the monarch. But it is rather pedantic to insist on the point in treaties.   [11] UKTS (1998) 35. See UKTS (1999) 55.

[12] 78 UNTS 277 (No. 1021); UKTS (1970) 58. For other examples, see Blix and Emerson, pp. 156–62.

[13] See the Convention on the Recovery Abroad of Maintenance 1956, Article 12 (268 UNTS 3 (No. 3850); UKTS (1975) 85).

1. Any Contracting Party may, at the time of signing this Convention without reservation of ratification or of depositing its instrument of ratification or accession, *or at any time thereafter*, declare by notification given to the depositary that this Convention shall *extend to all or any of the territories for whose international relations it is responsible*. Such notification shall take effect three months after the date of the receipt thereof by the depositary. However, this Convention shall not apply to the territories named in the notification before this Convention has entered into force for the Contracting Party concerned.

2. Any Contracting Party which has made a notification under paragraph 1 of this Article extending this Convention to any territory for whose international relations it is responsible may notify the depositary, under the procedure of Article 31 [denunciation] of this Convention, *that the territory in question will no longer apply this Convention.*[14]

Although most clauses tend to be rather simpler, and the drafting of this one is somewhat ponderous, it nevertheless has the merit of stating precisely what has to be done and its legal effect. In doing so it reflects well-established practice, in particular that an extension can be made at any time after ratification, and can be revoked. Such clauses are now more likely to be found in treaties on matters which involve existing domestic legislation, such as customs matters and extradition, where it cannot be assumed that overseas territories will be able to implement a treaty, or even that they will want to have it applied to them – most inhabited overseas territories now have a considerable degree of internal self-government.

Article 35(8) of the International Labour Organisation Constitution is unusual in that it requires members to give reasons if they do not extend an ILO Convention to one or more of their overseas territories.

Declaration on signature or ratification

When a treaty does not by its nature clearly apply to all the territory of a party, yet is silent as to its territorial scope and lacks a territorial clause, there is a well-established practice by which a state decides to which, if any, of its overseas territories the treaty will be extended. The state makes its position clear, at the time of signature or ratification, either that the treaty

---

[14] UKTS (1999) 60.

applies only to the metropolitan territory, or that it extends also to an overseas territory or territories.[15]

In the case of legally binding instruments made by an organ of an international organisation, or pursuant to a treaty,[16] and which are not subject to a process analogous to ratification, the declaration should be made at the time of adoption of the instrument, but much will depend on the rules and practice of the organisation or under the treaty.

United Kingdom practice

When expressing consent to be bound by a multilateral treaty the United Kingdom declares in writing to the depositary to which, if any, of its overseas territories the treaty will extend. If it is to apply, at least for the moment, only to the metropolitan United Kingdom, the instrument of ratification will state that the treaty will apply to 'the United Kingdom of Great Britain and Northern Ireland'. The name requires a little excursion into history. It derives from the uniting in 1801 of the Kingdoms of Great Britain (England, Wales and Scotland) and of Ireland, the reference to 'Ireland' being changed in 1922 to 'Northern Ireland' on the independence of the rest of the island. Although the Channel Islands (Guernsey and Jersey) and the Isle of Man are part of the geographical area known as 'the British Isles', they are *not* part of the United Kingdom. The Channel Islands were part of the Duchy of Normandy when William, Duke of Normandy, conquered England in 1066, since when they have been under English (and later United Kingdom) sovereignty by virtue of succession to the Dukes of Normandy. The Isle of Man is an ancient kingdom which did not finally come under British sovereignty until 1765. Although they are overseas territories for the purposes of international law, for United Kingdom constitutional purposes the Channel Islands and the Isle of Man are internally self-governing 'Crown dependencies'. They are the responsibility of the Home Office (interior ministry), but the Foreign and Commonwealth Office (foreign ministry) is responsible for their international representation.[17] The three territories must therefore also be mentioned expressly if the treaty is to extend to them.

The Government of the United Kingdom consults fully with the govern-

---

[15] For the text of two recent UK declarations included in instruments of accession, see BYIL (1997), pp. 478–80.   [16] See p. 97 above.
[17] For a short statement of the constitutional relationship between the United Kingdom and its overseas territories, see BYIL (1997), pp. 548–9.

ments of each of the Crown dependencies and its other overseas territories on whether a treaty should be extended to them. This process, as well as the drafting and enactment of any necessary implementing legislation for them, can be lengthy. The United Kingdom will therefore ratify the treaty either for the United Kingdom of Great Britain and Northern Ireland or also for all or certain overseas territories. If necessary, the ratification may be extended later, by means of a diplomatic note to the depositary specifying further territories. The extension will be effective as from the date of receipt of the note. Any necessary implementing legislation for the overseas territories will either be made by the territories themselves or by the United Kingdom, in the latter case usually by an Order in Council extending to the territories concerned, with suitable modifications, the provisions of the Act by which the United Kingdom implemented the treaty.[18]

When extending a treaty to a territory, and subject to its terms, any reservations made on ratification will apply to the territory, unless otherwise specified in the notification to the depositary; additional or modified reservations and declarations may also be attached.[19]

The ILC's Special Rapporteur recently suggested that the practice by which a state 'excludes' the application of a multilateral treaty to its overseas territories amounts to a reservation.[20] The suggestion is surprising. The purpose is not to exclude certain provisions of the treaty, but is to establish a different intention for the purposes of Article 29, which recognise that a treaty will not be binding in respect of the entire territory of a state if a different intention appears from the treaty 'or is otherwise established'. The UN Secretary-General takes the view that the constant practice of certain states in respect of territorial application, and acquiescence by other states, has established a different intention for the purposes of Article 29.[21] Even when territorial extension clauses were not popular, there was general absence of objections to the practice. The suggestion was made with only a brief study of state practice even though, as a cursory study of UN Multilateral Treaties will show, there is abundant practice.[22] The

---

[18] See, for example, the Antarctic Act 1994 (Overseas Territories) Order 1995 (SI 1995 No. 490).

[19] As was the case when the United Kingdom extended the Convention on the Rights of the Child to certain of its territories (UN Multilateral Treaties, Chapter IV.11).

[20] See the Third Report (1998) of the ILC's Special Rapporteur on Reservations to Treaties, UN Doc. A/CN.4/491/Add.3, pp. 18–20, and ILC Report 1998, UN DOC. A/53/10, pp. 182–3, 195 and 206–9.   [21] UN Depositary Practice, paras. 284–5.

[22] See, for example, the statements made by Denmark, the Netherlands and the UK on ratifying the Espoo Convention 1991 (ILM (1991), p. 802), recorded in UN Multilateral Treaties, Chapter XXVII.4.

practice is based on the premise that, unless *in order to be effective* the treaty has to apply to all overseas territories,[23] it does not apply to them unless extended to them specifically. It is not therefore a question of excluding overseas territories, but of applying treaties to them only when appropriate. The suggestion does not take account of this particular interest of overseas territories. Today, as in the past, many territories are small (some very small), but most have internal self-government. Given their circumstances, they do not necessarily want, or need, every multilateral treaty to apply to them.[24] One should contrast this state practice with the reservations made by federations regarding implementation of treaties by their metropolitan political sub-divisions (see below).

Application of a treaty to an overseas territory alone

It is possible for a treaty to apply only to an overseas territory. This is more usual for bilateral treaties and can happen in two ways. The parent state can become a party to the treaty solely in respect of the territory.[25] Alternatively, the state can authorise the territory to enter into a treaty, or a category of treaties, in its own name. In the case of the United Kingdom, this is done by an 'Instrument of Entrustment' granted to the government of the territory.[26] Of course, the other party can decline to deal only with the territory and, whichever method is employed, the parent state will remain ultimately responsible for ensuring that the territory fully implements the treaty, and for any breach of it.

The parent state may also denounce a treaty in respect of its metropolitan territory only, leaving the extension to overseas territories in effect. This could happen if the treaty has been amended and the parent state wishes to become a party to the amended treaty, but its overseas territories either do not yet have the legislation in place to implement the amended treaty or do not want it to be extended to them.

Objections to territorial extensions

Sometimes a contracting state objects to an extension to an overseas territory, usually because of a dispute over sovereignty of the territory.

---

[23] See p. 163 above.   [24] See pp. 166–7 above on UK practice.
[25] See p. 53 and p. 163 above.   [26] See p. 52 above.

Argentina regularly objects to the extension by the United Kingdom of treaties to the Falkland Islands, South Georgia and the South Sandwich Islands and the British Antarctic Territory, to all of which Argentina asserts territorial claims. In such a case the depositary, usually the UN Secretary-General, will circulate the text of the objection and any response.[27]

Political sub-divisions of a metropolitan territory

Many states, such as federations, have constitutions that divide the metropolitan territory into political sub-divisions. Even when it is only the federation which can be party to treaties, their implementation may require action by the governments and legislatures of the sub-divisions, yet the federation remains responsible in international law for the due performance of all treaties.[28] Under Article 36(1)(b) of the Vienna Convention on Consular Relations 1963 a person accused of a crime must, if he is an alien, be informed of his right to communicate with a consulate of his state.[29] In the case of *Breard*, a Paraguayan national arrested for murder in the US state of Virginia was not told of this right, and was convicted and sentenced to death. On an application by Paraguay, in 1998 the International Court of Justice indicated, as a provisional measure, that the United States should take all measures at its disposal to ensure that Breard was not executed pending the Court's final decision.[30] The State Department therefore sought a stay of execution, but the US Supreme Court declined to intervene and the execution was carried out. The case was later settled.[31]

Some treaties expressly provide that their provisions 'extend to all parts of federal states without any limitation or exception'.[32] If a treaty ratified by the Australian Government requires legislation by the Australian states,

---

[27] *UN Depositary Practice*, para. 183.
[28] See pp. 49–50 above. See generally B. Opeskin, 'Federal States in the International Legal Order', NILR (1996), pp. 353–86; and B. Opeskin, 'International Law and Federal States', in Opeskin and Rothwell (eds.), *International Law and Australian Federalism* (1997), pp. 1–33.
[29] 596 UNTS 261 (No. 8638); UKTS (1973) 14; TIAS 8620.
[30] ILM (1998), pp. 810 (ICJ) and 824 (Supreme Court). See also AJIL (1998), pp. 666–712; and AJIL (1999), pp. 170–4.
[31] A similar application to the ICJ was made by Germany against the United States on 2 March 1999 (ILM (1999), p. 308).
[32] Article 50 of the International Covenant on Civil and Political Rights 1966 (999 UNTS 171 (No. 14688); ILM (1967), p. 368; UKTS (1977) 6).

and they refuse, the Australian Government would be internationally responsible.[33] There are certain methods by which these problems can be reduced: territorial clauses, federal clauses and federal reservations.

Territorial clauses

Article 93(1) of the UN Convention on Contracts for the International Sale of Goods 1980 provides that:

> If a Contracting State has two or more territorial units in which, according to its constitution, different systems of law are applicable in relation to matters dealt with in this Convention, it may, at the time of signature, ratification, acceptance, approval or accession, declare that this Convention is to extend to all its territorial units or only to one or more of them, and may amend its declaration by submitting another declaration at any time.[34]

When acceding to that Convention Canada declared that it would extend it to nine of its then provinces and territories, and the following year added the other three.[35] Where it is possible to agree on the inclusion of the clause, the above example represents the modern formula.[36] The clause is also a territorial application clause, though expressed in a way which applies also to political sub-divisions of the metropolitan territory.[37] Use of the clause is mostly confined to treaties on commercial law, private law or private international law, such as those concluded within the UN Commission on International Trade Law (UNCITRAL) and the Institute for the Unification of Private Law (UNIDROIT).[38] It reflects the fact that in a federation such matters are often regulated by the sub-divisions. Although the clause has been criticised less than the clause which is mentioned next, it has been viewed as detrimental to those treaties which depend for their effectiveness on their uniform application.

---

[33] *R. v. Burgess, ex parte Henry* (1936) 55 CLR 608; *Commonwealth v. Tasmania* (Tasman Dam Case) (1983) 158 CLR 1.   [34] 1489 UNTS 3 (No. 25567); ILM (1980), p. 671.

[35] See *UN Multilateral Treaties*, Chapter X.10, for the Canadian declarations. Since 1 April 1999 there has been a thirteenth province, Nunavut, created from part of the Northwest Territories.

[36] For earlier examples, see Opeskin, 'Federal States' (note 28 above).

[37] Australia has not extended to Western Australia the Convention on the Settlement of Investment Disputes between States and Nationals of other States 1965 (575 UNTS 159 (No. 8359); ILM (1965), p. 524; UKTS (1967) 25). See *UN Multilateral Treaties*, Chapter X.10.

[38] See Article 40 of the Hague Convention on the Civil Aspects of International Child Abduction 1980 (1343 UNTS 89 (No. 22514); UKTS (1986) 66).

Federal clauses

Article 34 of the UNESCO Convention for the Protection of World Cultural and Natural Heritage 1972 provides:

> The following provisions shall apply to those State Parties to this Convention which have a federal or non-unitary constitutional system:
> (a) with regard to the provisions of this Convention, the implementation of which comes under the legislative jurisdiction of the federal or central legislative power, the obligations of the federal or central government shall be the same as for those States Parties which are not federal States;
> (b) with regard to the provisions of this Convention, the implementation of which comes under the legislative jurisdiction of individual constituent states, countries, provinces or cantons that are not obliged by the constitutional system of the federation to take legislative measures, the federal government shall inform the competent authorities of such states, countries, provinces or cantons of the said provision, with its recommendation for their adoption.[39]

These provisions limit the obligation of a federal state party when certain matters are outside its constitutional power. Although such clauses are not popular with unitary states, they do make it that much easier for federations to become parties. This is especially so if the constitution is of the 'dualist' type, in which treaties are not the supreme law.[40] But they have the disadvantage that they create uncertainty as to the extent of the obligations undertaken by the federation, and result in unequal treatment between parties.[41]

Federal reservations

It is only in the last forty years that federal states have sought to use reservations to deal with their problems in participating in treaties. In 1988 Canada made the following reservation to the Espoo Convention on Transboundary Environmental Impact Assessment 1991:

> In as much as under the Canadian constitutional system legislative jurisdiction in respect of environmental assessment is divided between the provinces

---

[39] 1037 UNTS 151(No. 15511); ILM (1972), p. 1358; UKTS (1985) 2; TIAS 82250.
[40] See p. 150 above.
[41] For other examples, see Opeskin, 'Federal States', at pp. 370–4 (note 28 above).

and the Federal Government, the Government of Canada in ratifying this Convention makes a reservation if respect of proposed activities . . . that fall outside of federal legislative jurisdiction exercised in respect of environmental assessment.[42]

Where federal legislative power extends to the implementation of treaties (as in Australia, India and the United States[43]), a federal reservation expressed in such terms would be improper.

An alternative course is for a federal state to make a statement on ratification explaining *how* the treaty will be implemented within the federal structure. In 1984 Australia replaced its federal reservation to the International Covenant on Civil and Political Rights with a 'Declaration':

> Australia has a federal constitutional system in which legislative, executive and judicial powers are shared or distributed between the Commonwealth and the constituent States. The implementation of the treaty throughout Australia will be effected by the Commonwealth, State and Territory authorities having regard to their respective constitutional powers and arrangements concerning their exercise.[44]

Since the statement does not purport to exclude or modify the treaty in its application to the state, it is not objectionable, and the Australian Government remains internationally responsible for implementation.

---

[42] *UN Multilateral Treaties*, Chapter XXVII.4

[43] See also the US 'understanding' on ratifying the Racial Discrimination Convention, the ICCPR and the Torture Convention (*UN Multilateral Treaties*, Chapter IV. 2, 4 and 9, respectively).

[44] *UN Multilateral Treaties*, Chapter IV.4.

12

Successive treaties

A particularly obscure aspect of the law of treaties.

This grim warning by Sinclair[1] may encourage the reader to turn to the next chapter; and it has to be said that, although the relationship between successive treaties which deal with the same subject matter is difficult and sometimes important, it does not cause daily consternation in the legal departments of foreign ministries. But the topic is gaining in importance. Because of the greater number and complexity of multilateral treaties, particularly on the environment, questions increasingly arise as to the relationship between successive treaties.

There should be no problem when the parties to both treaties are identical. If the earlier treaty is not considered as terminated or suspended (Article 59), the earlier treaty applies only to the extent that its terms are compatible with those of the later treaty (Article 30(3)).

The problems occur when the parties are not identical. When drafting final clauses of a new multilateral treaty it is therefore important to consider whether anything needs to be said about the relationship between it and existing treaties (and sometimes future treaties) which deal with the same subject matter. As will become apparent, these questions are related to the rules on amendment of treaties, and this chapter should therefore be read with Chapter 15.

Bilateral treaties

Problems should not arise with successive bilateral treaties between the same parties, even if there is an inconsistency. With careful interpretation

---

[1] Nevertheless, Sinclair has a typically incisive survey of the topic, at pp. 93–8. See also *Oppenheim*, paras. 590–2; and the short, but thought-provoking, passage in Reuter, paras. 200–3. For a more recent examination of the question, and a useful bibliography, see J. Mus, 'Conflicts between Treaties in International Law', NILR (1998), pp. 208–32.

it should be possible to apply both treaties. Where this is not possible the earlier treaty will be considered as terminated or suspended in accordance with Article 59. If the obligations in a treaty between State A and State B are incompatible with the obligations which State A has to State C under an earlier treaty, the obligations under that earlier treaty will be unaffected. State A will have to seek to amend or terminate one or other of the treaties, or risk being in breach of one of them.

Multilateral treaties

Similar problems could arise if one of the treaties is bilateral and the other is multilateral, but the real difficulties come when both treaties are multilateral and the parties to each are not the same. It is this problem which Article 30 seeks primarily to address, though not entirely satisfactorily given the developments in multilateral treaty-making since 1969. The rules in the article are residuary (though not expressed as such).[2] Prevention being better than cure, today a multilateral treaty may contain a clause (called a 'conflict clause' by the International Law Commission)[3] which seeks to regulate the relationship between it and another treaty or treaties. The clause may concern a prior treaty, a future treaty or any (unspecified) treaty past or future. Although the interpretation and application of such clauses is not always simple, especially when the treaties are not adopted within the same international organisation or are for different purposes,[4] they can be useful. A number, mostly from the 1950s and 1960s, are to be found in Blix and Emerson.[5] Here are some more examples.

Express provisions

The treaty prevails over all other treaties, past and future

The prime example of this kind of clause is Article 103 of the UN Charter:

> In the event of a conflict between the obligations of the Members of the United Nations under the present Charter and their obligations under any other international agreement, their obligations under the present Charter shall prevail.

---

[2] Sinclair, p. 97.   [3] ILC YB (1966), vol. II, p. 214.
[4] See Article XIV of the Convention on International Trade in Endangered Species (CITES) 1973 (999 UNTS 243; ILM (1973), p. 1085; UKTS (1976) 101).   [5] See pp. 210–22.

The interpretation and application of this fundamental provision of the Charter is before the International Court of Justice in the *Lockerbie* cases, in which one of the issues raised is whether the obligations of Members under Resolution 748 (1992), and other mandatory resolutions adopted by the Security Council under Chapter VII of the Charter, prevail over obligations under the 1971 Montreal Convention.[6] Although the Court has not determined the issue definitively, in 1992 the Court decided that, in accordance with Article 103, the obligation to carry out decisions of the Security Council prevailed over obligations under any other treaty, including the Montreal Convention, and that *prima facie* the Charter obligation extended to Resolution 748.[7] The application of Article 103 is comprehensive ('any other international agreement'). It applies to new Members in respect of their existing, not just future, obligations.[8] It applies also to Members as regards their agreements with non-Members, though the extent to which it affects the rights of non-Members is no longer a question of much practical importance now that almost all states are Members.[9]

Since there is no international organisation comparable to the United Nations in terms of its universality, purposes and powers, for so long as the United Nations exists it would not be possible to adopt a clause as extensive in effect as Article 103. The importance of Article 103 is recognised by Article 30(1) of the Convention, which provides that the residuary rules in Article 30 are subject to Article 103.

The parties shall not enter into later inconsistent treaties

Article 8 of the North Atlantic Treaty 1949 provides:

> Each Party declares that none of the international engagements now in force between it and any other of the Parties or any third State is in conflict with the provisions of this Treaty, and undertakes not to enter into any international engagement in conflict with this Treaty.[10]

The purpose of the clause is to maintain the integrity of the regime created by and under the Treaty. It therefore prohibits all kinds of inconsistent later

---

[6] 974 UNTS 177 (No. 14118); UKTS (1974) 10.
[7] *ICJ Reports* (1992), p. 3, at para. 39. See also the dissenting opinion of Judge Schwebel in the 1998 judgment (*ICJ Reports* (1998), p. 9 at p. 71).
[8] Goodrich and Hambro, *Charter of the United Nations* (3rd edn, 1969), p. 614.
[9] See p. 6 above.   [10] 34 UNTS 243; UKTS (1949) 56.

treaties, whether bilateral or multilateral, with another party or a third party, but does not prohibit treaties which merely supplement the Treaty. The Treaty is more in the nature of a framework instrument,[11] under which the parties established the North Atlantic Treaty Organisation and concluded many multilateral and bilateral treaties, and MOUs, on defence matters.

Article 28 of the European Convention on Extradition 1957 provides, in part:

(1) This Convention shall, in respect of those countries to which it applies, supersede the provisions of any bilateral treaties, conventions or agreements[12] governing extradition between any two Contracting Parties.

(2) The Contracting Parties may conclude between themselves bilateral or multilateral agreements *only* in order to supplement the provisions of this Convention or to facilitate the application of the principles contained herein.[13]

An existing treaty shall not be affected

Somewhat unnecessarily in view of Article 103 of the UN Charter, Article 7 of the North Atlantic Treaty provides that the Treaty shall not be interpreted as affecting rights and obligations under the Charter. This article would therefore appear to have been included more for (understandable) political reasons. But in many cases there might be a conflict between obligations under a new treaty and an existing treaty. Given the wide scope of the Treaty of Rome 1957 which established the EEC (now the European Community), a general provision was made in Article 234 (now Article 307) for those treaties which had been concluded previously by Member States with third states and remained in force, but which were not compatible with the Treaty:

The rights and obligations resulting from agreements concluded before 1 January 1958 or, for acceding States, before the date of their accession, between one or more Member States on the one hand, and one or more third countries on the other, shall not be affected by the provisions of this Treaty.[14]

[11] See p. 97 above.
[12] The use of the three terms may be because the existing bilateral treaties were variously designated; paragraph 2 refers only to agreements.
[13] 359 UNTS 273 (No. 5146); UKTS (1991) 97.
[14] Text as amended and renumbered by Article 6 I. (78) of the Treaty of Amsterdam 1997 (ILM (1998), p. 56 at p. 139). See MacLeod, Hendry and Hyett, *The External Relations of the European Communities* (1996), pp. 229–31.

Although this states the obvious, it is an assurance both to the Member States and third states. The provision applies to all treaties, whatever the subject, which might affect the operation of the Treaty. An EC Member State is not prevented from performing its obligations to non-EC parties under such treaties, but it must not assert rights under them if the effect would be incompatible with its obligations to other Member States under the Treaty. The article goes on to require Member States to take 'all appropriate steps to eliminate' any incompatibility of treaty obligations.

Sometimes it is relatively easy to identify the treaties concerned, or at least some of them. The 1991 Protocol on Environmental Protection to the Antarctic Treaty[15] seeks to protect the Antarctic environment in a comprehensive manner, but because there already existed treaties, mostly within the Antarctic Treaty System, which dealt with discrete aspects of the Antarctic environment, it was felt necessary to make it clear that they would not be affected. Article 4(2) provides that '[n]othing in this Protocol shall derogate from the other instruments in force within the Antarctic Treaty system'. The Final Act of the meeting at which the Protocol was adopted noted that 'nothing in the Protocol shall derogate from the rights and obligations of parties under the Convention on the Conservation of Antarctic Marine Living Resources [CCAMLR], the Convention for the Conservation of Antarctic Seals and the International Convention for the Regulation of Whaling', and that the environmental impact assessment procedure provided for in the Protocol was not intended to apply to activities under CCAMLR or the Seals Convention. The parties to the Protocol and to the three other treaties are not all the same. Despite these provisions, there are no doubt other general environmental treaties to which parties to the Protocol are, or will be, parties and which may be incompatible with the Protocol. Their relationship with the Protocol will have to be determined by applying the residual rules in Article 30 (see below).

For parties to it the treaty prevails over earlier treaties

Such a clause is employed when a later treaty is concluded between states which do not include all the parties to the earlier treaty. And, even when they are identical, it is useful to deal expressly with the matter; otherwise

---

[15] ILM (1991), p. 1460; UKTS (1999) 6.

Article 59 (implied termination or suspension) would apply.[16] By 1961 there were nine multilateral treaties concerning narcotic drugs. In that year the Single Convention on Narcotic Drugs sought to replace all of them, and included this clause:

> The provisions of this Convention, upon its coming into force, shall, *as between the Parties hereto*, terminate and replace the provisions of the [nine] treaties.[17]

The fact that the later treaty cannot deprive a state which is not a party to it of its rights under the earlier treaty is reflected in Article 30(4)(b) of the Vienna Convention:

> When the parties to the later treaty do not include all the parties to the earlier one . . . as between a State party to both treaties and a State party to only one of the treaties, the treaty to which both States are parties governs their mutual rights and obligations.

The Single Convention was amended by a Protocol in 1972[18] and supplemented by the Convention on Psychotropic Substances 1971[19] and the Convention against Illicit Traffic in Narcotic Drugs and Psychotropic Substances 1988.[20] Article 25 of the 1988 Convention provides that for the parties to it the Convention does not derogate from any rights enjoyed or obligations undertaken by them under the 1961 Convention, as amended by the Protocol, or under the 1971 Convention. This results in a number of possible permutations. Leaving aside the Protocol, let us assume that State A is a party to only the 1961 Convention; State B is a party to the 1961 and 1971 Conventions; and State C is a party to the 1971 and 1988 Conventions. Assuming that none of them denounce any of the Conventions, *as between themselves* States A and B will be bound by the 1961 Convention and States B and C by the 1971 Convention, but States A and C will be bound, as between themselves, by none of the three Conventions. This can lead to most undesirable results when there is a need for uniformity of obligations. The situation is close to that produced by a series of amending treaties which have differing sets of parties, and is

---

[16] See pp. 235–6 below.   [17] 520 UNTS 151 (No. 7515); UKTS (1965) 34.
[18] 976 UNTS 3 (No. 14151); ILM (1972), p. 804; UKTS (1979) 23. For the consolidated text, see 976 UNTS 105 (No. 14152). See also *UN Multilateral Treaties*, Chapter VI.18.
[19] 1019 UNTS 175 (No. 14956); ILM (1971), p. 261; UKTS (1993) 51.
[20] ILM (1989), p. 493; UKTS (1992) 26; UN Reg. No. 27627.

unavoidable unless there is built into the *initial* treaty a suitable amendment mechanism.[21]

Compatible supplementary treaties are permitted

Article 73 of the Vienna Convention on Consular Relations 1963 provides:

(1) The provisions of the present Convention shall not affect other international agreements in force as between States Parties to them.

(2) Nothing in the present Convention shall preclude States from concluding international agreements *confirming or supplementing or extending or amplifying* the provisions thereof.[22]

Paragraph 1 preserves consular agreements concluded before the parties to them become bound by the Convention. This was necessary since numerous consular agreements existed before the Convention was adopted, and it was not considered necessary or desirable to replace them by the uniform provisions of the Convention; states should be free to enter into agreements which do not simply repeat the Convention. Paragraph 2 therefore enables parties to conclude supplementary consular agreements which do not derogate from the obligations of the Convention, but prohibits, though by implication, the conclusion of treaties which, by providing for more limited rights or obligations, would so derogate. These provisions are necessary because of the need for certain uniform minimum standards.[23]

Comprehensive provisions

Given the importance of its subject matter, its universal application and the many existing treaties, bilateral and multilateral, on the same topic, the drafters of the UN Convention on the Law of the Sea 1982 (UNCLOS) took care to ensure that its relationship to other treaties was clearly and precisely spelled out.[24] Inspired by the Vienna Convention,[25] Article 311 has three key provisions:

---

[21] See pp. 215–19 below. For how the amendment of the UN Convention on the Law of the Sea 1982 was handled, see p. 222–3 below.

[22] 596 UNTS 261 (No. 8638); UKTS (1973) 14; TIAS 6820.

[23] See further L. Lee, *The Vienna Convention on Consular Relations* (2nd edn, 1991), pp. 623–9.

[24] ILM (1982), p. 1261; UN Reg. No. 31363; UKTS (1999) 81.

[25] See M. Nordquist (ed.), *The United Nations Law of the Sea Convention: A Commentary*, (1982) vol. V, pp. 229–43.

(1) This Convention shall prevail, as between the States Parties, over the Geneva Conventions on the Law of the Sea of 29 April 1958.

(2) This Convention shall not alter the rights and obligations of States Parties which arise from other agreements compatible with this Convention and which do not affect the enjoyment by other States Parties of their rights or the performance of their obligations under this Convention.

(3) Two or more States Parties may conclude agreements modifying or suspending the operation of provisions of this Convention, applicable solely to the relations between them, provided that such agreements do not relate to a provision derogation from which is incompatible with the effective execution of the object and purpose of this Convention, provided further that such agreements shall not affect the application of the basic principles embodied herein, and that the provisions of such agreements do not affect the enjoyment by other States Parties of their rights or the performance of their obligations under this Convention.

Successive constituent instruments of an international organisation

There are several international organisations which regularly replace their constituent instruments. The Unions created by the Paris and Berne Conventions have been revised on several occasions by treaties (called 'Acts'). Each Act is a revised version of the original Convention, which continues to exist, as does the Union as constituted by the original Convention. When a state accedes to the most recent Act, but is silent as to whether its accession is valid for previous Acts, the practice of the Unions is to regard the acceding state as having tacitly accepted the original Convention and all subsequent Acts. The practice has long been accepted, and, although not a formal rule, is preserved by the saving provision in Article 5 of the Vienna Convention.[26] In any event, the problem which the practice seeks to deal with might also be said to be resolved by application of the rules in Article 40 on the amendment of multilateral treaties.[27]

In contrast, relatively modern treaties can cause enormous difficulties when insufficient thought has been given when the original treaty was being drafted to providing for future changes. This was so with the International Convention on the Establishment of an International Fund for Compensation for Oil Pollution Damage 1971, which had to be

---

[26] See p. 9 above.　　[27] Sinclair, p. 95, and p. 220 below.

amended by a Protocol in 1992. Some of the difficulties experienced then are reflected in Article 28, which is not a model of lucid drafting, including as it does the following:

(6) A State which is a party to this Protocol but is not a party to the 1971 Fund Convention shall be bound by the provisions of the 1971 Fund Convention as amended by this Protocol in relation to other parties hereto, but shall not be bound by the provisions of the 1971 Fund Convention in relation to parties thereto.

(7) Any instrument of ratification, acceptance, approval or accession deposited after the entry into force of an amendment to the 1971 Fund Convention as amended by this Protocol shall be deemed to apply to the Convention *so amended, as modified by such amendment.*[28]

The 1994 Implementation Agreement,[29] which effectively amends the UN Convention on the Law of the Sea 1982 (UNCLOS)[30] and which was adopted before UNCLOS had entered into force, has a much simpler and more elegant formula:

(1) After adoption of this Agreement, any instrument of ratification or formal confirmation of or accession to the Convention shall also represent consent to be bound by this Agreement.

(2) No State or entity may establish its consent to be bound by this Agreement unless it has previously established or establishes at the same time its consent to be bound by the Convention.

The residuary rules of Article 30

The relationship with other treaties relating to the same subject matter, including future treaties, should always be borne in mind when drafting a new treaty, and it is preferable to include a clause whenever possible. But if this is not done, and though some other articles, such as Articles 5, 40 and 59, may be relevant, one must rely on the residual rules in Article 30, which codified customary law.[31] Article 30 is worth setting out in full:

(1) Subject to Article 103 of the Charter of the United Nations, the rights and obligations of States parties to successive treaties relating to the

---

[28] UKTS (1996) 87.   [29] ILM (1994), p. 1313; UN Reg. No. 31364.
[30] ILM (1982), p. 1261; UN Reg. No. 31363 UKTS (1999) 81.
[31] Mus, 'Conflicts between Treaties', p. 213, note 25 (note 1 above). See also E. Vierdag, 'The Time of the Conclusion of a Multilateral Treaty: Article 30', BYIL (1988), at pp. 90–111.

same subject-matter shall be determined in accordance with the following paragraphs.

(2) When a treaty specifies that it is subject to, or that it is not to be considered as incompatible with, an earlier or later treaty, the provisions of that other treaty prevail.

(3) When all the parties to the earlier treaty are parties also to the later treaty but the earlier treaty is not terminated or suspended in operation under Article 59, the earlier treaty applies only to the extent that its provisions are compatible with those of the later treaty.

(4) When the parties to the later treaty do not include all the parties to the earlier one:

(a) as between States parties to both treaties the same rule applies as in paragraph 3;

(b) as between a State party to both treaties and a State party to only one of the treaties, the treaty to which both States are parties governs their mutual rights and obligations.

(5) Paragraph 4 is without prejudice to Article 41, or to any question of the termination or suspension of the operation of a treaty under Article 60 or to any question of responsibility which may arise for a State from the conclusion or application of a treaty the provisions of which are incompatible with the obligations towards another State under another treaty.

Particular points to note include the following.

(1) The article applies only if both treaties are in force and in operation, not when one of the treaties has been terminated or its operation suspended by implication under Article 59[32] (paragraph 3).

(2) The rules in paragraph 4 determine the mutual rights and obligations of the particular parties in each situation *only as between themselves*; they do not relieve any party of international responsibility for concluding or applying a treaty the provisions of which are incompatible with its obligations towards *another* state under *another* treaty. If the rights of a party to another treaty are infringed, all the normal consequences of breach of treaty will follow. The injured party may terminate or suspend the operation of the treaty under Article 60 or invoke the international responsibility of the infringing party.[33] On the other hand, nothing in paragraph 4 prevents some of the parties to a multilateral treaty concluding an agreement to modify it among themselves provided the conditions in Article 41[34] are met (paragraph 5).

---

[32] See pp. 235–6 below.   [33] See p. 300 below.   [34] See p. 222 below.

(3) In determining which treaty is the earlier and which the later, the relevant date is the date of adoption, not entry into force (cf. the reference in Article 59(1) to the conclusion of a later treaty).[35]

(4) The obligations under Article 30 apply to a state only as from the date it becomes a party to the treaty.

(5) The meaning of the expression 'relating to the same subject-matter' is not clear but should probably be construed strictly, so that the article would not apply when a general treaty impinges indirectly on the content of a particular provision of an earlier treaty.[36]

---

[35] See also p. 74 above.
[36] The problems in applying Article 30 are well illustrated by Vierdag, 'The Time of the Conclusion (note 31 above), especially pp. 92–111, and by Mus, 'Conflicts between Treaties' (note 1 above).

13

Interpretation

> The interpretation of documents is to some extent an art, not an exact science.

This understatement by the International Law Commission[1] will come as no surprise to any lawyer, domestic or international. It is especially true for treaties, which are the product of negotiations leading to compromises to reconcile, often wide, differences. For multilateral treaties, the greater the number of negotiating states, the greater is the need for imaginative and subtle drafting to satisfy competing interests. The process inevitably produces much wording which is unclear or ambiguous. Despite the care lavished on drafting, and accumulated experience, there is no treaty which cannot raise some question of interpretation. Most disputes submitted to international adjudication involve some problem of treaty interpretation. Just as the interpretation of legislation is the constant concern of any government lawyer, treaty interpretation forms a significant part of the day-to-day work of a foreign ministry legal adviser.

A simple, but troublesome, example of an interpretation problem is to be found in the Comprehensive Nuclear-Test-Ban Treaty 1996 (CTBT).[2] Article XIV(2) envisages a conference being convened if the CTBT has not entered into force 'three years after the date of *the anniversary of* its opening for signature'. Some signatories argued that the emphasised words referred to the date twelve months after the opening for signature, and therefore the required period was one-plus-three years; others asserted that the words were tautological and must be a mistake, and that therefore the period was only three years. We will come back to this as we examine Articles 31 and 32 of the Vienna Convention (Article 33 is considered at the end of the chapter).

---

[1] ILC Commentary, p. 218, para. (4). See also M. Bos, 'Theory and Practice of Treaty Interpretation', NILR (1990), pp. 31–8 and 135–70; Sinclair, pp. 114–58; and Yasseen, *Hague Recueil* 151 (1976), III, pp. 1–114.   [2] ILM (1996), p. 1443.

In its Commentary on the draft of the two articles[3] the International
Law Commission surveyed the differing views of jurists on whether there
were any rules of international law governing the interpretation of treaties
and, if there were, what they were. The International Law Commission
rejected the view that in interpreting a treaty one must give greater weight
to one particular factor, such as the text ('textual' or 'literal' approach), or
the supposed intentions of the parties, or the object and purpose of the
treaty ('effective' or 'teleological' approach). Reliance on one to the detriment of the others was contrary to the jurisprudence of the International
Court of Justice.[4] Placing undue emphasis on the text, without regard to
what the parties intended; or on what the parties are believed to have
intended, regardless of the text; or on the perceived object and purpose in
order to make the treaty more 'effective', irrespective of the intentions of
the parties, is unlikely to produce a satisfactory result.[5] McNair was also
sceptical about the various doctrines of interpretation espoused by his
fellow jurists, and his views on interpretation and those of O'Connell still
contain much good sense.[6] This is O'Connell:

> The problem of treaty interpretation . . . is one of ascertaining the logic inher-
> ent in the treaty, and *pretending* that this is what the parties desired. In so far as
> this logic can be discovered by reference to the terms of the treaty itself, it is
> impermissible to depart from those terms. In so far as it cannot, it is permis-
> sible. These two propositions underlie the so-called 'canons [i.e., principles]
> of treaty interpretation', which are no more than logical devices for ascertain-
> ing the real area of treaty operation. Writers have divided into those who
> believe it is possible to formulate definite rules for interpretation and those
> who believe that this is a delusion. In several decided cases the courts have pref-
> aced their remarks by laying down rules for interpretation and have immedi-
> ately departed from them because it was found that the text required it.[7]

The International Law Commission took a middle course which avoided a
doctrinaire approach. In what are two of the most elegantly drafted articles, it formulated what it regarded as the comparatively few general principles governing treaty interpretation. The International Court of Justice

---

[3] Previously numbered as draft Articles 27 and 28; see of the ILC Commentary, 218–23; and
Sinclair, pp. 115–19.
[4] See on this H. Thirlway, 'The Law and Procedure of the International Court of Justice
1960–1989', BYIL (1991), pp. 16–17 and generally pp. 16–75.
[5] On the 'effective' approach, see O'Connell, pp. 253–5.
[6] McNair, pp. 364–473; and O'Connell, pp. 251–65.   [7] O'Connell, p. 253.

has held that the principles embodied in Articles 31 and 32 reflect customary international law.[8] Although the two articles are concerned with the interpretation of treaties, they contain much which is of practical value to the treaty-maker or to anyone involved in implementing a treaty.

Let us now examine them. Article 31 (General rule of interpretation) provides:

(1) A treaty shall be interpreted in good faith in accordance with the ordinary meaning to be given to the terms of the treaty in their context and in the light of its object and purpose.

(2) The context for the purpose of the interpretation of a treaty shall comprise, in addition to the text, including its preamble and annexes:

(a) any agreement relating to the treaty which was made between all the parties in connexion with the conclusion of the treaty;

(b) any instrument which was made by one or more parties in connection with the conclusion of the treaty and accepted by the other parties as an instrument related to the treaty.

(3) There shall be taken into account, together with the context:

(a) any subsequent agreement between the parties regarding the interpretation of the treaty or the application of its provisions;

(b) any subsequent practice in the application of the treaty which establishes the agreement of the parties regarding its interpretation;

(c) any relevant rules of international law applicable in the relations between the parties.

(4) A special meaning shall be given to a term if it is established that the parties so intended.

Article 32 (Supplementary means of interpretation) provides:

Recourse may be had to supplementary means of interpretation, including the preparatory work of the treaty and the circumstances of its conclusion, in order to confirm the meaning resulting from the application of article 31, or to determine the meaning when the interpretation according to article 31:

(a) leaves the meaning ambiguous or obscure; or

(b) leads to a result which is manifestly absurd or unreasonable.

Article 31 is entitled 'General *rule* of interpretation'. The singular noun emphasises that the article contains only one rule, that set out in para-

---

[8] *Libya* v. *Chad, ICJ Reports* (1994), p. 4, at para. 41. See also p. 11, n. 22 above.

graph 1. One must therefore consider each of the three main elements in treaty interpretation – the text, its context and the object and purpose of the treaty. By 'context' is meant material related to the conclusion of the treaty; and the reference to 'context' in the opening phrase of paragraphs 2 and 3 is designed to link those paragraphs with paragraph 1. Although at first sight paragraphs 1, 2 and 3 might appear to create a hierarchy of legal norms, this is not so: the three paragraphs represent a logical progression, nothing more. One naturally begins with the text, followed by the context, and then other matters, in particular subsequent material.

Supplementary elements such as the preparatory work of the treaty (*travaux préparatoires*) are not included in Article 31, since that article is limited to the primary criteria for interpreting a treaty. Interpretation involves an elucidation of the meaning of the text, not a fresh investigation as to the supposed intentions of the parties. Furthermore, the preparatory work of a treaty is by its nature less authentic than the other elements, being often incomplete and misleading. Nevertheless, Article 32 provides that, in certain circumstances, recourse may be had to supplementary elements to 'confirm' the meaning resulting from the application of Article 31.

Let us now examine the two articles in detail.

Article 31

Paragraph 1 (basic rule)

The first principle – interpretation *in good faith* – flows directly from the principle of *pacta sunt servanda* enshrined in Article 26. Interpretation is part of the performance of the treaty, and therefore the process of examining the relevant materials and assessing them must be done in good faith. Even if the words of the treaty are clear, if applying them would lead to a result which would be manifestly absurd or unreasonable (to adopt the phrase in Article 32(b)), the parties must seek another interpretation. When in 1971 the Government of the People's Republic of China replaced the Government of the Republic of China as the representative of China in the United Nations, there was never any question of the specific reference in Article 23(1) of the Charter to 'the Republic of China' having to be amended. A similar approach was adopted in 1991 when, with the gaining of independence by various Soviet republics, the 'Union of Soviet Socialist

Republics' (also specifically mentioned in Article 23(1)) was renamed the Russian Federation.[9] Any other approach would have led to a manifestly unreasonable result. The fact that in both cases the result was *politically desirable*, even necessary, should not disguise the fact that the approach taken by the Members of the United Nations followed correctly a basic principle of the law of treaties, even if their representatives may not have been conscious of it at the time.

It is important to give a term its *ordinary meaning* since it is reasonable to assume, at least until the contrary is established, that the ordinary meaning is most likely to reflect what the parties intended. As McNair put it, the task of interpretation is:

> the duty of giving effect to the expressed intention of the parties, that is, their intention *as expressed in the words used by them in the light of the surrounding circumstances.*[10]

The determination of the ordinary meaning cannot be done in the abstract, only in the *context* of the treaty and in the light of its *object and purpose*. The latter concept, as we have seen in relation to reservations to treaties,[11] can be elusive. Fortunately, the role it plays in interpreting treaties is less than the search for the ordinary meaning of the words in their context, and, in practice, having regard to the object and purpose is more for the purpose of confirming an interpretation. If an interpretation is incompatible with the object and purpose, it may well be wrong. Thus, although paragraph 1 contains both the textual (or literal) and the effectiveness (or teleological) approaches, it gives precedence to the textual.[12]

Paragraph 2 (context)

This paragraph specifies what comprises the context. We all think we know what an 'aircraft' is, but when a treaty uses that term, does it include all aircraft, civil and military, and what about microlights, hovercraft or balloons? Any term can be fully understood only by considering the context in which it is employed. Does the term 'public official', as used in the Torture Convention 1984,[13] include a head of state?[14] One must look at the

---

[9] See *UN Multilateral Treaties*, Chapter I, notes to entries for China and Russia.
[10] McNair, p. 365; emphasis in the original.   [11] At p. 110 above.   [12] O'Connell, p. 255.
[13] 465 UNTS 85 (No. 24841); ILM (1984), p. 1027; UKTS (1991) 107. See Article 1(1).
[14] See *R. v. Bow St. Magistrates' Court, ex parte Pinochet* (No. 3) [1999] 2 All ER 97; [1998] 2 WLR 827; ILM (1999), p. 581

treaty as a whole, including the preamble and any annexes. For example, Article I of the CTBT[15] prohibits 'any nuclear weapon test explosion *or any other nuclear explosion*'. This apparently all-inclusive formula might lead one to conclude that the CTBT also bans the use of nuclear weapons. This thought is dispelled however by, among other things, the unambiguous title of the treaty and the aspirations for nuclear disarmament expressed in the preamble.

In the example, also taken from the CTBT, given at the beginning of this chapter, paragraph 2 of Article XIV must be seen in the context of the preceding and succeeding paragraphs:

(1) This Treaty shall enter into force . . . in no case earlier than two years *after its opening for signature.*

(2) If this Treaty has not entered into force three years after the date of *the anniversary of its opening for signature*, the Depositary shall convene a Conference . . .

(3) . . . this process shall be *repeated* at *subsequent anniversaries of the opening for signature . . .*

The absence of any reference in paragraph 1 to the *anniversary* of the opening for signature might suggest that inclusion of that term in paragraph 2 was deliberate and therefore effect must be given to it (this is an example of interpretation *a contrario* – see below). However, the phrase in paragraph 3, 'subsequent anniversaries', would make perfect sense even if paragraph 2 had no reference at all to anniversary, the phrase in paragraph 3 being clearly a reference to the anniversaries of the opening for signature which will occur *after* the Conference has been convened. If it had really been intended that the Conference would be convened only after four years, why did it not say so explicitly? Nevertheless, the meaning of paragraph 2 is not clear.

Paragraph 2 of Article 31 is very important for treaty-making. It provides that, in addition to the text, including the preamble and annexes, the context comprises the following.

(1) *Any agreement relating to the treaty which was made between all the parties in connexion with the conclusion of the treaty.* The agreement does not have to be part of the treaty, or be itself a treaty; but it must be a clear expression of the intention of the parties. A good example is to be found in the Final Act of the conference which adopted the Convention on the Conservation of Antarctic

---

[15] ILM (1996), p. 1443.

Marine Living Resources 1980.[16] Attached to the Final Act is a formal statement regarding islands within the area of application of the Convention. The purpose of the statement is to permit the islands to be taken out of the normal application of the Convention. The statement was read out by the chairman of the conference, and is known as the 'Chairman's Statement'. The Final Act records that no objection was made to the statement (it having been carefully negotiated during the conference). When the ENMOD Convention 1977 was negotiated, a series of 'Understandings' were agreed regarding the interpretation or application of the Convention.[17]

(2) *Any instrument made by one or more parties in connexion with the conclusion of the treaty and accepted by the other parties as an instrument related to the treaty.* The Dayton Agreement 1995 included many such instruments.[18] The need for acceptance distinguishes this case from unilateral interpretative declarations made by a state when signing or ratifying.[19] It is common practice for treaties of the European Communities or the European Union to have various instruments associated with them which have been produced by one or more Member States, the texts having been agreed during the negotiation of the treaty.[20] They are also made in connection with bilateral treaties. The US–USSR 'START' Treaty 1991 was accompanied by many assurances and explanations in correspondence between the parties and in joint and national declarations.[21]

Such agreements and instruments are usually made on the conclusion of the treaty, or soon afterwards. They should not be seen only as an aid to interpretation, but as a valuable tool of the treaty-maker. There is often no reason why, as a matter of law, the content of the agreement or instrument could not have been put into the treaty. One reason for employing such devices is therefore political. One or more parties may insist on a particular point, but others, while accepting that it has to be made, may find it difficult politically to have it in the body of the treaty, but could agree to it being made in a separate document which is expressed to be made by certain negotiating states or by the chairman of the conference. The need

---

[16] 402 UNTS 71; ILM (1980), p. 840; UKTS (1982) 48; TIAS 10240.

[17] 1108 UNTS 151; ILM (1977), p. 16; TIAS 9614. See *Status of Multilateral Arms and Disarmament Agreements* (4th edn, UN, 1992), vol. 1.

[18] General Framework Agreement for Peace in Bosnia and Herzegovina 1995 (ILM (1996), p. 75).

[19] See p. 101 above.

[20] See the Declarations attached to the Europol Convention 1995 ((UK) European Communities Series No. 13 (1995)).

[21] Treaty on the Reduction and Limitation of Strategic Offensive Arms, 31 July 1991 (for references, see ILM (1992), p. 246).

for such devices has increased with the greater use of consensus in the adoption of treaties. But sometimes they are used simply for convenience. An agreed minute or exchange of letters regarding the detailed application of terms used in a treaty may be neater than overloading the treaty with lengthy definitions.[22]

The explanatory reports approved by the government experts involved in drafting conventions of the Council of Europe, and adopted at the same time as the conventions and published with them, provide an invaluable guide to their interpretation, and should be seen as part of the 'context' in which the conventions were concluded.[23] As such, they must be distinguished from 'official' commentaries which are later produced and, depending on the circumstances, may come to be regarded as authoritative. The *Handbook on Procedures and Criteria for Determining Refugee Status*, published by the UN High Commissioner for Refugees (UNHCR), is generally regarded as an authoritative commentary on the Refugees Convention, and much relied upon by domestic courts and tribunals. Commentaries published by other organisations, such as those by the ICRC on the Geneva Conventions of 1949, can be highly persuasive.[24]

Paragraph 3 (subsequent agreements and practice)

Sub-paragraph (a) provides that, together with the context, there shall be taken into account any 'subsequent agreement' between the parties regarding the interpretation of the treaty or the application of its provisions. Given that the parties can agree later to modify the treaty, they can also subsequently agree on an authoritative interpretation of its terms, and this can amount, in effect, to an amendment. There is no need for a further treaty,[25] since the paragraph refers deliberately to an 'agreement', not a treaty. The agreement can take various forms,[26] including a decision adopted by a meeting of the parties, provided the purpose is clear.[27] In

---

[22] See the exchange of interpretative letters accompanying the UK–US Air Services Agreement 1977 (1079 UNTS 21 (No. 16509); UKTS (1977) 76).

[23] Sinclair, pp. 129–30. For an example, see ILM (1994), p. 943.

[24] J. Pictet (ed.), *The Geneva Conventions 1949, Commentary* (4 vols. 1952–60). But see also S. Rosenne, *Practice and Methods of International Law* (1984), pp. 50–1.

[25] But see the 1996 Czech–UK Exchange of Notes regarding the interpretation of the Consular Convention 1975 'for the purposes of paragraph 3, Article 31 of the Vienna Convention on the Law of Treaties' (UKTS (1997) 5).

[26] See the example given in R. Gardiner, 'Treaties and Treaty Materials: Role, Relevance and Accessibility', ICLQ (1997), p. 643 at pp. 648–9.   [27] See p. 214 below, note 9.

1993 the states parties to the Treaty on Conventional Forces in Europe (CFE) 1990 concluded a 'Document of the States Parties' which included an 'understanding' as to how certain provisions of the CFE Treaty would be interpreted and applied, and which are in effect amendments to the Treaty.[28] The Treaty of Rome establishing the European Economic Community, as amended, refers to the 'ECU' (European currency unit). When in 1995 the Member States decided to replace the ECU with the 'Euro', instead of amending the Treaty, which would have involved a lengthy ratification procedure and parliamentary scrutiny, the heads of state and government of the Member States recorded in the 'Conclusions' of their meeting in Madrid that:

> The specific name Euro will be used instead of the generic term 'ECU' used in the Treaty to refer to the European currency unit. The Governments of the fifteen Member States have achieved the common agreement that this decision is the agreed and definitive interpretation of the relevant Treaty provisions.[29]

Under the (rather accident-prone) Ramsar Wetlands Convention 1971, as amended in 1982 to include an amendment clause, the acceptance of 'two thirds of the Contracting Parties' is needed for an amendment to come into force. However, it was not clear if the phrase referred to the contracting parties at the time the amendment was adopted, or at any given moment. Therefore at a conference of the parties in 1990 a resolution was adopted that it should be interpreted to refer to the time of adoption of the amendment.[30]

Article IX(1) of the Antarctic Treaty of 1959[31] provides for certain of the parties (known as 'Consultative Parties') to *recommend* to their governments *measures* in furtherance of the principles and objectives of the Treaty. Article IX(4) provides that the measures 'shall become effective' when they have been 'approved' by all of the Consultative Parties. Between 1961 and 1995 over 200 measures were recommended. But, until 1995 there had been a misunderstanding, and a consequent

---

[28] UKTS (1994) 21. See also UKTS (1993) 44 at pp. 97–108.

[29] Conclusions of the Madrid European Council 1995 (*Bulletin of the EU*, 12-1995, p. 10). For another example, see D. Howarth, 'The Compromise on Denmark', *Common Market Law Review* (1994), p. 765.

[30] 996 UNTS 245 (No. 14583); ILM (1972), p. 963; UKTS (1976) 34 (for the consolidated text see UKTS (1996) 13). See M. Bowman, 'The Multilateral Treaty Amendment Process – A Case Study', ICLQ (1995), p. 540 at p. 552.   [31] 402 UNTS 71 (No. 5778); UKTS (1961) 97.

misapplication, of Article IX(1). From the very beginning the Consultative Parties had adopted instruments termed 'Recommendations', of which the majority were no more than exhortatory, ephemeral or procedural. Nevertheless, they were treated as measures subject to the full approval procedure of Article IX(4). This resulted in most Recommendations not becoming 'effective' until many years after their adoption. This unsatisfactory situation was corrected in 1995, when the Consultative Parties agreed that in future they would recommend under Article IX(1) only 'Measures' properly so-called (i.e., intended to be legally binding): in future other matters would be the subject of 'decisions' or 'resolutions', and would be effective on their adoption at the annual Antarctic Treaty Consultative Meeting (ATCM). This agreement was embodied in Decision 1 of the 1995 ATCM.[32] The new arrangements were explained by the proposers to be an agreement for the purposes of Article 31(3)(a).

This last example is more in the nature of corrective action; the earlier examples amounted more to modifications or amendments to the treaties. Foreign ministry legal advisers are familiar with the question of how to modify a treaty without an amending treaty? If the treaty does not have a built-in amendment procedure, the process of amendment can be lengthy and uncertain, and especially if it is a multilateral treaty subject to ratification.[33] Much will depend on the circumstances but, particularly where the modification is essentially procedural, it may be possible to embody it in an agreement as to the application of the treaty. This technique is particularly useful if there is a need to fill a lacuna, to update a term or postpone the operation of a provision. The time for the first election of judges of the International Tribunal for the Law of the Sea was specified in the UN Convention on the Law of the Sea 1982, but since the date turned out to be premature, the election was postponed by a consensus decision of a meeting of the parties, the decision being recorded in the record of the meeting.[34] But the use of such means should be done cautiously and sparingly. The distinction between application and amendment is not always easy to draw. Problems could be caused if such means are used for a purpose which is safer done by a formal amendment to the treaty.

---

[32] ILM (1996), p. 1188.   [33] See pp. 212–13 below.   [34] SPLOS/3 of 28 February 1995.

Subsequent practice

Sub-paragraph (b) provides that, together with the context, there shall be taken into account any subsequent practice in the application of the treaty which establishes the agreement of the parties regarding its interpretation. This is a most important element in the interpretation of any treaty, and reference to practice is well established in the jurisprudence of international tribunals. However precise a text appears to be, the way in which it is actually applied by the parties is usually a good indication of what they understand it to mean, provided the practice is consistent, and is common to, or accepted by, all the parties.[35] In its Award in the US–UK Heathrow User Charges Arbitration, the Tribunal found that a 1983 UK–US MOU was of value as 'consensual subsequent practice' by the parties.[36]

Article 37(1) of the Vienna Convention on Diplomatic Relations 1961 refers to the 'members of the family of a diplomatic agent forming part of his household'.[37] The phrase is not defined, and even in 1961 there was doubt as to which persons formed part of a diplomat's household: did it include a 30-year-old perpetual student son or daughter? Given the changes in society since then (and to which even diplomats are not entirely immune) might other persons be considered as members of the family? Does it now include unmarried partners? And, if so, what about partners of the same sex? In interpreting the phrase great weight must necessarily be given to the practice of states. Most states have had to face such problems, either as a sending or receiving state, or both.[38]

On the face of it, Article 5 of the Chicago Convention, which governs charter air services, does not require a charter airline to obtain permission to land en route, provided it does not pick up or set down passengers or cargo. However, the practice of the parties over many years has been to require charter airlines to seek permission to land in all cases, and the article is now so interpreted.[39]

Perhaps the best, and most oft-quoted, example of interpretation by subsequent practice is the way in which Members of the United Nations have interpreted and applied Article 27(3) of the Charter. This provides

---

[35] See the US–France Air Services Arbitration 1963 (54 ILR 303).
[36] 102 ILR 261, p. 353, paras. 6.7–6.8.   [37] 500 UNTS 95 (No. 7310); UKTS (1965) 19.
[38] See further E. Denza, *Diplomatic Law* (2nd edn, 1998), pp. 321–8.
[39] 15 UNTS 295 (No. 102); UKTS (1953) 8. See B. Cheng, 'Air Law', *Max Planck Encyclopaedia of Public International Law* (1989), vol. 11, pp. 8–9.

that decisions of the Security Council on non-procedural matters shall be made by the 'affirmative' vote of nine of its members 'including the *concurring votes* of the permanent members'. Although at first sight this would appear to mean that all five permanent members must cast an affirmative vote, the practice of the Council from as early as 1946 was to interpret 'concurring' as meaning 'not objecting'. Therefore, if a permanent member wishes to block a decision it is not enough for it to abstain, or even be absent; it must cast a negative vote (known colloquially as 'the veto'). Thus during the early stages of the Korean war in 1950 the Soviet representative was, by staying away from meetings of the Council, not able to prevent the Council taking action.[40] The practice was upheld by the International Court of Justice in the *Namibia* case,[41] even though, ironically, it would seem from the *travaux* of the Charter that it was not what had been originally intended by the permanent members.[42]

It is not necessary to show that each party has engaged in a practice, only that all have accepted it, albeit tacitly. But, if a clear difference of opinion between the parties exists, the practice may not be relied upon as a supplementary means of interpretation.

Relevant rules of international law

Sub-paragraph (c) provides that, together with the context, there shall be taken into account any relevant rules of international law applicable in the relations between the parties. For example, in certain cases reaching an interpretation which is consistent with the intentions (or perceived intentions) of the parties may require regard to be had to not only international law at the time the treaty was concluded (the 'inter-temporal rule'), but also to contemporary law.[43] In interpreting today a reference in a treaty of 1961 to the continental shelf, it would probably be necessary to consider not only the Geneva Convention on the Continental Shelf 1958, but also the United Nations Convention on the Law of the Sea 1982.[44]

---

[40] Bailey and Daws, *The Procedure of the United Nations Security Council* (3rd edn, 1998), at p. 257.   [41] *ICJ Reports* (1971), p. 16, at paras. 20–2.

[42] See Goodrich and Hambro, *Charter of the United Nations* (1969), at p. 229.

[43] See H. Thirlway, 'The Law and Procedure of the International Court of Justice 1960–1989', BYIL (1991), pp. 57–60; R. Higgins, 'Some Observations on the Inter-Temporal Rule in International Law', in J. Makarczyk (ed.), *Theory of International Law at the Threshold of the 21st Century*, (1996), pp. 173–81; R. Higgins, 'Time and the Law: International Perspectives on an Old Problem', ICLQ (1997), pp. 501–20.

[44] See Sinclair, pp. 138–40; and *Oppenheim*, p. 1281.

Special meaning

A special meaning must be given to a term if it is established that the parties so intended (paragraph 4). Notwithstanding the apparent meaning of a term in its context, it is open to a party to invoke any special meaning, but the burden of proof of the special meaning will rest on that party.[45] In the passage in the 'Chairman's Statement'[46] which refers to islands 'over which the existence of state sovereignty is recognised by all Contracting Parties', the word 'existence' was carefully chosen to indicate that the passage covered also islands where sovereignty is disputed, such as South Georgia and the South Sandwich Islands.[47]

International organisations

When interpreting the constituent instrument of an international organisation, one may need to take into account also the relevant rules of the organisation (see Article 5).[48] In most cases this will not be necessary; Articles 31, 32 and 33 are adequate for the purposes of the constituent instruments of the United Nations and other (classic) international organisations, being copied word for word in Articles 31, 32 and 33 of the Vienna Convention on the Law of Treaties between States and International Organizations or between International Organizations 1986.[49] However, the situation may well be different in the case of regional international organisations, especially when the organisation has powers over the social or economic structure of its member states. The Court of Justice of the European Communities, on the basis of its understanding of the object and purpose of the Treaty of Rome, has certainly adopted an effective or teleological approach in interpreting and applying the Treaty.[50] Similarly, the European Court of Human Rights has seen the object and purpose of the European Convention on Human Rights as requiring it to broaden the ordinary meaning of the terms of that Convention.[51]

---

[45] See Sinclair, pp. 126–7; Thirlway, 'Law and Procedure', pp. 27–9 (note 43 above).
[46] See p. 190 above.
[47] A British territory to which Argentina asserts a claim, as well as disputing this interpretation.
[48] See p. 9 above.   [49] ILM (1986), p. 543.
[50] See p. 99 above; and J. Bengoetxea, *The Legal Reasoning of the European Court of Justice* (1993).
[51] Sinclair, pp. 131–5; J. Merrills, *The Development of International Law by the European Court of Human Rights* (2nd edn, 1993), pp. 76–81.

Article 32

Supplementary means of interpretation

The preparatory work (*travaux préparatoires*, or *travaux* for short) of a treaty is not a primary means of interpretation, but is an important supplementary means. International tribunals have for long had recourse to the *travaux* for the purpose of *confirming* the meaning arrived at by the application of the general rule as set out in Article 31.[52] In order to try to come to an understanding of what those who negotiated the treaty had intended, they may have recourse to supplementary means of interpretation, in particular the *travaux* and the circumstances of the conclusion of the treaty,[53] and this is recognised by Article 32. In the *Lockerbie* case the United Kingdom maintains that it was not intended that the UN Charter should give the International Court of Justice a power of judicial review over Security Council decisions, and that this is supported by the *travaux* of the Charter.[54] The rest of Article 32 provides that recourse may also be had to the same supplementary means of interpretation when reliance on the primary means produces an interpretation which (a) leaves the meaning 'ambiguous or obscure' or (b) leads to a result which is 'manifestly absurd or unreasonable'. In this case the purpose is not to confirm, but to determine, the meaning.

It has been suggested that, even when the ordinary meaning appears to be clear, if it is evident from the *travaux* that the ordinary meaning does not represent the intention of the parties, the primary duty in Article 31(1) to interpret a treaty in good faith requires a court to 'correct' the ordinary meaning.[55] This is no doubt how things work in practice; for example, the parties to a dispute will always refer the tribunal to the *travaux*, and the tribunal will inevitably consider them along with all the other material put before it. The suggestion is therefore a useful addition to the endless debate on the principles of interpretation.[56]

The International Law Commission did not seek to define what is

---

[52] See, for example, McNair, p. 413, note 3, and p. 422, note 4. [53] O'Connell, p. 263.

[54] See *Libya* v. *United Kingdom* (*Preliminary Objections*), *ICJ Reports* (1998), p. 9, paras. 4.17–4.18; ILM (1998), p. 587; and the submissions of the Lord Advocate (CR 97/17, para. 5.46), and the dissenting opinion of President Schwebel (all available on the ICJ website, http://www.icj-cij.org).

[55] S. Schwebel, 'May Preparatory Work be Used to Correct Rather than Confirm the "Clear" Meaning of a Treaty Provision?', in Makarczyk (see note 43 above), at pp. 541–7.

[56] See p. 234–5 below about withdrawal from the UN; and p. 201 below regarding implied terms.

included in the *travaux*, but it is generally understood to include written material, such as successive drafts of the treaty, conference records, explanatory statements by an expert consultant at a codification conference, uncontested interpretative statements by the chairman of a drafting committee and ILC Commentaries: in O'Connell's words, 'the amorphous mass of documentation which goes under the name *travaux prépara-toires*.[57] The value of the material will depend on several factors, the most important being authenticity, completeness and availability. The summary record of a conference prepared by an independent and skilled secretariat, such as that of the United Nations, will carry more weight than an unagreed record produced by a host state or a participating state. However, even the records of a conference served by an independent and expert secretariat will generally not tell the whole story. It is not the practice of the EC/EU to keep written records of the negotiation of their constituent instruments. The most important parts of a negotiation, and of drafting, often take place informally with no agreed record being kept. The negotiations at the Third United Nations Law of the Sea Conference which met, intermittently, from December 1973 until the adoption of the UN Convention on the Law of the Sea in 1982 are a good example. The reason why a particular compromise formula was adopted, and what it was intended to mean, may be difficult to establish.[58] This will be especially so if the form of words was deliberately chosen to overcome a near irreconcilable difference of substance. The final drafting of new Article 3*bis* (prohibition on use of force against civil aircraft) of the Chicago Convention was done by hectic, highly visible and informal (*literally* back-of-the-envelope) negotiations during a mayoral reception held at the end of a three-week conference. As a result it shows all the signs of the last-minute compromises which are needed to reach consensus. Here is the key paragraph:

> The Contracting States recognise that every State must refrain from resorting to the use of weapons against civil aircraft in flight and that, in case of interception, the lives of persons on board and the safety of aircraft must not be endangered. This provision shall not be interpreted as modifying in any way the rights and obligations of States set forth in the Charter of the United Nations.[59]

---

[57] O'Connell, p. 263.
[58] See, for example, E. Denza, *Diplomatic Law* (2nd edn, 1998), pp. 127–9, regarding whether service of legal process can be made on a diplomatic mission.   [59] ILM (1984), p. 705.

In fact the main purpose of the second sentence is to indicate, in an oblique manner, that force may be used against a civil aircraft if it is done in the proper exercise of the inherent right of self-defence as reflected in Article 51 of the UN Charter. Here is an example of even more tortuous drafting:

> The activities of armed forces during an armed conflict, as those terms are understood under international humanitarian law, which are governed by that law, are not governed by this Convention, and the activities undertaken by the military forces of a state in the exercise of their official duties, inasmuch as they are governed by other rules of international law, are not governed by this Convention.

This opaque text in Article 19(2) of the Terrorist Bombing Convention 1997[60] reflects a sharp difference of opinion on the extent to which acts by members of armed forces should be subject to that Convention. The formula does not paper over the cracks very well, reading as it does rather like an explanation by Sir Humphrey Appleby.[61]

Travaux must therefore always be approached with care. Their investigation is time-consuming, and their usefulness often marginal and very seldom decisive.

In the case of a multilateral treaty which is open to states which did not take part in its negotiation, the *travaux* can probably be invoked in a dispute to which they are parties, at least if they have been published or were otherwise available before those states became parties. Any other rule would be extremely inconvenient given the number of new states which have emerged since the Second World War, and the quantity of multilateral treaties made during that period to which new states have subsequently become parties.[62]

An examination of the *travaux* did not resolve the question of interpretation posed by Article XIV(2) of the CTBT mentioned at the start of this chapter, the official records of the Conference on Disarmament not throwing any light on the matter. But it was agreed eventually that the inclusion of the phrase 'the anniversary of' before the reference to the opening for signature was simply a mistake; the words should have been omitted. This would have brought the provision into line with the rest of the article. Because of an oversight, this was not done.

---

[60] ILM (1998), p. 251.
[61] A fictional senior civil servant in the venerable BBC TV series, 'Yes Minister', about ministers and their officials. [62] *ILC Commentary*, p. 223, at para. 20; Sinclair, pp. 142–4.

Other supplementary means of interpretation

Article 32 gives only examples of the principal supplementary means of interpretation. One may also look at other treaties on the same subject matter adopted either before or after the one in question which use the same or similar terms. It is also legitimate to assume that the parties to a treaty did not intend that the treaty would be incompatible with customary international law.[63]

There are several other means of interpretation, though it is not always easy to distinguish them from familiar legal techniques, often based on commonsense or grammatical rules. Many derive from principles of domestic law, especially Roman law. *Oppenheim* lists the most important, as well as giving a wealth of examples of their application and other sources.[64] It will therefore be enough to mention briefly some of the more useful, remembering always that none of them should be followed slavishly, being no more than *possible* aids to interpretation. Most relate to discovering the ordinary meaning.

(1) *A contrario.* The International Covenant on Civil and Political Rights has no denunciation clause, but its Optional Protocol does. One might therefore argue that it was not intended that a party would have the right to withdraw from the Covenant. This is interpretation *a contrario*. Article IV of the Genocide Convention 1948[65] provides that heads of state can be prosecuted for genocide in the country where the crime was committed or before an international tribunal. Article 27 of the Statute of the International Criminal Court 1998 provides expressly that a head of state is subject to the jurisdiction of the Court.[66] Since neither the Hostages Convention 1979[67] nor the Torture Convention 1984[68] have such provisions, it could be argued that it could not have been intended that those treaties should apply to heads of state. But in these examples this argument alone would not be likely to be decisive.[69]

(2) Acquiescence. If a party has made plain its understanding of the meaning of a provision, and it later applies it in that sense without objection, other parties may not be able to insist on a different interpretation. Article 31(3)(b) might also apply.

[63] O'Connell, p. 261.
[64] At paras. 631 and 633. See also McNair, pp. 393–410; and O'Connell. pp. 253–8.
[65] 78 UNTS 277 (No. 1021); UKTS (1970) 58.   [66] ILM (1998), p. 1002.
[67] ILM (1979), p. 1460; UKTS (1983) 81.
[68] 465 UNTS 85 (No. 24841); ILM (1984), p. 1027; UKTS (1991) 107.   [69] See note 14 above.

(3) *Contra proferentem.* If it is possible to interpret a provision in two ways, the meaning which is less favourable to the party which proposed it, or for whose benefit it was included, should be adopted. The principle is applied more often to standard contracts; it is rarer for a treaty (and especially a multilateral treaty) to contain a provision for which only one party is clearly responsible.

(4) *Ejusdem generis.* When general words follow special words, the general words are limited by the *genus* (class) indicated by the special words. Taking as an example Article I of the CTBT, in the phrase 'any nuclear weapon test explosion *or any other nuclear explosion*' the scope of the italicised words is limited by the preceding words, thereby excluding from the CTBT the actual use of nuclear weapons.[70]

(5) *Expressio unius est exclusio alterius.* Express mention of a circumstance or condition excludes others.

(6) *Lex posterior derogat legi priori.* When two rules apply to the same matter, the later in time prevails.

(7) *Lex specialis derogat legi generali.* A specific rule prevails over a general rule.

All these supplementary means of interpretation need to be used with special care. They are no more than aids to interpretation, and might well produce wrong results if followed blindly.

Implied terms

Although it is not for an international tribunal to revise a treaty by reading into it provisions which it does not contain by necessary implication, it is sometimes necessary to imply a term, and this has been the approach of the International Court of Justice[71] and the European Court of Human Rights.[72] Here is an example, though it did not go to court. At the end of the Falklands conflict there was not enough accommodation in the territory for the some 10,000 prisoners of war (POWs) captured in the final stage, the tents intended for them having been lost at sea when the ship carrying them was sunk. Following consultations with the International Committee of the Red Cross, it was decided that the POWs could be kept on merchant ships and warships in Falklands waters until they could be repatriated. Although Article 22 of the Third Geneva Convention[73]

[70] See also p. 189 above.
[71] The Court will not 'revise' a treaty on the pretext that it has found an omission: see S. Rosenne, *The Law and Practice of the International Court of Justice* (3rd edn, 1997), pp. 172–3. And see H. Thirlway, 'The Law and Procedure of the International Court of Justice', BYIL (1992), pp. 42–3. [72] See McNair, Chapter 26; and Merrills (note 51 above), pp. 84–90.
[73] 75 UNTS 3 (No. 972); UKTS (1958) 39.

prohibits holding on ships POWs who are captured on land, given that the primary object and purpose of that Convention is the welfare of POWs, one could properly imply a term to the effect that when, for reasons beyond its control, a party to a conflict was unable to comply with Article 22, it may hold POWs on ships if that is preferable to leaving them on land without sufficient protection from the elements. Good interpretation is often no more than the application of commonsense.

Thus one has to look at the treaty *as a whole*, plus all other relevant materials, assessing their respective weight and value. This is, in fact, what international lawyers and international courts and tribunals do when confronted by a difficult question of interpretation.

Interpretation of treaties in more than one language

Most treaties, bilateral as well as multilateral, are bilingual or plurilingual. The exceptions are mostly very old treaties or treaties between states which have the same mother tongue or official language. Even then a (non-authentic) text in another language may be produced for certain purposes. It is also quite common for two states with different languages to negotiate a treaty in a third language (which these days is often English), and for the only authentic text to be in that language. Ironically, these include even cultural agreements.[74] The language of one of the negotiating states may not be widely spoken, and to produce a draft and hold the negotiations in that language may be unduly burdensome. Bilateral negotiations are therefore frequently held in the language of only one of the states, or in a third language common to both. This may be reflected in the languages in which a treaty is concluded and in the choice of a language text to prevail in the case of a difference. The Holy See–Israel Fundamental Agreement 1993 is in English and Hebrew, the English prevailing in case of divergence.[75] Similarly, the Israel–Jordan Treaty of Peace 1994 has equally authentic texts in Arabic, English and Hebrew, but again the English text prevails.[76] Air services negotiations are frequently conducted only in English, even if that is not the first language of either delegation, because it is the *lingua franca* of the world of aviation, not just of pilots, and some-

---

[74] Japanese–Pakistan Cultural Agreement 1957 (325 UNTS 22 (No. 4692)); Finland– Netherlands Cultural Agreement 1988 (1540 UNTS 257 (No. 26718))).
[75] ILM (1994), p. 154.   [76] ILM (1995), p. 43.

times an English text will prevail,[77] or the text will be in English only.[78] The *Estonia* Agreement 1995 between Estonia, Finland and Sweden was concluded only in English.[79]

Multilateral negotiations are most likely to be held in more than one language, though there are notable exceptions. All but the most formal sessions of the fifty-four member Organisation for Security and Co-operation in Europe (OSCE) are held only in English, and the OSCE Convention on Conciliation and Arbitration of 1992[80] was negotiated on the basis of an English draft. Although the proceedings of the General Assembly of the United Nations and its committees are conducted in the six official languages, informal meetings (of which there are many) are often held, and drafting done, in English.

The reasons for using one language in multilateral negotiations are various, and will depend on the circumstances. Today the cost of translation and simultaneous interpretation is an important factor. Even when these can be afforded, it is sometimes easier, and therefore quicker, to hold negotiations in one language. On the other hand, technical reasons or national policies may require that negotiations are conducted in other languages, or at least that the resulting treaty is in several. This can lead to treaties, particularly regional treaties, being produced in numerous languages. A recent, and extreme, example is the 1997 Protocol further amending the Eurocontrol Convention of 1980. This is in no less than nineteen European languages, all of which are equally authentic, even though it was negotiated on the basis of only English and French texts. Fortunately, it provides that in the case of divergence between the languages the French text prevails.

Treaties which have been concluded in more than one language can cause problems of interpretation if there are material differences between the language texts. These can be to some extent avoided if before the texts are authenticated there is a thorough combing through of the texts (as part of the process known, appropriately, as the *toilette finale*) to clean them up and straighten out inconsistencies. This has the added advantage that one usually discovers at least minor errors, and sometimes major substantive problems. The process is most easily done with bilateral treaties. In practice the translations of multilateral treaties are done by translators

---

[77] Netherlands–Saudi Arabia Air Transport Agreement 1985 (1480 UNTS 143 (No. 25244)).
[78] Bahrain–UK Air Services Agreement 1998 (UKTS (1999) 4).
[79] Finnish Treaty Series 1995, No. 49; UKTS (1999) 74 (including Additional Protocol regarding accession).   [80] ILM (1993), p. 557.

who, though highly professional, will not have been at the negotiations, and may not necessarily appreciate all the nuances of the final text. When the negotiations have been primarily on the basis of a draft in one language, it is essential that delegations into whose mother tongue the text is to be translated check the translations carefully.

But, if despite all these efforts there is a discrepancy, the problem can be overcome if the treaty provides that in the case of inconsistency the text in one language shall prevail. The 1955 Protocol to amend the Warsaw Convention 1929 has three authentic texts, English, French and Spanish, but provides that 'in the case of any inconsistency, the text in the French language, *in which language the Convention was drawn up*, shall prevail'.[81] Because the Warsaw Convention was concluded so long ago, has been amended several times, and is specifically designed to be given effect in domestic law, consistency in its interpretation is of prime importance. This can only be achieved by maintaining the French text of the Convention, and the amendments to it, as the authoritative (i.e., only true) text, even if this causes difficulties for judges in non-French-speaking countries.[82] The British legislation implementing amendments to the Convention therefore schedules the French and English texts.[83]

When a treaty has no antecedents it may still be prudent to provide for one language to be authoritative. The Kuwait Regional Marine Environment Convention 1978 was concluded in Arabic, English and Persian, but provides that in the case of divergence the English text prevails.[84] The Convention was almost certainly drafted in English. In other cases the treaty may be concluded in one authentic, and 'neutral', language (such as English or French) and provide for 'official' (but non-authentic) translations into the languages of the parties to be made later.

Article 33[85]

These treaty practices are reflected in Article 33. Unless the treaty provides, or the parties otherwise agree, that in the case of divergence between

---

[81]   UKTS (1967) 62.

[82]   R. Gardiner, 'Treaty Interpretation in the English Courts since Fothergill v. Monarch Airlines', ICLQ (1995), pp. 620–8.

[83]   Carriage by Air Act 1961 and Carriage by Air (Supplementary Provisions) Act 1962.

[84]   ILM (1978), p. 511.

[85]   See the useful article by C. Kuner, 'The Interpretation of Multilateral Treaties: Comparison of Texts versus the Presumption of Similar Meaning', ICLQ (1991), pp. 953–64, though it over-

the texts a particular text shall prevail, the text is equally 'authoritative' in each language in which it has been authenticated (paragraph 1). Some treaties are silent on the matter of authenticity; and in the absence of any provision to the contrary, each text is equally authentic. But the usual practice is to state expressly in the treaty if the various language texts are equally authentic (see, for example, Article 85 of the Vienna Convention itself).

If a version of a treaty is produced in a language other than those in which the treaty has been authenticated (e.g., an 'official' text or one made for the purposes of registration with the United Nations), it is not an authentic text, unless the treaty so provides or the parties so agree (paragraph 2).

If there are two or more authentic texts the normal rules of interpretation in Articles 31 and 32 still remain the starting point. Although the existence of discrepancies between different language texts can complicate interpretation, when the meaning is ambiguous or obscure in one text it may be clearer in another and there may be no need to attempt to reconcile them. Paragraph 3 reflects this approach: the terms of a treaty are presumed to have the same meaning in each authentic text.

Paragraph 4 lays down the residual rule that, provided there is no provision for a particular text to prevail, when a comparison of the authentic texts discloses a difference of meaning, which the application of Articles 31 and 32 does not remove, one must adopt the meaning which best reconciles the texts. In *France v. Commission* the European Court of Justice interpreted Article 228 of the Treaty of Rome by considering the authentic English, Danish, Dutch, French and German texts.[86]

Of course, in most cases each party will use only one authentic language version of the treaty (as it is entitled to do under paragraph 3), and if there are discrepancies they may never come to light. But this does not mean that the most restrictive interpretation, or the lowest common denominator must be adopted.[87] Nor does it mean that each language text will carry the same weight. If the treaty was negotiated and drafted in only one of the authentic languages, it is natural to place more reliance on that text, particularly if it is unambiguous. This approach is not incompatible with paragraph 4, and the jurisprudence of the International Court of Justice

states somewhat the scale of the problem. As regards the *Young Loan* arbitration (59 ILR 495), see Sinclair, pp. 121–2, 143–4, and 150–2.   [86] [1994] ECR I-3641.
[87] ILC Commentary, pp. 225–6, para. (8); Sinclair, pp. 149–51.

would seem to support it in suitable cases.[88] The Dayton Agreement 1995 was negotiated entirely in English, even though there are supposed to be authentic texts in Bosnian, Croatian and Serbian.[89] The European Space Agency Convention 1975 was concluded in seven 'equally authentic' languages. The Convention provides for texts to be drawn up in other official languages of the Member States and 'authenticated by a unanimous decision of all Member States'. In this particular case, although such texts are equally authentic, in practice they may not carry quite the same weight as the originals. Similarly, the testimonium of the Convention on Temporary Admission 1990 has two authentic texts, English and French, but provides for 'authoritative translations' into Arabic, Chinese, Russian and Spanish.[90]

The Court itself almost always consults only the English and French texts of treaties, those being the official languages of the Court. There can be a danger in this. In the dispute between Qatar and Bahrain the question whether the Court had jurisdiction depended largely on a passage in an Arabic text. In its 1995 judgment the Court, instead of finding the ordinary meaning of the disputed words in their Arabic context, interpreted them, and in particular the word 'may' (in French 'pourront'), by reference to English and French translations. This was despite having heard expert evidence from both parties as to the meaning of the Arabic text.[91]

---

[88] Sinclair, pp. 147–52.   [89] ILM (1996), p. 75.   [90] UKTS(1999)60.
[91] *ICJ Reports* (1995), p. 6, paras. 34–40; ILM (1995), p. 1207. See also J. McHugo, 'The Judgments of the International Court of Justice in the Jurisdiction and Admissibility Phase of Qatar v. Bahrain', NYIL (1997), p. 171.

14

Third states

Who is the third who walks always beside you?[1]

In relation to a treaty, a third state is a state which is 'not a party to the treaty' (Article 2(1)(h)). A range of states fall within this definition, from a state which is not eligible to become a party, to a state which has ratified but for which the treaty is not yet in force.

General rule

The general rule is rather obvious: a treaty does not create either obligations or rights for a third state without its consent (Article 34). Similar rules apply in laws of contract, but the rule in the Convention rests firmly on the sovereignty and independence of states. Thus a treaty, whether bilateral or multilateral, cannot, by its own force, impose an obligation on a third state, nor modify in any way the legal rights of a third state without its consent.[2] By the same token, a right cannot arise for a third state from a treaty which makes no provision for that state.

In a more general sense, even if a treaty does not purport to affect the rights or obligations of third states, it may nevertheless affect them. For example, a treaty establishing a regional economic integration organisation, such as the European Community, may have the effect of limiting the ability of non-Member States to compete with the Member States. But that is well beyond the scope of this book.

Articles 35 and 36 elaborate the general rule by setting out those circumstances in which a treaty can apply to a third state.

[1] T. S. Eliot, *The Waste Land* (1922), Part 5.
[2] See p. 176 above concerning Article 307 (previously 234) of the Treaty of Rome.

Treaties providing for obligations for third states

Two conditions must be satisfied before a state can be bound by an obligation arising from a provision in a treaty to which it is not a party: first, the parties must intend the provision to be the means of establishing the obligation of the third state. Secondly, the third state must have expressly accepted the obligation in writing (Article 35). Conduct consistent with acceptance of the obligation will not, of itself, bind the third state. Even when a third state has accepted an obligation in a treaty, it does *not* become a party to the treaty.

Treaties providing for rights for third states

There is nothing in international law which prevents two or more states creating by treaty a right in favour of a third state. An intention to create only a *benefit* (such as an agreement between the parties to restrict noxious emissions which will, as a matter of fact, benefit also a third state) does not confer any *right* on the third state. Whether states have created a right for a third state depends on their intention. Thus a right arises for a third state (or a group of states to which it belongs) from a provision of a treaty if the parties to it so intend and the third state assents. But, since the right accorded to the third state does not require it to do anything, its assent is presumed as long as the contrary is not indicated, unless the treaty provides otherwise (Article 36(1)). Peace treaties concluded after the two World Wars provided for the defeated states to waive claims arising out of the wars in favour of certain states which were not parties to the peace treaties. Article 109 of the Treaty of Versailles contained stipulations in favour of Denmark, and Articles 358 and 374 in favour of Switzerland.[3]

Erga omnes status or regime

Certain treaties have been held to create a status or regime valid *erga omnes* (for all the world).[4] Examples include treaties which provide for neutral-

---

[3] 225 CTS 188; UKTS (1919) 4. See H. Thirlway, 'The Law and Procedure of the International Court of Justice', BYIL (1992), pp. 43–7, on the *South West Africa, Monetary Gold* and *Northern Cameroons* cases.

[4] See M. Ragazzi, *The Concept of International Obligations Erga Omnes* (1997), pp. 24–7.

isation or demilitarisation of a certain territory or area, such as Svalbard[5] or outer space;[6] for freedom of navigation in international waterways, such as the Suez Canal,[7] the Turkish (or Black Sea) Straits[8] and the Straits of Magellan;[9] or for a regime for a special area. The Antarctic Treaty 1959[10] has been given as an example of the latter since it creates a unique (or objective) regime for the area south of 60° south latitude, even though it has no more than forty-three parties, and of which only twenty-seven have decision-making powers under the Treaty, although they come from all continents.[11] It has even been suggested that the *Estonia* Agreement may create an objective regime.[12]

The Vienna Convention does not deal with *erga omnes* rights and obligations, as such. The International Law Commission considered that the rule in Article 36(1), by which a right can be accorded to 'all States', and the process recognised by Article 38 (see below), furnished a sufficient legal basis for the establishment of treaty rights and obligations valid *erga omnes*.[13]

When exercising a right conferred on it, the third state must comply with the conditions for its exercise provided for in the treaty or established in conformity with it (Article 36(2)). The latter phrase takes account of the fact that the conditions may be laid down in a supplementary instrument or, if consistent with the treaty, unilaterally by a party. Provisions on freedom of navigation on specific international rivers or waterways are usually subject to the right of the territorial state to lay down conditions for its exercise.[14] Similarly, Article 35(2) of the UN Charter gives a non-Member the right to bring a dispute to which it is a party to the attention of the Security Council or the General Assembly, provided it accepts in advance for the purposes of the dispute the obligations of peaceful settlement of disputes provided for in the Charter.

---

[5] 2 LNTS 8; UKTS (1924) 18.
[6] Outer Space Treaty 1967 (610 UNTS 205 (No. 8843); ILM (1967), p. 386; UKTS (1968) 10; TIAS 6347).   [7] 171 CTS 241.   [8] 173 LNTS 213; UKTS (1937) 30.
[9] 159 CTS 45.   [10] 402 UNTS 71 (No. 5778); UKTS (1961) 97.
[11] For a detailed justification for regarding the Antarctic Treaty as creating an objective regime, see A. Watts, *International Law and the Antarctic Treaty System* (1992), pp. 295–8.
[12] UKTS (1999) 74; J. Klabbers, 'Les cimtieres marins sont-ils établis comme des régimes objectifs', *Espaces et Ressources Maritimes* (1997), pp. 121–33.
[13] For a critical assessment of these provisions of the Convention, see C. Chinkin, *Third Parties in International Law* (1993), pp. 25–50 and 134–44.
[14] See, for example, *Oppenheim*, pp. 641–3 regarding the Bosphorus and the Dardanelles.

Revocation or modification of obligations or
rights of third states

When an *obligation* has arisen for a third state in conformity with Article 35, unless it has been agreed otherwise, the obligation may be revoked or modified only with the consent of the parties *and* the third state (Article 37(1)). The initiative for revocation may come from the third state, in which case the consent of the parties to the treaty is necessary; but if they wish to renounce their right to call for the performance by the third state of the obligation, the consent of the third state would be a formality. On the other hand, the third state's obligations may involve a complex relationship with the parties to the treaty, and possibly involve also the rights of the third state. It is therefore desirable that any change in the obligations should be by mutual consent.

When the parties create *rights* in favour of a third state, especially in matters such as freedom of navigation in international waterways or transit through territory, it is desirable that such rights should have a measure of solidity and firmness. The parties may not therefore revoke or modify rights if it is established that they were intended not to be revocable or subject to amendment without the consent of the third state (Article 37(2)). If the parties wish to have such options, they can provide for this in the treaty or by other means when creating them. If they have not done so, and if the treaty creates a status or regime which is valid *erga omnes*, there is a presumption that the right cannot be changed without the consent of third states.

There is no need to provide for revocation by the third state of its rights, since it can always decline to exercise them.

Rules in a treaty becoming binding on third states through
international custom

A treaty may formulate a rule or establish a regime which later becomes generally accepted by states which are not parties to the treaty. Nothing in Articles 34–37 precludes a rule set forth in a treaty from becoming binding upon a third state as a rule of customary international law, recognised as such (Article 38). In respect of the rules of land warfare in the Hague Conventions 1899 and 1907, the Nuremberg Tribunal decided that by 1939 the rules 'were regarded as being declaratory of the laws and customs of war'.[15] Similarly a treaty purporting to codify customary law may come to be regarded as representing the customary rules. The Vienna Convention is itself a good example.[16] These are not cases where a treaty has legal effects for third states: for them the binding force of the rules remains custom. It was nevertheless decided to include Article 38 so as to make it clear that nothing in the immediately preceding articles precluded such a result.

---

[15] *International Military Tribunal,* vol. XXII, p. 497, quoted in R. Woetzel, *The Nuremberg Trials in International Law* (1960), p. 497.   [16] See p. 10 above.

15

Amendment

D'ora innanzi ogni cosa deve camminare alla perfezione[1]

The amendment of treaties is a subject of great practical importance, and needs always to be thought about seriously when drafting a treaty: afterwards is too late. Although amending a bilateral treaty causes no great technical difficulty, amending a multilateral treaty can raise a multitude of problems. In domestic law most contracts are between two parties and are short-term. In contrast, a multilateral treaty may have as many as 150 or more parties and be of unlimited duration. These factors lead to two basic problems. First, the process of agreeing on amendments and then bringing them into force can be nearly as difficult as negotiating and bringing into force the original treaty. Secondly, because of their long life multilateral treaties are more likely to need amendment.

Before that watershed for treaties, the Second World War, when a treaty needed to be amended it usually required unanimity, since this was then the rule of customary international law. It was relatively rare for a multilateral treaty to have a built-in amendment procedure, and when it did the procedure would normally incorporate the unanimity rule. This is generally still the rule for the constitutions of regional international organisations like the Council of Europe and the European Community. But in other cases, because of the difficulty of obtaining unanimity, a practice gradually developed by which amendments entered into force between only those states willing to accept them. This meant that the *original* treaty remained in force both as between the parties which did not accept the amendments *and* between those parties and the parties which did accept the amendments.

This unsatisfactory state of affairs is made worse when there is a series of

[1] 'From now on everything must function to perfection.' Benito Mussolini to a railway stationmaster (G. Pini, *Mussolini* (1939), vol. 2, p. 251).

amending treaties. The Convention for the Unification of Certain Rules relating to International Carriage by Air 1929 (Warsaw Convention) was amended by Protocols in 1955 and 1971 and four Additional Protocols in 1975, and was supplemented by a Convention in 1961.[2] The 1971 Protocol and one of the four 1975 Additional Protocols have even now not yet entered into force. Moreover, the parties to the various amending and supplementing instruments vary; some states remain parties to just the Convention; some to the Convention and to one or more of the other instruments; and some to one or more of those instruments only.[3] This has resulted in the limits of liability of an airline to its passengers being dependent primarily on which treaty obligations have been accepted by the state concerned, instead of a uniform regime applying throughout international aviation, as was the objective of the Convention. Establishing which version of the Warsaw Convention applies in a particular case can be sometimes difficult, especially for national courts, and it is they which have to enforce the regime.[4]

The International Law Commission was well aware of these problems, but, perhaps wisely, did not attempt to suggest solutions. Instead the Vienna Convention laid down certain basic rules. Article 39 states the general rule regarding the amendment of treaties, whether bilateral or multilateral: a treaty may be amended by 'agreement' between the parties. The use of this word recognises that it is perfectly possible to supplement a treaty by an agreement which does not itself constitute a treaty,[5] or by an oral agreement, the legal force of which is preserved by Article 3.[6] Subsequent practice in the application of a treaty by one party can also have the effect of modifying it if there is tacit or implied consent to it. This is only possible if the other party or parties had the possibility of raising objections to a regular course of conduct, but did not.[7]

A treaty can also be effectively amended by a subsequent 'agreement'

---

[2] 137 LNTS 11; UKTS (1933) 11. For 1955, see UKTS (1967) 62; for 1961, see UKTS (1964) 23.
[3] See Shawcross and Beaumont, *Air Law* (ed. P. Martin, looseleaf) Appendix A, Part 1.C.
[4] See generally R. Gardiner, 'Revising the Law of Carriage by Air: Mechanisms in Treaties and Contract', ICLQ (1998), pp. 278–305; and N. Pickelman, 'Draft Convention for the Unification of Certain Rules for International Carriage by Air: The Warsaw Convention Revisited for the Last Time?', *Journal of Air Law and Commerce* (1998), pp. 273–306.
[5] See p. 189 above about Article 31(2)(a).   [6] See p. 7 above.
[7] See pp. 194–5 above. *United States* v. *France (Air Transport Services) Arbitration* (38 ILR 182, at pp. 248–55); *United States* v. *Italy (Air Transport) Arbitration* (45 ILR 393); and *Egypt* v. *Israel (Taba Arbitration)* (80 ILR 224).

(again not necessarily a treaty) between the parties regarding the interpretation or application of the treaty (Article 31(3)(a)).[8] The Convention on International Trade in Endangered Species 1973 (CITES) was effectively modified by a resolution of the Conference of the Parties in 1986 despite an amendment procedure having been built into the Convention.[9]

Article 39 provides that the rules laid down in Part II (Conclusion and Entry into Force of Treaties) apply to an agreement to amend a treaty 'except in so far as the treaty may otherwise provide'. This phrase recognises that many treaties, especially multilateral, now have built-in amendment mechanisms. It is wrong to think that the Vienna Convention is a rigid structure[10] which places obstacles in the way of treaty modification: rather, it allows states to include in treaties such amendment provisions as they wish.

Bilateral treaties

Naturally, bilateral treaties can be amended more easily than multilateral. The parties can always agree to an amendment, the only question is the form in which it is to be expressed. Sometimes the treaty will contain an amendment clause. Here is a simple example from an air services agreement:

> Any amendments or modifications of this Agreement agreed by the Contracting Parties shall come into effect when *confirmed* by an Exchange of Notes.[11]

Similar provisions are found in many other air services agreements. They leave the procedure for *adopting* the amendment to be determined by the parties, the agreement to amend coming into effect when confirmed by an exchange of notes. The amendment will often be recorded first in an MOU, which may also provide for the amendment to be put into effect 'administratively' pending confirmation. The provision for confirmation by an exchange of notes is a prudent means of ensuring that not only will each amendment be properly recorded, but that there will be no doubt that the decision to amend is legally binding. This is important since, as

---

[8] See pp. 191–3 above.
[9] 999 UNTS 243; ILM (1973), p. 1085; UKTS (1976) 101; Proceedings of the Sixth Meeting of the Conference of the Parties (Doc. 6.19; Res. 6.2.4).   [10] See p. 3, note 2, above.
[11] UK–US Air Services Agreement 1977 (1079 UNTS 21 (No. 16509); UKTS (1977) 76).

has been pointed out,[12] it is not necessary for an amendment to be in writing. Nevertheless, it is undesirable to effect amendments to treaties orally, or by other informal means such as an MOU, unless this is later confirmed formally. Otherwise there may be doubt as to what was agreed, or as to its effect, or indeed whether anything had been finally agreed. After all, that is why one has treaties. It is also a good way of testing that the amendment will work in relation to the rest of the treaty, and whether any consequential changes need to be made. There are numerous other examples of bilateral amendment clauses.[13]

There may be reasons why an amendment clause is not wanted or is not desirable. It would probably not be right to contemplate amendments to a treaty which establishes a border.

There seems to be a recent trend among some European states to conclude treaties, bilateral or multilateral, on collaborative projects which have no provision enabling other states to join later, even though the parties envisage that this will happen. There will then be need for an amending protocol. The reason for the omission is usually political, the founding states wishing to keep tight control on the substance and future membership. This is short-sighted and unnecessary. It is always possible to provide for the adherence of other states in a way which protects the interests of the founding states.[14]

Multilateral treaties

States have devised methods of amending multilateral treaties designed to avoid the problems inherent in amending by means of another treaty. The tremendous increase in multilateral treaty-making, the advent of multilateral treaties of great complexity and the constantly changing needs of international society have made it essential to include in most multilateral treaties an effective mechanism for their amendment.

Automatically binding amendment mechanisms

The treaties establishing international organisations ('constituent instruments') need to have built-in amendment procedures under which once an amendment has been approved by a specified percentage of the

---

[12] See p. 213, note 6, above.   [13] See Blix and Emerson, pp. 223–5.   [14] See p. 89 above.

members it is binding on *all* members. Article 108 of the Charter of the United Nations has perhaps the most succinct and elegant procedure:

> Amendments to the present Charter shall come into force for all Members of the United Nations when they have been adopted by a vote of two thirds of the members of the General Assembly and ratified in accordance with their respective constitutional processes by two thirds of the Members of the United Nations, including all the permanent members of the Security Council.

The essential characteristic of this procedure is that, once an amendment has entered into force, it also binds *all those who did not vote for or ratify it*, and in this sense it may be described as automatically binding. The amendment clause of the Inmarsat Convention 1976 is even more blunt about the effect of its amendment procedure:

> Upon entry into force, the amendment shall become binding upon all Parties . . ., *including those which have not accepted it*.[15]

The amendment procedures built into treaties in recent years are often elaborate. No two are the same, each being tailored to suit the particular needs of the organisation or treaty,[16] but they usually provide for:

(1) the number of parties, or votes in the plenary body or meeting, needed to support an amendment before it has to be put to all the parties;
(2) the majority needed for adoption of the amendment;
(3) whether the adopted amendment needs to be ratified or accepted (some treaties enable technical annexes to be amended simply by a decision of a body or meeting);
(4) if so, the number of parties which need to ratify or accept for the amendment to come into force;
(5) where ratification or acceptance is not required, whether the amendment can be adopted by tacit agreement; and
(6) whether the amendment binds those parties which do not accept it.

These points can be illustrated by looking at two recent examples. Under Article XIII of the FAO Agreement to Promote Compliance with International Conservation and Management Measures by Fishing Vessels

---

[15] 1143 UNTS 105 (No. 17948); ILM (1976), p. 1051; UKTS (1979) 94; TIAS 9605.
[16] Blix and Emerson, pp. 225–39, has many examples from before 1966. See also the UN *Handbook of Final Clauses* (ST/LEG/6 (1957), pp. 130–52; updated by ST/LEG/SER.D/1, Annex and Supplements 1 to 11).

on the High Seas 1993 (Compliance Agreement)[17] a proposed amendment requires the approval of the FAO Conference by two thirds of the votes cast, and comes into force after acceptance by two thirds of the parties.[18] However, if an amendment involves new obligations for parties (which is assumed unless the Conference decides otherwise by consensus) it comes into force for each party only when it has been accepted by that party. The subject matter of the Agreement is not only important, but contentious. The less than automatically binding amendment procedure reflects the reluctance of states to be bound by amendments they do not accept. To be fully effective therefore, any amendments are likely to need approval by consensus. Article 9 of the Vienna Convention on the Protection of the Ozone Layer 1985 has – no doubt for similar reasons – a similar procedure.[19]

Contrast the Compliance Agreement procedure with Article VII of the Comprehensive Nuclear-Test-Ban Treaty 1996 (CTBT).[20] Any party can propose amendments to the Treaty. If a majority of the parties support consideration of the proposal a conference must be held. An amendment is adopted by the vote of a simple majority of the parties at the conference, provided no party casts a negative vote. The amendment enters into force for *all* parties thirty days after *all those parties which voted for the amendment* have deposited instruments of ratification.

The article provides also that, in order to ensure the 'viability and effectiveness' of the Treaty, parts of the Protocol and its Annexes (but not the Treaty itself) can be 'changed' if the changes relate only to 'administrative or technical' matters. Any party may propose a change. After the proposal has been evaluated by the Director-General, it is examined by the Executive Council. If the Council recommends adoption of the change, it is 'considered approved' if no party objects within ninety days. If the Executive Council recommends rejection, it is considered rejected if no party objects within ninety days. But if a party objects to a recommendation to adopt or to reject a proposal, the proposal must be considered by the next conference of the parties. If consensus cannot be reached, a decision is taken by a two thirds majority of the parties present and voting at the conference. Changes which have been adopted by any of these

---

[17] ILM (1994), p. 968.   [18] For the FAO acceptance procedure, see p. 87 above.
[19] 1513 UNTS 324 (No. 26164); ILM (1987), p. 1529; UKTS (1990) 1.
[20] ILM (1996), p. 1443. Article VII is modelled on Article XV of the Chemical Weapons Convention 1993 (ILM (1993), p. 804; UKTS (1996) 45; UN Reg. No. 33757).

procedures enter into force 180 days after they have been notified to the parties, and all are bound. This longer period is to give time for the parties to make arrangements for the implementation of the change, such as modifying legislation.

The tacit procedure for minor changes to the Protocol to the CTBT and its Annexes enables them to become effective more quickly than substantive amendments to the Treaty, since there is no need for the changes to be ratified. This procedure avoids the delay which is inevitably caused by having to submit amendments to a ratification process, though some constitutions may require that all recommendations for amendment or changes be scrutinised in some way by parliament. In any case, all amendments and changes which are adopted should be published by each party. Once in force, they will be registered by the depositary with the UN Secretary-General.

Where parties are not required to ratify an amendment for it to enter into force for them, they must nevertheless take any necessary steps to implement the amendment (including any legislation) should it enter into force. This is particularly important for parties with a 'dualist' constitution.[21] It is therefore desirable when enacting legislation to implement a treaty which is likely to last for a long time and need amendment, to provide for a simple and quick means of amending or supplementing the legislation, if possible by secondary legislation.[22]

The percentage problem

Some amendment clauses provide for entry into force of an amendment after a specified percentage of 'the parties' have ratified it, but do not say to which parties the percentage has to be applied; and one cannot imply that it excludes later parties. It is important therefore to exclude expressly those states which become parties *after* the amendment is adopted. If this is not done the percentage must be applied to the parties from time to time, and thus if a number of states become parties following adoption of the amendment, even more parties will have to ratify before the amendment can enter into force (entry into force clauses can have similar problems[23]). Unfortunately the drafters of several treaties have fallen into this trap.

---

[21] For an explanation, see p. 150 above.
[22] See p. 132, para. (3), above.   [23] See p. 133, para (4), above.

Article 20 of the Convention on the Physical Protection of Nuclear Material 1980 provides that the amendment shall enter into force 'after two thirds of the States Parties have deposited their instruments of ratification'.[24] The same mistake was made in the Ramsar Wetlands Convention 1971, ironically when it was amended in 1982 to include an amendment article.[25] Article XIII(4) of the recent FAO Compliance Agreement 1993 (see above) also has the same error. The problem could arise in an acute form if the clause provides that 'all parties' have to accept the amendment. The way to avoid the problem is to use a simple formula, such as that in Article XVII of the Intelsat Agreement 1971:

> An amendment . . . shall enter into force . . . after the Depositary has received notice of approval . . . from . . . two thirds of the States *which were parties as of the date upon* [sic] *which the amendment was approved.*[26]

Non-automatic amendment procedures

Some (usually older) built-in amendment procedures contain no automatic element. Under Article XVI of the Convention on the Establishment of the European Space Agency 1975 (ESA), any Member State can recommend an amendment, but it will enter into force only if all Member States ratify it.[27] This is no more than a formalisation of the basic rule on amendment in Article 39 of the Vienna Convention. Article 26 of the Convention on the Elimination of all Forms of Discrimination Against Women 1979 (CEDAW) provides simply that a party may request revision of the Convention, and the UN Secretary-General shall decide upon the steps to be taken, 'if any'.[28]

Review clauses

Article 109 of the UN Charter provides for its review. It is, however, no different in substance from Article 108[29] as regards the process for the adoption and entry into force of an amendment resulting from a review; the only additional provisions being those for the calling of a general

---

[24] ILM (1979), p. 1419; UKTS (1995) 61.
[25] See p. 192 above for how the mistake was corrected.   [26] ILM (1971), p. 909; UKTS (1973) 80.
[27] 1297 UNTS 161 (No. 21524); ILM (1975), p. 864; UKTS (1981) 30. See also Article 17 of the Eumetsat Convention 1983 (UKTS (1990) 32).
[28] 1249 UNTS 13 (No. 20378); ILM (1980), p. 33; UKTS (1989) 2.   [29] See p. 216 above.

conference for the purpose of reviewing the Charter. The International Law Commission saw no essential *legal* difference in the processes of amendment and review, regarding amendment as including review. This book also does not deal with review clauses as such, for which there are numerous precedents.[30]

Residual rules

It is evident, therefore, that there are multilateral treaties, including quite modern ones, which have no effective built-in amendment procedures. And even where there is a procedure, it does not always cover all eventualities. One has then to apply the residual rules in Articles 40 and 41.

Proposal to amend a treaty as between all the parties

Any proposal to amend a multilateral treaty as between all the parties must be notified to all the contracting states (i.e., those who have consented to be bound by the treaty even if it is not yet in force); each of them has the right to take part in the decision on the action (if any) that should be taken, and to participate in the negotiation and conclusion of any amendment treaty (Article 40(1) and (2)). There can be problems in determining exactly which are the contracting states, and in excluding a state which is regarded as not suitable (e.g., an aggressor). In an extreme case one may be able to avoid such problems only by some of the states negotiating a new treaty incorporating the amendments, and withdrawing from the original.

Every state entitled to become a party to the treaty is also entitled to become a party to the treaty as amended (Article 40(3)). This would apply to a state which had taken part in the conclusion of the treaty but which had not yet expressed its consent to be bound. An amending agreement does not bind a party to the treaty which does not become a party to the amending agreement (Article 40(4)). As between such a party and a party to the amending agreement, only the *un*amended treaty applies.

It is not uncommon for a state to consent to be bound by a treaty for which an amending agreement is already in force, but for the state not to

---

[30] For some (pre-1970s) examples, see Blix and Emerson, pp. 240–5; and *UN Depositary Practice*, para. 251.

indicate whether it intends to be bound by the amending agreement. Article 40(5) reflects the established practice of the UN Secretary-General: unless the state expresses a different intention, it is considered to be a party to the treaty as amended, and in relation to any party to the treaty which is not bound by the amending agreement it is regarded as a party to the *una-mended* treaty. This rule is reflected in the 1972 Protocol amending the Single Convention on Narcotic Drugs 1961, which provides that any state which becomes a party to the Convention after the entry into force of the Protocol shall, unless it expresses a different intention, be considered a party to the amended Convention, but as a party to the unamended Convention in relation to any party to the Convention which is not a party to the Protocol.[31]

Although an amendment treaty is often called a 'protocol', the title is not legally significant.

Supplementary treaties

It is important to distinguish between treaties which *amend* and treaties which *supplement*. The right to become a party to a supplementary treaty is not necessarily extended or limited to parties to the earlier treaty. This will be so if the supplementary treaty, although linked to the earlier treaty, stands alone and to be effective does not need the parties to it to be parties to the earlier treaty. The Protocol relating to the Status of Refugees 1967 does not amend the Convention relating to the Status of Refugees 1951, but requires the parties to the Protocol to apply the substantive provisions of the Convention, as broadened by the Protocol. It is, in effect, open to all states.[32] Although it does not amend the Antarctic Treaty 1959, because the provisions of the 1991 Protocol on Environmental Protection are so closely related to the Treaty, and the need to preserve the integrity of the Antarctic Treaty System, the Protocol provides in effect that before a party to the Treaty can be accepted as a Consultative Party (with the right to take part in decision-making under the Treaty) it must first become a party to the Protocol.[33]

[31] 976 UNTS p. 3 (No. 14151); ILM (1972), p. 804; UKTS (1979) 23. See also p. 178 above.
[32] 606 UNTS 267 (No. 8791) (Protocol); 189 UNTS 137 (No. 2545) and UKTS (1954) 39 (Convention).   [33] ILM (1991), p. 1460; UKTS (1999) 6 (Article 22(4)).

Agreement to modify a multilateral treaty between certain parties only

There are instances where some of the parties to a treaty make an agreement for the purpose of modifying the treaty only as between themselves. Such an *inter se* agreement may have an aim and effect incompatible with the object and purpose of the treaty. If so, in relation to the other parties to the treaty it may amount to a breach. But an *inter se* agreement is permissible if the possibility of such a modification is provided for in the treaty (Article 41(1)(a)). Alternatively, provided the modification is not prohibited by the treaty, an *inter se* agreement is permissible if it meets *both* of two conditions. First, it must not prejudice the rights or add to the burdens of the other parties. Secondly, it must not relate to a provision derogation from which would be incompatible with the effective execution of the object and purpose of the treaty as a whole (Article 41(1)(b)). It could therefore be permissible for some of the parties to an environmental treaty to enter into an agreement to enforce higher standards in their territory than required by the treaty. The prospective parties to an *inter se* agreement must notify the other parties to the treaty of their intention and of the modification, unless the possibility of the proposed *inter se* agreement is provided for in the treaty and the treaty does not provide for notification (Article 41(2)).

The provisions of Article 30(4) (application of successive treaties relating to the same subject matter)[34] will *not* apply if an agreement to amend satisfies the conditions in Article 41 (see the saving provision in Article 30(5)).

Amendment before entry into force

It is may be necessary to amend a multilateral treaty even before it has entered into force. Before it had entered into force the Olive Oil Agreement 1956 was amended in 1958 by a Protocol.[35] The more famous example is the 1994 Agreement relating to the Implementation of Part XI of the UN Convention on the Law of the Sea 1982.[36] The provisions in Part XI on mining of the deep sea-bed were unacceptable to industrialised states, and so they would not adhere to the Convention. It would therefore

---

[34] See p. 182 above.   [35] 336 UNTS 177; UN Juridical Yearbook (1974), pp. 194–5.
[36] ILM (1994), p. 1313; UN Reg. No. 31364; UKTS (1999) 81.

have entered into force with mostly developing states as parties. Such a situation would have been very unsatisfactory, not only to developing states who would have to pay all the costs of the institutions established by the Convention, but because it would have denied the Convention its universal character. There was, however, understandable reluctance by those developing states which had already ratified the Convention to amend it (or at least to be seen to amend it) before it had entered into force. After difficult and lengthy negotiations it was agreed to supplement the Convention with an Agreement.[37] The parties to the 1994 Agreement 'undertake to *implement* Part XI in accordance with this Agreement'. For this purpose the Annex to the Agreement is an integral part of it and contains what are, in effect, amendments to Part IX. Furthermore, the parties agree that the provisions of the Agreement and Part IX 'shall be interpreted and applied together as a single instrument', and that in the case of any inconsistency *the Agreement shall prevail*. The Agreement also provides that any future ratification of the Convention would amount to consent to be bound by the Agreement; and that one cannot become a party to the Agreement without being a party to the Convention.[38] A simplified procedure by which existing parties to the Convention can express consent to be bound without having to ratify the Agreement is also provided.[39] The Agreement was adopted on 28 July 1994 and was applied provisionally[40] with effect from 16 November 1994, the date on which the Convention entered into force.

It is not uncommon for bilateral treaties to be amended before they have entered into force.[41]

---

[37] See D. Anderson, 'Further Efforts to Ensure Universal Participation in the [UNCLOS]', ICLQ (1994), pp. 886–93.   [38] See p. 181 above.   [39] See p. 91 above.   [40] See p. 140 above.
[41] See p. 106 above.

16

Duration and termination

En toute chose il faut considérer la fin.[1]

As always, La Fontaine is quite right: consideration of the duration and termination of a new treaty should not be left until last. Not only may the necessary provisions raise difficult technical questions, but they can also raise sensitive points of policy which should be discussed earlier rather than later in the negotiations. But, first, a note on terminology:

> *Denunciation* denotes a unilateral act by which a party seeks to terminate its participation in a treaty. Lawful denunciation of a *bilateral* treaty *terminates* it. Although denunciation is also used in relation to a multilateral treaty, the better term is *withdrawal*. Withdrawal of a party from a multilateral treaty will not normally result in its termination.[2]

Part V of the Convention, Articles 42–45 and 54–64, set out the various circumstances in which a treaty can be denounced, terminated or its operation suspended, other than on grounds of invalidity (for which see Chapter 17). In each case it is for the party claiming that a treaty has been terminated or suspended to establish that the necessary grounds exist. To be effective denunciation, termination or suspension may take place only as a result of the application of the provisions of the treaty or the Vienna Convention (Article 42(2)). These days most treaties contain provisions on duration and termination. Where there is none one must consider not only the relevant article in Part V, but other articles in that Part which govern the conditions for applying the article, such as Articles 65–68 concerning the procedure to be followed. Certain other articles of the Convention may also be relevant, for example, Article 5 if the treaty is the constituent instrument of an international organisation.

---

[1] 'In all matters one must think of the end' (La Fontaine, *Fables*, III.5, 'Le Renard et le Bouc').
[2] While 'denunciation' is a technical term when used in relation to treaties, it may be seen by non-lawyers as carrying undertones of its ordinary, condemnatory meaning, and for this reason should be avoided if possible.

Express provisions

A treaty may terminate, or a party may withdraw from it, in conformity with its provisions (Article 54(a)). In practice most difficulties arise over the drafting of a suitable clause or its interpretation, or when a party seeks to terminate or suspend the operation of a treaty on the ground of breach. Although one occasionally finds a treaty which makes provision only for its duration, or only for denunciation or withdrawal, or which is silent on all such matters, it is more usual to find a clause providing for both duration and denunciation or withdrawal, and often in the same article. This is so whether the treaty is bilateral or multilateral. The following examples illustrate the great variety of clauses.[3]

Indefinite duration with right to terminate

Many *bilateral* treaties make no provision for duration and their subject matter is such that they could remain in force indefinitely but, since it is possible that either of the parties may want to terminate it at some time, they include a termination clause. Typically this provides:

> Either party may terminate this treaty by means of a written notice to the other party. Termination shall take effect six months following the date of notification.[4]

Air services agreements can last for many decades because they are usually in general terms, can be amended easily and be supplemented by MOUs.[5] Some will contain the following provision:

> Either Contracting Party may at any time give notice in writing to the other Contracting Party of its decision to terminate this Agreement. Such notice shall be simultaneously communicated to the International Civil Aviation Organisation. This Agreement shall terminate *at midnight (at the place of receipt of the notice) immediately before the first anniversary of the date of receipt of the notice by the other Contracting Party,* unless the notice is withdrawn by agreement before the end of this period. In the absence of acknowledgement of receipt by the other Contracting Party the notice shall be deemed to have been received 14 days after receipt of the notice by the International Civil Aviation Organisation.

[3] See also Blix and Emerson, pp. 96–113.
[4] UK–US Treaty on Mutual Legal Assistance in Criminal Matters 1994 (UKTS (1997) 14).
[5] See pp. 36–7 above.

This rather elaborate (but fairly common) formula in the Azerbaijan–UK Air Services Agreement 1994[6] is necessary because of the special nature of the subject matter. An air services agreement provides the framework for important legal and economic relations between two states and their airlines. It is essential to be able to determine precisely when termination will take effect. Unlike most other treaties, the effect of termination on this type of commerce can be immediate: once the agreement has terminated the aircraft of each state will have no treaty right to land in or take off from the other state with fare-paying passengers or cargo. Although termination takes effect on the expiration of the last day the agreement is in force (i.e., at midnight),[7] because the parties to an air services agreement may well be in different time zones, there is a need to know exactly when termination will take effect, in particular, *whose* midnight.

Most *multilateral* treaties of unlimited duration will allow a party an unconditional right to withdraw. In this the International Convention for the Suppression of Terrorist Bombings 1997 is typical of practice within the United Nations:

(1) Any State Party may denounce this Convention by written notification to the Secretary-General of the United Nations.

(2) Denunciation shall take effect one year following the date on which notification is received by the Secretary-General of the United Nations.[8]

Other multilateral treaties place certain limitations on when a party may withdraw. The Convention concerning the European Synchrotron Radiation Facility 1988 was concluded:

for an initial period ending on 31 December 2007 and shall remain in force after that date. It may be denounced with three years notice, such notice to be given to the [Depositary]. Withdrawal can only take effect on 31 December 2007 or at the end of each successive period of three years.[9]

Conventions adopted within the International Labour Organisation often require a lengthy period of notice and impose strict conditions on when notice can be given. For example, ILO Conventions 163 to 166 of 1987, concerning seafarers' welfare, each provide that a Member State cannot denounce it until after ten years from the date on which the Convention 'first comes into force' (i.e., not just for the Member State concerned), and

---

[6] UKTS (1995) 20.   [7] See McNair, pp. 198–9.   [8] ILM (1997), p. 251 (Article 23).
[9] Cm 911.

if a Member State does not denounce it within twelve months of the expiration of the ten-year period, it may not then denounce it until the expiration of a *further* ten-year period, and so on.[10]

In calculating in this case the precise date when denunciation will take effect, similar considerations apply as for entry into force.[11]

Duration for a fixed period with possibility of extension

The Netherlands–United Kingdom Agreement concerning a Scottish Trial in the Netherlands 1998 provides in Article 29 that:

(1) This Agreement shall enter into force on a date to be agreed by the Parties, provided that they may agree in the meantime to apply provisionally any of its provisions.

(2) ... this Agreement shall remain in force for one year from its entry into force, with the possibility of extending it by mutual agreement.[12]

The one-year period was chosen to avoid delay. Under the Dutch law on treaties some treaties which are for no more than a year do not have to be submitted to Parliament for approval, though extension of the period may be possible.[13] Nevertheless, the provision that the Agreement would enter into force on a date to be agreed was to reduce the likelihood of the need for the term of the agreement to be extended. It has now been.

Indefinite duration with conditional right to withdraw

Article XVI of the Chemical Weapons Convention 1993 states that the Convention 'shall be of unlimited duration',[14] but provides for withdrawal, albeit subject to special conditions based on those in the Nuclear Non-Proliferation Treaty 1968 (NPT):[15]

Each State Party shall, in exercising its national sovereignty, have the right to withdraw from this Convention *if it decides that extraordinary events, related to the subject-matter of this Convention, have jeopardised the supreme interests of its country.* It shall give notice of such withdrawal 90 days in advance to all other States Parties, the Executive Council, the Depositary and the United Nations Security Council. *Such notice shall include a statement of the extraordinary events it regards as having jeopardised its supreme interests.*

---

[10] ILM (1987), pp. 633–67.   [11] At p. 135 above.   [12] ILM (1999), p. 926; UKTS (1999) 43.
[13] See p. 148 above.   [14] ILM (1993), p. 804; UKTS (1997) 45; UN Reg. No. 33757.
[15] 729 UNTS 161 (No. 10485); ILM (1968), p. 809; UKTS (1970) 88; TIAS 6839 (Article X(1)).

Given that a treaty must be performed in good faith,[16] even though the above provision gives a discretion to the withdrawing party ('if it decides'), it must have grounds for its decision. Furthermore, the extraordinary events must be 'related to the subject-matter of this Convention'. The need for these elements is reinforced by the requirement to state what are the extraordinary events. On 12 March 1993 the Democratic People's Republic of Korea (DPRK), following a period of non-cooperation with the IAEA with regard to the safeguards agreement required by the NPT, gave ninety days' notice of withdrawal from the NPT, giving as the reason US military exercises (which according to the DPRK threatened it with nuclear war) and the conduct of the IAEA. The three depositaries of the NPT (Russia, the United Kingdom and the United States) issued a joint statement which questioned whether, as required by the NPT, the DPRK's reasons were 'extraordinary events related to the subject-matter' of the NPT. The UN Security Council, in Resolution 825 (1993) called upon the DPRK to reconsider its decision. Following DPRK/US talks, the DPRK and the United States announced on 11 June 1993, just before the end of the ninety days, that the DPRK 'had decided unilaterally to suspend as long as its considers necessary the effectuation [*sic*] of its withdrawal'.[17]

Duration until a specific event with no termination provision

The Agreement between Egypt and the United Nations on the Status of the UN Emergency Force 1957 provided for it to remain in force until the departure of UNEF from Egypt, the date to be defined by the Secretary-General and the Government of Egypt.[18]

Duration for a specified period of years with no provision for extension or withdrawal

This is unusual. The UK–USSR Exchange of Notes on Inspection Rights relating to the INF Treaty 1987 was entered into for thirteen years from the date of entry into force of the Treaty, with no provision for termination or extension.[19] The Convention on the Declaration of Death of Missing

---

[16] See p. 144 above.   [17] See UN Docs. S/25405; S/25515; and S/RES/825(1993).
[18] 260 UNTS 62 (No. 3704): see para. 44.   [19] UKTS (1991) 30; UN Reg. No. 28537.

Persons 1950 provided for it to be valid for five years from its entry into force, but, perhaps not surprisingly, a Protocol was later concluded to extend the Convention for ten more years.[20]

Comprehensive clauses

When the parties are not sure how long they envisage the treaty lasting, they will often include a clause which provides for an initial term which can be extended, either expressly or tacitly, as well as for withdrawal. Such flexible provisions enable the parties to keep their options open, and are normally found in bilateral treaties. The Slovenia–United Kingdom Cultural Co-operation Agreement 1996 provides that it:

> shall remain in force for a period of five years and *thereafter* shall remain in force until the expiry of six months from the date on which either Contracting Party shall have given written notice of termination to the other through the diplomatic channel.[21]

This example does not, however, make it clear *when* notice of termination may be given. The placing of 'thereafter' after 'period of five years' might imply that it can be given only after five years have elapsed, but this would mean that the minimum term would be five and a half years, a rather curious result. One could argue that the notice may be given at any time before the end of the five years to take effect *on or after* the expiry of the five years. A clause which puts the matter beyond doubt is:

> [The treaty] shall terminate on 31 December 1998 upon notification by either party *not less than six months before this date* that it is opposed to renewal; otherwise the Agreement's duration shall be extended automatically for periods of one year, subject to notification of opposition to renewal by either party *not less than six months before the end of any one-year period.*[22]

It might have been better if the clause had ended there, for the next paragraph provides:

> This Agreement may be terminated by denunciation by either party. The party wishing to denounce the Agreement shall notify the other of this step not less than *one year* before the intended date of termination.

---

[20] 119 UNTS 99 and 258 UNTS 392 (No. 1610).   [21] UKTS (1996) 14 (Article 18).
[22] European Space Agency–UK Agreement establishing an Ariane Station on (appropriately) Ascension Island 1989 (UKTS (1990) 27, Article 90).

Since this paragraph stands alone it must mean that the Agreement could be terminated at any time, even before 31 December 1998, provided twelve months' notice was given. If so, it would have been clearer if the paragraph had begun:

> Notwithstanding the provisions of paragraph 1, this Agreement may be terminated at any time . . .

That example shows just how easy it is, even today, to formulate imprecise or ambiguous clauses. The France–United Kingdom Film Co-Production Agreement 1994 gets it right, almost:

> This Agreement shall remain in force initially for a period of eighteen months from the date of its entry into force. Either Contracting Party wishing to terminate it shall give written notice to the other [at least] three months before the end of that period and the Agreement shall then terminate at the end of the eighteen months. If no such notice is given the Agreement shall automatically remain in force for successive periods each of eighteen months, unless written notice to terminate is given by either contracting party *at least* three months before the end of any period of eighteen months, in which case it shall terminate at the end of that period.[23]

Given the wording of the second sentence, the words in square brackets seem to have been omitted by mistake. Of course, even if a clause does not specify 'at least X months' or 'not less than X months', but merely says that 'X months' notice must be given, the notice can be given more than X months before the date on which it is meant to take effect, provided that date is stated in the notice.

A simpler, but effective, clause for a bilateral treaty is:

> The present treaty shall enter into force on the date of signature and shall remain in force for a period of ten years. Unless, twelve months before the expiry of the said period of ten years, either Contracting Party shall have given notice to the other of its intention to terminate the treaty, this treaty shall remain in force *thereafter* until the expiry of twelve months from the date on which notice of such intention is given.[24]

Note that in this example the placing of 'thereafter' after 'remain in force' means that the notice can be given, say, three months before the end of the ten-year period to take effect nine months after the expiry of that period.

---

[23] UKTS (1995) 82.   [24] 824 UNTS 93 (No. 11810); UKTS (1972) 4.

Transitional provisions

If a treaty concerning a co-operative project is *bilateral* it will usually contain a provision which keeps the treaty alive until the project has been completed, and provide for certain obligations to continue indefinitely:

> The termination of this Agreement shall not affect the carrying out of any project or programme undertaken under this Agreement and not fully executed at the time of termination of this Agreement.[25]

An investment promotion and protection agreement (IPPA) will provide that, in respect of investments made while the IPPA is in force, its provisions will continue in effect with respect to those investments for a certain period (usually at least ten or fifteen years) after the date of termination, and without prejudice to the application thereafter of the rules of general international law.[26]

Sometimes the withdrawal of a party from a *multilateral* treaty may cause problems for the remaining parties. Some treaties anticipate this and provide for any financial consequences.[27] Since they can be complex, and will probably depend largely on the circumstances at the time of withdrawal, the clause will of necessity be in general terms.[28]

Article 317(2) of the UN Convention on the Law of the Sea 1982 provides that:

> A State shall not be discharged by reason of the denunciation [of this Convention] from the financial and contractual obligations which accrued while it was a party to this Convention, nor shall the denunciation affect any right, obligation or legal situation of that State created through the execution of this Convention prior to its termination for that State.[29]

Sometimes negotiating states agree that the arrangements for termination cannot be laid down, even in outline, before the event. The agreements between Norway and the United Kingdom relating to the exploitation of

---

[25] South Africa–UK Science and Technology Co-operation Agreement 1995 (UKTS (1995) 62); see also Article 10 of the ESA–UK Agreement (UKTS (1990) 27).

[26] UK–Venezuela IPPA 1996 (UKTS (1996) 83). See also the texts of model IPPAs in Dolzer and Stevens, *Bilateral Investment Treaties* (1995).

[27] See Article 10 of the ESA–UK Agreement (UKTS (1990) 27). See also p. 246–7 below.

[28] For example, Article XXIV of the ESA Convention 1975 (1297 UNTS 161 (No. 21524); ILM (1975), p. 864; UKTS (1981) 30); and Articles 21 and 30 of the Inmarsat Convention 1976 (1143 UNTS 105 (No. 17948); ILM (1976), p. 1051; UKTS (1979) 94; TIAS 9605).

[29] ILM (1982), p. 1261; UN Reg. No. 31363; UKTS (1999) 81.

several oil and gas fields are of indefinite duration and each provide that
the two governments 'may amend or terminate this Agreement at any time
by agreement', so leaving the conditions to be agreed at the time and in the
light of the situation then.[30] The Convention concerning the European
Synchrotron Radiation Facility 1988 provides that:

> The conditions and effects of withdrawal or termination, in particular the
> costs, shall be settled by agreement among the Contracting Parties before . . .
> withdrawal or termination.[31]

Termination or withdrawal by consent

A treaty may of course be terminated, or a party withdraw from it, at any
time by consent of all the parties (Article 54(b)). This can be done even if
the treaty provides for a minimum period of notice.[32] Although individual
parties may have to take into account their own constitutional requirements, the parties are free to choose the form their consent will take. The
International Law Commission did not accept that the civil law principle of
acte contraire (a rule can be altered only by a rule of the same legal nature)
applied. Although it is desirable that the parties' consent is formalised in
writing, the agreement of the parties does not have to be in the same form
as the treaty (cf. amendment of a treaty other than by another treaty).[33] If
the treaty creates rights for a third state in accordance with Article 36, or an
obligation has arisen for a third state from the treaty in accordance with
Article 37, the consent of the third state may also be needed.[34] The consent
does not have to be expressed in any particular form.

Article 54(b) imposes one pre-condition, applicable only to a multilateral treaty: before taking action the parties must consult the contracting
states, that is, states which have consented to be bound but for which the
treaty is not yet in force. By the same means the parties may suspend the
operation of the treaty (Article 57(b)).

Although these provisions would appear to envisage the power to terminate or suspend the whole treaty, the parties are of course free to agree
to terminate or suspend only a part or parts of the treaty.

---

[30] For example, Article 24(2) of the 1979 Agreement on the Murchison Field (UKTS (1981) 39).
[31] Cm 911.
[32] See the 1996 Exchange of Notes between Armenia and the United Kingdom to terminate the
UK–USSR Visa Abolition Agreement 1964 (UKTS (1998) 57).   [33] See p. 213 above.
[34] See p. 210 above.

The operation of a multilateral treaty may be suspended by agreement between only certain parties if this is done in accordance with Article 58, the terms of which are substantially similar to Article 41 (agreement to modify a multilateral treaty between certain parties only).[35]

Reduction of parties below the number necessary for entry into force

In the past, a few multilateral treaties provided that they would terminate if the number of parties fell below a certain number. Although the International Law Commission did not cite an example, it thought it desirable to make it clear that if the number of parties were to fall below the number required for entry into force this would not affect the continuance of the treaty, unless the treaty provided otherwise (Article 55).[36] If the remaining parties are unhappy with the situation – which may leave them with a greater financial burden – they would generally be free to withdraw, individually or collectively, or to join together and conclude a new treaty.

No provision for termination or withdrawal

Some general law-making conventions are naturally silent as to their duration, but have provisions for withdrawal, for example, the Genocide Convention 1948[37] and the Geneva Conventions 1949.[38] Does this mean that when other similar conventions (including the Vienna Convention itself), or other treaties, bilateral or multilateral, are silent as to their duration and have no provision for withdrawal, one cannot imply a right? Article 56(1) prohibits a party from denouncing or withdrawing *unless*:

(a) it is established that the parties intended to admit the possibility of denunciation or withdrawal; or
(b) a right of denunciation or withdrawal may be implied by the nature of the treaty.

Since this is expressed as an exception, the onus is on the party wishing to invoke it. Unless another period is established, it must give the other party or parties at least twelve months' notice of its intention (Article 56(2)).

---

[35] See p. 222 above.
[36] See p. 95 above on the effect of withdrawal of consent to be bound before entry into force.
[37] 78 UNTS 277 (No. 1021); UKTS (1970) 58.   [38] 75 UNTS 3 (Nos. 970–3); UKTS (1958) 39.

Since it is now very common to include provisions on withdrawal, when a treaty is silent it may be that much harder for a party to establish the grounds for the exception. A party will not be able to withdraw from a treaty transferring territory or establishing a boundary (cf. Article 62(2)(a)),[39] except in the (highly unlikely) event of the treaty allowing for this. The same may apply in the case of some codification conventions. Although Article 317(1) of the UN Convention on the Law of the Sea 1982 permits denunciation, its predecessors did not. When Senegal in 1971 purported to denounce two of the Law of the Sea Conventions of 1958, several parties objected that this was not possible.[40] In any event, in many cases the rules in such conventions reflect, or have become accepted as, customary law, and so withdrawal might make little or no legal difference.[41] Article 317(3) of the UN Law of the Sea Convention 1982 confirms that denunciation:

> shall not in any way affect the duty of any State Party to fulfil any obligation embodied in this Convention to which it would be subject under international law independently of this Convention.[42]

Other treaties which are unlikely to be capable of withdrawal are treaties of peace and disarmament treaties, and those establishing permanent regimes, such as for the Suez Canal.[43] Most universal human rights treaties do not provide for withdrawal. In the case of the International Covenant on Civil and Political Rights 1966, the Human Rights Committee established under it has expressed the view that the omission of such a right, as well as the nature of the Covenant, precludes the existence of such a right.[44] Although the views of the Committee are not determinative of the matter, and must be treated with due caution, they would seem to be correct.[45]

Treaties which are by their nature more likely to fall within the exception in Article 56(1) are treaties of alliance, commercial or trading agreements, and cultural relations agreements. The commercial character of a treaty will, however, not be decisive, particularly when the treaty concerns a joint endeavour.

Although most of the constitutions of international organisations

---

[39] See p. 242 below.   [40] Sinclair, p. 187.   [41] See pp. 9–10 above.
[42] ILM (1982), p. 1261; UKTS (1999) 81.   [43] See pp. 208–9 above.
[44] General Comment No. 26 (61) (CCPR/C/21/Rev. 1/Add. 8/Rev. 1). The text is in ILM (1995), p. 839.   [45] See also p. 200, para (1), above on the *a contrario* argument.

provide for a member state to withdraw, the right is probably implicit. This was certainly the view of the drafters of the UN Charter, as expressed by a committee of the San Francisco Conference and accepted in plenary session.[46]

It will usually be possible to withdraw from a general treaty for the settlement of disputes between the parties even when it has no withdrawal provision. That a party may do so is consistent with the consensual nature of international jurisdiction: a state can be made subject to the jurisdiction of an international court or tribunal only if it consents, either in advance or *ad hoc*.[47] Moreover, states have withdrawn from such optional dispute settlement protocols to several United Nations treaties without (at least legal) objection, even when they contain no provision for this; and declarations under Article 36 of the Statute of the International Court of Justice (which is an integral part of the UN Charter) can be, and have been, withdrawn. However, the other party or parties will be able to invoke the jurisdiction of the Court or tribunal during any period of notice in order to deal with an existing dispute.[48]

Even where the treaty has no express provision on duration or termination, the position will be different if there is an inherent time factor conditioning the application of the treaty. Thus, the International Court of Justice rejected the contention of Iceland that it could denounce a treaty with the United Kingdom of 1961 which provided that either party could have recourse to the Court if Iceland purported to extend her fishery limits. Since the right to invoke the jurisdiction of the Court was deferred until the occurrence of such a well-defined future event, the treaty could not be denounced by Iceland before that event had occurred.[49]

Termination or suspension by conclusion of a later treaty

Two or more states conclude a treaty on the same subject matter as an earlier treaty to which they are parties, but the terms of the treaties are not compatible. What effect is there on the earlier treaty in the absence of an express provision? If the parties to both treaties are identical, they are

[46] K. Widdows, 'The Unilateral Denunciation of Treaties Containing No Denunciation Clause', BYIL (1982), p. 83 at pp. 98–102.   [47] See p. 290 below.
[48] H. Thirlway, 'The Law and Procedure of the International Court of Justice 1960–1989', BYIL (1992), pp. 63–71.
[49] *ICJ Reports* (1973), p. 15, paras. 25–9; Thirlway, 'Law and Procedure', pp. 64–5.

competent to abrogate the earlier one, and may include an express provision to this effect in the later treaty. The same would apply even if the parties to the later treaty are not the same as for the earlier one, provided they include *all* the parties to the earlier one. But can the conclusion of the later treaty impliedly terminate the earlier one? Article 59(1) provides that if *all* the parties to the earlier treaty are also parties to the later one, *and* the two treaties relate to the same subject matter, the earlier treaty will be terminated if:

(a) it appears from the later treaty or is otherwise established that the parties intended that the matter should be governed by that treaty; or

(b) the provisions of the later treaty are so far incompatible with those of the earlier one that the two treaties are not capable of being applied at the same time.

The question is therefore one of interpretation of the two treaties to determine what the parties intended. Although a later treaty for a fixed term will not necessarily abrogate an earlier treaty with a longer or indefinite duration, there is likely to be a presumption that the parties intended that effect. The earlier treaty will be considered as only suspended in operation if it appears from the later treaty, or it is otherwise established, that that was the intention of the parties (Article 59(2)).[50]

Despite their apparent similarities, Article 59 does not cover the same ground as Article 30.[51] The latter is concerned with the application of successive treaties relating to the same subject matter, and deals only with the *priority* of inconsistent obligations in treaties when there is no doubt that *both* are in force. It therefore comes into play only once it has been determined, by the application of the rules in Article 59, that the parties did not intend to abrogate or suspend the earlier treaty. There is no reason in principle why both articles should not apply also to treaties where less than the whole of one, or of both, relates to the same subject matter, though more problems are likely then to arise.

Termination or suspension for breach[52]

Like the violation of any other international obligation, breach of a treaty obligation may entitle another party to terminate or withdraw from the

---

[50] See also O'Connell, pp. 272–4; E. Vierdag, BYIL (1988), pp. 90–2.   [51] See pp. 181–2 above.

[52] See generally S. Rosenne, *Breach of Treaty* (1985).

treaty or suspend its operation. If it causes harm to another party, that party may have the right to take reasonable countermeasures, or to present an international claim for compensation or other relief.[53]

Bilateral treaties

A 'material' breach of a bilateral treaty by one party entitles the other to invoke it as a ground for terminating the treaty or suspending its operation in whole or in part (Article 60(1)) (see below for the definition of 'material'). The use of 'invoke' means that a party may not simply declare a treaty at an end because of a perceived breach. Subject to such right as it may have to take countermeasures,[54] it must seek a peaceful settlement of the dispute, as required by Article 33 of the United Nations Charter, and, more particularly, follow the procedure in Articles 65–68 of the Vienna Convention.[55] To entitle a party to invoke material breach, the breach must be of the treaty itself, not of another treaty or of rules of general international law.[56] Nor can a party which is itself already in breach, and which has prevented the other party from complying with the treaty, invoke a breach by that other party.[57]

Multilateral treaties

Multilateral treaties pose different problems, since a material breach by one party may not necessarily affect all other parties, whose interests must also be taken into account. Article 60(2) therefore deals with three different situations:

(1) The other parties, by unanimous agreement, are entitled to suspend the operation of the treaty in whole or in part, or to terminate it, in the relations between themselves and the defaulting state *or* to terminate or suspend the operation of the treaty completely. It is not clear if in taking action the other parties must follow the procedure in Articles 65–68,[58] though given the reason for those articles there would seem good reason why they should.[59]

(2) A party 'specially affected' by the breach may invoke it as a ground for suspending the operation of the treaty in whole or in part in the relations between itself and the defaulting state.

---

[53] See pp. 300–4 below.   [54] See p. 302 below.   [55] See p. 245 below.
[56] *Gabcikovo, ICJ Reports* (1997), p. 7, para. 106.   [57] *Ibid.*, para. 110.
[58] See Sinclair, p. 189; and *Oppenheim*, p. 1302, note 5.   [59] See, pp. 244–5 below.

(3) If the treaty is 'of such a character' that a material breach 'radically changes the position of every party with respect to the further performance of its obligations under the treaty', any party, other than the defaulting party, may invoke the breach as a ground for *suspending* the operation of the treaty in whole or in part with respect to itself. This provision is designed to deal with certain special types of treaty, such as disarmament treaties, where breach by one party could well to undermine the whole treaty regime. In such a case, the provisions in (1) and (2) above may not adequately protect the interests of an individual party, which could not suspend the performance of its own obligations in relation to the defaulting party without at the same time breaching its obligations to the other parties, yet if it does not do so it may be unable to protect itself against the threat resulting from, for example, rearming by the defaulting state.

Material breach

Determining what is a 'material breach' will depend upon the circumstances of each case. Article 60(3) defines it as:

(a) a repudiation of the treaty not sanctioned by the Convention; or
(b) the violation of a provision 'essential to the accomplishment of the object and purpose of the treaty'.

This last-quoted phrase is not the same as 'fundamental' breach (see below). It can therefore be breach of an important ancillary provision. If a party to the Chemical Weapons Convention (CWC) obstructs the conduct on its territory of international inspections to verify that it is complying with the CWC, this could be a material breach since the inspection regime is a key means of monitoring the effectiveness of the CWC.[60]

Article 60(4) preserves the rights of the parties under any specific provisions of the treaty which would apply in the event of breach. Article 60(5) makes it clear that Article 60(1)–(3) does not apply to breach of provisions in treaties relating to the protection of the human person and, in particular, provisions prohibiting any form of reprisals against persons protected by such treaties. Although it was the Geneva Conventions of 1949 which were in mind, the paragraph would apply equally to other conventions of a humanitarian character, or to human rights treaties, since they create rights intended to protect individuals irrespective of the conduct of the parties to each other.

---

[60] ILM (1993), p. 804; UKTS (1996) 45; UN Reg. No. 33757.

Fundamental breach

A fundamental breach is one which goes to the root of a treaty. Although it is not mentioned expressly in the Convention, the concept is contained within that of a material breach. On 1 September 1983 Korean Airlines flight KAL 007 was unlawfully shot down by Soviet forces. Several states with air services agreements with the Soviet Union unilaterally suspended them, for varying periods and with immediate effect, so preventing Aeroflot from landing in their territory. They were entitled to do so because the Soviet action undermined the fundamental basis of all air services agreements: that each party will ensure the safety of the other party's aircraft.[61] The previous year, in response to the failure of Afghanistan to extradite or prosecute the alleged hijackers of a Pakistan airliner, contrary to its obligations under the Hague Convention for the Suppression of Unlawful Seizure of Aircraft 1970,[62] certain states had terminated their air services agreements with Afghanistan, but only by giving the twelve months' notice required under them.[63] The breach by Afghanistan had not been considered so fundamental as to justify immediate suspension of air services. The action taken was an example of retorsion.[64]

Supervening impossibility of performance

If an *object* which is indispensable for the execution of a treaty disappears permanently or is destroyed, thereby making the performance of the treaty impossible, it is hardly surprising that a party can invoke this as a ground for terminating or withdrawing from the treaty, and Article 61(1) so provides. The rule has been much criticised,[65] and there are few precedents. In its judgment in *Gabcikovo*, the International Court of Justice held that the object of the treaty had not definitively ceased to exist, there being in the treaty means by which the parties could negotiate necessary adjustments.[66] The International Law Commission mentioned as possible examples of impossibility of performance the

---

[61] See G. Richard, 'KAL 007: The Legal Fallout', *Annals of Air and Space Law* (1983), p. 146 at p. 150; K. Chamberlain, 'Collective Suspension of Air Services', ICLQ (1983), p. 616 at pp. 630–1.
[62] 860 UNTS 105; UKTS (1972) 39.
[63] Chamberlain, 'Collective Suspension', pp. 626–8.   [64] See p. 304 below.
[65] See Sinclair, pp. 191–2.   [66] *ICJ Reports* (1997), p. 7, paras. 102–3; ILM (1998), p. 162.

submergence of an island (which global warming may now make a practical possibility), the drying-up of a river (though it may not be permanent) or the destruction of a dam. Another example might be the loss by fire of national treasures which a state has agreed to loan to another. The total extinction of the international personality of one of the parties[67] has also been suggested, but was not included because it also involves issues of state succession, which the Commission did not address. If the impossibility of performance is temporary, it is only ground for suspension.

At the end of the Falklands conflict in 1982, the complete loss by enemy action of the tents intended for the POWs could have been regarded as providing grounds for the temporary suspension of the provision, in Article 22 of the Third Geneva Convention 1949, which prohibits the holding of POWs on ships, since that was then the only means of protecting POWs from the rigours of the Falklands winter.[68]

Impossibility of performance may not be invoked by a party if it is the result of a breach by it either of an obligation under the treaty (as was the case with Hungary in *Gabcikovo*) or of any other international obligation owed to any other party to the treaty (Article 61(2)). As *Gabcikovo* made clear, serious financial difficulties would not be enough.[69]

Fundamental change of circumstances (*rebus sic stantibus*)

The principle, recognised by domestic law, that a person may no longer be bound by a contract if there has been a fundamental change in the circumstances which existed at the time it was signed (in English common law, the doctrine of frustration[70]), has been acknowledged to apply also to treaties. But there has been a lively debate about the conditions under which it could be invoked. Because the concept was abused in the past, particularly between the two World Wars, Article 62 was drawn in restrictive terms. On the other hand, the International Law Commission did not limit it, as had been suggested by jurists, to treaties with unlimited duration and no termination clause, though the Commission noted that, since most treaties now have either express duration or termination clauses, the scope for invoking the article is more limited.

---

[67] See p. 307, para. 3, below.   [68] See also pp. 201–2 above.
[69] *ICJ Reports* (1997), p. 7, para. 102.
[70] See *Halsbury's Laws of England* (4th reissued edn, 1998) vol. 9(1), para. 897.

Paragraph 1

Paragraph 1 defines strictly the (cumulative) conditions under which a change of circumstances may be invoked (the principle has no automatic effect) as a ground for terminating a bilateral treaty or withdrawing from a multilateral treaty:

(1) the change must be of circumstances existing at the time of the conclusion of the treaty;
(2) the change must be fundamental;
(3) it must not have been foreseen by the parties (i.e., when they concluded the treaty);
(4) the existence of the circumstances must have constituted an essential basis of the consent of the parties to be bound by the treaty; and
(5) the effect of the change must be to transform radically the extent of the obligations still to be performed under the treaty.

Thus, a state may not invoke its own conduct. Whether a change of policy by the government of one party would be enough would depend entirely on the circumstances, but certainly only if the effect were to alter fundamentally a circumstance which constituted an essential basis of the consent of the parties to the treaty.

The principle has been *invoked* many times, and recognised by treaties.[71] But the principle has not so far been *applied* by an international tribunal, though no tribunal has denied its existence.[72] Article 62 was considered by the International Court of Justice in the *Icelandic Fisheries Jurisdiction* cases.[73] In *Gabcikovo* the International Court of Justice rejected Hungary's argument that profound political changes, diminishing economic viability of a project, progress in environmental knowledge and the development of new norms of international environmental law constituted a fundamental change of circumstances. The Court emphasised that the stability of treaty relations requires that Article 62 be applied only in exceptional cases.[74] In *Racke* the European Court of Justice upheld a Decision of the Council of Ministers in 1991 denouncing the operation of the Cooperation

---

[71] *Oppenheim*, para. 651, note 2.
[72] See *Oppenheim*, para. 651, note 8; and *Free Zones*, PCIJ Reports (1932), Series A/B. No. 46, at p. 158.
[73] See Sinclair, pp. 195–6; McNair, pp. 681–91; and Thirlway, 'Law and Procedure', (note 48 above) pp. 75–81.   [74] *ICJ Reports* (1997), p. 7, para. 104; ILM (1998), p. 162.

Agreement between the European Community and Yugoslavia.[75] The Court accepted that, since the changed conditions in Yugoslavia could amount to a fundamental change of circumstances, in adopting the Decision the Council of Ministers had not made 'a manifest error of assessment'. However, the Court approached the matter as one of judicial review, and the Article 62 point was not dealt with in much depth. The Court said, in effect, that the Council had not been clearly wrong; it did not say the Council had been right to apply the principle.

Paragraph 2

In addition to the strict conditions for the application of the principle, paragraph 2 makes two exceptions. First, the principle cannot be invoked if the treaty 'establishes' a boundary, that term being used so as to include treaties which cede territory, not merely delimit a boundary. The International Law Commission resisted suggestions that the exception might be inconsistent with the principle of self-determination, but accepted that the operation of that principle was not excluded in any case where the conditions for its legitimate operation existed.[76] Secondly, the principle cannot be invoked if the fundamental change is the result of a breach by the party invoking it of either an obligation under the treaty or any other international obligation owed to any other party to the treaty. This is an application of the general principle of law that a person cannot take advantage of his or her own wrongdoing, which is applicable to any of the grounds for termination which might be invoked. It is mentioned here, and in Article 61 (impossibility of performance), because of the risk that the grounds dealt with by them might well result from a breach of treaty.

Paragraph 3

If the ground can be invoked, it may also be invoked as a ground for suspending the operation of the treaty.

Severance of diplomatic or consular relations

The severance of diplomatic or consular relations between parties to a treaty does not affect the legal relations established between them by the

---

[75] Case C-162/96; ILM (1998), p. 1128. See AJIL (1999), pp. 205–9.
[76] ILC Commentary, p. 259, para. (11).

treaty, except in so far as the existence of diplomatic or consular relations is indispensable for the application of the treaty (Article 63). The rule applies both to bilateral and multilateral treaties. In fact, the severance of diplomatic relations may not make a substantial difference. The widespread practice of establishing 'interest sections' in the embassies of third states, and contacts at the United Nations and other international organisations, means that, depending on the level of staffing of the interest sections, fairly normal relations can be maintained.[77] Diplomatic relations between Iraq and the United Kingdom were broken off in 1990 following the invasion of Kuwait. Nevertheless, since then Iraq has applied thrice under the Iraq–UK Extradition Treaty 1932 for the extradition of Iraqi nationals.[78] In each case the application was refused, but not on the basis that the Treaty was suspended. In each case the applications and responses were transmitted through third states.[79]

Outbreak of hostilities

The legal effect of the outbreak of hostilities between parties to a treaty is still uncertain,[80] and the only comprehensive treatment of the subject is now out of date.[81] The topic is outside the scope of the Convention (Article 73), the International Law Commission having adopted the, perhaps rather high-minded, attitude that 'in the international law of today [1966] the outbreak of hostilities between states must be considered as an entirely abnormal condition, and that the rules governing its legal consequences should not be regarded as forming part of the general rules of international law applicable in the normal relations between states'.[82]

It is clear that there is no presumption that hostilities, however intensive or prolonged, will necessarily have the effect of terminating or suspending the operation of treaties between the parties to the conflict. These days it is less usual for hostilities to consist of one state attacking and occupying another, as when the Soviet Union invaded Afghanistan in 1979, Argentina invaded the Falkland Islands in 1982 and Iraq invaded Kuwait in 1990. These were classic examples of aggression. Although states still

---

[77] E. Denza, *Diplomatic Law* (2nd. edn, 1998), pp. 399–402; *Oppenheim*, p. 1120, note 4.
[78] UKTS (1933) 13. Ironically, the Treaty followed the Treaty of Alliance 1931 (UKTS (1931) 15).
[79] See also Article 74 about new treaties.   [80] *Oppenheim*, para. 655.
[81] *Oppenheim* (7th edn), vol. II, para. 99. See also McNair, pp. 693–728; and O'Connell, pp. 268–71.   [82] ILC Commentary, p. 267, para. (2).

intervene militarily in the affairs of other states, it is not so easy to categorise and is generally more limited in scale.[83] The situation created by the outbreak of hostilities might be regarded, at least for treaty relations, as somewhat analogous to that of severance of diplomatic relations, treaties continuing to apply except in so far as their continuation or operation is not possible during a period of hostilities. A 'political' treaty of alliance or friendship will certainly terminate. Certain commercial treaties, such as air services agreements may be suspended. Treaties like investment protection agreements may not be suspended, given that their purpose is the mutual protection of nationals of the parties. Treaties creating special regimes or fixing boundaries will continue in force, although their practical application may be affected by military operations. As between even the belligerent parties, multilateral treaties whose purpose is to regulate the affairs of belligerents (such as the Geneva Conventions 1949) will of course continue to apply. Nor does the state of belligerency prevent the parties concluding at least certain treaties between themselves, such as prisoner-exchange and armistice agreements. When the conflict is over the parties will need to assess to what extent it has affected their treaty relations. They may have to go though a joint process similar to that which some states carry out on succession of a state.[84]

Procedure

It would be wrong to think that the above heading of this section of Part V of the Convention means that the content is less important than that of the preceding sections, though it might be slightly less exciting. The International Law Commission was concerned that the grounds for termination or suspension might be invoked as a pretext for casting off inconvenient treaty obligations. When one of the grounds is invoked, whether it is justified will turn upon facts, the determination or appreciation of which may well be controversial; if the facts are agreed then it is much more likely that the parties will be able to agree to modify or terminate the treaty. The danger for the security of treaties is particularly great if the ground invoked is based on an alleged material breach or fundamental change of circumstances, both of which can produce a substantial degree of subjectivity.

---

[83] See *Oppenheim*, paras. 128–33.   [84] See pp. 311–19 below.

Article 65 is thus a key provision, its procedural safeguards being designed to deter states from arbitrary action, though it is often not followed.[85] A party wishing to invoke provisions in Part V in order to terminate, withdraw from or suspend the operation of a treaty must *notify* the other parties of its claim. The notification must be in writing (Article 67(1)) and indicate the measure proposed to be taken and the reasons for it. The other parties must be given time to reply. Except in cases of special urgency, this must not be less than three months from receipt of the notification. If no party raises any objection within the notice period, the proposed measure can be carried out in the manner provided for in Article 67 (see below). However, if an objection is raised, Article 65(3) provides that the parties are under an obligation to seek a solution through the means indicated in Article 33 of the United Nations Charter by, for example, negotiation, mediation or arbitration (see Chapter 20), although existing agreements between the parties on dispute settlement remain unaffected. A party may, by way of answer to a demand by another party that it perform the treaty, or to a complaint that it is in breach, make a notification. A party may not have invoked the ground in question before being confronted with the complaint, but the failure to make prior notification does not prevent that party from making it in answer to a complaint. This is, however, without prejudice to Article 45, concerning the effect of inaction in debarring a party from invoking a ground.[86]

In *Racke*[87] the European Court of Justice, when considering Article 62 (fundamental change of circumstances) found that Article 65 did not form part of customary international law. But, as indicated above, the Court approached the case as one of judicial review and did not consider the international law in depth.

Article 66

Article 66 did not figure among the International Law Commission's draft articles. It was included at the Vienna Conference in order to strengthen Article 65(3), which would have been little more than a pious hope if the parties in dispute were not bound by a mechanism for settling their disputes. A number of states were not prepared to accept articles representing

---

[85] See p. 302–4 below about countermeasures. [86] See p. 249 below.
[87] See pp. 241–2 above.

progressive development of treaty law without procedural safeguards.[88] Paragraph (b) of Article 66 provides for conciliation of most disputes under Part V. Paragraph (a) deals only with *jus cogens* disputes.[89]

Instruments for termination, withdrawal or suspension

Because the withdrawal from a treaty, or the threat to do so, is sometimes made in a public speech not addressed directly to the other states concerned, to avoid any uncertainty as to the status of the announcement Article 67 provides that any act terminating, withdrawing from or suspending the operation of a treaty under Article 65(2) or (3) must be done by an instrument communicated to the other party or parties. Because of the importance of the effect of such an act, the article provides also that, unless the instrument is signed by the head of state, head of government or foreign minister,[90] the representative of the state communicating it can be called upon to produce full powers. No special form of words is needed.[91]

If the instrument does not specify the date on which it is to become effective, the date will be calculated in accordance with the withdrawal provisions of the treaty. It is, however, normal practice to specify the date. This must be calculated in accordance with the period of notice prescribed in the treaty, though a later date may always be specified.

A notification under Article 65 or an instrument under Article 67 may be revoked at any time before it takes effect (Article 68).[92]

Consequences of termination, withdrawal or suspension

Article 70 does not deal with any question of state responsibility if, for example, a treaty has been terminated because of the breach of it by another party; and many treaties, including law-making treaties, do not contain provisions on the consequences of termination. But a treaty, whether bilateral or multilateral, pursuant to which acts are likely to be taking place at and after termination may, as the opening words of Article 70(1) recognise, have transitional provisions applying the treaty in whole or in part to such acts even after termination. Thus, Article 65 of the

---

[88] For the history of the negotiation of Article 66, see Sinclair, pp. 226–32.
[89] See pp. 257–9 below.   [90] See p. 60–1 (para. (1)) above.
[91] See also examples in Blix and Emerson, pp. 114–16.
[92] See AJIL (1966), p. 826; Whiteman, vol. 14, pp. 446–8.

European Convention on Human Rights 1950 provides that denunciation shall not release a party from its obligations in respect of any acts which, being capable of constituting a violation of those obligations, may have been done before the denunciation becomes effective.[93] The same will apply to treaties on the settlement of disputes.[94] Transitional provisions are especially important when the treaty deals with a project which involves joint financing. Such provisions have to be tailor-made to suit the circumstances of the particular treaty, and can be complex.[95]

Article 70(1) provides, somewhat obviously, that, in the absence of any transitional provisions, if a treaty is terminated under its provisions or in accordance with the Convention the parties are released from any obligation further to perform it, but that this does not affect any right, obligation or legal situation 'of the parties' created through the execution of the treaty before its termination. The words in quotes are to make clear that the provision is not concerned with the question of vested interests of individuals.

No rule is laid down in the Convention to deal with the situation where a treaty has been terminated because of supervening impossibility of its performance (Article 61), yet has been partially executed by one party only. Given the difficulties which would be likely to be experienced in such a situation, the matter is left to be decided by the parties acting in good faith.

During a period of suspension the parties must refrain from acts tending to obstruct the resumption of the operation of the treaty (Article 72(2)).

Miscellaneous

Articles 43–45 contain some general considerations.

Obligations imposed by international law independently of a treaty

The termination or suspension of a treaty, or withdrawal of a party, does not affect the duty of a state to fulfil any obligation in the treaty to which it would be subject under general international law (Article 43). For

---

[93] 213 UNTS 221 (No. 2889); UKTS (1953) 71.   [94] See p. 235 (Iceland) above.
[95] See Article XXIV of the ESA Convention 1975 (1297 UNTS 161 (No. 21524); ILM (1975), p. 864; UKTS (1981) 30); and Articles 29 and 30 of the Inmarsat Convention 1976 (1143 UNTS 105 (No. 17948); ILM (1976), p. 1051; UKTS (1979) 94; TIAS 9605).

example, the substantive provisions of the four Geneva Conventions of 1949 are now accepted as representing customary international law. Thus, if a party were to withdraw from the Conventions it would still be bound by customary law to respect the substantive rules set out in them. This is reflected in each of the Conventions which provide that denunciation shall in no way impair the obligations of the parties to a conflict under general international law.[96] Similarly, Article 318(3) of the UN Convention on the Law of the Sea 1982 provides that:

> denunciation shall not in any way affect the duty of any State Party to fulfil any obligation embodied in this Convention to which it would be subject under international law independently of this Convention.[97]

Separability of treaty provisions

In the past it was thought that if one had the right to terminate a treaty on the ground that another party was in breach, one could do so only in respect of certain provisions, but not if termination was based on other grounds. Article 44(1) makes no such distinction. If a treaty provides a right to withdraw or to suspend its operation, this may be exercised only with respect to the *whole* treaty, unless the treaty provides or the parties agree otherwise. Paragraph 2 provides that, where no such right is included, a party may invoke a ground recognised in the Convention only with respect to the *whole* treaty, except as provided in paragraph 3, or in Article 60 (termination for breach). Paragraph 3 permits separability if the ground relates *solely to particular clauses*. It may be invoked only with respect to those clauses if all three conditions are met:

(a) the clauses are separable from the remainder of the treaty with regard to their application, in that it must be possible to sever them without affecting the clauses which remain; *and*

(b) it appears from the treaty, or is otherwise established, that acceptance of the clauses was not an essential basis of the consent of the other party or parties to be bound by the treaty as a whole (this condition is the most difficult to apply and would require an examination of the subject matter of the clauses, their relationship to the other clauses, and perhaps also the *travaux* and the circumstances of the conclusion of the treaty); *and*

---

[96] See, for example, Article 142 of the Third Geneva Convention (75 UNTS 3 (NO. 972); UKTS (1959) 39).　　[97] ILM (1982), p. 1261; UN Reg. No. 31363; UKTS (1999) 81.

(c) continued performance of the remainder of the treaty would not be unjust. Severance might affect the balance of the treaty; and an examination under condition (b) would not necessarily take into account how the balance of interests might have changed over the years the treaty has been operated.

(Paragraphs 4 and 5 are relevant only to invalidity.)

Loss of rights by acquiescence

A state may not invoke certain grounds for terminating, withdrawing from or suspending the operation of a treaty if, after it had become aware of the facts, it either (a) expressly agreed that the treaty remain in force or continue in operation, or (b) by reason of its conduct it must be considered as having acquiesced in its maintenance in force or in operation (Article 45). The article applies to grounds under Articles 46 to 50, 60 and 62.

Can one validly withdraw from a treaty and then immediately accede?

One can envisage reasons why a state may wish to withdraw from a multilateral treaty and then rejoin it; the United Kingdom withdrew from UNESCO, only resuming its membership several years later. Probably the only reason a state would withdraw and then *immediately* accede would be to make a reservation. Although depositaries may allow a certain latitude to states which make reservations a little while after they ratified,[98] this would not be permissible years afterwards. Therefore, if, say, a year or more after ratifying a state still wishes to be a party but decides that it must limit its obligations by a reservation, the only possible course may be to withdraw from the treaty (assuming this is permissible) and immediately accede. This is what Trinidad and Tobago purported to do in 1998. It had become a party to the International Covenant on Civil and Political Rights 1966 (ICCPR) in 1978, and to the Optional Protocol to it in 1980.[99] Parties to the Protocol agree to individuals communicating with (i.e., petitioning) the Human Rights Committee established by the Covenant. By 1998 Trinidad and Tobago had decided that this procedure was being increasingly 'abused' by prisoners sentenced to death. It therefore gave the

---

[98] See p. 129 above.
[99] ICCPR and Optional Protocol (1999 UNTS 171 (No. 14668); ILM (1967), p. 368; UKTS (1977) 6). The United Kingdom is not a party to the Optional Protocol since it is a party to the ECHR and has accepted the right of individual petition to the European Court of Human Rights.

required three months' notice to withdraw from the Protocol, but at the same time deposited an instrument of accession. The new instrument included a reservation that the Human Rights Committee would not be competent to receive and consider communications from such prisoners. Although the withdrawal from the Optional Protocol would seem to be valid in itself, other parties may object to the reservation and to the Protocol re-entering into force between them and Trinidad and Tobago.[100]

Other grounds for termination

Article 42(2) makes it clear that a treaty may be terminated only as a result of the application of its provisions or those of the Convention. The International Law Commission has been criticised for excluding from the draft Convention other suggested grounds of termination.[101] However, those usually mentioned may not really be grounds for termination. They include the following.

Execution

This may seem too obvious a case to need mention, but if *all* the provisions of a treaty have been carried out, and none of them has any residual purpose, then one may say that the treaty has terminated by its execution. The Egypt–UK treaty of 1971 for the loan for six months of the treasures of Tutankhamen would fall into this category.[102] A treaty for the transfer of territory is executed once the transfer has taken place in accordance with its terms, unless it has conditions which continue to apply to the parties in respect of the territory. In any event, the actual transfer of the territory will have continuing legal effects.

Desuetude (disuse)[103] or obsolescence

Although the International Law Commission did not dismiss these as grounds, since it saw the basis for them being the consent of the parties as evidenced by their conduct, it saw no need for separate treatment.[104] In

---

[100] See p. 130 above and *UN Multilateral Treaties*, Chapter IV.4.   [101] Sinclair, pp. 163–5.
[102] 824 UNTS 71 (No. 11809); UKTS (1972) 19.   [103] See McNair, pp. 516–18 and 681–91.
[104] But see H. Thirlway, 'Law and Procedure', pp. 94–6 (note 48 above).

1990 Austria declared that certain provisions of the Austrian State Treaty 1955[105] had become obsolete. There were no objections.[106] In the case of a bilateral treaty it is, however, desirable for the parties to record their agreement that the treaty has become obsolete. This avoids any doubt on the matter. The simplest procedure is to have an exchange of notes either terminating the treaty or confirming that the parties do not consider it as any longer in force.

Extinction of the international legal personality of a party

These days this is more likely to occur when two states join to form one state (Yemen), or a state splits into two or more new states (Yugoslavia). This could, of course, also amount to a supervening impossibility of performance[107] or a fundamental change of circumstances,[108] or, perhaps more likely, simply raise a question of treaty succession.

---

[105] 217 UNTS 223 (No. 2249); UKTS (1957) 58; TIAS 3298.
[106] Kennedy and Specht, 'Austrian Membership in [*sic*] the European Communities', *Harvard International Law Journal* (1990), p. 407.   [107] See p. 239 above.   [108] See p. 240 above.

Invalidity

> a matter upon which there exists abundant literary authority, a little
> diplomatic authority, and almost no judicial authority.[1]

Not much has changed since McNair made this dispiriting observation,
except that the Convention has nine main articles on invalidity of treaties
(Articles 46–53 and 64). It has to be said, however, that the subject is not of
the slightest importance in the day-to-day work of a foreign ministry.
The author does not recall during more than thirty years of practice a
single serious suggestion that an existing treaty might be invalid. The
International Law Commission was well aware that invalidity was a rarity,
there being a natural presumption that a treaty is valid and its continuance
in force being the normal state of things. Nevertheless, learned works continue to devote considerable space to the topic, which has a certain fascination for lawyers.[2] What follows is a short account, in which we can step
back in time a little.

Violation of internal law on competence to conclude treaties

The overriding need for certainty in treaty relations is clearly reflected in
the wording of Article 46, which provides that:

(1) A State may not invoke the fact that its consent to be bound by a treaty
    has been expressed in violation of a provision of its internal law regard-
    ing competence to conclude treaties as invalidating its consent unless
    that violation was manifest and concerned a rule of its internal law of
    fundamental importance.

(2) A violation is manifest if it would be objectively evident to any State
    conducting itself in the matter in accordance with normal practice and
    in good faith.

---

[1] McNair, p. 207, on duress.   [2] Sinclair, pp. 159–81 and 203–26, contains a thorough account.

The provision is expressed in negative form ('may not invoke . . . unless') to emphasise the exceptional character of the cases in which this ground might be invoked. There are a number of procedures in treaty-making, such as ratification, which have been specifically designed to enable a state to reflect fully before deciding whether or not to become a party, and to comply with any constitutional requirements. States are entitled to regard other states as having acted in good faith when its representatives express their consent to be bound.

Although not directly relevant, the judgment of the European Court of Justice in *France* v. *Commission*[3] is instructive. The Court held that the European Community (EC) had concluded a treaty with the United States in contravention of internal EC rules governing the competence of various EC organs to conclude treaties. However, the Court did not claim that the treaty was not binding on the EC in international law. Given the complexity of EC internal rules,[4] if the EC enters into a treaty in breach of those rules any internal irregularity is most unlikely to be manifest. It is therefore unlikely that the EC could invoke any rule of customary international law which might be reflected in Article 46, or rather the equivalent article in the 1986 Convention.[5]

If a state seeks to invoke constitutional defects after the treaty has entered into force and after the state has been carrying it out, it will be estopped[6] (i.e., prevented) from asserting the invalidity of its consent to be bound.

Article 46 must be distinguished from Article 27, which provides that a party may not invoke the provisions of its internal law as justification for its failure to perform a treaty.[7] That rule applies unless the treaty has been held to be invalid.

Violation of specific restrictions on authority to express consent

An omission by the representative of a state to observe a specific (internal) restriction on his authority to express the consent of his state to be bound may not be invoked as invalidating that consent unless the restriction was

---

[3] [1994] ECR V-3641.   [4] See pp. 55–6 above.
[5] The EC is not party to the 1986 Convention, but the European Court of Justice has held that the rules in the 1969 Convention apply to the EC to the extent that they reflect rules of customary international law: *Racke* (Case C-162/96; ILM (1998), p. 1128) AJIL (1999) 205–9.
[6] See p. 45 above.   [7] See p. 144 above.

previously notified to the other negotiating state or states (Article 47). Moreover, this rule is limited to those cases where the treaty is not subject to ratification or similar process, since in that case the state would have an opportunity to repudiate any unauthorised act of its representative.

Error

Because the treaty-making process is such that the risk of material errors is reduced to the minimum, almost all the recorded cases where error has been invoked to invalidate a treaty have concerned errors in maps.[8] Sometimes the matter was disposed of by a further treaty; sometimes the error was treated more as affecting the application of the treaty rather than its validity, and the matter settled by arbitration. A state may invoke an error as invalidating its consent to be bound if the error relates to a fact or situation which was assumed by the state to exist at the time when the treaty was concluded and formed an essential basis of its consent to be bound, provided that it did not contribute to the error by its own conduct, and if the circumstances were not such as to put it on notice of a possible error (Article 48).[9] The following additional points should be noted:

(1) The error cannot for this purpose be one of law, although it is not always easy to draw a line between law and fact.[10]

(2) The error can be mutual or unilateral.

(3) The error does not make the treaty void automatically: the ground must first be invoked, but if invalidity is established the treaty will be void *ab initio* (i.e, from the start).

(4) An error which relates only to the wording of the text does not affect its validity, and failure by one party to read properly the final text will not be a ground for invoking Article 48; the only recourse is to the correction procedures of Article 79.[11]

Fraud

It is heartening that no clear case of fraud having been used to procure the conclusion of a treaty has ever been cited; and fraudulent misrepresenta-

---

[8] See *Oppenheim*, p. 1288.

[9] The formula was taken from the *Temple of Preah Vihear* case (*ICJ Reports* (1962), p. 26).

[10] See H. Thirlway, 'The Law and Procedure of the International Court of Justice', BYIL (1992), pp. 27–8. The different consequences of a mistake of law and of fact are now less distinct in English law: *Kleinwort Benson* v. *Lincoln City Council* [1998] 3 WLR 1095.

[11] See p. 270 below.

tion of a material fact which induced an error would be likely to be caught by the provisions on error. Nevertheless, if a state has been induced to conclude a treaty by the fraudulent conduct of another negotiating state, the first state may invoke the fraud as invalidating its consent to be bound (Article 49). The expression 'fraudulent conduct' includes any deliberately false statements, misrepresentations or other deceitful proceedings by which a state is induced to give consent which it would not otherwise give. The detailed connotations given to the concept of fraud in domestic law are not necessarily applicable. Fraud may be invoked with respect to particular clauses only, provided they are separable, are not essential to the treaty, and it would not be unjust to continue performance of the rest of the treaty (Article 44(4)).

Corruption

If the consent of a state to be bound by a treaty has been procured through the corruption of its representative by another negotiating state, directly or indirectly, the first state may invoke it as invalidating its consent (Article 50). But the state may only rely on acts calculated to exercise a substantial influence on the disposition of its representative to conclude the treaty; a small courtesy or favour is not enough. It is unlikely that Article 50 could be invoked if the treaty is subject to ratification. As with fraud, corruption may be invoked either with respect to the whole treaty or, subject to conditions, to particular clauses (Article 44(4)). Surprisingly, perhaps, there does not appear to be any recorded example of such corruption.

Coercion of a representative of a state (duress)

If a state's consent to be bound has been procured by coercion of its representative by acts or threats directed against him, the consent is without any legal effect (Article 51). Even if it were possible to separate out provisions of the treaty to which the state would have no objection, this is not permitted: the whole treaty will be void (Article 44(5)). The acts or threats, such as a physical threat to him or his family or blackmail, must affect the representative as an individual, not as the representative of his state. Such coercion is therefore unlikely to be used in order to procure ratification. There have been a few cases of personal coercion, such as the extreme pressure put on the President and Foreign Minister of Czechoslovakia in 1939 to get them to sign the treaty creating a German protectorate over Bohemia and Moravia.[12]

Coercion of a state by the threat or use of force

Article 52 provides that a treaty is void if its conclusion has been procured by the threat or use of force in violation of the principles of international law embodied in the UN Charter. No separation of the provisions of the treaty is permitted (Article 44(5)). The principle, as set out in Article 2(4) of the UN Charter, does not include economic or political pressure.[13] Since the prohibition of the use of force is a rule of general international law of universal application, Article 52 applies also to non-Members of the United Nations. The article does not itself have any retrospective effect (Article 4), but, since the Charter is regarded as setting out modern customary law on the use of force, the rule laid down in Article 52 recognises, by implication, that it will apply to all treaties concluded at least since the entry into force of the Charter.

If the treaty is multilateral, the participation of the coerced state will be void, but not the treaty itself, the provisions of Article 44(5) being applicable to the provisions of the treaty, not to its parties. The Nationality Treaty of 1938 between Czechoslovakia and Germany, which gave effect to provisions of the notorious Munich Agreement, was void because of the pressure on the Czech Government.[14] The Agreement concerning the restoration of the Government of President Aristide, signed in Port au Prince on 18 September 1994 by the provisional President of Haiti and ex-President Jimmy Carter on behalf of President Clinton, might at first sight appear to have been obtained by the threat of force, since at the time American bombers were on their way to Haiti. However, the Security Council had adopted on 16 October 1993 Resolution 875 which authorised the use of force to restore the legitimate government of Haiti. Article 52 does not apply to the threat or use of lawful force.

---

[12] *Oppenheim*, para. 641, note 1.
[13] *Oppenheim*, para. 641, note 5; and Sinclair, pp. 177–9.
[14] As to the Munich Agreement, see *Oppenheim*, p. 1291, note 8.

Peace treaties

It might seem as if a peace treaty must involve some degree of coercion of the vanquished by the victor. Nowadays a peace treaty forced on a state which has been the victim of aggression would be void. But the Vienna Convention provides expressly that its provisions are without prejudice to any obligation in relation to a treaty which may arise for an aggressor state in consequence of measures taken in conformity with the UN Charter with reference to that state's aggression (Article 75).

'Unequal treaties'

So-called 'unequal' or 'Leonine' treaties are those which are said to have been forced upon a weaker state by a stronger one. However, the concept has never been accepted in international law. No two states are ever equal, and to allow a state to avoid its treaty obligations on this ground could undermine the stability of treaty relations.

Conflict with a peremptory norm of general international law (jus cogens)

The concept of *jus cogens* (peremptory norm of general international law) was controversial at the time of the Vienna Conference. Now it is more the scope and applicability of the concept which is debated.[15] *Jus cogens* is defined in Article 53 for the purposes of the Convention as:

> a norm accepted and recognised by the international community of States as a whole as a norm from which no derogation is permitted and which can be modified only by a subsequent norm of general international law having the same character.

There is no agreement on the criteria for identifying which norms of general international law have a peremptory character. Whether a norm of general international law has it depends on the particular nature of the subject matter. Perhaps the only generally accepted example is the prohibition on the use of force as laid down in the UN Charter. The prohibitions on genocide, slavery and torture may also be said to be *jus cogens*. This is so even where such acts are prohibited by treaties which parties to them can

---

[15] For an in-depth discussion of *jus cogens*, see Sinclair, pp. 203–26.

denounce. But it would be rash to assume that all prohibitions contained in human rights treaties are *jus cogens*, or even part of customary international law. Some rights, such as the freedom of association, are far from being generally accepted as customary law. Article 53 does not therefore attempt to list examples of *jus cogens*, leaving that to be worked out by state practice and in the jurisprudence of international tribunals.

If part only of a treaty conflicts with an existing *jus cogens* the whole of the treaty is void, not just the offending part (Article 44(5)).

Article 53 has no retrospective effect (Article 4). It must, however, be read with Article 64, which provides that, if a new peremptory norm of general international law emerges, any existing treaty which is in conflict with that norm 'becomes void and terminates'. Since this provision is not retrospective, the treaty is invalid only as from the time the new norm is established.

The vast majority of rules do not of course have the character of *jus cogens*, and states are therefore free to contract out of them; and a treaty which conflicts with general international law is not necessarily void. Similarly, if a treaty provides that no derogation from it is permitted, but later a party concludes a treaty which conflicts with it, the latter treaty is not void although the party may be liable for breach of the earlier treaty.[16]

There are no reported instances of Articles 53 or 64, as such, being invoked.

Consequences of invalidity (other than for *jus cogens*)

With the exception of *jus cogens*, the invalidity of a treaty is rooted in the invalidity of the *consent* of a party to be bound. If it is a bilateral treaty it will be void *ab initio* and its provisions will never have had legal force (Article 69(1)). If it is a multilateral treaty, an invalid consent will normally mean that the treaty will nevertheless remain valid for the other parties (Article 69(4)). Article 69 is concerned only with the immediate legal effects of the invalidity of a treaty: it does not deal with any question of state responsibility arising from the act which was the cause of the invalidity, such as fraud or coercion (see Article 73).

Nevertheless, since the parties may have in good faith been performing acts under an invalid treaty for some years, each party can require another party to re-establish, as far as possible, in their mutual relations the posi-

---

[16] See p. 174 above.

tion that would have existed if the acts performed under the treaty had not been performed, that is to say, to re-establish the *status quo ante*; and if an act performed in good faith under an invalid treaty is not otherwise unlawful, it will not be rendered unlawful by the invalidity of the treaty (Article 69(2)). But a party whose fraud, corruption or coercion was the cause of the invalidity cannot benefit from these provisions (Article 69(3)).

The consequences of the invalidity of a treaty which conflicts with *jus cogens* under Article 53 or Article 64, are dealt with in Article 71.

Procedure

Article 65 is a key provision, its procedural safeguards being designed to deter states from arbitrary action. In particular, a party wishing to invoke any of the grounds for impeaching the validity of a treaty must notify the other parties. The procedure in respect of termination applies equally to cases of invalidity.[17]

There is an additional provision for cases of *jus cogens*. Article 66 did not figure among the final draft articles produced by the International Law Commission, but was included at the Vienna Conference in order to strengthen the obligation in Article 65(3) to seek a peaceful solution. That obligation would have had little substance if the parties in dispute were not already bound by a mechanism for settling their disputes. A number of states were not prepared to include an article representing such a development in the law of treaties without some procedural safeguards.[18] Article 66(a) thus provides that if a dispute as to the applicability of the *jus cogens* rules (Articles 53 and 64) to a particular treaty cannot be resolved in accordance with procedure laid down in Article 65(3), any party to the dispute may invoke the compulsory jurisdiction of the International Court of Justice, unless the parties agree to arbitration. In contrast, Article 66(b) provides only for conciliation of other disputes under Part V. On ratifying the Convention some states have sought to exclude the compulsory effect of Article 66(a), but other states have rejected these attempts.[19]

---

[17] See pp. 244–6 above.
[18] For the history of the negotiation of Article 66, see Sinclair, pp. 226–32.
[19] See the reservations concerning Article 66(a), and the objections to them, in *UN Multilateral Treaties*, Chapter XXIII.1; and Sinclair, pp. 65–8.

General points

In each case it is for a party to establish that the necessary grounds for invalidity exist. To do this it must apply the provisions of the Convention (Article 42(1)). In all cases one must consider not only the article dealing with the particular ground invoked, but other provisions in Part V and the rest of the Convention which govern the conditions for applying the article in question, including the special procedures laid down in Articles 65–68. Articles 44 and 45 contain some other general considerations. The comments on them in Chapter 16 (Duration and termination) also apply, where relevant, to cases of invalidity, subject to the following points.

Separability of treaty provisions

Article 44(4) lays down a different separability rule for cases of fraud and corruption. Article 44(5) rules out separability altogether in cases of coercion or where part of a treaty conflicts with an existing *jus cogens.*

Loss of rights by acquiescence

Article 45 prevents a state from invoking grounds for invalidating a treaty if, after it had become aware of the facts, it either (a) expressly agreed that the treaty was valid or (b) by reason of its conduct must be considered as having acquiesced in the validity of the treaty. The article applies to grounds of invalidity under Articles 46–50 (lack of competence, restrictions on authority, error, fraud or corruption), but not to grounds for invalidity under Articles 51–53 and 64 (coercion or conflict with *jus cogens*).

18

The depositary

Neither a borrower nor a lender be.[1]

If Shakespeare had only taken a closer interest in treaty procedures he would surely have had Polonius add, 'nor a depositary'. Although not of much concern to others, and little appreciated, the exacting and onerous duties of a depositary are vital to the effective functioning of multilateral treaties. Yet not all states which act as depositaries are fully aware of their responsibilities or how they should be carried out. On the other hand, their work can be made more difficult by the lack of knowledge by governments of depositary procedures. This chapter will attempt to de-mystify the role of the depositary.

The term 'depositary' means a person to whom something is entrusted. Even when used in the context of a treaty it is sometimes wrongly spelled as depositary, which means a storehouse.

Bilateral treaties

A bilateral treaty is usually signed in duplicate, so that each of the contracting states keeps one signed original. In the most exceptional case of a bilateral treaty having only one original text, the contracting states would have to decide which of them should keep it. Alternatively, they could deposit it with a third state or an international organisation, as depositary. The depositary would then provide both states with a copy certified to be true and accurate. Apart from that, there should be little more, if anything, for the depositary to do. But the depositary of a multilateral treaty has plenty to do.

---

[1] *Hamlet*, I, iii, 75.

Designation of the depositary

The increase in the number of parties to multilateral treaties led to the practice of designating a depositary for each treaty. The depositary plays an essential role in ensuring throughout the life of the treaty that the necessary formalities and procedures which have to be performed in connection with the treaty are properly observed and recorded. The duties may appear at first sight to be routine, and although much of the work is of that nature, the duties are of vital importance. They require a responsible attitude, a methodical approach and attention to detail. The designation of a depositary may be made by the negotiating states either in the treaty or in some other manner. The depositary may be one or more states, an international organisation or its chief administrative officer (Article 76(1)).

A word of warning: when a state is a depositary its duties should be carried out only by the foreign ministry. These days when other ministries often take the lead on negotiating treaties on technical subjects, there may be a temptation for the depositary functions to be 'sub-contracted' to another ministry or public body which is responsible for the substance of the treaty. This should not happen. Depositary functions are the same whatever the subject matter of the treaty, and the necessary expertise is found only in a foreign ministry or an international organisation. In a recent case a small European state appears to have largely delegated its depositary functions under a regional treaty to a semi-commercial public authority. Some of the procedures which were then followed were rather unusual.[2]

One or more states as depositary

If a multilateral treaty has not been adopted within an international organisation or at a conference convened by one, it is customary (though not a rigid rule) for the treaty to be deposited with the state which hosted the conference. The Charter of the United Nations, having been adopted at the San Francisco Conference, provides for it to remain deposited in the archives of the Government of the United States. This tradition is in recognition of the (not always easy) task which the host state has had to perform. It is also practical, the host state having probably provided most of the secretariat for the conference and produced the final text of the treaty.

[2] Information on file with the author.

During the Cold War certain treaties, such as the Partial Test Ban Treaty 1963[3] and the Outer Space Treaty 1967[4] each had three depositaries: the Soviet Union (now Russia), the United Kingdom and the United States.[5] A state wishing to sign, ratify or accede to treaties with such provisions was (and still is) able to do so with any *one* of them. This arrangement was to avoid the embarrassment caused by the differences between any one of the three depositaries and other states on the then question of the status of the German Democratic Republic (East Germany) and the right of the Government of the People's Republic of China to represent China. Although contrary to normal practice, it was understood that if it would embarrass a depositary to accept a signature or receive an instrument of ratification or accession from an entity which it did not recognise, it could decline to do so. Deposit of the instrument with one of the other depositaries which did recognise it would be sufficient. The arrangement also allowed a depositary which did not recognise an entity which had deposited an instrument with another of the depositaries to object (as a party, not as a depositary) to the entity taking part in any amendment conference. There is at present no compelling need for such arrangements for new treaties. Nevertheless, there are still entities which are recognised as states by a number of states (sometimes for political reasons), but not generally, Taiwan being the prime example.[6] This may present problems for a depositary (see below on the duty to act impartially).

The Cambodia Agreement 1991 has two depositaries, France and Indonesia, simply, it seems, because they co-hosted the conference.[7]

An international organisation as depositary

Most multilateral treaties are now adopted within an international organisation or at an international conference convened by one. Although there are some exceptions,[8] it is the chief administrative officer of the organisation which the treaty will designate as the depositary. He will not normally

---

[3] 480 UNTS 43 (No. 6964); UKTS (1964) 3; TIAS 5433.
[4] 610 UNTS 205 (No. 8843); ILM (1967), p. 386; UKTS (1968) 10; TIAS 6347.
[5] See Schwelb, 'The Nuclear Test Ban Treaty and International Law', AJIL (1964), p. 642 at pp. 651–3; *Oppenheim*, vol. I, para. 50, note 6; UN Juridical YB (1980), pp. 207–8.
[6] It is equally true that sometimes recognition has been withheld for political reasons, the Federal Republic of Yugoslavia having been the most recent example.   [7] ILM (1992), p. 1820.
[8] The Convention on the Marking of Plastic Explosives for the Purposes of Detection 1989 (ILM (1991), p. 726) designated ICAO (i.e., the organisation itself).

agree to be depositary of a treaty with which his organisation has no substantial connection.[9] It would therefore be a mistake to believe that
because all treaties have to be registered with the United Nations its
Secretary-General is willing to be the depositary of all multilateral treaties.
One must therefore seek the concurrence of the Secretary-General, or of
the chief administrative officer of another international organisation,
before designating them.

The UN Secretary-General as depositary

A treaty adopted within the United Nations, or at a conference convened
by it, will include a provision that it shall be deposited with the UN
Secretary-General. He will usually agree to be the depositary of other treaties only if satisfied that they are intended to be of universal application
(open to all states) and there are no provisions (such as for the participation of certain non-state entities) which might be embarrassing for him
politically.

In carrying out depositary functions the Secretary-General is guided
also by any particular rules laid down by the UN General Assembly. Thus,
when a treaty has an 'all states' participation clause[10] the Secretary-General
will follow the resolutions and practice of the General Assembly in applying it, and when necessary will ask it for its opinion before agreeing to
receive the signature or an instrument of ratification of an entity if there is
doubt whether it is a state.[11] The chief executive officers of the UN specialised agencies follow a similar practice, and their assemblies and general
conferences tend to follow the lead given in such matters by the UN
General Assembly. In practice the depositary duties of the UN Secretary-
General will be performed by the Treaty Section of the Office of Legal
Affairs in the UN Secretariat.

Between 1945 and 1998 over 500 multilateral treaties were deposited
with the Secretary-General. No other international organisation is the
depositary of so many. The UN publication *Multilateral Treaties Deposited
with the Secretary-General* (referred to in this book as *UN Multilateral
Treaties*) gives the status of those treaties (i.e., lists of parties, dates of entry
into force, etc.). It is published annually in English and French. The

---

[9] *UN Depositary Practice*, paras. 28–30.   [10] See p. 92 above.
[11] *UN Depositary Practice*, paras. 82–7.

English version is available on the Internet, where it is updated daily.[12] The *Summary of Practice of the Secretary-General as Depositary of Multilateral Treaties* (1994) (referred to in this book as *UN Depositary Practice*),[13] prepared by the UN Office of Legal Affairs, provides invaluable guidance on the depositary practice of the United Nations, and is a good guide for any depositary, whether an international organisation or a state.

Duty to act impartially

Multilateral treaties cause problems which require action by the depositary. It is a long-established customary law principle that the functions of a depositary are, in the words of Article 76(2), 'international in character' and that the depositary is under an obligation 'to act impartially in their performance'.[14] This is particularly important when the depositary was one of the negotiating states. The depositary must at all times keep a clear distinction between its views and national interests as a state and its functions as depositary. For example, problems can be caused by changes to the structure of a state or the emergence of a new state. When a depositary receives an instrument or communication from a state with which it has no diplomatic relations, or from an entity which it does not recognise as a state, or which it knows is not recognised by other states, it must *not* seek to pass judgment on the validity of the instrument or communication. If necessary, the depositary should circulate a note to the interested states (which are usually contracting states, signatory states and other states entitled to become parties to the treaty) about the instrument or communication, but without comment. It is for those states to form a view as to the legal position.

On 21 June 1989 the Permanent Observer of Palestine to the United Nations lodged a purported instrument of accession of the 'State of Palestine' to the Geneva Conventions of 1949. The depositary, Switzerland, circulated a note to the parties stating that, because of the uncertainty within the international community as to whether there is a State of Palestine, the depositary was not in a position to decide whether deposit of the instrument amounted to a valid act of accession. The instrument was therefore circulated for the information of the parties, leaving it

---

[12] See p. 282 below. [13] ST/LEG/8 (1994).
[14] Article 77(2) of the 1986 Convention has identical wording.

to them to decide whether it could be accepted. There was no need for the parties to reply to the note and, given the circumstances, silence could not have been taken as tacit acceptance of one view or the other. In the event, the matter was not pursued.

When the depositary is the chief administrative officer of an international organisation, it may be necessary for the assembly of the organisation to be consulted about difficult cases. The UN Secretary-General will be guided by the resolutions of the General Assembly and practice within the United Nations.[15]

As we have seen,[16] due to a drafting error there was doubt whether under the Comprehensive Nuclear-Test-Ban Treaty 1996 (CTBT) a conference could be held in 1999 or 2000. In the event, the contracting states agreed on 1999. Although the UN Secretary-General has under the CTBT the duty of convening the conference if a majority of the contracting states so request, it was not for him to give an opinion as to the date unless he was asked to do so by the negotiating (not just the contracting) states.[17]

The corollary of the impartiality principle is that nothing which a state does as a depositary will prejudice it *as a state*. By notifying the adherence to a treaty of an entity which it does not recognise, a depositary state does not thereby accord recognition to the entity. But its position as depositary does not prevent it from making known its position, as a state, in a *separate* communication to the other interested states.

A depositary may sometimes experience difficulties in drawing up a list of contracting states; a task which should be done each time a new instrument of ratification etc. is received, and the list circulated to the contracting states and other states entitled to become parties. In the early 1990s, the break-up of Yugoslavia and the gaining of independence by certain republics of the former Soviet Union caused problems for depositaries. In 1994 the newly independent Ukraine lodged with the depositary state an instrument of *succession* to the Convention on the Conservation of Antarctic Marine Living Resources 1980 (CCAMLR),[18] on the basis that it was a successor state to the Soviet Union, though the latter (as Russia) remained a party. The depositary state duly notified the parties. Although two parties claimed that, in view of the particular membership provisions

---

[15] See p. 264, above.   [16] See p. 184 *et seq.* above.

[17] See Article 2(1)(e) and (f) of the Vienna Convention as to the definitions of negotiating states and contracting states.

[18] 402 UNTS 71; ILM (1980), p. 837; UKTS (1982) 48; TIAS 10240.

of CCAMLR, no state could become a party by succession, the depositary accepted the instrument of succession. Although they had no objection to Ukraine becoming a party, as a matter of principle and to prevent an undesirable precedent, the same two parties sent notes to the depositary indicating that they would treat the instrument as one of *accession*. The depositary then notified all parties that Ukraine had become a party on the date of deposit of the instrument (not on the date of independence, as would have been appropriate in a case of succession), and without saying on what basis it had become a party.[19]

But where it is indisputable that an instrument is unacceptable, the depositary must refuse it. In 1977 the depositary of the World Meteorological Organisation Convention did not accept a purported instrument of accession from the 'Turkish Federated State of Cyprus' because it did not meet the (factual) pre-condition for participation: membership of the United Nations.[20] This is clearly distinguishable from the case where there is a difference of view as to the status of an entity.

A difference between a state and the depositary as to the performance of the latter's functions can usually be resolved by informal contacts. When this is not possible, the depositary must bring the question to the attention of the interested states or, where appropriate, to the competent organ of the international organisation concerned (Article 77(2)).

If a depositary state were itself to cease to exist, or be unwilling or unable to act as depositary, no doubt the parties to the treaty would agree on a pragmatic solution, which might be to ask an international organisation to act as depositary.

Functions of the depositary

In the past when a treaty designated a depositary it would list his functions, or at least some of them, and this is often still done (see below). Subject to any provisions in the treaty or as may be agreed by the contracting states, the principal functions are listed in Article 77(1):

(1) Keeping custody of the original text of the treaty[21] and any full powers.
(2) Preparing certified copies of the original text and any further texts in such additional languages as may be required by the treaty, and transmitting them

---

[19] Information on file with the author.   [20] Information on file with the author.
[21] In the past, several original copies might be made so that, like at a chilren's party, each plenipotentiary could take away an original which had his signature first.

to the parties and to 'the states entitled to become parties to the treaty' (which formula is not always easy to apply). A certified copy is usually needed by the negotiating states for the purpose of official publication and any parliamentary procedure which may be necessary. Unless the Final Act contains substantive provisions, normally neither it, nor the signature pages, are included in the certified copies.

(3) Receiving any signatures and receiving and keeping custody of any instruments of ratification, acceptance, approval, accession or succession, and all other notifications and communications relating to the treaty.

(4) Examining whether the signature, or any instrument, notification or communication relating to the treaty, is in due and proper form and, in case of doubt, bringing the matter to the attention of the state in question. If the instrument is in a foreign language, the depositary notes the date of deposit as the date on which it was received, but does not acknowledge receipt until the instrument has been translated and checked. It is therefore desirable that a state depositing an instrument in a language foreign to the depositary should provide a translation. Since it is not part of the functions of the depositary to adjudicate on the legal validity or effect of an instrument, notification or communication, if it appears that there may be an irregularity, the proper course is to draw the matter to the attention of the state concerned and, if that does not resolve the matter to the satisfaction of the depositary, to bring the question to the attention of the interested states or competent organ in accordance with Article 77(2).

(5) Informing the parties, and states entitled to become parties, of acts, notifications and communications relating to the treaty. This is elaborated in Article 78 (see below).

(6) Informing the states entitled to become parties to the treaty when the number of signatures or instruments of ratification, acceptance, approval or accession required for the entry into force of the treaty has been received or deposited. The date of entry into force of the treaty is a matter which requires the depositary to form a view as to the validity of the signatures received or instruments deposited in order to reach a, at least preliminary, view as to the date of entry into force. If the depositary's appreciation of the date of entry into force were to be challenged (e.g., on the basis that an instrument was invalid), it would be bound to consult all interested states in accordance with Article 77(2).

(7) Following entry into force, registering the treaty with the Secretariat of the United Nations (see Article 80).

(8) Performing the functions specified in other provisions of the Vienna Convention or the treaty, such as the convening of a review conference, though this may be regarded more as an administrative function (see below).

Now that depositary functions are so well established and largely codified in the Convention, it is enough simply to designate a depositary on the understanding that the duties will be performed in accordance with the law of treaties and established practice. Including a list of functions in the treaty can, however, provide a useful reminder or checklist, especially if the depositary is a state which is not so familiar with the duties of a depositary. Any list should, however, be illustrative and not attempt to be exhaustive. The Convention for the Establishment of the Lake Victoria Fisheries Organisation 1994[22] lists the functions of the depositary as:

(1) sending true copies of the Convention to the contracting states;
(2) informing the contracting states of:
    (a) signature of the Convention and the deposit of instruments of ratification or accession;
    (b) the date of entry into force of the Convention;
    (c) proposals for amendments to the Convention and of the adoption of amendments;
    (d) notices of withdrawal from the organisation;
    (e) any other notification received from the contracting states; and
    (f) registration of the Convention with the United Nations.

Notifications and communications

Article 78 provides that, except as the treaty or the Convention otherwise provides, any notification or communication which the Convention requires a state to make:

(a) shall be made to the depositary or, if there is none, direct to the states for which it is intended;
(b) is considered as having been made only when it is received by the depositary or the states, as the case may be;
(c) if transmitted to a depositary, is considered received by the state for which it is intended only when that state has been informed by the depositary in accordance with Article 77(1)(e).

These rules are important for the calculation of time limits fixed by the Convention, including that in Article 20(5) for making objections to reservations, where this is applicable.[23]

---

[22] ILM (1997), p. 672 (Article XXII).   [23] See pp. 127 and 130 above.

The reference, in the *chapeau* of Article 78, to the Convention otherwise providing is to prevent any misconception as to the relationship between that article and Article 16 (exchange or deposit of instruments of ratification, etc.) and Article 24 (entry into force). Although the depositary has a duty to notify states of the deposit of an instrument of ratification, that is only for the purpose of information; the notification is not a *substantive* part of the transaction by which the depositing state establishes treaty relations with the other states. The act of deposit will have the legal effect provided for under the treaty even if the notification of it by the depositary is delayed or even overlooked. Similarly, late notification by the depositary of the date of entry into force will not affect that date.

The depositary *as a state*

If a state is the depositary of a treaty, that is not an obstacle to it becoming party to the treaty, though it has no obligation, legal or moral, to become a party. It is therefore good practice for a depositary state to maintain a clear distinction between the two roles. This is especially important if, as will often be the case, the same official is responsible for, say, both preparing and depositing the instrument of ratification of the state, and then, as depositary, receiving and recording it. Steps must be taken to avoid simple mistakes, such as overlooking the need to include the name of the depositary state in the list of states which have ratified. The depositary state itself should therefore treat itself as if it were just another state. Its officials do not have to go quite so far as sending diplomatic notes to themselves; it is enough if a memorandum concerning an act by the depositary state (signature, ratification, etc.) is recorded in the same way as acts by the other states.

Correction of errors

Unfortunately, it is quite common for errors to occur in the texts of treaties. This happens with both bilateral and multilateral treaties, though the problem is increasing in the case of multilateral treaties due to their length and complexity and the time pressure under which some of them are negotiated these days. The errors may be typographical, spelling, punctuation, numbering or cross-referencing, or a lack of concordance between the authentic language texts. It may be a simple drafting mistake, such as use of inconsistent terminology. But correcting anything which is more than an obvious 'physical' error, or mistake of spelling or numbering, may affect the substance. Punctuation is an aspect of grammar which is perhaps more crucial for some languages, including English, than others which have more precise grammatical rules. Occasionally an error of drafting, usually caused by lack of time to check the text before adoption or signature, can cause a major problem. In the form in which it had been adopted, the Statute of the International Criminal Court 1998 contained some incomplete cross-references which, if not corrected, could have had a substantive effect.[24]

Attention may be drawn to an error by a state or the depositary. If there is a dispute as to whether there is an error, the problem may have to be decided in accordance with Article 48 (Error),[25] not Article 79, which deals with corrections only where there is no dispute as to the existence of the error. It is more likely, however, that there will be no dispute, merely a difference of view as to how to deal with the matter.

In January 1997 the Preparatory Commission for the Comprehensive Nuclear-Test-Ban Treaty 1996 informed the negotiating states that the text of the attachments to the Treaty contained several errors. The location or names of some monitoring stations were wrong, and in some cases the location had been found to be unsuitable. The errors did not come to light until after the authentic text had been prepared by the depositary, the UN Secretary-General, and would have been obvious only to someone with an intimate knowledge of the technical details. It was suggested that, once agreement had been reached by the negotiating states on what to do, the text could be 'corrected' in accordance with the procedure in Article 79 of the Convention. However, although corrections to the *details* of locations and names might be done in this way, to replace the entries for the stations which had been found to be unsuitable with other ones would amount to a substantive change, and this could only be done by amending the text, if necessary before entry into force.[26]

Since the subject of corrections is discrete, the reader is referred to the text of Article 79 in which the procedure for correcting errors is set out in detail. It is enough to draw attention to certain points:

---

[24] ILM (1998), p. 1002. Article 121(5) should have cross-referred to Articles 6, 7 and 8 as well.
[25] See p. 254 above.   [26] See p. 222 above.

(1) Paragraph 1 deals with the case where there is *no depositary*, as is normally the case with a bilateral treaty, and applies even if the treaty has not yet entered into force (note the reference to 'the signatory states and the contracting states', rather than to the parties). The paragraph lays down a residuary rule, it being essentially for the states concerned to decide what, if anything, to do about the error. In the case of a bilateral treaty there will normally be two original texts, possibly in two languages, whether the treaty is in a single instrument or an exchange of notes. Making corrections therefore needs to be done with particular care. If the error is only typographical, and the treaty has not yet been published, one method is for one foreign ministry to send the other, under cover of a third-person diplomatic note, a photocopy of the original text with the corrections written-in clearly by hand. Once the corrections have been agreed, an authorised official on each side can then make them on the original held by it, initialling each correction. If required by one of the states, the corrections can be confirmed by a further third-person note. But, if the error is more than typographical, or the treaty has been published, the most prudent course is for the agreed corrections to be set out in an exchange of notes (Appendix N). Since the notes will be recording only corrections, not amendments, the exchange should *not* be expressed to constitute an agreement (which could make the exchange itself a treaty).[27] There will be no need to publish the exchange, a corrigendum to the published text being sufficient.

(2) Paragraph 2 deals with the case where there is a depositary. It does not lay down a residuary rule, and applies even before the treaty has entered into force. Whether he has been alerted to the error, or discovered it himself, the depositary must initiate the correction procedure by notifying the signatory states and contracting states of the error and the proposed correction. In practice, the UN Secretary-General will communicate proposed corrections to all states which participated in the elaboration of the treaty, even though only the signatory and contracting states have the right to object to a correction.[28] No rule is laid down in the Convention, or otherwise, as to the legal effect of an objection to a proposed correction, though when an objection is not soundly based the depositary can usually negotiate its withdrawal.[29] The United Nations follows customary practice in usually specifying a ninety-day time limit for any objections, but will sometimes set a shorter one, especially if the errors were already well known to the states. If there is no objection, an authorised official of the depositary makes the correction to the text of the deposited treaty, initialling each correction. The depositary then draws up a *procès-verbal* recording this, and circulates it for informa-

---

[27] Cf. pp. 355–8 below.   [28] *UN Depositary Practice*, paras. 53–4.   [29] *Ibid.*, paras. 61–2.

tion to the signatory and contracting states (when consulting the states it may be useful to include a draft *procès-verbal*). A specimen by a depositary state is at Appendix O.

(3) The rules in paragraphs 1 and 2 apply also where there is a divergence between texts authenticated in more than one language. Although this can be due to simple errors in translation, sometimes the difference can raise a point of substance. This can happen when the treaty was negotiated in only one language and this has resulted in a misunderstanding. It might, for example contain a *faux ami*. In contemporary English 'alternatives' can refer to two *or more* options. In French, 'alternatives' refers to two options; more than two being 'options'. The matter may then have to be dealt with under Article 48.[30]

(4) The corrected text is deemed to operate from the date of the original text, unless otherwise agreed.

(5) Where the error is found only in the certified copies of the treaty provided by the depositary (which is all that the interested states will usually hold), the depositary does not have to go through the procedure of paragraph 2: it is sufficient for it to execute a *proces-verbal* and communicate it to the interested states.

Administrative functions

Although not strictly depositary functions, a depositary may also be entrusted by the treaty with functions such as maintaining a list of conciliators (see the Annex to the Vienna Convention) or convening meetings of the parties. Under the Partial Nuclear-Test-Ban Treaty 1963 (PTBT), the three states designated as the depositaries, the Soviet Union (now Russia), the United Kingdom and the United States, have the additional functions of circulating proposed amendments and convening amendment conferences. Although such functions are also often given to a depositary, they are more difficult for a state depositary to discharge, and even more difficult when they are joint depositaries, as well as being parties to the treaty. The PTBT has an 'all states' participation clause[31] which can cause the three depositaries a particularly acute problem when they are faced with the question whether, for example, an entity is a state which has succeeded to the PTBT and is thus entitled to be invited to attend a review conference.[32]

As discussed earlier,[33] the UN Secretary-General, as depositary of the Comprehensive Nuclear-Test-Ban Treaty 1996 (CTBT), might have been

---

[30] See p. 254 above.   [31] See p. 92 above.   [32] See p. 316 below.   [33] See p. 266 above.

faced with the problem of whether to convene a conference in 1999 or 2000 if the contracting states had not reached agreement on this. In such circumstances a wise depositary will consult the states concerned and take no action until there is a consensus.

19

Registration and publication

Order is heaven's first law.[1]

McNair emphasised the importance of registering and publishing treaties, and saw the *United Nations Treaty Series* (UNTS) as 'an indispensable piece of international apparatus'.[2] As we shall see, it can be surprisingly difficult to find the text of many treaties, particularly recent ones. This chapter will explain the procedure for registering a treaty and offer suggestions on how find the texts of treaties and information about their status.

Registration

Although the successful negotiation of a treaty may require secrecy, its adoption requires openness. Abhorrence at the discovery of secret treaties during and in the immediate aftermath of the First World War, and President Woodrow Wilson's call for 'open covenants', resulted in Article 18 of the Covenant of the League of Nations.[3] This required every new treaty entered into by any member of the League to be registered forthwith with the Secretariat and published by it as soon as possible. Until registered the treaty was not binding. No less than 4,834 were registered.

Article 102(1) of the United Nations Charter requires that 'every treaty *and every international agreement*' entered into by any Member of the United Nations after the Charter comes into force be registered with the Secretariat as soon as possible, and then published by it. Article 80 of the Vienna Convention requires a party to it to register any treaty to which it is a party once it is in force. By the end of 1998 over 40,000 treaties had been registered. In the ten years from 1988 to 1998, on average 1,200 treaties were registered each year.

---

[1] Alexander Pope (1688–1744), *An Essay on Man*, IV, 49.   [2] McNair, p. 179.
[3] See the quotation at the beginning of p. 26; and McNair, p. 179.

The term 'international agreement' was intended to embrace unilateral engagements of an international character made by one state in favour of another and accepted by the other state, implied acceptance being enough. The Secretariat therefore treats such engagements as agreements.[4] Thus declarations under Article 36(2) of the Statute of the International Court of Justice accepting its compulsory jurisdiction are registered. The unilateral declaration of 1957 by Egypt by which it reaffirmed its respect for the Constantinople Convention 1888, and specified the future arrangements for the Suez Canal, stated that it contained obligations and constituted an international instrument which would be registered with the United Nations, which it was.[5]

Some treaties are required to be registered also with other international organisations. Article 83 of the Chicago Convention on International Civil Aviation 1944 requires the parties to register 'arrangements' with the ICAO Council, although there is no sanction for not registering. The requirement does not, however, avoid the need to register air services agreements with the United Nations.[6]

Regulations and procedure

Detailed regulations on registration have been drawn up by the UN General Assembly in consultation with the Secretariat.[7] The main rules are:

(1) A treaty is not registered until it has entered into force for at least two parties. This important pre-condition is sometimes overlooked by states. There is no time limit for registration.

(2) Registration may be done by any party and relieves all other parties of the obligation to register.

(3) The United Nations must register *ex officio* every treaty which authorises the United Nations to register it; which designates the United Nations as the depositary; or to which the United Nations is a party.

(4) All subsequent actions effecting changes in a treaty, such as amendment or termination, must be registered. By the end of 1998 some 40,000 such actions had been registered.

(5) A treaty which has already been terminated may still be registered.

---

[4] M. Tabory, 'Registration of the Egypt–Israel Peace Treaty: Some Legal Aspects', ICLQ (1983), p. 981 at p. 989.   [5] 265 UNTS 299; AJIL (1957), pp. 673–5; McNair, p. 11.
[6] See also pp. 35–6 above.   [7] 859 UNTS xii.

(6) The date of receipt of the treaty by the Secretariat, or the date of entry into force in the case of registration *ex officio*, is deemed to be the date of registration. Since the Secretariat has a duty to effect the registration of any treaty lodged with it for that purpose – provided it has entered into force – the act of registration is regarded as that of the registering state, not of the Secretariat. This can be important if the status of the instrument is disputed.[8]

The Regulations are at Appendix P.

To register a treaty one must file the following documents with the Treaty Section of the Office of Legal Affairs of the United Nations:

(1) A copy of the treaty (certified true and complete) in *all* its authentic languages.

(2) Either *two* additional copies *or* a copy on diskette (preferably WordPerfect 6.1 for Windows) and one hard copy. If the treaty is not in English and/or French, a translation into one or both languages should be supplied in the same form and with the same number of copies. Eventually it is hoped that texts can be transmitted to the Secretariat by e-mail.

(3) The text of any reservations or declarations.

(4) If it is not clear from the text, the title of the treaty, the names of those who signed, and the date and place of signature.

(5) The date on which the treaty entered into force for each party and the method by which this was done.

A checklist of the material to be provided, and a model certification statement, is at Appendix Q.

The text of the treaty and related documents will appear, usually some years later, in the UNTS in all the authentic languages, and if these do not include English and French with translations into those languages.

Associated documents

Provided it meets the basic conditions of the regulations, any document lodged with the Secretariat for registration will be registered. If the treaty provides that certain protocols, annexes, maps, etc. are integral to it they must be registered, and they will be published with the treaty in the UNTS even if they are ephemeral. A treaty will not be registered if an associated document which is an integral part of the treaty has not been submitted for registration. If a treaty presented for registration refers to a previous, but

---

[8] See pp. 278–80 below.

unregistered, treaty or to unpublished non-treaty texts, such as unilateral notes, it is the practice of the Secretariat to ask the registering state to supply copies for registration, and publication with the treaty in due course.[9]

However, states must take care over MOUs. As explained earlier, an MOU can either stand alone or be supplementary to a treaty.[10] It may be confidential; and of course it is not a treaty. Therefore, before an MOU which is referred to in a treaty, or which is associated with it, is supplied to the Secretariat, it is important that its non-treaty *and* non-confidential status has been confirmed by all states concerned.

Joint registration

On rare occasions the parties to a bilateral treaty will, as a political gesture, each submit it for registration. An example is the Sino-British Joint Declaration on the Question of Hong Kong 1984.[11] But problems can arise if the two texts differ or each party lodges a different set of associated documents. The difficulties in the latter case were well illustrated in the (admittedly special) case of the Treaty of Peace between Egypt and Israel of 1979, which was accompanied by a complex of minutes, letters and other documents. Since the parties could not agree which of these should be registered, the Secretariat registered and published separately the set of documents lodged by each party.[12]

Article 80 of the Convention goes further than Article 102 of the UN Charter, in that it requires parties to the Convention to transmit treaties to the United Nations even if they are not Members of the United Nations. In the latter case, the United Nations will not register them as such, but will 'file and record' them, and publish them in Part II of the UNTS. A state which is neither a party to the Convention, nor a Member of the United Nations, may nevertheless transmit a treaty to the United Nations, where it will also be filed and recorded, and published in Part II.

Legal effect of registration or non-registration

The Secretariat will check that an instrument which is presented for registration is, on the face of it, a treaty. Now and then it has refused registra-

---

[9] UN Juridical YB (1979), pp. 195–7.   [10] See pp. 34–5 above.
[11] 1399 UNTS 33 (No. 23391); ILM (1984), p. 1366; UKTS (1985) 26.
[12] Tabory, 'Registration', (note 4 above) pp. 981–1003, especially notes 10 and 11; ILM (1979), pp. 362–89 and 530–6.

tion.[13] Although the vast majority of instruments presented for registration are without doubt treaties, some which would generally be regarded as MOUs are on rare occasions registered.[14] But the act of registration, as such, has no effect on the status of the instrument. The UN Secretariat in registering an instrument does not pass judgment on its status, and registration does not confer on it any status which it does not already have.[15] When registration has been effected, the Secretariat notifies only the registering party. In a small number of cases a party will register as a treaty an instrument which another party regards as an MOU, yet the latter will probably remain unaware of the registration unless a dispute about the instrument arises.[16]

When there is a dispute as to whether it is a treaty, the fact that the instrument has, or has not, been submitted for registration may, depending on the circumstances, be evidence of the intention of the states concerned as to its status. Article 102 does not say on whom the obligation to register rests, and registration by one party (which is usual) is evidence only that that party regards the instrument as a treaty. Nor is the lack of any protest at the registration necessarily evidence that other parties accept that the instrument is a treaty, since states do not routinely monitor registrations. The 1963 Agreed Minutes between Iraq and Kuwait, which formed the basis of the decision by the UN Security Council to help arrange for their common boundary to be demarcated, were registered by Kuwait in 1964. After its invasion of Kuwait in 1990, Iraq maintained that it had never been bound by the Agreed Minutes.[17] In *Qatar v. Bahrain*, Qatar submitted for registration 'Minutes' of December 1990 (which it claimed constituted the agreement of the two states to submit their dispute to the International Court of Justice) in June 1991, only ten days before it made its application to the Court. The Court admitted the Minutes since it found them to constitute a treaty, their status being unaffected by the objections of Bahrain or late registration.[18]

Equally, non-registration is, at least on its own, not evidence that the

---

[13] *Repertory of Practice of the United Nations Organs*, vol. V, pp. 295–6.   [14] See pp. 33–4 above.
[15] See p. 29 above; and see generally D. Hutchinson, 'The Significance of the Registration or Non-Registration of an International Agreement in Determining Whether or Not it is a Treaty', *Current Legal Problems* (1993), pp. 257–90.   [16] See pp. 33–4 above.
[17] 485 UNTS 321 and UN Security Council Resolution 687(1991). See Mendelson and Hulton, 'The Iraq–Kuwait Boundary', BYIL (1993), pp. 135–95; and by the same authors, 'La Revendication par l'Iraq de la Souveraineté sur le Koweït', *Annuaire Français de Droit International* (1990), p. 195.
[18] *ICJ Reports* (1994), p. 112, paras. 21–30; ILM (1994), p. 1461. And see p. 276, para. (1), above.

instrument is not a treaty. There are many reasons why what are obviously treaties are not registered: ignorance of the requirement or of the rules or procedures, inertia, lack of staff or simple oversight.

The intention of the parties as to the status of the instrument can be put beyond doubt by an express provision that it is (or is not) eligible for registration, as was done at the end of the Helsinki Final Act 1975,[19] and it would be a bold step indeed for any court to disregard such a clear indication of the common will of the parties.

It has been suggested that as many as 25 per cent of treaties are not registered.[20] Article 102(2) of the Charter of the United Nations provides that no party to any treaty entered into by a Member of the United Nations which has not been registered may invoke it before any organ of the United Nations. However, the principal judicial organ of the United Nations, the International Court of Justice, does not apply the provision strictly, or perhaps at all. In *Qatar v. Bahrain*, the 1987 double Exchange of Letters which the parties did agree constituted a treaty, but which had not been registered, were invoked before the Court, which gave full regard to its terms.[21] Other organs of the United Nations have on occasion allowed states to invoke an unregistered treaty; and it is unthinkable that the Security Council would ignore a treaty which is relevant to a matter of international peace and security just because it was not registered. The sanction in Article 102(2) would appear from the practice of principal organs of the United Nations to be more honoured in the breach than the observance.[22]

Publication

There is no international rule requiring a state to publish a treaty. Finding the text of a treaty, especially a new treaty, or even finding proof of a treaty's existence, is not at all easy.[23] The problem affects practitioners as

[19] ILM (1975), p. 1293. See also p. 28 above.
[20] P. Reuter, *Introduction to the Law of Treaties* (2nd English edn, 1995), note to para. 86.
[21] *ICJ Reports* (1994), p. 112, paras. 17–19 and 22; ILM (1994), p. 1461.
[22] *Hamlet*, I, iv, 14. See also Hutchinson, 'Significance', (note 15 above), p. 279; R. Higgins, *The Development of International Law through the Political Organs of the United Nations* (1963), p. 334; and McNair, pp. 186–9.
[23] R. Gardiner, 'Treaties and Treaty Materials: Role, Relevance and Accessibility', ICLQ (1997), pp. 643–66; S. Rosenne, *Practice and Methods of International Law* (1984), pp. 48–51; C. Parry, 'Where to Look for Your Treaties', *International Journal for Law Libraries* (February 1980); A. Sprudzs, 'Status of Multilateral Treaties: Researcher's Mystery, Mess or Muddle?,' AJIL (1972), p. 365.

much as scholars and students. Because a treaty cannot be published in the UNTS until it has entered into force and has been registered, and the publication of both the UNTS and its *Index* are still some years behind (though things should now improve), one has to rely heavily on governmental or commercial sources.

Publication by the United Nations

Article 102 requires the Secretariat of the United Nations to publish treaties registered with it. It does this by publishing them in the single series of the UNTS, although it no longer publishes in full (1) treaties of assistance and co-operation on financial, commercial, administrative or technical matters, (2) treaties relating to the organisation of conferences, seminars or meetings, and (3) treaties that are published by a specialised or related agency (e.g., the IAEA).[24] Publication is done in all the authentic languages, and if these do not include English and French, with translations into those languages. By the end of 1998 the UNTS consisted of some 1,550 volumes, containing over 30,000 of the treaties which had been registered. However, because a treaty can be registered only once it has entered into force, and publication of the UNTS was in 1998 some four to five years behind, the UNTS is not, at present, a good source for the texts of treaties which entered into force less than about four years ago. At the root of the problem has been lack of money. However, by the end of 2001, it is hoped that all treaties will be published (on paper) within one to two years of registration.

All treaties which have been registered are available on the UN website (http://www.un.org/depts/treaty), but only once they have been published in the UNTS, and so far only in English. The UN website is accessed for the UNTS over 40,000 times a week. New treaties are added on a regular basis. But it is intended that by about the end of 2001 the full text of every treaty will be available, on the website only, immediately after registration. The *Index* to all treaties in the UNTS is now also available on the website. However, as with the paper version of the *Index*, it is out of date, although the search mechanism has made the paper index largely obsolete.

Unfortunately, searching for a treaty on the website is not that easy unless one knows if it has been registered and, if so, the registration

---

[24] UN Doc. A//RES/53/153, para. 7.

number (which is why this book often gives the registration number). But, if one has the reference to the volume of the UNTS in which the treaty is published, or an *International Legal Materials* (ILM) reference, and easy access to those publications, it may be simpler and quicker to look up the treaty there.

The UN Secretary-General is also the depositary of over 500 multilateral treaties. The annual publication, *Multilateral Treaties Deposited with the Secretary-General* (in this book referred to as *UN Multilateral Treaties*), is an authoritative guide to the status of those treaties, containing as it does information on signatures, ratifications, accessions, successions, declarations, reservations, objections and entry into force. It is published in English and French. It is normally published each year in March or April. The English version (and in the future the French) is available on the website, where it is updated every two to three days. It is accessed over 3,000 times a week.[25]

Publication by states

Whether, or when, a treaty is published by a state is dependent on its constitution, legislation and practice. Publication may be in an official gazette or journal, or in an official treaty series. Although most states publish treaties, the extent to which this is done varies greatly, publication by some states being not comprehensive. The increasing number of treaties has led to some states dispensing with the publication of 'routine' treaties, such as those dealing with short-term aid projects. Where a treaty has to be submitted to parliament before it can be signed or ratified, it will usually have to be published.

In the United Kingdom all treaties which the United Kingdom has concluded, and which are subject to ratification, accession, acceptance, approval, or a similar procedure, are laid before (i.e., formally presented to) Parliament in accordance with the constitutional practice known as the 'Ponsonby Rule'.[26] Although such treaties are not published in an official journal, they are published by the Government as *Command Papers* in the *Country, European Communities* or *Miscellaneous Series.*

---

[25] Further information about the UN treaty collection can be provided by: Treaty Section, Office of Legal Affairs, United Nations, New York NY10017, USA (fax: ++1 212 963 3693; e-mail: treaty@un.org).   [26] See p. 151 above.

Since 1 January 1997, each treaty laid before Parliament under the Ponsonby Rule is accompanied by a brief explanatory memorandum, which is published on the internet,[27] but not the text of the treaty.[28]

The United Kingdom is, or has been, party to over 12,400 treaties. Since 1892 every treaty, once it has entered into force for the United Kingdom, has been published in the *United Kingdom Treaty Series* (UKTS). If it enters into force on signature, it will generally be published only in the UKTS, not as a Command Paper. The UKTS is not published in volumes, each treaty being issued separately. Since 1973 only the English text of multilateral treaties has been published. Earlier British treaties dating back to at least 1812 can be found in *British and Foreign State Papers* (BFSP).

In contrast to some (chiefly monist) states, neither laying a treaty before Parliament, nor its publication in the *United Kingdom Treaty Series* has legal effect; neither procedure makes the treaty part of the law of the United Kingdom.[29]

Other sources of treaty texts

A prime source of modern treaty texts is *International Legal Materials* (ILM) which has been published by the American Society of International Law since 1962. Published six times a year, it has become an invaluable source for texts of recently concluded treaties (and some MOUs), whether bilateral or multilateral, which may be of general interest to public international lawyers, whether practitioners, academics or students. It is very often the quickest, or only, way to find a new treaty or one whose entry into force, or publication in the UNTS, is considerably delayed.

Texts of multilateral treaties and related material are also available on the internet through the Multilaterals Project begun in 1992 at the Fletcher School of Law and Diplomacy at Tufts University, Massachusetts, USA. The data includes a list of treaty secretariats with their web addresses (http://www.tufts.edu/fletcher/multilaterals.html). Up-to-date information on developments of interest to the more computer-literate lawyer is

---

[27] http://www.fco.gov.uk/treaty.asp.

[28] *Hansard*, House of Lords, 16 December 1996, column 101; BYIL (1996), p. 753.

[29] See p. 151 above. Further information can be obtained from: Treaty Section, Records and Historical Department, Foreign and Commonwealth Office, London, SW1A 2AH, UK (fax: ++44(0)20 7 210 3841; e-mail: treaty.rhd.fco@gtnet.gov.uk; website: http://www.fco.gov.uk/treaty.asp).

given regularly in *What's Online in International Law*, published in the news-letters of the American Society of International Law (http://www.asil.org). The website of the Lauterpacht Research Centre for International Law at Cambridge, England (http://www.law.cam.ac.uk/rcil/home.htm) may also be worth a browse.

For the text of treaties concluded between 1648 (Treaty of Westphalia) and 1919 the best source is the 231-volume *Consolidated Treaty Series* (CTS), though not all the treaties have been translated into English or French. For those concluded between 1919 and 1946, one should consult the 205-volume *League of Nations Treaty Series* (LNTS). For US treaties there is *Treaties and other International Acts Series* (TIAS) issued in single pamphlets, and *United States Treaties and other International Agreements* (UST) published in annual volumes since 1950.[30] The 100-plus volumes of the *International Law Reports* (ILR), with its excellent index, are an impor-tant source for the decisions of courts and tribunals, international and national, on treaty matters.

Treaty indexes

Apart from the UN treaty publications, there are certain other indepen-dent treaty indexes. Treaty collections are listed in the *United Nations List of Treaty Collections*,[31] though it is now out of date. For the main multilat-eral treaties since 1856 there is Bowman and Harris, *Multilateral Treaties, Index and Current Status* and its cumulative supplements (London and Nottingham, 1984–). Rohn's *World Treaty Index* (2nd edn, 1984) may also be worth consulting. The annual index to *Treaties and other International Acts Series* (TIAS) can be a useful source.

For United Kingdom bilateral and multilateral treaties there is Parry's four-volume *Index of British Treaties 1101 to 1988* (HMSO, 1970 and 1991). The UKTS has annual (but not cumulative) indexes and quarterly *Supplementary Lists of Ratifications, Accessions, Withdrawals etc.* These contain information on reservations, participation, etc., and are not limited to actions by the United Kingdom.

---

[30] Now available on the internet: see the Oceana website at http://www.oceanalaw.com.
[31] ST/LEG/5 (2nd edn, 1981).

20

Settlement of disputes

war settles *nothing* . . . to win a war is as disastrous as to lose one!

So shrewdly wrote, Agatha Christie.[1] This chapter outlines the main methods of settling disputes between states, with particular reference to disputes under treaties. The account is simplified. For example, it should not be assumed that all dispute settlement clauses refer to only one method of settlement. Many provide a choice, a sort of 'mix and match'. There are no hard and fast rules. The means devised for settling disputes are many and various. The reader is advised to consult the many works on the subject, and, in particular, that by Professor Merrills[2] and the UN *Handbook on the Peaceful Settlement of Disputes between States.*[3]

Treaties give rise to numerous disputes about their interpretation or application. Although the two terms are usually mentioned in the same breath, strictly speaking when the meaning is clear, the text is applied; when it is not clear, it has to be interpreted.[4] The methods are no different to those used for other disputes in international law, except that many treaties prescribe how disputes about them may be settled. Many disputes are settled quickly and informally; others can take many years to resolve; some are never resolved; and some it is better to manage rather than attempt a resolution.[5] There is no one method by which disputes of a certain kind are dealt with; not even one generally used method. The means used for disputes under a multilateral treaty are essentially the same

---

[1] *Autobiography* (1977), Part 10 (Miss Christie's emphasis).
[2] J. Merrills, *International Dispute Settlement* (3rd edn, 1998). See also the short but invaluable practical guide by Professor Bowett, 'The Conduct of International Litigation', in Gardner and Wickremsinghe (eds.), *The International Court of Justice, Process, Practice and Procedure* (British Institute for International and Comparative Law, 1997), pp. 1–20.
[3] Published by the United Nations in 1992.   [4] McNair, p. 365, note 1.
[5] See R. Jennings, 'The Role of the International Court of Justice', BYIL (1997), p. 1 at p. 51, note 100, where he cites as an example the Antarctic Treaty 1959 (402 UNTS 71 (No. 5778); UKTS (1961) 97) in which the parties have effectively frozen their sovereignty disputes.

as for a bilateral treaty, since the dispute is usually between only two of the parties. Nor is the method necessarily dictated either by the importance or magnitude of the dispute or how long it has lasted. There are treaty disputes which are never settled even when a method is specified in the treaty (it will now be obvious that 'settle' is here being used in the more general sense of 'resolve', and not in its narrow meaning of agreeing terms upon which pending litigation will be ended).

Article 33 of the United Nations Charter elaborates on the basic principle enunciated in Article 2(3) of the Charter, that all Members shall settle their international disputes by peaceful means, and lists the most usual means: negotiation, mediation, conciliation, arbitration and judicial settlement. The methods can be broadly divided into voluntary and compulsory, depending on whether or not the parties to a dispute are under a treaty obligation to enter into a particular means of settlement. But this does not mean that under a voluntary process the parties will never be bound by the result; nor that under a compulsory process the result will always be binding: it depends entirely on the terms agreed.

Voluntary settlement

Negotiations and consultations

There is of course nothing to prevent the parties to a dispute seeking to resolve it by direct negotiations. In fact, this is normally the first step in any dispute, and even if the dispute is to be referred to arbitration or judicial settlement it is desirable that the point at issue should be defined by negotiation. Since negotiations can be held in decent privacy, it may be easier to reach a settlement. Once a dispute is elevated to a more formal or public level, it may be more difficult, at least politically, to settle it; positions become entrenched and public 'face' requires that neither side is seen to compromise.

Negotiating procedures are infinitely flexible, the process being completely under the control of the parties. Once a third party is brought in to help reach a settlement, negotiations may gain a momentum of their own which the parties (at least individually) may not be able to stop or influence effectively. This may be one reason why most disputes are settled by negotiation; though it may also be true that most disputes are not so intractable that the parties have to resort to more formal methods. One should treat with caution proposals for still further general treaties on dispute settlement. There are already sufficient for those states which wish to use them. And, although formal methods of dispute settlement have an important role to play, they are generally no substitute for a carefully negotiated settlement.

There is no significant difference between consultations and negotiations, though consultations are often made a formal pre-condition for moving to a third-party settlement procedure. The settlement of disputes provision in the UK–US Air Services Agreement 1977 ('Bermuda 2') provides for a dispute to be the subject of a 'first round of consultations' before it can be submitted by either party to third-party settlement,[6] and 'first round' is generally understood to mean at least two meetings with a gap in between.

Some treaties require the parties to a dispute to do no more than enter into consultations or negotiations with a view to reaching a settlement or to agreeing on another method of settlement. These have to be implemented in good faith (Article 26). Thus, the negotiations must be conducted purposefully.

Negotiations can last as long as the parties wish, and may be stopped and resumed at any time. Some dispute settlement clauses, however, prescribe a time limit after which either party is free to invoke whatever third-party means of settlement is provided for in the treaty.

If the negotiations are successful it is essential for the parties to record what they have agreed. The form will depend on the circumstances. It may involve an amendment to the treaty or a public statement. If the parties do not want publicity they may record the terms of settlement in an unpublished MOU. For the reasons already given, the MOU, though not itself legally binding, may nevertheless have legal consequences, as was demonstrated in the award in the UK–US User Charges Arbitration.[7]

If the negotiations are not successful, one of the parties may decide to terminate the treaty. This could be described as *the other way of settling a dispute*. Since 1945 the United Kingdom has, because of unresolved disputes, terminated at least four air services agreements: with the Philippines (1953 and 1984), the United States (1976) and Lebanon (1981)).[8]

---

[6] 1079 UNTS 21 (No. 16509); UKTS (1977) 76.
[7] 102 ILR 215, especially pp. 561–4. And see p. 46 above.
[8] A. Aust, 'Air Services Agreements: Current United Kingdom Procedures and Policies', *Air Law* (1985), p. 189, at pp. 198–9.

Sometimes a dispute becomes so bad that termination and starting afresh is the only way out of the impasse. It does not, of course, mean that the dispute may not still be settled by reference to a third party if the treaty provides for this (a disputes clause may remain in force in relation to matters occurring before termination of the treaty),[9] or if the parties agree to this course. But termination can have the advantage of drawing a line under the dispute and enabling the parties to negotiate a new treaty to their mutual satisfaction.

Involvement of third parties

If it is not possible to settle a dispute by negotiation, it may be necessary to seek the help of a third party. Whether this will be successful – and even whether it will be possible – will depend on various factors. One will be the degree of co-operation between the parties. Despite the existence of several general treaties on the settlement of disputes, in many cases there will be no agreement binding the parties to any means of third-party settlement for the particular dispute. It will then be necessary to negotiate – probably in unfavourable circumstances – an *ad hoc* agreement on a means of settlement. If the method is mediation or conciliation, unless the agreement provides for the parties to accept the recommendations of the third party (which is not usual), neither party will be bound by them.

Conciliation

Conciliation may be provided for in the treaty itself or in a general treaty on the settlement of disputes to which the parties in dispute are both bound,[10] or it may be agreed *ad hoc*. The nature of conciliation is neatly expressed in the Annex to the Vienna Convention itself, which provides for the conciliation of disputes between parties to the Convention in certain limited circumstances. Part of it provides that:

(4) The [Conciliation] Commission may draw the attention of the parties to the dispute to any measures which might facilitate an amicable settlement.

---

[9] See pp. 246–7 above.
[10] The OSCE Convention on Conciliation and Arbitration 1992 (ILM (1993), p. 557) provides for compulsory conciliation, though the outcome is not binding: see A. Bloed (ed.), *The Conference on Security and Co-operation in Europe* (1993), p. 870.

(5) The Commission shall hear the parties, examine the claims and objections, and make proposals to the parties with a view to reaching an amicable settlement of the dispute.

This formula became a model for multilateral treaties, in particular for the
United Nations Convention on the Law of the Sea 1982.[11]

A conciliation commission is usually composed of three to five
members, one (or two) members being appointed by each party and a
third member chosen by the appointed members to serve as chairman. If a
party fails to appoint its member (or members), or there is no agreement
on the choice of the third member, it is customary to provide for the necessary appointments to be made by an eminent independent person, such
as the President of the International Court of Justice or the UN Secretary-
General. It is therefore essential to set time limits for all appointments
so as to avoid one party obstructing the process. The Annex to the
Convention itself provides a useful model for multilateral treaties, and was
a model for provisions which, by providing for a permanent list of conciliators, avoid the problem of leaving the appointments of conciliators
solely in the hands of the parties in dispute.[12]

Conciliation is inevitably more expensive than negotiation, since each
party will not only have to pay its own expenses, including the fees of any
outside lawyers or experts it engages, but it will normally have to pay half
of the costs of the conciliators, their accommodation and staff.

The results of a conciliation are almost invariably non-binding. Once
again the matter is well expressed in the Annex to the Convention:

(6) . . . The report of the Commission, including any conclusions stated
therein regarding the facts or questions of law, shall not be binding
upon the parties and it shall have no other character than that of recommendations submitted for the consideration of the parties in order to
facilitate an amicable settlement of the dispute.

Thus, conciliation is, from one point of view, usually less effective
than arbitration or judicial settlement, the results of which are binding,
yet it can be as expensive and time-consuming. If conciliation has not
led to a settlement, unless the parties can then agree to take the dispute to

[11] ILM (1982), p. 1261; UN Reg. No. 31363; UKTS (1999) 81 (Annex V, Articles 5 and 6).
[12] For a bilateral precedent, see the Switzerland–United Kingdom Treaty for Conciliation,
Judicial Settlement and Arbitration 1965 (605 UNTS 205 (No. 8765); ILM (1965), p. 943;
UKTS (1967) 42).

arbitration or judicial settlement (further expense), there may be no practicable means for settling it.

Mediation and good offices

Mediation is usually an *ad hoc* method involving the intervention of a third person in an attempt to reconcile the claims of the parties by advancing ideas of his own for a compromise. It is more of a political process and, as such, it may not be suitable for the resolution of a dispute about the interpretation or application of a treaty. Good offices are very similar in nature (indeed, the terms are almost interchangeable) and consist in a third person (these days often the UN Secretary-General, or rather his special representative) giving his impartial assistance in an effort to help resolve the dispute. The process therefore suffers from the same weaknesses as mediation, at least as far as treaty disputes are concerned.

Compulsory binding settlement

As with the hydrogen bomb, the real value of compulsory binding settlement is that a party should not have to resort to such a means, the party in the wrong being only too well aware that if it persists in its unlawful action it risks all the trouble and expense of international legal proceedings, and probably judgment against it. Of course, governments do not always act rationally, and some will take a risk or view legal proceedings as a useful way of buying time. In many cases there will, of course, be a genuine dispute which cannot be settled in any other way. Nevertheless, even though one cannot know to what extent the threat, or simply the possibility, of compulsory settlement influences the decisions of states, on the analogy of domestic legal disputes it is reasonable to assume that the deterrent factor is significant.

The settlement of a dispute between states by compulsory means requires their consent. Therefore, whether a party to a dispute is legally bound to submit the dispute to any method of dispute settlement depends on whether it has agreed to do so, either in advance of the dispute arising or subsequently.

The two principal characteristics of compulsory binding settlement are a prior agreement to submit disputes to a third party and a decision by the third party which is legally binding on the parties. This may be provided for in the treaty which is the subject of the dispute, in a general treaty on the settlement of disputes to which the parties in dispute are bound, or *ad hoc*. But even if a treaty provides for a method of compulsory third-party settlement, unless the provision is tightly drafted one party may, in practice, be able to delay the process.

Arbitration

Arbitration is the submission of a dispute to a judge or judges in principle chosen by the parties who agree to accept and respect the judgment. The judges are termed 'arbitrators' and their judgment is usually referred to as an 'award'. Although some arbitrations are conducted by a single arbitrator, this is really only suitable for a relatively simple case involving a narrow, essentially factual, point. It is normally better to have only one arbitrator appointed by each party and one, or preferably three, other arbitrators, the appointments being made as for a conciliation commission (see above).[13] Not only will those appointed by each party be able to explain further their state's position, they will be able to share what may be a considerable workload. Although it may be more common to have only three arbitrators (as in the Iran–US Claims Tribunal), this is not ideal since the chairman will then need the support of one of the arbitrators appointed by a party in order to reach a decision. To do this he may have to compromise; three 'neutral' arbitrators do not have the same obstacles to reaching an honest decision.[14]

Many multilateral and bilateral treaties contain arbitration clauses and, apart perhaps from a regional court such as the European Court of Justice, many more treaty disputes are decided by arbitration than by judicial settlement. Although it is unquantifiable, the possibility that another party to a treaty could take a dispute to arbitration is a powerful deterrent to a state contemplating breach of the treaty, especially if it is a bilateral treaty. It is for this reason that many arbitrations about treaties concern genuine differences of view, not blatant flouting of treaty obligations.

That arbitration is more common is certainly not because it is necessarily quicker, cheaper or less complicated, but because the parties are better able to control the process. If they want a quick decision they can more easily direct the tribunal to finish by a specific date. This is helped by the

---

[13] See, for example, *ibid.*, Article 16.   [14] Bowett, 'Conduct', (note 2 above), p. 9.

fact that, even with five arbitrators, reaching a decision will be that much easier than with the fifteen judges of the International Court of Justice. But, such advantages have to be weighed against the fact that all the costs of the arbitrators, the registrar, other staff and accommodation have to be borne by the parties (normally split equally whatever the outcome), in addition to their own costs. And, since an arbitral tribunal has to be constituted for each case and its rules of procedure may have to be agreed, the mere setting up of the tribunal can take many months. As we shall see, judicial settlement has certain distinct advantages over arbitration. In 1998, in the *M/V Saiga (No. 2)* case, the parties, Saint Vincent and the Grenadines and Guinea, after beginning arbitration proceedings, then agreed to take their dispute to the International Tribunal for the Law of the Sea.[15]

It is often said that the nature of the arbitration process is such that the result is usually a compromise. This may be so, but it would seem from some recent judgments of the International Court of Justice that even fifteen judges sometimes reach compromise decisions.

Since arbitration is a consensual process, the parties must first agree that the dispute will be taken to arbitration. This can be done by the following methods.

(1) A treaty under which the parties agree to submit future disputes (not just about treaties) to arbitration. The treaty can be multilateral or bilateral. The 'Jay Treaty' of 1794,[16] between Great Britain (as it then was)[17] and the United States led to a series of arbitrations. The first multilateral treaties concerning dispute settlement (but without compulsory settlement) were the Hague Conventions for the Pacific Settlement of International Disputes 1899 and 1907, which established the Permanent Court of Arbitration (PCA).[18] They were followed by other such general treaties, though they have been little used.[19] States have sometimes entered into general bilateral treaties by which they agree to settle their disputes by arbitration, such as the Swiss–UK Treaty for Conciliation, Judicial Settlement and Arbitration 1965.[20]

(2) A clause in a treaty (known as a 'compromissory clause') under which the parties agree to submit all or part of their future disputes regarding the inter-

---

[15] ILM (1998), p. 360.   [16] 52 CTS 243.
[17] See p. 166 above on the evolution of the United Kingdom.
[18] See p. 296 below.
[19] General Act for the Pacific Settlement of International Disputes 1928 (93 LNTS 343); the Revised General Act 1949 (71 UNTS 101 (No. 912)); European Convention for the Peaceful Settlement of Disputes (320 UNTS 102).   [20] See note 12 above.

pretation or application of the treaty to arbitration.[21] In the past such clauses were usually drawn in general terms and left most of the important details to be worked out only when one of the parties had invoked the clause, which is the worst possible time. Many such clauses are to be found in treaties still in force. It is better, however, to put into the clause as much detail as possible, omitting only those matters which cannot easily be worked out until the dispute has arisen. Such an approach will avoid some of the considerable delay which will ensue if crucial matters, such as the method of appointment of the arbitrators are not laid down with sufficient detail. The arbitration clause of the UK–US Air Services Agreement, which was invoked by the United States in 1988 over the dispute about the aircraft user charges at London (Heathrow) Airport,[22] contains the necessary basic provisions. Even then, they were soon found to be inadequate for what turned out to be a very long and complicated arbitration. The Rules of Procedure of the Arbitral Tribunal were modified several times during the course of the arbitration.[23]

(3) A *compromis*. If there is no existing agreement, or if it does not contain enough detail, it will be necessary for the parties to conclude a treaty called a *compromis* (sometimes termed in English 'special agreement', even though the more elegant term, in English, is *compromis*, never 'compromise'). The *compromis* sets out all the details of the establishment and procedure of the arbitral tribunal. It usually covers the following:

• composition of the tribunal;
• appointment of its members, including the filling of vacancies;
• appointment of agents of the parties;
• question(s) to be decided;
• rules of procedure and methods of work;
• languages;
• applicable law;
• seat of the tribunal;
• appointment of the secretary of the tribunal and his staff;
• costs;
• the binding nature of the award.

It may not be necessary to cover all points. For example, the agreement may provide that the working methods of the tribunal will be determined by the tribunal itself. For an example of a *compromis*, see that between France and the United Kingdom in 1975 to delimit part of the continental shelf.[24]

---

[21] For older examples, see Blix and Emerson, pp. 122–4.   [22] 102 ILR 215.
[23] For the text, see 102 ILR 551–61.   [24] 999 UNTS 137 (No. 14664); UKTS (1975) 137.

A trap to be avoided is failure to provide for a third party to make the appointment of a 'national' or 'neutral' arbitrator, if the appointment has not been made. An example of this omission is to be found in the arrangements in Annex 2 to the Dayton Agreement, which provides for arbitration by three arbitrators of the dispute over territory in the Brcko area of Bosnia.[25] Although there is provision for the President of the International Court of Justice to appoint the 'neutral' chairman, if the two arbitrators do not agree on who it should be, the Annex makes no provision for the President to appoint a 'national' arbitrator if one of the parties fails to do so. In the event, the parties appointed their arbitrators. There may, however, be no need to include such provision if the reference to arbitration is 'friendly', as in the case of the France–United Kingdom arbitration just mentioned.

Giving the President of the International Court the power to make such appointments normally has a good effect. However, he has had to exercise the power infrequently, and usually because the arbitrators (in reality the governments which appointed them) could not agree on appointment of the chairman. This occurred in the Brcko arbitration.[26]

It is also essential to agree on precisely the subject matter of the dispute.

Non-retroactivity

Following the decision of the International Court of Justice in the *Genocide (Bosnia v. Yugoslavia)(Preliminary Objections)* case,[27] it has been suggested that, unless a compromissory clause expressly excludes from the jurisdiction of the court or tribunal disputes about matters arising *before* the entry into force of the treaty concerned, the jurisdiction will include them.[28] It is doubtful if it is correct to draw this inference, which goes against the consensual nature of a compromissory clause.

Judicial settlement

Although a judgment of the International Court of Justice is, like an arbitral award, legally binding on the parties, being a permanent body the

---

[25] ILM (1996), p. 75. The arbitration was not between states, but the principle is the same.
[26] See also the *US* v. *France Air Transport Arbitration* 1963 (38 ILR 182).
[27] *ICJ Reports* (1996), p. 595.
[28] Chua and Hardcastle, 'Retroactive Application of Treaties Revisited', NILR (1997), pp. 414–20.

Court has certain advantages over an arbitral tribunal. Being already established, it has judges who are always available to hear cases. The parties do not have to pay anything towards the costs of the International Court of Justice, apart from what they pay anyway as part of their contribution to the budget of the United Nations. Although the Court has been criticised for being leisurely, it probably takes no more time to dispose of a complex case (and most cases coming before the Court are complex) than would an arbitral tribunal, yet at much less direct cost to the parties. Developing country litigants may also be able to have part of their legal costs met from a trust fund administered by the UN Secretary-General. The scope of the jurisdictional competence of the Court will be known in advance, as will its rules of procedure and methods of work. Moreover, since the Court has built up a body of jurisprudence, states and their advisers may be better able to predict how it may approach a case. All these factors should in principle enable the proceedings to take place more quickly (provided that is what the parties want), and with less trouble and more cheaply. Given the Court's current increased workload, and underfunding, considerable delays are, however, being experienced. Although there are similar bodies, such as the International Tribunal for the Law of the Sea, in contrast to the International Court of Justice their jurisdiction is restricted by their constituent instruments to specific areas of international law.

As with arbitration, a dispute can come before a standing court or tribunal only if the parties to the dispute have so agreed. Their agreement can be constituted in the following ways.

(1) By adherence to a general bilateral or multilateral treaty which provides for disputes between them to be referred, at the request of either, to the Court. Certain treaties of friendship provide for this. Iran successfully invoked the Iran–United States Treaty of Amity 1955 as the basis for the Court's jurisdiction to hear the dispute it has with the United States over attacks on its oil platforms.[29] Earlier, Nicaragua successfully invoked its Treaty of Friendship, Commerce and Navigation with the United States 1956.[30]

(2) By adherence to an optional protocol to the treaty which is the subject of the dispute. Such a protocol is essentially a compromissory clause but, being a separate treaty, a party to the principal treaty will need to adhere to the protocol in order to accept the jurisdiction of the Court. A good example is the

---

[29] 284 UNTS 93 (No. 4132); TIAS 3853. *ICJ Reports* (1996), p. 803 at p. 820.
[30] 367 UNTS 3 (No. 5224); *ICJ Reports* (1984), p. 392.

Optional Protocol to the Vienna Convention on Diplomatic Relations 1961,[31] which the United States invoked successfully in its dispute with Iran over the Tehran hostages,[32] and the Optional Protocol to the Vienna Convention on Consular Relations 1963,[33] under which Paraguay took the United States to the Court in 1998.[34]

(3) By the compromissory clause of the treaty which is the subject of the dispute. The *Lockerbie* cases were brought by Libya under the compromissory clause of the Montreal Convention for the Suppression of Unlawful Acts against the Safety of Civilian Aviation 1971.[35]

(4) By the conclusion of a *compromis*, as in the *ELSI* case.[36]

(5) By the making of reciprocal declarations under Article 36 of the Statute of the International Court of Justice accepting in advance the general jurisdiction of the Court to decide 'all cases which the parties refer to it and all matters specially provided for ... in treaties and conventions in force'. Over sixty have been made by a wide geographical spread of states.[37] Most states which have made declarations have attached conditions to their acceptance of the general jurisdiction of the Court.[38] In order to confer jurisdiction on the Court over a dispute the declarations of each party must match in all necessary particulars.

The Permanent Court of Arbitration

The Hague Convention for the Pacific Settlement of International Disputes 1899 established the Permanent Court of Arbitration (PCA) at The Hague (for which the Peace Palace, home also to the International Court of Justice, was built in 1913).[39] These days its secretariat, the International Bureau, is very active.[40] The PCA's name is misleading. It is not a court, but a permanent facility (including a courtroom, chambers, offices, library, secretariat services and a list of potential arbitrators) available to states and international organisations to help them conduct arbitrations, whether under the 1899 (or the 1907) Hague Convention, or

---

[31] 500 UNTS 241 (No. 7132); UKTS (1965) 19.   [32] *ICJ Reports* (1980), p. 4.
[33] 596 UNTS 469 (No. 8639); UKTS (1973) 14.   [34] See p. 169 above (*Breard*).
[35] 974 UNTS 177 (No. 14118); UKTS (1974) 10 (Article 14).   [36] *ICJ Reports* (1989), p. 15.
[37] J. Merrills, 'The Optional Clause Revisited', BYIL (1993), p. 197.
[38] A list of current declarations, including conditions, can be found in *UN Multilateral Treaties,* Chapter I.4 and in the *Yearbook of the International Court of Justice.*
[39] UKTS (1901) 6. A more recent but so far unused body, conceived somewhat hastily yet elaborately, is the OSCE Court of Conciliation and Arbitration (see note 10 above).
[40] Its address is Peace Palace, 2517 KJ, The Hague (tel ++ 31 70 302 4242; fax 4167; e-mail pca@euronet.nl).

otherwise. The cost of its services are met by the parties in dispute, although they are less than those of other arbitrations because the basic running costs of the International Bureau are met by the eighty-six parties to the two Conventions. Since 1902 the PCA has provided various types of services to nearly 150 arbitrations. Recent examples include the US–UK Heathrow User Charges Arbitration 1988–1993[41] and the Eritrea–Yemen Arbitration 1996–. In 1997 the PCA was involved in twenty-two arbitrations. In recent years the PCA has developed modern procedural rules for fact-finding, conciliation and various types of arbitration.[42] Whatever the nature of the dispute, or the parties, the parties are free to determine most aspects of the procedure and to decide the extent to which the International Bureau should be involved. Increasingly the PCA is involved with international commercial arbitrations between states or international organisations and private persons or entities, with the Secretary-General of the PCA being called upon to designate arbitrators in default of their appointment by the parties. He also designates appointing authorities in commercial arbitrations conducted under the UNCITRAL Arbitration Rules, and the International Bureau services arbitrations under those Rules.

Settlement of disputes within international organisations

This chapter has so far dealt mainly with disputes between states when they arise outside international organisations. A dispute between members of an international organisation, or between the organisation and its members, about the interpretation or application of its constituent instrument is settled in accordance with the provisions of that instrument. However, as with other disputes, it would be expected that the members would first consult fully in an attempt to settle the matter. And, even if that is unsuccessful, it does not follow that the dispute settlement procedures of the organisation will be activated. There may be various reasons why the members, or some of them, will not want to formalise the dispute. There are many disputes within international organisations which remain unresolved, often because they are not so important (or at least not important for enough of the members) that they have to be resolved.

---

[41] 102 ILR 261.
[42] PCA Optional Rules for Arbitrating Disputes between Two States (ILM (1993), p. 575).

The United Nations

It may seem surprising, but the United Nations Charter has no built-in procedure specifically for settling disputes within the Organisation about the Charter. There are many differences of view, some long-standing, about the interpretation or application of the Charter, but these are dealt with by negotiations, mostly informal and often inconclusive. Some are on major issues (such as the effective exclusion of South Africa during the period of apartheid). Some are resolved, often by a compromise or 'fudge'[43] (such as over the question of the arrears of South Africa's contributions following the resumption of its seat). Others remain unresolved. Many matters are often best settled by a political fix rather than by the use of formal mechanisms.

However, under Article 96 of the United Nations Charter, the International Court of Justice may give advisory opinions on, among other things, legal questions arising within the scope of the activities of the United Nations and the UN specialised agencies. The opinion is not binding unless otherwise agreed, but is persuasive as to the law. Opinions have been given on treaties concerning the work of the Organisation, for example, the application of the headquarters agreement between the United Nations and the United States in relation to the observer mission of the Palestine Liberation Organisation.[44] The Court can, if so requested, give an opinion very quickly; within eight weeks in the PLO case.

The Court has in contentious proceedings been asked to interpret the Charter in order to decide fundamental questions regarding the respective powers of principal organs of the United Nations, as in the *Expenses* case[45] and the *Lockerbie* case.[46]

The UN specialised agencies

Most disputes within the specialised agencies are settled by negotiation, but if there is a need to pursue a more formal procedure the dispute will be referred in most of the agencies to one of the main organs; and if it cannot be settled it may then be referred to arbitration or to the International

---

[43] To put together in a temporary or dishonest way (OED).

[44] *ICJ Reports* (1988), p. 12; ILM (1988), p. 808.   [45] *ICJ Reports* (1962), p. 151.

[46] *ICJ Reports* (1992), p. 3 and (1998) p. 9; ILM (1992), p. 662 and ILM (1998), p. 587, respectively.

Court of Justice for an advisory opinion. The International Civil Aviation Organisation (ICAO) and the International Labour Organisation (ILO) have different procedures. The World Trade Organisation has elaborate formal procedures for settling disputes between its members.

Human rights treaty-monitoring bodies

Many post-war human rights conventions, such as the International Covenant on Civil and Political Rights 1966,[47] have established a body to which a party (and sometimes an individual) can take a claim that another party is in breach. Although the provision is an integral part of the Covenant, it only applies if both parties have declared their acceptance of it.

---

[47] 999 UNTS 171 (No. 14668); ILM (1967), p. 368; UKTS (1977) 6. See Articles 41–42.

21

Remedies for breach

'Tis a sharp remedy, but a sure one for all ills.

Sir Walter Raleigh was reportedly referring to the executioner's axe. The use of force in response to a breach of treaty is now severely limited by the prohibition, in Article 2(4) of the UN Charter, on the threat or use of force in international relations. It is now most unlikely that a breach of treaty would, in itself, entitle another party to respond with force. The breach of a treaty of non-aggression by one party invading the other would certainly entitle the invaded state to use force, but it would be done in exercise of the inherent right of self-defence, as recognised in Article 51 of the UN Charter. But there are several peaceful responses which a party may make to a breach of treaty. Here we enter into the realm of state responsibility, that is to say, the responsibility which a state bears for conduct in breach of its international obligations.[1] Discussion of remedies will therefore be brief.[2]

Breach of an international obligation constitutes an international wrong, from which flow certain legal consequences.[3] The law governing the topic is customary international law. The International Law Commission decided not to deal with remedies in its draft articles on the law of treaties; and Article 73 provides that the provisions of the Convention do not prejudge any question that may arise in regard to a treaty from the international responsibility of a state. Nevertheless, the Commission has been working hard since 1956 on codifying the law on state responsibility and, largely due to antipodean efforts, in 1996 adopted provisionally a set of draft articles on state responsibility.[4] The Commission hopes to complete its work in 2001. Although it may not result in

---

[1] As to the relationship between the law of treaties and the law of state responsibility, see the *Rainbow Warrior*, 82 ILR 499 at 547–51.

[2] For further reading, see M. Evans (ed.), *Remedies in International Law* (1995).

[3] See generally, *Oppenheim*, paras. 145–67.   [4] A/51/10; ILM (1998), p. 440.

the adoption of a convention, the draft articles contain some useful indications as to the current state of the law, though they have certain controversial aspects.

The previous chapter outlined the means by which a dispute about the interpretation or application of a treaty may be settled. Such disputes usually involve allegations that a party is in breach; and many disputes about treaties involve mutual accusations of breach, as in the *Gabcikovo* case.[5] If a party to a treaty has been injured by a breach of it by another party, in addition to the remedies which may be available under the Convention,[6] it may seek one or more of the following:

* cessation of the wrongful conduct;
* assurances and guarantees of non-repetition;
* satisfaction;
* restitution in kind; and
* compensation,

or it may be entitled to resort to countermeasures; and there is always retorsion.

Cessation of wrongful conduct

If the breach has a continuing character, the state in breach is under an obligation to cease the conduct causing the breach. To do so would not of course absolve it from responsibility for the consequences of the breach.

Assurances and guarantees of non-repetition

A promise not to do it again is an even more obvious remedy which may be sought along with other remedies.

Satisfaction

Particularly when the damage is intangible, the injured state may seek satisfaction by way of an apology, nominal compensation or, if the breach is especially grave, exemplary damages. However, in the case of breach of a treaty, it is more likely that satisfaction would be sought in addition to another remedy.

---

[5] *ICJ Reports* (1997), p. 7; ILM (1998), p. 162.   [6] See pp. 236–8 above.

Restitution in kind (*restitutio in integrum*)

Provided it is possible, and would not involve a burden out of all propor-
tion to the benefit which the injured state would gain from compensation,
the injured state is entitled to the re-establishment of the situation which
existed before the breach occurred. Restitution may, of course, be combined with other remedies. If a state agrees by treaty to lend another state
national treasures, and the borrower does not return them, the lender will,
in addition to compensation for the consequent loss of opportunity to
display the treasures, and expenses, naturally be able to claim restitution
of the objects.[7] On the other hand, for the breach of an air services agreement which prevented the airlines of the other party from flying, an end to
the unlawful conduct and compensation would be the only feasible remedies. Although, in principle, a state should only seek other remedies if restitution is not possible, in practice many do not seek restitution even when
it would be possible.

Compensation

Compensation is the most likely remedy to be sought, particularly when
nationals of the injured party have suffered loss. Today those nationals are
often companies. Compensation can include any economically assessable
damage, including loss of profit and interest. Even if a breach has been
admitted, the amount of compensation may have to be determined by
arbitration or other means of settlement. A leading case in the field of
international aviation arose in 1988 under the UK–US Air Services
Agreement 1977 ('Bermuda 2'), concerning the lawfulness of the user
charges for US aircraft using London's Heathrow Airport.[8]

Countermeasures

We have seen how a material breach of a treaty may entitle another party to
terminate or suspend the operation of the treaty in whole or in part, in
which case the rules of the Convention will apply.[9] There are sometimes
other ways in which a state can respond *in kind* to a breach of treaty. Apart

---

[7] See the 1971 Egypt–UK treaty for the loan of the treasures of Tutankhamen (824 UNTS 71 (No.
11809); UKTS (1957) 19). The treasures were returned on time.   [8] 102 ILR 261.
[9] See pp. 236–9 above.

from, or perhaps in addition to, compensation, resort to countermeasures can be the most effective remedy for breach of treaty. Because bilateral treaties create reciprocal rights and obligations between only two parties, countermeasures can offer a convenient, quick, and therefore effective, means of dealing with a breach. The taking of countermeasures in response to the breach of a multilateral treaty can raise more complex issues. Countermeasures usually consist in the injured party not complying with one or more of its obligations under the treaty, or, possibly, under another treaty (see below).

Article 30 of the ILC's draft articles on state responsibility defines a countermeasure as 'a measure legitimate under international law against another state, in consequence of an internationally wrongful act of that other state'. This definition recognises that an otherwise unlawful act loses its unlawful character when it is taken in response to an unlawful act. In its 1997 judgment in the *Gabcikovo* case, the International Court of Justice held that for a countermeasure to be justified it has to meet four conditions:

(1) it must be taken in response to a previous international wrong of another state and directed against that state;

(2) the injured state must have called on the other state to discontinue its wrongful conduct or make reparation for it;

(3) the purpose must be to induce the other state to comply with its obligations (i.e., to resolve the dispute, not escalate it); and

(4) the effects of the countermeasure must be proportionate to the injury suffered, taking account of the rights in question, and therefore the countermeasure must be reversible.[10]

A simple, and typical, example of a countermeasure in the field of international aviation is for one party to an air services agreement, in response to a breach of the agreement by the other party or its airlines, to restrict the number of weekly flights to its territory by the airlines of the other party. Such action naturally has an immediate effect and concentrates minds wonderfully. Of course, unless the other party admits the breach, or the existence of the breach has been determined by some mutually agreed means, the party taking countermeasures leaves itself open to the claim that it is in breach; and countermeasures can provoke counter-counter-measures.

---

[10] *ICJ Reports* (1997), p. 7 at paras. 82–7; ILM (1998), p. 162, at p. 191.

The additional proposal in the ILC draft articles, that before taking countermeasures a state must negotiate or go through a dispute settlement process provided for in the treaty, has no basis in customary law.[11] The reason is not difficult to see. Air services agreements govern civil air transport between the territory of the parties, regulating the routes which can be flown, the number of flights and the size of aircraft. Any interruption or restriction of the services is a serious matter for an airline, for revenue lost can never be recouped, except by compensation. Disputes about air services agreements are constant, and, because of the money which is at stake, countermeasures often have had to be taken very swiftly, and sometimes this has resulted in arbitrations.[12]

What is not clear is whether countermeasures must always be related to the subject matter of the treaty concerned.

Retorsion

Retorsion (not 'retortion') is a term used only in international law. It describes the imposing of a penalty which does not involve any unlawful measure. A simple example would be the unilateral withdrawal of an ambassador, cancellation of an official visit by a head of state or a decision not to offer financial help. The reason does not have to be a breach of treaty or of some other international legal obligation; nor do the interests of the retorsioning state have to be directly affected. In 1999 several EU states sought to block the participation of Israel in a £10.5bn scientific and research programme because of its failure to implement the Wye peace accord.[13] The point is to show displeasure in a way which may have an effect, but without making matters significantly worse.

---

[11] See the US comments on the draft articles in AJIL (1998), at pp. 253–4.
[12] For example, *Italy* v. *US* (45 ILR 393); *US* v. *France* (54 ILR 303).
[13] *Financial Times*, 1 February 1999.

22

Succession to treaties

> The international lawyer seeking a way out of this marshland is as
> likely as ever to be led into the centre of the miry bog itself.[1]

Despite this warning ringing in our ears, we must explore in some detail
this important subject, particularly because it is not covered by the
Convention (Article 73). When a state becomes party to a treaty, a legal
nexus (connection) is established between the treaty and the territory of
the state.[2] Problems can arise when another state then becomes responsible for the international relations of all or part of the territory. This
process is described as succession of states. In the forty-five years following
the end of the Second World War the problems arose chiefly when colonies
became independent. But the end of the Cold War, and the subsequent
fragmentation of states, created very different problems of treaty succession. Although the process of solving them is by no means complete, there
is already developing a useful body of recent state practice in addition to
that from the era of decolonisation. The value of state practice before the
Second World War as a guide to today's problems of treaty succession must
now be doubtful.

Vienna Convention on Succession of States in
respect of Treaties 1978[3]

This Convention resulted from work done by the International Law
Commission. Even though only fifteen ratifications or accessions were
needed for it to enter into force, it did so only in 1996, and by the end of
1998 the Convention still had only fifteen parties. Until 1990 only eight

---

[1] See T. Maluwu, 'Succession to Treaties in Post-Independence Africa', *African Journal of
International and Comparative Law* (1992), p. 791.   [2] See p. 162 above.
[3] ILM (1978), p. 1488; UN Reg. No. 33356.

states[4] had adhered to the Convention. Those which have become parties since then are new states of eastern Europe.[5] Their reason is obvious, but why did it take eighteen years for the Convention to enter into force? Some states may not have seen its relevance or importance to them, the era of decolonisation having almost come to an end, and during the period from the Treaty of Versailles 1919 until the end of the Cold War the division of the territory of states (outside the context of decolonisation) was a rare occurrence. But there were other reasons. At the time when the draft articles were being developed by the International Law Commission most state practice related to former colonies, and was not consistent. Consequently, those rules of the 1978 Convention which are concerned with newly independent states are excessively complex, yet do not give adequate weight to the abundant state practice of concluding devolution agreements or making declarations of succession. Moreover, decolonisation was almost at its end by 1978, and, unless the successor state agrees otherwise, the Convention does not apply to a succession of states which occurs before its entry into force (6 November 1996). Nor did the rules in the Convention about the break-up of states reflect modern state practice, though admittedly at the time there was little on which to draw. Therefore, until recently states may have seen little advantage in becoming parties.

Although the Convention is largely an example of the progressive development of international law, rather than a codification of customary law, and is not therefore a reliable guide to the rules of customary law on treaty succession, its eventual entry into force, recent practice following the end of the Cold War, and decisions of the International Court of Justice, may have now breathed life into some of its provisions.

The rules of customary international law on the subject are not easy to determine. This is hardly surprising: the circumstances vary widely and the subject is politically sensitive. The interests and perception of a successor state may differ significantly from those of the predecessor state (if it still exists) and of third states. In practice much depends on what can be agreed, expressly or tacitly, between the successor state and other states. When it is possible for the successor state and its predecessor to reach

---

[4] Dominica, Egypt, Ethiopia, Iraq, Morocco, the Seychelles, Tunisia and Yugoslavia.
[5] Bosnia, Croatia, Estonia, Macedonia, Slovakia, Slovenia and Ukraine. All but Estonia and Ukraine deposited, appropriately, an instrument of succession, Czechoslovakia and the *Socialist* Federal Republic of Yugoslavia (SFRY) having been contracting states.

agreement this will be important to third states, even though they will not be bound by such agreement.[6] It is therefore a particularly uncertain and controversial area of international law. Although recent state practice may prove to be valuable, for the moment it may be safer to say that there are only certain customary law principles; for the rest, there is evolving state practice. Indeed, almost all problems (particularly with bilateral treaties) are resolved on the basis of agreements between the states concerned (successor state and third state). Such residual rules of customary international law as may exist play a secondary role.

The customary law principles

Certain general principles can be deduced with reasonable confidence. They apply whether a treaty is bilateral or multilateral.

(1) A new state does not succeed automatically to a treaty if the subject matter is closely linked to the relations of the predecessor state with the other party (it will usually, but not always, be a bilateral treaty). Examples include 'political treaties' such as treaties of alliance or defence co-operation.

(2) A new state will succeed, without any action by it, to treaties (or at least to the legal situation created by them) relating to matters such as the status of territory, boundaries or the navigation of rivers. Although this principle is well established, its exact extent is not.[7] Although accession to the Austrian State Treaty 1955[8] is restricted to 'any Member of the United Nations which on 8 May 1945 was at war with Germany and which then had the status of a United Nation and is not a signatory of the present Treaty', because the Socialist Federal Republic of Yugoslavia (SFRY) had acceded to the Treaty in 1955, on the dissolution of the SFRY the former republics succeeded to the Treaty automatically.

(3) When a state has been absorbed by another, such as the German Democratic Republic by the Federal Republic of Germany in 1990,[9] and South Vietnam by North Vietnam in 1976, almost all treaties entered into by the absorbed state will either simply lapse or their fate will need to be discussed with the other parties. Under the 'moving-boundary principle', treaties of the absorbing state will generally extend to the absorbed state. But when there is a true union of two states, such as that of the Republic of Yemen and the People's Democratic Republic of Yemen in 1990, most treaties will continue to bind

---

[6] As to treaty succession for Hong Kong and third states, see p. 327 below.
[7] See *Oppenheim*, p. 213; and Articles 11 and 12 of the 1978 Convention.
[8] 217 UNTS 223 (No. 2249); UKTS (1957) 58; TIAS 3298.   [9] See BYIL (1997), pp. 520–9.

the successor state, at least as regards that part of its territory for which the treaties were in force before the union.[10] This is also the approach of Article 31 of the 1978 Convention.

(4) A new state will not normally succeed automatically to multilateral treaties. Some writers consider that treaties which embody or reflect generally accepted rules of international law (in particular those concerned with human rights or international humanitarian law) bind a successor state by virtue of the concept of the acquired rights of the inhabitants of the state.[11] There is no authority for this view.[12] As regards the International Covenant on Civil and Political Rights, the Human Rights Committee has taken the position that '[t]he rights enshrined in the Covenant belong to the people living in the territory of the State Party . . . such protection devolves with the territory and continues to belong to them, notwithstanding . . . State succession'.[13] But the sounder view is that in so far as such a human rights treaty represents rules of customary international law a successor state will be bound by those rules, but only as a matter of customary international law.[14] The International Court of Justice avoided deciding the issue in its judgment in 1996 in the *Genocide Convention* (*Bosnia v. FRY*) (*Preliminary Objections*) case, the Court concluding that the Federal Republic of Yugoslavia was a party to the Genocide Convention because it had declared its intention to remain bound by the treaties to which the Socialist Federal Republic of Yugoslavia had been a party.[15] But, even if the new state is bound by customary rules reflected in a human rights treaty rather than the treaty itself, this will have important practical consequences. The state will not have the right to attend meetings of the states parties. Nor will it be under any obligation to report to any monitoring body established by the treaty.

(5) The transfer of part of the metropolitan territory of a state to another state will not usually, unless the two states have agreed otherwise, involve succession of treaties. Under the 'moving-boundary principle', when Alsace-Lorraine was returned to France at the end of the First World War, German treaties ceased to apply and French treaties to it applied as to any other part of France.[16]

---

[10] And see *UN Multilateral Treaties*, Chapter I.2, footnote to the entry for Yemen.
[11] See R. Mullerson, 'The Continuity and Succession of States, by Reference to the Former USSR and Yugoslavia', ICLQ (1993), p. 473 at pp. 490–2.
[12] See M. Shaw, 'State Succession Revisited', *Finnish Yearbook of International Law* (1994), p. 34; and M. Kamminga, 'State Succession in Respect of Human Rights Treaties', EJIL (1995), pp. 469–84.   [13] General Comment No. 26(61); see ILM (1995), p. 839.   [14] See pp. 9–10 above.
[15] *ICJ Reports* (1996), p. 4, paras. 17 and 23; but see the separate opinion of Judge Weeramantry, para. 17. See M. Wood, 'Participation of Former Yugoslav States in the United Nations and in Multilateral Treaties', *Max Planck Yearbook of United Nations Law* (1997), pp. 231–58, and the many articles it refers to.
[16] D. O'Connell, *Law of State Succession* (1967), pp. 221 and 374–81.

(6) A new state will not succeed to membership of international organisations if the predecessor state still exists. Some organisations, such as the United Nations, have a formal admission procedure; and a precondition for membership of most of the UN specialised agencies is membership of the United Nations, as well as any admission procedure under the constituent instrument. If, however, a new state is the result of the union of two states, at least one of which was a member of the organisation before the union, the new state will usually be accepted as a member under its new name and without having to apply for membership. When the two Yemens joined together as one state they retained a seat in the United Nations under the name of Yemen, no application for membership being required.

These general principles do not take one very far, but may be better understood by an examination of some of the more recent state practice.

Former colonies and other dependent territories

Although since the Second World War some ninety colonies or other dependent territories, such as protectorates, protected states and trust territories, have attained independence, the practice of newly independent states has not been consistent. It is therefore not possible to promulgate a set of rules of customary law on state succession applicable in such situations. The most one can do is to summarise the main approaches which have been taken.

There are two *theoretical* starting points. The first is the nineteenth-century theory of universal succession, which persisted up to the 1960s. According to this a new state inherited all the treaty rights and obligations of the former power in so far as they had been applicable to the territory before independence. This approach was reflected in the *devolution agreements* entered into by Iraq in 1931 and by some former Asian colonies in the 1940s and 1950s.[17] From 1955 all former British colonies in West Africa, except for the Gambia, concluded devolution agreements with the United Kingdom. These provided that, as from the date of independence, all obligations and responsibilities of the United Kingdom which arose from 'any valid international instrument' would be assumed by the new state 'in so far as such instruments may be held to have application' to it; and the rights and benefits previously enjoyed by the United Kingdom by

---

[17] Iraq (UKTS (1931) 15); Indonesia 1949 (69 UNTS 266); Vietnam 1954 (161 BFSP 649); Malaya 1957 (Cmnd 346).

virtue of the application of such instruments to the former colony would be enjoyed by the new state. Although these agreements created a presumption that a treaty which could have application to the new state would apply to it, they naturally left many questions unanswered.[18] A devolution agreement could not bind a third state which is party to a devolved treaty unless it consents.[19] Nevertheless, a devolution agreement was useful in serving as a formal and public statement of the general attitude of the new state.

Although they did not enter into devolution agreements, most former French colonies in Africa regarded themselves as successors to pre-independence treaties, and made declarations to that effect which they notified to the UN Secretary-General.[20]

The other starting point is the so-called *clean slate* doctrine, under which the new state is free to pick and choose which treaties it will succeed to. This approach was followed most famously by the United States when it gained its independence. However, even when the clean slate doctrine is applied, treaties which concern territorial rights, such as boundary treaties and those granting rights of navigation or passage, will usually bind the new state.[21]

The doctrine has been applied in different ways. Following the so-called 'Nyerere Doctrine', a number of former British colonies made unilateral declarations in which they undertook that, for a specified period following independence, they would continue to apply all bilateral treaties validly concluded by the United Kingdom, unless abrogated or modified by agreement. After that period the new state would 'regard such of these treaties which could not by application of the rules of customary international law be regarded as otherwise surviving, as having terminated'.[22] Such declarations do not, however, in the longer term resolve all succession problems. Once the time limit has been reached the effect of the declaration is uncertain, unless the position of the new state in respect of all bilateral and multilateral treaties which might apply to the new state has by then been made clear. This is particularly so for treaties entered into expressly for the territory by the former colonial power, which the International Court of

---

[18] Maluwa, 'Succession to Treaties', (note 1 above), p. 804.   [19] See p. 208 above.

[20] For the Malagasy Republic's declaration see UN Doc. A/CN. 4/150, p. 31, para.87, and Maluwa, 'Succession to Treaties', pp. 792–3.   [21] See p. 307, para (2), above.

[22] See the Declaration by Malawi on 24 November 1964 in the ILA study, *The Effect of Independence on Treaties* (1965), p. 388; Maluwa, 'Succession to Treaties', pp. 806–7; and *Oppenheim*, p. 231, note 21.

Justice has held bind the new state.[23] Another clean slate approach, adopted by Zambia in 1964, was to avoid any general commitment to confirm or deny the continuing applicability of treaties within any specific period of time.

When a *clean slate* declaration has been made by a former British colony, it has been the (not strictly necessary) practice of the United Kingdom to circulate to UN Members a disclaimer of any continued responsibility for the treaties formerly applied by it to the territory.[24]

The two German states

The Unification Treaty entered into by the Federal Republic of Germany (FRG) and the German Democratic Republic (GDR) provided that, in principle, most treaties entered into by the FRG would apply to the whole of the unified state ('moving-boundary principle'), and for consultations with the other parties regarding treaties to which only the former GDR had been a party.[25] Although other parties were not bound by the Treaty, most accepted what had been agreed, the terms of which had been notified to all UN Members and to the depositaries of multilateral treaties. Consultations with over 135 states resulted in their agreement that most of the GDR's bilateral treaties had lapsed. Treaties which the FRG and the GDR had with Czechoslovakia and Poland concerning borders were discussed with the other parties and various agreements reached. Germany became party to only a few multilateral treaties to which the GDR alone had been a party.[26] Thus the arrangements did not follow Article 31(2) of the 1978 Convention.

The former Soviet Union

Russia

The dramatic changes to the Union of Soviet Socialist Republics in 1991 had some similarity to the process of decolonisation in that several repub-

---

[23] *United States Nationals in Morocco Case, ICJ Reports* (1952), pp. 176 and 193–4.
[24] For such a disclaimer in relation to Hong Kong, see p. 324 below. Because of the special circumstances, the arrangements made by China and the United Kingdom for Hong Kong's treaties are described at the end of this chapter.
[25] Articles 11 and 12 (ILM (1991), p. 457).
[26] See *UN Multilateral Treaties*, Chapter I.2, footnote to entry for Germany; AJIL (1992), pp. 152–73; and D. Papenfuss, 'The Fate of the International Treaties of the German Democratic Republic within the Framework of German Unification', AJIL (1998), pp. 469.

lics broke away and became independent states, yet the state which had exercised sovereignty over them *continued*, though under the name of the principal constituent part of the Union, the Russian Federation (or Russia for short). The process was, however, different from decolonisation in that the republics had been part of the Soviet Union. The continuation of the Soviet/Russian state has been reflected most prominently in the United Nations and other international organisations where the name of the USSR was simply replaced by that of the Russian Federation without any requirement to apply for membership.[27] Nevertheless, Russia formally declared that it would continue to comply with all the international obligations entered into by the Soviet Union.[28] Since Russia's assertion that it is the continuation of the USSR has been accepted,[29] the declaration would seem to have a purpose more political than legal. Similarly, Russia has sought to agree with certain states a list of the bilateral treaties which would continue to apply between them. This is desirable for the sake of good order. There were treaties entered into by the Soviet Union which in practice concerned only a part or parts of the Soviet Union which are now independent, and therefore have no application to Russia. The approach taken by Russia and other states is consistent with Article 35 of the 1978 Convention.

The former Soviet republics

In contrast to Russia, the former Soviet republics had each to apply for UN membership, except for Belarus (previously Byelorussian SSR) and Ukraine (previously Ukrainian SSR), which were already, for political reasons, Members of the United Nations and of the specialised agencies in their own right, even though not previously recognised as sovereign by most states. The practice with regard to treaty succession of Armenia, Azerbaijan, Belarus, Georgia, Kazakhstan, Kyrgyzstan, Moldova, Tajikistan, Turkmenistan, Ukraine and Uzbekistan (the Baltic states will be dealt with separately below) is instructive, given the number of states and the recentness of the practice, even though it is not consistent. At first the United States asserted that as successor states of the Soviet Union the

---

[27] Y. Z. Blum, 'Russia Takes over the Soviet Union's Seat at the United Nations', EJIL (1992), p. 354.
[28] See the footnote to the entry for the Russian Federation in *UN Multilateral Treaties*, Chapter I.1.   [29] BYIL (1992), pp. 652–4.

former republics were obliged by international law to fulfil the treaty obligations of the Soviet Union, and sought to make it a pre-condition for the
establishment of diplomatic relations that they should commit themselves
to fulfil those obligations.[30] Although the responses from most of the new
states were suitably equivocal, diplomatic relations were soon established.
The United States then proceeded to conclude exchanges of notes with
each of them concerning their succession to *bilateral* treaties between the
United States and the former Soviet Union. The notes recorded that, following a review which had identified treaties which had expired or had
become obsolete, the parties *confirmed* that treaties dating from as long
ago as 1854, and listed in an annex, would *continue* in force.[31] This formulation is more consistent with the continuity principle than the *clean slate*
approach.

The exchanges of notes recorded that the governments took 'as a point
of departure' the continuity principle in Article 34 of the 1978
Convention. That article provides that, when a part or parts of the territory of a state separate to form one or more states, and whether or not the
predecessor state continues to exist, any treaty in force at the date of succession in respect of the *entire* territory of the predecessor state continues
in force in respect of each successor state so formed; and any treaty in force
at the date of succession in respect only of *that part* of the territory of the
predecessor state which has become a successor state continues in force in
respect of that successor state alone. These rules do not apply if (a) the
states concerned otherwise agree, or (b) it appears from the treaty or is
otherwise established that the application of the treaty in respect of the
successor state would be incompatible with the object and purpose of the
treaty or would radically change the conditions for its operation. The
article thus envisages the possibility of agreements between the new state
and other states about which treaties would continue in force; the need for
such agreements being amply demonstrated by the difficulty otherwise of
applying the rule in (b).

The United Kingdom informed all the former republics of the Soviet
Union that, as appropriate, it regarded all *bilateral* treaties to which the
United Kingdom and the Soviet Union were parties immediately before
the new states' independence as remaining in force between them and the

---

[30] P. Williams, 'The Treaty Obligations of the Successor States of the Former Soviet Union,
Yugoslavia, and Czechoslovakia: Do They Continue in Force?' *Denver Journal of International
Law and Policy* (1994), pp. 1–37.   [31] See, for example, AJIL (1995), pp. 761–2.

United Kingdom.[32] The United Kingdom is seeking to conclude exchanges of notes with each former republic confirming which treaties are regarded as continuing in force.

The practice of the former Soviet Republics with regard to *multilateral* treaties has been mixed and often unclear. For example, although the Soviet Union was a party to the Vienna Convention, Georgia, Kazakhstan, Moldova, Tajikistan, Turkmenistan and Uzbekistan have now *acceded* to it. On the other hand, in 1994 Ukraine purported to *succeed* to the Convention on the Conservation of Antarctic Marine Living Resources 1980[33] on the basis of succession to the Soviet Union which, as Russia, remained a party. But, since that Convention laid down certain pre-conditions for accession, the United Kingdom and the United States were unable to accept the validity of the instrument of succession. However, since Ukraine had fulfilled the conditions for accession the two states informed the depositary that they would treat the instrument as one of *accession.*[34]

The Baltic states

Since Estonia, Latvia and Lithuania had been annexed unlawfully by the Soviet Union in 1940, when they regained their independence in 1991 they did not regard themselves as successor states to the Soviet Union, but as states which had regained their sovereignty. Each informed the UN Secretary-General that they did not regard themselves as parties by succession to any treaties entered into by the Soviet Union.[35] They then acceded to many multilateral treaties to which the Soviet Union had been (and to which Russia continues to be) a party. There was, however, a problem with bilateral treaties entered into by the Soviet Union during the period of unlawful occupation: to maintain that they had no relevance would have been to ignore the reality of fifty years. With admirable pragmatism, agreements were therefore reached with some neighbouring states to regard certain of these treaties as in force, at least for the time being; and some bilateral treaties entered into in the period between the two World Wars, when the three states were first independent, were agreed to be still

---

[32] BYIL (1992), pp. 652–5 and (1997), pp. 535–6.
[33] 402 UNTS 71; ILM (1980), p. 837; UKTS (1982) 48; TIAS 10240.   [34] See pp. 266–7 above.
[35] *UN Multilateral Treaties*, Chapter I.2, see footnotes to the entries for the three states; Mullerson, 'Continuity and Succession' (note 11 above), pp. 480–7.

applicable, the rest being obsolete or irrelevant by the 1990s. In principle, multilateral treaties entered into during that period will, again, be in force for the three states.[36]

The former Yugoslav republics

By 1992 or 1993, with the exception of Serbia and Montenegro, the constituent republics of the former *Socialist* Republic of Yugoslavia (SFRY) had been recognised as independent sovereign states. Although the dissolution of the SFRY was anything but amicable, it created similar succession questions as the break-up of Czechoslovakia (see below), though the attitude of Serbia and Montenegro, which relabelled itself the Federal Republic of Yugoslavia, has been a complication.[37]

Bosnia and Herzegovina, Croatia, Macedonia and Slovenia

Each of these four new states informed the United Nations Secretary-General that it considered itself bound, by virtue of state succession, to multilateral treaties to which the SFRY had been bound. The SFRY was a party to the 1978 Convention, and the four new states each deposited instruments of succession to it. In doing so they were apparently guided by Article 9(1) of that Convention, which provides that the making of a unilateral declaration is not enough to make the successor a party to a treaty, as well as by Article 34 of the same Convention. They therefore lodged instruments of succession with the relevant depositaries. The United Nations gives as the date of succession the date of deposit of the instruments (cf. Article 23 of the 1978 Convention). This may be because the dates on which each of the former Yugoslav republics became independent were not clear.[38]

Former republics of the SFRY have also entered into bilateral treaty succession arrangements with various other states. Croatia[39] and Slovenia[40] have concluded exchanges of notes with the United Kingdom confirming which treaties (and some MOUs) remain in force. Slovenia has concluded such confirmations with over twenty states.

---

[36] See *UN Multilateral Treaties*, Part II, Chapter 14(a).
[37] See Wood, 'Participation' (note 15 above), and ILM (1992), p. 1488.   [38] See p. 321 below.
[39] Third Supplementary List (UKTS (1997) 80).
[40] Second Supplementary List (UKTS (1998) 39).

The Federal Republic of Yugoslavia

Even though Serbia and Montenegro, now known as the Federal Republic of Yugoslavia (FRY) asserts that it is the continuation of the SFRY, the other former republics of the SFRY, as well as most third states, do not accept this or the FRY claim to the seat of Yugoslavia in the United Nations and other international organisations.[41] In September 1992 the UN General Assembly decided that the FRY could not continue automatically the membership of the SFRY; that it should apply for membership; and that therefore it could not take part in the work of the General Assembly.[42] The consistent advice from successive UN Legal Counsel is that the effect of this decision is that the membership of 'Yugoslavia' is not terminated or suspended, but its practical consequence is that FRY representatives can no longer take part in the work of the General Assembly, its subsidiary organs, or conferences or meetings convened by the General Assembly.[43]

The assertion by the FRY of continuation was reflected in its attitude to treaties to which the SFRY had been a party. A formal FRY declaration of 27 April 1992 stated that the 'FRY, continuing the state, international legal and political personality of the SFRY, shall strictly abide by all the commitments that the SFRY assumed internationally'. This did at least accord with the wishes of the EU Member States, and other states, that the FRY should abide by the international obligations of the SFRY, albeit as one of its successor states. Other states were therefore faced with a dilemma: they wanted the FRY to respect the treaties, and especially human rights conventions, to which the SFRY had been a party, but they could not accept the FRY as a party on the basis of continuation of statehood. It was not only a matter of principle: acceptance of the FRY's assertion of continuation could have an effect on the important question of succession to other rights and obligations of the SFRY, especially with regard to property and debts. The dilemma persisted even after the FRY was formally recognised as a state in 1996. It has also caused problems for meetings of treaty parties in which the FRY has wished to participate.

---

[41] BYIL (1992), pp. 655–8. See also the report of the Badinter Commission (92 ILR 162 at 166). The ICJ dodged the question in *Genocide* (*Bosnia* v. *Yugoslavia*), *ICJ Reports* (1993), p. 3 at pp. 20–3; ILM (1993), p. 888: see p. 308, para. (4), above.

[42] See UN Security Council Resolutions 757, 777, 821 and 1074; and UNGA Resolutions 47/1, 47/229 and 48/88; ILM (1992), p. 1421.   [43] See UN Doc. A/47/485.

A more comprehensive – and neater – solution to the 'continuity or succession' problem would have been for the FRY to have written to the depositaries of the various multilateral treaties to which the SFRY was a party, confirming that it (the FRY) regarded itself as a party, but without saying on what basis. Each depositary could then have circulated the letter to the parties which, if they made no objection, would have been deemed to have accepted the FRY as a party, though without specifying on what basis.[44] The great advantage of this course is that it would not have prejudiced the position of either the FRY or other states, including the other former Yugoslav republics, on the issue of continuity or succession.

When the United Kingdom recognised the FRY on 9 April 1996, a letter from the Foreign Secretary to the FRY President confirmed that 'as appropriate, we regard treaties and agreements in force to which the United Kingdom and the SFRY were parties as remaining in force between the United Kingdom and the FRY'.[45] On the basis of this letter, and the FRY Declaration of 27 April 1992, the United Kingdom treats the FRY as party to *multilateral* treaties on a case-by-case basis.

The problem of *bilateral* treaties has been resolved pragmatically by some states separately agreeing with the FRY a list of those treaties between them and the SFRY which would remain in force. The United Kingdom signed on 3 April 1998 a 'record of a meeting' confirming this arrangement, to which was annexed a list of twenty-five treaties.[46]

For the moment, the most one can say about treaty succession with regard to the FRY is that the situation has to be viewed and assessed in the light of its own particular facts.

The former Czechoslovakia

At midnight on 31 December 1992 the state of Czechoslovakia was dissolved and was succeeded by two states: the Czech Republic and Slovakia. Both declared themselves to be successors to Czechoslovakia and committed to fulfilling the treaty and other obligations of Czechoslovakia.[47] In this

---

[44] Known to Antarctic legal experts as the 'bifocal' approach: see Joyner and Chopra (eds.), *The Antarctic Legal Regime* (1988), p. 111.   [45] BYIL (1996), p. 707.

[46] See the entry for Yugoslavia, Federal Republic of, in the First Supplementary List of 1998 (UKTS (1998) 28).

[47] *UN Multilateral Treaties*, Chapter I.2, footnote to entry for the Czech Republic; V. Mikulka, 'The Dissolution of Czechoslovakia and Succession in Respect of Treaties', *Development and International Co-operation* (1996), pp. 45–63.

they consciously applied the rules in Article 34 of the 1978 Convention.[48] There was no suggestion that the Czech Republic, though the larger of the two states, was the continuation of Czechoslovakia.

The policy adopted by both states with regard to *multilateral* treaties to which Czechoslovakia had been a party was that each would be bound, as from the dissolution, by all of them, including any reservations or declarations. Both states regarded themselves as bound by virtue of a state succession which left them no discretion in the matter.[49] In addition, each state regarded itself as a signatory of all those multilateral treaties which had been signed, but not ratified, before the dissolution. The two states each sent notes to this effect to the UN Secretary-General and other depositaries, who circulated them to the interested states. No objections were raised.[50]

Membership of international organisations raised a special problem because neither state purported to be the continuation of Czechoslovakia. Each therefore had to apply to join those organisations of which it wished to be a member. Where Czechoslovakia had been a member of certain bodies within a particular organisation, the two states agreed which of them should seek election to the seat, and this choice was respected and endorsed by the East European Regional Group. This civilised approach was generally accepted by the other members.

Bilateral treaties entered into by Czechoslovakia were regarded by the two new states as continuing to apply except in so far as it would not be appropriate. For example, the application of certain treaties had always been limited to the territory of Slovakia, in particular the 1977 treaty regarding the Danube Dam Project. In *Gabcikovo* (*Hungary* v. *Slovakia*) the International Court of Justice decided that Article 12 of the 1978 Convention (succession does not, as such, affect territorial regimes) reflected a rule of customary international law and applied to the treaty; thus the succession of Slovakia to Czechoslovakia did not affect the application of the treaty to Slovakia, and it became binding on Slovakia alone on the dissolution of Czechoslovakia.[51]

The Czech Republic and Slovakia each had discussions with certain states which had had bilateral treaties with Czechoslovakia. The main purpose was to seek confirmation that, unless there was a special reason,

---

[48] See p. 313 above.   [49] Mikulka, 'Dissolution of Czechoslovakia' (note 47 above), pp. 47–8.
[50] *UN Multilateral Treaties*, Chapter I.2; see the notes for the Czech Republic and Slovakia.
[51] *ICJ Reports* (1997), paras. 116–24.

all the treaties would continue to apply to the new states. The discussions were also an opportunity to consider whether some treaties might be terminated or be replaced by new ones, particularly taking into account the political changes which had taken place with the end of the communist regime. In 1996, following a joint examination of bilateral agreements and 'arrangements' (i.e., MOUs), the Czech Republic and the United Kingdom entered into an exchange of notes confirming that eighteen treaties and MOUs, some dating from the 1920s, would be regarded as remaining in force. The exchange was expressed to 'constitute *joint confirmation* of the position regarding bilateral agreements and arrangements between our two countries'. Accordingly, the exchange, not being a treaty, was not published as one and the United Nations was not informed. Instead an information note was included in the *United Kingdom Treaty Series*.[52] By the end of 1998 the Czech Republic had made similar arrangements with some seventy states; and Slovakia had made about thirty. The arrangements the Czech Republic made with Germany and with Bosnia and Herzegovina were unusual since they included, respectively, some treaties between Czechoslovakia and the German Democratic Republic which had remained in force after reunification, and treaties between Czechoslovakia and the former Socialist Federal Republic of Yugoslavia.[53]

The European Community

It has been suggested that when Member States of European Community (EC) are parties to a treaty and the EC cannot itself be a party, but the subject matter is one for which the EC has exclusive competence, the EC can be the successor to its Member States.[54] The European Court of Justice so found in respect of the GATT.[55] The Court's judgment was, of course, binding only on the EC and its Member States, and should therefore be seen as determining only that, for the purposes of the EC Treaty, the EC has succeeded to the GATT obligations of the EC Member States. The other parties to GATT would still regard the Member States as responsible for their GATT obligations. But in later cases the Court held that the

---

[52] See the Third Supplementary List for 1996 (UKTS (1996) 96; BYIL (1996), pp. 755–9).
[53] Mikulka, 'Dissolution of Czechoslovakia' (note 47 above), pp. 56–62.
[54] See MacLeod, Hendry and Hyett, *The External Relations of the European Communities* (1996), pp. 235–6, though the suggestion is not that of the authors.
[55] *International Fruit Company* [1972] ECR 1219.

Community had not succeeded to the European Convention on Human Rights or to certain treaties on pollution.[56]

Multilateral treaties: role of the depositary

If a successor state does not deposit an instrument of succession, the depositary is under no obligation to enquire as to its position. If asked by the successor state about procedure a depositary should do no more than indicate the possible options.[57] However, due to his particular position, when the UN Secretary-General is depositary of a multilateral treaty to which the predecessor state was a party, it is now his practice to write to the new state inviting it to confirm whether it considers itself to be bound by the treaty.

Information issued by a depositary about the status of a treaty should distinguish between states which have deposited (1) instruments of ratification, acceptance or approval, (2) instruments of accession, and (3) notifications of succession. In noting a succession in its records the depositary should not delete the details of when and by what means the predecessor state became a party, since this may be historically important. If a treaty is no longer open for signature, ratification or accession (i.e., is 'closed'), the depositary should notify the parties of the communication from the successor state and await their responses.

'Yugoslavia'

The present untidy status of the Federal Republic of Yugoslavia (FRY)[58] is also reflected in its position with regard to multilateral treaties deposited with the UN Secretary-General. Since neither the UN General Assembly, nor any other intergovernmental organ representative of the international community as a whole, nor any treaty organ with regard to a particular treaty, has taken a decision on this matter, the Secretary-General has stated that he is not in a position to decide on disputed questions related to the participation of the FRY in a particular treaty for which he is depositary. Since the General Assembly has not terminated or suspended the membership of 'Yugoslavia' in the United Nations, the Secretary-General

---

[56] *Dorca Marina* [1982] ECR 3949; *Peralta* [1994] ECR I-3453.
[57] See Article 76.   [58] See p. 316 above.

continues to list under 'Yugoslavia' treaty actions (ratifications, etc.) by both the SFRY and the FRY.[59]

Date of succession

There is no consistent practice as to the date on which succession takes effect, but the better (and logical) view is that it is the date of independence, since the essence of succession to treaty rights and obligations is that it is an automatic process, the notification of succession being no more than formal confirmation of what has already happened by operation of law, even though the confirmation may take some time in coming. But the matter may be treated differently when it is not possible to determine the exact date on which a new state came into being.[60] If the new state does not wish to be bound immediately, the correct course would be to accede when it is ready to become a party.

Domestic implications of treaty succession

Treaty succession is not a subject of concern only to states and international lawyers: it can cause problems for others. Where a treaty has to be given effect in domestic law, the question whether a new state has succeeded to it can cause a very real problem. The operation in domestic law of a treaty, such as the Convention on the Recovery Abroad of Maintenance 1956[61] or the New York Convention on the Recognition and Enforcement of Foreign Arbitral Awards 1958,[62] will depend on whether the states concerned are parties to it. How that is decided depends on the relevant national legal system, but in all cases a decision has to be taken at the national level as to whether a state has succeeded to the treaty. In taking that decision the national courts may look for guidance from government. But, as we have seen, in some cases government will be in no position to give authoritative advice. There is no easy solution; each case has to be dealt with in the light of its own particular circumstances. In some ways the problem of the FRY is not as difficult to deal with as some others where

---

[59] Advice of the UN Legal Counsel annexed to ICAO Doc. A32–WP/175 of 25 September 1998. See also the entry for 'Yugoslavia' in *UN Multilateral Treaties*, Chapter I.1.
[60] See p. 315 above regarding the former Yugoslav republics.
[61] 268 UNTS 3 (No. 3850); UKTS (1975) 85.
[62] 330 UNTS 3 (No. 4739); UKTS (1976) 26; TIAS 6997.

the position of the successor state is also not clear. The FRY is definite that it is a party to all the treaties to which the SFRY was a party: it is just that it takes a different view to others as to the *basis* on which it is a party. Thus, taking its cue from the judgment of the International Court of Justice in the *Genocide Convention* (*Bosnia* v. *Yugoslavia*) case,[63] it is legitimate, to conclude that the FRY is a party to all treaties to which the SFRY had been a party.

Hong Kong: 'one country, two systems'

The circumstances of the handover of Hong Kong to China at midnight on 30 June 1997 were unique and do not provide much in the way of insight into the more usual treaty problems. But because the arrangements made for the continuation of Hong Kong's treaty relations are of interest far beyond China and the United Kingdom, and will last for at least fifty years, they need to be explained in some detail.

Continued application of treaties

It was essential that there should be substantial continuity in Hong Kong's treaty relations after the handover. As the United Kingdom's most economically developed colony, and one of the world's larger economies, a considerable number of bilateral and multilateral treaties already applied to Hong Kong, either by virtue of their extension by the United Kingdom (over 200) or because Hong Kong had become a party in its own right.[64] It was thus important for the future health and development of the Hong Kong economy that the framework of treaties within which Hong Kong operated should continue, and that there should be no doubt as to which treaties would continue to apply after handover. The matter was therefore approached in a highly methodical way.

The future status of Hong Kong was agreed between China and the United Kingdom in a treaty of 19 December 1984, entitled Joint Declaration on the Question of Hong Kong.[65] After handover Hong Kong

---

[63] See p. 308, para (4), above.
[64] See p. 52 above regarding entrustment of treaty-making powers to dependent territories.
[65] 1399 UNTS 33 (No. 23391); ILM (1984), p. 1366; (1985) UKTS 26. The Joint Declaration entered into force on 28 May 1985. As to its treaty status, see p. 22 above. See P. Slinn, 'Le Règlement Sino-Britannique de Hong-Kong', *Annuaire français de droit international* (1985),

would have the status of a Special Administrative Region of China and be known as the 'Hong Kong Special Administrative Region' (HKSAR). It would enjoy a high degree of autonomy, except in foreign and defence affairs, which are the responsibility of the Central People's Government (CPG). Although the governing principles with regard to treaties were laid down, there was no mention of 'succession', since that might imply that China had previously validly ceded sovereignty to the United Kingdom, which China had never accepted. Section XI of Annex I to the Joint Declaration provides, in part, that:

> The application to the HKSAR of international agreements to which the People's Republic of China is or becomes a party shall be decided by the CPG, in accordance with the circumstances and needs of the HKSAR, and after seeking the views of the HKSAR Government. International agreements to which the People's Republic of China is not a party but which are implemented in Hong Kong may remain implemented in the HKSAR.

These general principles needed detailed elaboration by the Sino-British Joint Liaison Group (JLG) established by the Joint Declaration. The JLG was mandated in Annex II to the Joint Declaration with considering 'action to be taken by the two Governments to ensure the continued application of international rights and obligations affecting Hong Kong'. The JLG met until the end of 1999 as a forum in which the two governments were able to exchange views on matters relating to the implementation of the Joint Declaration. Multilateral and bilateral treaties were discussed separately.

Multilateral treaties

Over a ten-year period the JLG examined 225 multilateral treaties and agreed that all but twelve would continue to apply to the HKSAR. The treaties examined were (a) treaties to which the United Kingdom was a party and which it had extended to Hong Kong, whether or not China was a party (it was not a party to over eighty), but which would continue to apply to the HKSAR if China agreed, and (b) treaties to which China was a party but the United Kingdom was not.

p. 167; and P. Slinn, 'Aspects Juridiques du Retour de Hong-Kong à la Chine', *Annuaire français de droit international* (1996), p. 273. See also BYIL (1989), pp. 593–8; and BYIL (1997), pp. 529–35.

The JLG also agreed on the mechanism by which the other parties to the treaties would be informed of what had been agreed. This was done in two parts. First, on 20 June 1997, shortly before the handover, China sent a diplomatic note to the UN Secretary-General, with a request that he bring it to the attention of the Members of the United Nations and of the UN specialised agencies, notifying him that as from 1 July 1997 the treaties listed in Annex I to the note 'will be applied' to the HKSAR.[66] The Annex listed 126 multilateral treaties to which China was a party and which (a) had applied to Hong Kong before 1 July 1997; or (b) because they concern foreign affairs (e.g., the United Nations Charter) or defence (e.g., disarmament treaties) had to apply to the entire territory of China; or (c) were not applied to Hong Kong before 1 July 1997, but which it had been decided should apply to the HKSAR as from that date (e.g., the revised Berne Copyright Convention). Annex II to the note listed eighty-seven treaties which already applied to Hong Kong, but to which China was not then a party. The note said they would continue to apply to the HKSAR as from 1 July 1997. The effect of Annex II was to make China a party to those treaties in respect of the HKSAR only.

The Chinese note was matched by a note to the UN Secretary-General from the United Kingdom stating that from 1 July 1997 the United Kingdom would cease to be responsible for the international rights and obligations arising from the application of treaties to Hong Kong.[67] A list of 231 treaties was annexed. This was seventeen more than listed in the Chinese note, since the British note included treaties which would no longer apply to the HKSAR.

Secondly, with the exception of forty-nine ILO conventions, which were dealt with in a single note, China sent a separate note in respect of each treaty to its depositary in which it explained the legal basis for the continued application of the treaty to the HKSAR: as from handover, treaties to which China was also a party 'will apply', the ones to which it was not a party 'will continue to apply', and China would assume responsibility for the international rights and obligations arising from the application of treaties to the HKSAR. The notes specified also the reservations and declarations which would apply to the HKSAR. These were for the most part the same as those which had been made previously in respect of Hong Kong,

---

[66] ILM (1997), pp. 1675–83; UKTS (1997) 80, pp. 21–31.
[67] ILM (1997), pp. 1684–91; UKTS (1997) 80, pp. 9–21; BYIL (1997), pp. 536–7.

with suitable adaptations. Reservations and declarations made by China on becoming a party to them were not extended to the HKSAR, except where this had been agreed by the British and Chinese Governments. China's reservations regarding provisions for the compulsory jurisdiction of the International Court of Justice were extended to the HKSAR, as well as declarations about Taiwan. It was considered necessary for the parties to the treaties to be told formally of the continued application of reservations and declarations, and modifications to them, and no party has objected.

Thus, with a few exceptions, multilateral treaties which had applied to Hong Kong before handover continued to apply thereafter in all essential respects.

The Chinese notes to the depositaries were matched by notes from the United Kingdom by which it informed them that, as from 1 July 1997, it would cease to be responsible for the international rights and obligations arising from the application of treaties to Hong Kong. These included that most important human rights treaty, the International Covenant on Civil and Political Rights. China was not party to it,[68] and it was not included in Annex II to the Chinese note to the Secretary-General regarding treaties which China had agreed would continue to apply to the HKSAR. However, in Annex I, Section XIII, of the Joint Declaration it is provided that the 'provisions of [the Covenant] as applied to Hong Kong shall remain in force'. This was reiterated in the Chinese note to the UN Secretary-General of 20 June 1997.[69] In addition, the Basic Law (the constitution of the HKSAR) provides that the provisions of the Covenant 'shall be implemented through the laws of the [HKSAR]'. Information on the implementation in the HKSAR of the provisions of the Covenant is prepared by the HKSAR and transmitted by the CPG to the Human Rights Committee established by the Covenant. Reports on the HKSAR under those human rights treaties to which China is a party will be integrated into the reports submitted by China to the relevant treaty-monitoring bodies.

On all matters concerning pre-handover multilateral treaties (except those to which the HKSAR is a party in its own right, such as the World Trade Organisation Agreement), depositaries should, of course, communicate with the Chinese Foreign Ministry or the local Chinese embassy, not with the Government of the United Kingdom.

---

[68] In October 1998 China signed the Covenant and is expected to ratify it.
[69] See also the UK note of 1 July 1997 (BYIL (1997), pp. 537–8).

Bilateral treaties with third states

Bilateral treaties between the United Kingdom and third states (i.e. other than China) which had been extended to Hong Kong, and treaties concluded by Hong Kong under entrustment,[70] could, under the terms of the Joint Declaration, have continued to apply to the HKSAR. But, in contrast to a multilateral treaty where it is not necessarily a matter of great concern to other parties if a state succeeds to the rights and obligations under it, a bilateral treaty is the result of (often intense) bargaining, particularly if the subject is economic or commercial relations, or if it involves important aspects of sovereignty. Thus, as with newly independent states, it could not be assumed that a third state would be willing to accept that a bilateral treaty would continue to apply to the HKSAR, even with any necessary technical adjustments. It was agreed therefore in the JLG that *none* of the then existing bilateral treaties with third states would apply to the HKSAR after handover. Instead, a process was agreed by which, following agreement in the JLG, Hong Kong was entrusted by the United Kingdom to negotiate and conclude directly with third states the bilateral treaties which it would need in the future. Such treaties would then continue to apply to the HKSAR after handover.

Under this procedure, before handover a substantial number of states concluded treaties with Hong Kong on such matters as air services, investment promotion and protection, surrender of fugitive offenders, mutual legal assistance in criminal matters and transfer of prisoners, even though sometimes the third state already had a treaty on the same subject with China.[71] In some cases the treaties, such as air services agreements, replaced treaties between the third state and the United Kingdom to the extent to which they had applied to Hong Kong. Most of the replacement treaties concluded by Hong Kong recite in their preamble that the Government of Hong Kong was 'duly authorised to conclude this Agreement by the sovereign government which is responsible for its foreign affairs'. Since the handover more bilateral treaties have been entered into by the HKSAR.[72]

---

[70] See p. 52 above.
[71] For example, the HKSAR–US Agreement on Surrender of Fugitive Offenders 1996 (ILM (1997), p. 844); the HKSAR–US Agreement for the Transfer of Sentenced Persons 1997 (ILM (1997), p. 860); the HKSAR–Japan Investment Promotion and Protection Agreement 1997 (ILM (1997), p. 1425).   [72] See pp. 327–30 below.

Legal effect of the arrangements for third states

The UN Secretary-General, as depositary of some fifty of the multilateral treaties applicable to the HKSAR, has accepted that the arrangements are effective, as have other depositaries. The parties to various treaties have also taken the same view. No party to a multilateral treaty has objected to the continued application of a treaty to the HKSAR. For example, the Assembly of the International Oil Pollution Compensation Fund agreed that the Convention establishing the Fund[73] may continue to apply to the HKSAR even though China is not a party. A similar attitude has been exhibited by third states with respect to new bilateral treaties concluded by them with Hong Kong in the period leading up to the handover. Since they were all signed only after China had signified its approval in the JLG, and were designed to continue after the handover, they do not need further action by either China or the third state, and this was made abundantly clear to the negotiators of the third states.

The capacity of the HKSAR to conclude treaties

The Joint Declaration confers a 'high degree of autonomy' on the HKSAR, except for foreign and defence affairs, which are the responsibility of the CPG. Thus, section 3(9) and (10) authorise the HKSAR to establish economic relations with the United Kingdom and other countries, and provide that the HKSAR may on its own maintain and develop economic and cultural relations and conclude relevant agreements. The details of the treaty arrangements are elaborated in Annex I to the Joint Declaration, in particular in Section XI on foreign affairs, which provides, in part, that:

> The HKSAR may on its own, using the name 'Hong Kong, China', maintain and develop relations and conclude and implement agreements with states, regions and relevant international organisations in the appropriate fields, including the economic, trade, financial and monetary, shipping, communications, touristic, cultural and sporting fields.

This is repeated in the Basic Law. Thus, if the HKSAR wishes to conclude treaties in these fields, which because of the generality of the wording

---

[73] UKTS (1978) 95.

includes matters such as investment promotion and protection, double taxation, social security, intellectual property and customs co-operation,[74] it may do so without seeking authority from the CPG, general authority having been conferred by China in the Joint Declaration and reiterated in the Basic Law. Such treaties can be bilateral or multilateral, though many multilateral treaties will not be open to full participation by a non-state entity like the HKSAR.[75] Naturally, there cannot be bilateral treaties between China and the HKSAR, but *both* China and the HKSAR became or remained parties to certain multilateral treaties, such as the Asian Development Bank Agreement 1965, the Constitution of the Asia–Pacific Telecommunity 1976 and the Agreement on the Network of Aquaculture Centres in Asia and the Pacific 1988.

Annex I to the Joint Declaration makes specific provision for treaties in certain areas which involve particular aspects of sovereignty, and where it is therefore desirable that there should be no uncertainty as to the powers of the HKSAR. In the case of bilateral treaties for *reciprocal juridical assistance*, Section III provides that the CPG shall 'assist or authorise' the HKSAR to make appropriate arrangements. This means that the CPG must either take part in the negotiations or authorise the HKSAR to negotiate and conclude treaties on matters such as mutual legal assistance, reciprocal enforcement of judgments, surrender of fugitive offenders and transfer of prisoners. Authorisation may be given either generally or specifically. In practice, the CPG has given authorisations and not sought to participate in the negotiations: the HKSAR thus enters into bilateral treaties in these fields in its own right.

Section VI of Annex I provides that the HKSAR shall be a separate customs territory, and may participate in relevant *international trade agreements and organisations* (including preferential trade arrangements), and arrangements regarding international trade in textiles. For this purpose the HKSAR does not need authorisation from the CPG. The HKSAR has thus become a member of the World Trade Organisation even though China is not a member. Both China and the HKSAR are members of the International Textiles and Clothing Bureau, the World Tourist Organisation and the World Meteorological Organisation. As a member, the HKSAR has a vote in its own right.

---

[74] In November 1998 the EC and the HKSAR initialled a Customs Co-operation Agreement.
[75] See p. 53 above.

Detailed provisions are made in Section IX for *air services*. These provide, in particular, that 'acting under specific authorisations from the CPG', the HKSAR may:

(1) renew or amend air services agreements previously in force (in fact, air services agreements between the United Kingdom and third states which had been extended to Hong Kong by the United Kingdom were replaced before handover by new agreements between Hong Kong and the third states);[76] and

(2) negotiate and conclude, after handover, new air services agreements providing routes for HKSAR-based airlines. All scheduled air services to and from the HKSAR which do not operate to, from or through mainland China are regulated by such agreements.

The provisions of Section IX also contain standing authority for the HKSAR to negotiate and conclude all arrangements implementing air services agreements, i.e. MOUs. By these means the freedom of the HKSAR to continue to develop as a major centre for international air services, and to promote the interests of HKSAR-based airlines, has been assured.

Section XIV contains the undertaking of the CPG to 'assist or authorise' the HKSAR to conclude *visa abolition agreements*. Again, in practice the CPG has authorised the HKSAR to negotiate some agreements on its own.

By the end of 1998 the HKSAR had concluded twenty-six bilateral treaties on subjects such as investment promotion and protection, mutual legal assistance in criminal matters, surrender of fugitive offenders, transfer of prisoners, visa abolition and air services. The treaties specify in the preamble that the Government of the HKSAR has been 'duly authorised to conclude this Agreement by the Central People's Government of the People's Republic of China'.[77] Where necessary, the application article provides that the treaty shall apply, '[i]n relation to the Hong Kong Special Administrative Region of the People's Republic of China, to such region'. This makes it clear that it has no application to the rest of China.[78] All the treaties, are signed 'For the Government of the HKSAR of the People's Republic of China'.[79]

When a post-handover treaty to which the HKSAR may become a party in its own right is subject to ratification, the instrument of ratification is

[76] See p. 326 above.
[77] HKSAR–UK Agreement for the Transfer of Sentenced Persons 1997 (UKTS (1998) 51).
[78] HKSAR–UK Surrender of Fugitive Offenders Agreement (UKTS (1998) 30).
[79] HKSAR–UK Air Services Agreement 1997 (UKTS (1999) 27).

effected by the Government of the HKSAR, and in the case of a multilateral treaty the depositary should deal with the HKSAR.

Extension of treaties to the HKSAR by China

Before Hong Kong was returned to China the United Kingdom had extended many treaties to Hong Kong. The way these were dealt with on handover has been described above. Section XI of the Joint Declaration provides that after handover:

> The application to the HKSAR of international agreements to which the People's Republic of China is or becomes a party shall be decided by the Central People's Government (CPG), *in accordance with the circumstances and needs of the HKSAR, and after seeking the views of the HKSAR Government.*

The words emphasised are in recognition of the 'high degree of autonomy' which the HKSAR enjoys under the regime established by the Joint Declaration. It is also similar to the situation before handover when, in accordance with the general practice of the United Kingdom, Hong Kong was consulted about the extension of treaties, and only in an exceptional case would a treaty be extended against its objections.[80]

The Chinese note of 20 June 1997 to the UN Secretary-General envisaged in respect of treaties which were not listed in the note, but to which China was then or would become a party, that if it were decided to apply them to the HKSAR the CPG would separately carry out the formalities. This is a reference to the provisions of the Joint Declaration just quoted, pursuant to which China may, following consultations with the HKSAR, accept the obligations of a treaty in respect of the rest of China separately from its acceptance on behalf of the HKSAR. For the avoidance of doubt, the note also states that no separate formalities will need to be carried out by the CPG 'with respect to treaties which fall within the category of foreign affairs or defence or which, owing to their nature and provisions, must apply to the entire territory of a state'. However, even in those areas, to the extent that implementing legislation will be needed in the HKSAR to give effect to such treaties, the HKSAR will need to be consulted in order that the legislation can be made in good time. The HKSAR retains the dualist approach to giving effect to treaties in domestic law.[81]

---

[80] See pp. 166–8 above.   [81] See pp. 150–4 above.

Thus, despite the unique situation and its attendant difficulties – or perhaps because of them – the ingenious arrangements, devised by British and Chinese government lawyers, by which Hong Kong's treaty relations could be continued by the HKSAR, are more certain, effective and timely than those made for a normal post-colonial situation. The same procedure will apparently be used for Macau.[82] It will be interesting to see whether the arrangements may provide a precedent for any other special situations.

---

[82] See the statement by China recorded in *UN Multilateral Treaties*, Chapter XXV.2, note 3.

23

Drafting and final clauses

> The party of the first part shall be known in this contract as 'the party of the first part'. . . . the party of the second part shall be known in this contract as 'the party of the second part'.

This glorious comment on legal jargon by Otis B. Driftwood[1] is a useful reminder that even lawyers are not always good at drafting. This chapter will describe the way in which treaties, and to some extent MOUs, should be drafted, and what is good practice and what is not. It also suggests some drafting techniques. The views are inevitably subjective, though based on – sometimes bitter – experience.

Treaties do not have to be in any particular form.[2] But, with the principal exception of exchanges of notes (which are dealt with later in this chapter), most treaties consist of a single main instrument which follows a well-established pattern:

- title;
- preamble;
- main text;
- final clauses;
- testimonium and signature block;
- annexes (if any).

Title

The title consists of two elements: the designation (name) given the treaty and a description of its purpose.

---

[1] Aka Groucho Marx in *A Night at the Opera* (1935). But note the 1995 Interim Accord between Greece and the former Yugoslav Republic of Macedonia (ILM (1995), p. 1497) which, because of the opposition of Greece to the Republic of Macedonia using that name, refers to the parties as 'the party of the first part' and 'the party of the second part'. Such is the resourcefulness of the treaty-maker.   [2] See p. 17 above.

Name

As has been mentioned, there is no consistent practice in the naming of treaties.[3] Whereas Agreement, Convention and Treaty are perhaps the most common names given to treaties, other terms such as Act, Charter, Covenant, Pact and Protocol are also used. Although a self-standing treaty is sometimes called a Protocol, it is more common to use that name for an amending or subsidiary treaty. But, whereas a non-legally binding instrument like an MOU[4] would never be called – at least formally – an Agreement, terms such as Act, Charter and Protocol are also used for MOUs. In view of the importance of maintaining a clear distinction between treaties and MOUs, one should try to reflect this in the name. For treaties, unequivocal terms, such as Agreement, Convention and Treaty, should be used whenever possible. For MOUs, names such as Arrangement, Memorandum of Understanding or Understanding should be used. However, as previously mentioned, such names, in particular Memorandum of Understanding, are also used for treaties.[5] This may in the past have been because the parties, for political reasons, did not want the treaty to appear too formal. Since there is no legal difference between treaties and treaties in simplified form[6] – only between treaties and MOUs – it is regrettable that treaties are still called Memoranda of Understanding.

Purpose

There can be simple descriptions of the purpose of a treaty, and thoroughly bad descriptions. The descriptive titles of *multilateral* treaties are frequently far too long, and inevitably a shorthand title is used for all but the most formal purposes. The 'Agreement for the Implementation of the Provisions of the United Nations Convention on the Law of the Sea of 10 December 1982 relating to the Conservation and Management of Straddling Fish Stocks and Highly Migratory Fish Stocks' of 1995 is almost invariably referred to as the 'Straddling Stocks Agreement'. It is ironic that the Agreement supplements one of the longest and most important treaties of modern times, which happily enjoys the simple title of United Nations Convention on the Law of the Sea.

---

[3] See pp. 19–24 above.   [4] For an explanation of this term, see pp. 17–18 above.
[5] See p. 20 above.   [6] See pp. 14–15 above.

The Straddling Stocks Agreement is not quite the worse example. The prize for that may have to go to the 'Agreement concerning the Adoption of Uniform Technical Prescriptions for Wheeled Vehicles, Equipment and Parts which can be Fitted and/or Used on Wheeled Vehicles and the Conditions for Reciprocal Recognition of Approvals Granted on the Basis of these Prescriptions' of 1958. It was even increased to thirty-nine words from its original twenty-seven words.[7] One can only hope that those who have to implement the treaty have devised a shorthand name.

Sometimes the negotiating states will agree that the treaty should be known by a shorthand title.

We have already seen how some treaties, like the General Framework Agreement for Peace in Bosnia and Herzegovina 1995, are known by the place where they were adopted, but not necessarily signed: hence the 'Dayton Agreement'.[8] Many treaties with long titles are referred to by the acronyms of the shorthand version of the title. Thus the 'Convention on the Prohibition of the Development, Production, Stockpiling and Use of Chemical Weapons and on their Destruction' 1993, or 'Chemical Weapons Convention', is usually referred to as the 'CWC'. There is much to be said for the treaty or Final Act providing that the treaty may be referred to by a shorthand title.

The Comprehensive Nuclear-Test-Ban Treaty (the full title), or CTBT, is a good example of how things can be done better. Unless there is some important, political reason for a long title (and in most cases it is not obvious that there is), it should be possible to capture the nature and purpose of a treaty in a few words, as indeed was done for the Vienna Convention on the Law of Treaties. As with so many aspects of the law of treaties, the Convention is a sound and sensible model.

Titles pose less of a problem for *bilateral* treaties, if only because the parties will be the only ones affected by an impossibly long title. Unlike most multilateral treaties, bilateral treaties normally include in the title the full names of the parties. This is important if only to distinguish between the many bilateral treaties on the same subject. Thus a normal title will be:

Agreement on Co-operation in the Field of Tourism
between the Government of the United Kingdom of Great Britain and
Northern Ireland and the Government of the Republic of Albania[9]

---

[7] 335 UNTS 211 and 609 UNTS 290; *UN Multilateral Treaties*, Chapter XI.B-16.
[8] See p. 23 above.   [9] UKTS (1994) 42. See Appendix B.

An even simpler formula is:

Polaris Sales Agreement
between the Government of the United Kingdom of Great Britain and
Northern Ireland and the Government of the United States of America[10]

There should be no need to begin with the words 'Agreement on . . .'. The former treaty could have been entitled simply 'Tourism Agreement', since this is certainly how it will be referred to by those who will implement it.

Although the *full* names of the states should always be given in the title, they can be abbreviated in the main text. As we have seen, there can sometimes be a problem if, for political reasons, the name used by one of the states is not acceptable to the other.[11] Before the British–Irish Agreement of 10 April 1998,[12] the practice with a bilateral treaty between the Irish Republic and the United Kingdom had been for the title, preamble and testimonium of the original signed copy to be retained by the Republic to refer to 'the Government of Ireland' and 'the Government of the United Kingdom', and the one to be retained by the United Kingdom to refer to 'the Government of the United Kingdom *of Great Britain and Northern Ireland*' and 'the Government of *the Republic of* Ireland'. Starting with the 1998 Agreement, the practice has been for *both* originals to refer to the 'Republic of Ireland' and the 'United Kingdom of Great Britain and Northern Ireland'.[13]

Preamble

Multilateral treaties

The preamble should begin:

The States Parties to this Agreement/Convention/Treaty . . .

The term 'States Parties' (the words are usually given initial capital letters in treaty texts) is used in the Convention itself, and generally in multilateral treaties concluded within or under the auspices of the United Nations or the UN specialised agencies. It is the most accurate in that 'States'

---

[10] 479 UNTS 49 (No. 6871); UKTS (1963) 59. [11] See note 1 above on 'Macedonia'.

[12] ILM (1998), p. 777. The Agreement, as with earlier Irish–UK treaties on political matters, has no mention of the subject in the title.

[13] E.g., the 1998 Protocol to the Ireland–UK Double Taxation Agreement (UKTS (1999) 23).

reflects the fact that, although the treaty will be signed by representatives of governments, they do so on behalf of their states; and 'Parties' refers to the status the contracting states will have once they have consented to be bound by the treaty and it is in force for them (Article 2(1)(g)). But other terms are often found: Parties, Contracting Parties (often used in bilateral treaties), High Contracting Parties (e.g., in ICRC treaties), Contracting States, Contracting Governments, Signatory States, Partner Governments and Member States. None of these is necessarily wrong, and some may be more appropriate in particular circumstances, but unless there are special reasons, such as practice within a regional organisation, it is better to use 'States Parties' or, simply, 'Parties'. The latter is preferable if non-states, such as international organisations, are eligible to become parties.[14]

When the treaty is plurilateral (between only a few states) the preamble will often begin with the names of all the negotiating states. The Memorandum of Understanding (actually a treaty) on the Avoidance of Overlaps and Conflicts relating to Deep Sea-Bed Areas 1991[15] begins with the names of the negotiating states and then provides that they shall be 'hereinafter referred to as the "Parties"'. Despite the use of such a ponderous term as 'hereinafter', this formula is a useful way of simplifying the rest of the text of any treaty, not just a plurilateral treaty. Alternatively, after setting out the names of the parties, it is enough to add '("the Parties")'. One can thereafter use this term in the main text.

Preambular paragraphs

There is no rule or custom as to what the rest of the preamble should contain; everything depends on the circumstances. In fact, from the *legal* point of view there is no need to say more than:

> The Parties to this [Agreement], *have agreed* as follows . . .

But if more needs to be said, the primary aim should be to introduce the main text of the treaty by including a few paragraphs about the background and the purpose of the treaty. Sometimes the preamble contains what are essentially political statements. It may also refer to a matter which a negotiating state was unsuccessful in having included in the body of the

---

[14] See the Climate Change Convention 1992 (ILM (1993), p. 851; UKTS (1995) 28; UN Reg. No. 30822).   [15] UKTS (1991) 52.

treaty, though usually in a much watered-down version. As with UN resolutions, the preamble is a convenient repository for the remnants of
causes, large and small, which were lost during the negotiating process. In
this, it serves a valuable purpose. Often negotiations become bogged down
over a point insisted on by one delegation, or sometimes a few. By suggesting that it might be dealt with by including 'a suitable form of words'
(which will have to be agreed) in the preamble, further pointless arguments may be avoided, and the loser will be able to report to his government that, despite considerable pressure from others to exclude all
mention of the point, they had been persuaded to include it upfront in the
preamble. At the FAO Conference which adopted the Compliance
Agreement 1993, the first contentious issue was the problem of 'reflagging'
of fishing vessels,[16] but because it was not possible to reach a consensus
oblique references to it were included in the preamble.[17] By such means the
'face' of a government is saved, if not the credibility of its negotiator. But
the device should be used sparingly. The preamble is part of the context of
the treaty for the purposes of interpretation (Article 31(2)),[18] including for
determining the object and purpose of the treaty.[19] It is therefore important to ensure that the preambular paragraphs are not inconsistent with
the main text. The more one burdens the preamble with unnecessary, but
not always insubstantial, material, the greater the danger that it will come
to be relied on to support a particular interpretation of the main text.

   In addition to keeping the preamble as short as possible, another objective of the chairman of a conference is to postpone detailed consideration
of the preamble for as long as possible. Because it appears at the beginning,
there is a natural – but misguided – tendency to start the negotiations by
discussing it.[20] This is usually a mistake. Although preambles have their
uses, their value is insignificant compared with the rest of the treaty. The
final clauses, which are often not given as much attention as they should
be, are considerably more important. Much time can be wasted discussing
the preamble before the shape and content of the main text and the final
clauses have been determined.

   Each preambular paragraph begins with a participle such as 'Recalling',
'Recognising', 'Noting', 'Convinced', and suchlike. It is customary either

---

[16] The changing of the state of registry of a vessel, in this case to avoid fishing controls.
[17] ILM (1994), p. 968.   [18] See p. 188 above.   [19] See pp. 110–12 above.
[20] To start by discussing the preamble may be logical, but is, as a French diplomatic friend once
said, to put Déscartes before the horse.

to underline or italicise such opening words, but this is purely a matter of style. The preamble to the Convention is a good model. As a practical matter, when a draft preamble contains several paragraphs it is useful to number them for ease of reference. The numbers are removed once drafting has been completed.

The preamble, whatever its length, should end with a final paragraph:

Have agreed as follows:

Bilateral treaties

The preamble to a bilateral treaty will usually begin:

The Government of Freedonia and the Government of Utopia ('the Parties')
. . .

and end:

Have agreed as follows:

There is seldom need for more than a few preambular paragraphs, if any.

MOUs

The preamble of an MOU will look similar to that of a treaty, except that the governments will normally be described as such or as 'the Participants'. Instead of the formula, '*Have agreed* as follows', the preamble should end 'Have reached the following understanding(s)', or 'Have decided' or 'the Governments/Participants will'.

Main text

The main text is naturally the heart of the treaty. Some suggestions on how to approach its drafting are at the end of this chapter. For the moment we will concentrate on form and layout. One might be forgiven for thinking that the drafters of some multilateral treaties never have to use them. Treaties are tools of international life and in constant use; they should therefore be user-friendly. But they are becoming longer and more complex. The Vienna Convention itself, with eighty-five relatively short articles, is now dwarfed by treaties such as the UN Convention on the Law of the Sea 1982 (UNCLOS), the Chemical Weapons Convention 1993 (CWC) and the Comprehensive Nuclear-Test-Ban Treaty 1996 (CTBT). UNCLOS[21] has 320 articles and nine, sometimes lengthy, annexes, yet it is quite easy to navigate. This is because each article is kept as short as possible and has a heading, as have the annexes. The CWC[22] is much more difficult to use. The fact that it has only twenty-four articles is misleading. Some are quite unnecessarily long. Article VIII consists of no less than fifty-one paragraphs. Article IX has twenty-five paragraphs. Others have nineteen and seventeen paragraphs. But that is not all. There are three (unnumbered) annexes. The most often consulted, the Annex on Implementation and Verification, has eleven Parts, some of which stretch to no less than eighty-six, sixty-nine, sixty-six, thirty-two(twice) and twenty-seven paragraphs. The difficulty in using the CWC was recognised at the time by the inclusion of a table of contents of the Annex referred to, though it is not a substitute for splitting it into more manageable pieces. The same mistakes were made in the CTBT,[23] the form of which follows that of the CWC. The article on verification has sixty-eight paragraphs and the one on the Organisation has fifty-seven paragraphs. Although the CTBT has only two short annexes, it has a Protocol on Monitoring which is split into three Parts. The second has no less than 110 paragraphs.

Although one appreciates that complex subjects cannot be treated in short, simple treaties, that is no reason why they should not be reasonably simple to use, whether by lawyers, diplomats, legislators, technical experts, or indeed even by students and members of the public. With mammoth articles it becomes that much more difficult to find (or even to cite) a particular provision. This is especially so when there are no less than nine paragraphs each numbered 25, as in the CWC and its attachments. Dividing up an article or an annex by sub- and sub-sub-headings is not the answer; although it may give the appearance of order, it does not make the text any easier to read, or to refer to. Sometimes treaties have been drafted in this way is because what began as short, simple articles were later added to many times, and during the process of, no doubt lengthy and difficult negotiations, no one had the time, energy, initiative or simple good sense to concern themselves with how the treaty would look or read; and by the time the negotiations were over there was no time

---

[21] ILM (1982), p. 1261; UN Reg. No. 31394; UKTS (1999) 81.
[22] ILM (1993), p. 804; UKTS (1996) 45; UN Reg. No. 33757.   [23] ILM (1996), p. 1443.

or energy left to recast the text. Although this is understandable, a better laid-out text can be produced if a conscious effort is made from the start. Here are some suggestions.

Layout of the main text

The layout and numbering of the Vienna Convention itself (to which many draftsmen turn in time of need) is a good guide to the right way to do it. It consists of eighty-five articles, each with a heading. No article is longer than six paragraphs. The articles are grouped into eight 'Parts', each with a short heading. These are then divided into 'Sections'. The need for this latter grouping is marginal, though it does enable one to make reference to a group of articles on, say, reservations. But, in practice, it is necessary to refer to the numbers of the articles since they are always easier to find than a Part, or a Section of a Part. Even if the published version of the Convention comes with a table of contents (see below), this is chiefly of use in finding a particular article or series of articles.

Headings

Even today one finds new treaties where the articles have no headings. Even (perhaps especially) during drafting and negotiation, headings are extremely useful in helping to find one's way around the text, particularly if the numbers of the articles have to change during the negotiations. Headings may be added at any time, provided it is understood that until the substance of the draft has been agreed, they are only provisional. This can be emphasised by temporarily putting the headings in square brackets. As with the preamble, there should be *no* discussion of the headings until the end of the negotiations: otherwise much time may be wasted arguing over the wording of what is no more than a label. Although there can be arguments over exactly what should be in the heading, these are not generally serious, and should not discourage the draftsman from inserting headings in the very first draft. Most headings can be very short. Those in the Vienna Convention are rather different in that some of them are, in effect, summaries of the content of the articles (Article 18 is headed 'Obligation not to defeat the object and purpose of a treaty prior to its entry into force'), but for that reason are rather useful.

Numbering of the main text

The articles of the Vienna Convention itself have Arabic numbers (1, 2, 3 etc.); the Parts have Roman numerals (I, II, III etc.); and the Sections of the Parts have Arabic numbers. In the past it was customary to use Roman numerals for articles, and they are, regrettably, still found in some new treaties. This should be avoided, especially if the treaty has many articles. For those without the benefit of a classical education, Article 79 of the Vienna Convention is that bit easier to find than Article LXXIX. Roman numerals can, as in the Convention, be used for numbering the Parts (or Chapters). Since there are only eight Parts to the Convention and one Annex, this is acceptable; but when a treaty has more than one annex it may be better to use Arabic numbers for the Parts of the main text, and Roman numerals for the parts of the annexes, so distinguishing them clearly from the main text.

Paragraph numbering

Articles should be divided into paragraphs, sub-paragraphs and sub-sub-paragraphs, as follows:

1. A state whose vessels ...
2. A state shall authorise ...
3. Measures to be taken by a state in respect of vessels flying its flag shall include:

    (a) control of such vessels ... ;
    (b) establishment of regulations to:
       (i) apply terms ... ;
       (ii) prohibit fishing ... ;[24]

If an article has only one paragraph it should *not* be numbered, and if it has sub-paragraphs, they should continue to be numbered (a), (b), etc., (*not* 1, 2, 3 etc.). If it should be necessary to have *sub-sub*-sub-paragraphs, they should be numbered either (aa), (bb), or (A), (B), etc. One should avoid numbering which emulates that found in modern commercial contracts (1.1.1, 1.1.2, 1.2.1 etc.).[25] Not only is it inelegant, but, despite its

---

[24] See the Straddling Stocks Agreement 1995 (ILM (1995), p. 1542).
[25] See the 1996 Protocol to the London Dumping Convention (Cm 4078).

apparent simplicity, it is not as easy to use as one might think, and can (as the above example illustrates) lead to errors, especially typographical.

Cross-references

If one is referring to an article of the treaty itself, or in an article to a paragraph of that article, one should avoid pedantic cross-referencing, such as 'Article 4 *above*' or 'paragraph 6 *below*'. If there really might be doubt as to which particular article or paragraph is being referred to, one can add 'of this treaty' or 'of this article'.

When the reference is to a paragraph or sub-paragraph of another article one should use the formula 'Article 4(6)(a)(i)' rather than 'sub-sub-paragraph (a)(i) of paragraph 6 of Article 4' or 'Article 4, paragraph 6, sub-sub-paragraph (a)(i)'. The preferred form is more logical – one looks first for the article and then for the paragraph, etc. – as well as being neater than either of the alternatives.

Footnotes

It is not usual to find footnotes to a treaty text, except perhaps in the text as later published, and then only for information, such as a reference for a treaty mentioned in the text. There is, however, nothing in principle against the inclusion of footnotes in the text of a treaty, provided there is no more suitable way of dealing with the matter. A footnote should not, for example, be used to express the objection or reservation of one or more of the negotiating states to a provision. Footnotes should be used very sparingly and restricted to providing *information* to the reader which is more conveniently conveyed in this manner rather than in the body of the treaty, in the Final Act or in a resolution.[26]

MOUs

The points about layout and numbering apply generally to MOUs as well, except that one should use sections or paragraphs (with headings of course), rather than articles.

---

[26] For an example, see the 'Explanatory Notes' following Articles IX and XVI of the World Trade Organisation Agreement 1994, and the attached Understanding on Rules and Procedures Governing the Settlement of Disputes (ILM (1994), p. 1144).

Terminology

In order to make clear the intention to enter into a treaty, it is the established practice to use terms, both in the main text and in annexes, which convey the intention that it will be legally binding rather than an MOU.[27] The text should therefore use 'shall' (in French the present tense would be used), 'agree', and 'rights' and 'obligations'. A table contrasting the terminology which should be used for a treaty and for an MOU is at Appendix G. It may look comic, but it works.

Definitions

Most treaties have a list of definitions in the first or second article. Definitions help to keep the text simple and uncluttered by making it unnecessary to repeat long, descriptive phrases throughout the treaty. The Vienna Convention once again shows how it should be done. Article 2 contains only nine definitions, but each is a model of precision combined with lucidity and conciseness.

Some drafters prefer to put all the definitions into the definitions article. Logic, order and consistency are desirable in drafting, but should not be applied slavishly. If a term needs to be defined, but is used in only one article, it is better to define it in that article and not in the definitions article, though the latter might have a cross-reference to the definition. Once again, the CWC shows how *not* to do it. Article II contains definitions of eleven terms used throughout the CWC. The twelfth definition contains (as it says so itself) definitions for the purposes of Article VI only. It would therefore have been more sensible if they had been included at the beginning of that article.

It is not easy to say when definitions should be added to the text: so much depends on the circumstances, but it will become apparent during the course of drafting and redrafting when they are needed. Unless it is obvious when preparing the initial draft that particular definitions will be needed, it is better not to try to anticipate them, though a (blank) definitions article should be included, as the first or second article, in the first draft. This should at least avoid the need to renumber the whole text later.

---

[27] See p. 27 above.

Privileges and immunities

The matter of privileges and immunities is included here because, like final clauses, it is often regarded, albeit wrongly, as a routine matter, and rarely given proper attention at an early stage, yet will normally need legislation. Unlike final clauses, privileges and immunities are not solely the concern of foreign ministries. The subject, which includes conferring legal personality on a new international organisation, exemptions from taxation and immunity from the jurisdiction of national courts, touches upon the rights of the ordinary citizen. Moreover, the provisions will need implementing in domestic law, even if the rest of the treaty does not. Consultations with several ministries may therefore be necessary, and it is the task of the foreign ministry to co-ordinate this work. Since the process could be lengthy, ideally the proposed provisions should be considered in parallel with the main text.

Privileges and immunities will normally be required if, for example, the treaty is establishing a new international organisation or if it is necessary to confer certain privileges and immunities on, say, members of armed forces or inspection teams.[28] Although there are no model articles, as such, one should try to follow as closely as possible those in treaties on similar subjects.[29] If, as is usually the case, there are several articles, they may be put into an annex or even a self-contained treaty. MOUs, principally in the defence field, sometimes make provision for privileges and immunities.[30]

Table of contents

Even though its preparation is a purely mechanical operation, it is rare to find a table of contents even in a long and complex multilateral treaty. Notable exceptions are the Verification Annexes to the Chemical Weapons Convention, and the CTBT. Since a table is sometimes added by a state when it publishes the treaty, there is no reason why it should not more

---

[28] See Article VIII, paragraphs 48–51, and Part II, Section B, of the Verification Annex to the CWC (note 22 above).

[29] For European treaties a good starting point is Annex I to the Convention establishing the European Space Agency 1975 (1297 UNTS 161 (No. 21524); ILM (1975), p. 864; UKTS (1981) 30), though more recent provisions should also be considered, depending on the subject matter of the treaty.   [30] And see pp. 33–4 above.

commonly be included in the adopted text, or why the negotiating states should not request, perhaps in the Final Act, that the depositary include a table of contents in the certified copy of the treaty which he will provide to them.

Final clauses

Final clauses can be a trap for the unwary. Compared with the main body of a treaty, the final clauses may appear to anyone who is not a foreign ministry lawyer to be less important, and in a sense they are. But, as should be apparent from earlier chapters,[31] final clauses do play an essential, if different, role from the main text. Unfortunately they are not always given the care and attention they deserve, even though they are crucial to the smooth operation of any treaty. It may be because they come at the end of the treaty that they are not always given the same deep thought as the main text, or even the preamble. Too often they are perceived as purely formal provisions which have only to be copied or adapted from another similar treaty. Although they are usually based on precedents – and once again the Vienna Convention is a good starting point – it is vital that they are drafted with the needs of the particular treaty in mind. Although some clauses are truly technical, some will need policy decisions.

Now that so many treaties are negotiated primarily by specialists (even if they include lawyers), rather than generalist diplomats and foreign ministry lawyers, the importance of final clauses may not always be fully appreciated, and their drafting done too late. It is rare to find the first draft of a treaty with a full set of (or, for that matter, any) final clauses. This can lead to errors, some of which can be quite troublesome.[32] If a multilateral treaty is being negotiated within an international organisation, or at a conference at which an international organisation provides the secretariat, the legal department of the organisation should provide the necessary expertise. Otherwise delegations need to seek advice from their own foreign ministry lawyers at an early stage, and especially if they are not taking a direct part in the negotiations.

Final clauses can include articles on:

---

[31] See, for examples, those on consent to be bound and entry into force.
[32] See p. 218 above (the percentage problem); Chapter 13 regarding the interpretation of Article XIV of the CTBT; and p. 93, note 58, above (participation clause of the Climate Change Convention).

- relationship to other treaties
- settlement of disputes*
- amendment and review*
- status of annexes*
- signature*
- ratification*
- accession*
- entry into force*
- duration
- withdrawal/termination*
- provisional application
- territorial application
- reservations*
- depositary*
- registration
- authentic texts*

Those marked with an asterisk will be found in most multilateral treaties, and many bilateral treaties. Inclusion of the others will depend on the nature and content of the treaty. The length of the list illustrates the many different matters covered by final clauses, some of which, such as settlement of disputes, amendment, duration, termination and entry into force, may be of prime importance and raise difficult questions of policy (e.g., whether there should be compulsory arbitration). One article may deal with two or more of these subjects.

There are no rigid formulas for these various provisions, and therefore the examples given are not necessarily the 'right' ones. One of the problems is the very wide variety of final clauses. Earlier examples can be found in Blix and Emerson. In 1957 the United Nations published a *Handbook of Final Clauses* which is updated from time to time.[33]

MOUs

An MOU will possibly have provisions on settlement of disputes, amendment, duration and withdrawal/termination. Signature and coming into operation or effect will normally be dealt with in a simplified testimonium (see Appendix D).

---

[33] See ST/LEG/6 and ST/LEG/SER. D/1, Annex and Supplements 1 to 11.

Where appropriate, what follows should be read with earlier chapters.

Relationship to other treaties

A provision on this matter will not always be needed for multilateral treaties, and seldom for bilateral treaties (see Chapter 12). MOUs seldom include an equivalent provision.

Settlement of disputes

It is normal to find an article on the settlement of disputes concerning the interpretation or application of the treaty, whether it is bilateral or multilateral. There are many precedents, although they tend to follow a certain pattern (see Chapter 20). An MOU will have either no such clause or one on the following lines:

> Any dispute regarding the interpretation or application of this MOU will be resolved by consultations between the Participants, and will not be referred to any national or international tribunal or third party for settlement.

Some MOUs include near the end a formula such as:

> This Memorandum records the commitments of the Participants; it does not create legally binding obligations.[34]

Amendment and revision

It is increasingly common to find a provision about amendment or revision. In the past there was a tendency not to think that far ahead. As a result the amendment of treaties which included no such built-in provision caused, and continues to cause, considerable problems. Today's multilateral treaties are so complex, and need to be adjusted to meet changes, that an amendment clause is often essential (see Chapter 15).

MOUs will sometimes have a clause providing that:

> This MOU may be amended at any time, in writing, by the mutual consent of the Participants. No amendment will have effect until signed by [both] [all] Participants.

---

[34] See also p. 28 above.

Status of annexes

When a treaty has an annex it is normal to provide, though not necessarily in a separate article, that the annex is an integral part of the treaty. Since there are often other documents produced at the time the treaty is adopted, such as agreed minutes, declarations and interpretative exchanges of notes, it is important to know whether they are an integral part of the treaty, or merely associated with it. As a typical example, Article XVII of the CWC provides:

> The Annexes form an integral part of this Convention. Any reference to this Convention includes the Annexes.

Signature

This section should be read with pages 75–8 above. Treaties do not have to be signed,[35] and many, particularly bilateral, do not have a separate article on signature, it being implicit from the terms of the testimonium.[36] But most multilateral treaties have a specific article on signature. The formula chosen depends on whether the treaty will enter into force on signature or is subject to ratification. A treaty adopted within or under the auspices of the United Nations, a UN specialised agency or other international organisation, will today usually provide:

> This [treaty] shall be open for signature by [all States] and shall remain open for signature at [place] from [date] until [date].

As indicated, the article will normally set a deadline for signature. There is no legal requirement for this: the purpose is mainly political. Governments like to be able to say (particularly if it will take some time to ratify the treaty because of the need for parliamentary approval or new legislation) that they are 'a signatory'.[37] Setting a deadline thus encourages those states to sign, and the more that sign, the greater the effect politically, including on those parliaments which have to act before those states can ratify.

It is less common for a multilateral treaty to enter into force upon

---

[35] See p. 24 above.
[36] See the 1987 Agreement between six NATO members regarding inspections relating to the US–USSR Treaty on elimination of certain missiles (ILM (1988), p. 60; UKTS (1991) 31).
[37] See p. 91 on the misuse of the term.

signature, though this is provided for in some treaties which are between only a small number of states, provided no parliamentary procedure is needed before the treaties can enter into force for them all. Such a treaty will usually provide:

> This Agreement shall enter into force upon signature.

This simple formula assumes that the treaty will be signed by all on the same day, which will usually be the case for such treaties. Otherwise the treaty will provide that it 'shall enter into force on the date of the last signature'.

A bilateral treaty is usually signed by both parties on the same day, and frequently provides for entry into force upon signature.

Ratification

When ratification is required for a multilateral treaty, a normal provision would be as in Article 82 of the Vienna Convention:

> The present Convention is subject to ratification. The instruments of ratification shall be deposited with the [name of the depositary].

Sometimes the sentence about deposit of instruments of ratification is omitted, the matter being implicit from the article on the depositary. In the case of a bilateral treaty, it is usual to provide something on the following lines:

> This [treaty] shall be ratified, and the instruments of ratification shall be exchanged at [place] as soon as possible.

Sometimes the article will provide for a procedure analogous to ratification:

> Each Party shall notify the other of the completion of the constitutional formalities required by its laws for the entry into force of this Agreement.

Accession

Accession is only relevant to multilateral treaties. Nowadays those which are subject to ratification almost always include provision for accession during the period *before* entry into force and, depending on the terms of the accession article, a state will be able to accede after a specified date (e.g., the deadline for signature) or a specified event or at any time (for examples and further details, see pages 88–90 above) .

Entry into force

With a few exceptions, one will always find an express provision on entry into force (see pages 131–5 above). When there is none, it will be implicit from the terms of the treaty when entry into force will happen.

Duration and denunciation, withdrawal or termination

It is normal to provide for the duration of the treaty and the procedure by which a party may withdraw from it, or for the conditions under which it can be terminated, unless the treaty is such that that possibility is not envisaged. There are numerous examples of such clauses (see pages 225–32 above).

In a simple bilateral treaty the termination provision is often combined with other provisions:

(1) Each Party shall notify the other of the completion of the constitutional formalities required by its laws for the entry into force of this Agreement. This Agreement shall enter into force on the first day of the month following the expiration of one calendar month after the date of the later of the two notifications.

(2) It may be terminated by either Party by giving notice to the other through the diplomatic channel. It shall cease to be in force six months after the date of receipt of such notice.

Provisional application

It is not usual to include a provisional application clause. The matter is complex (see pages 139–41 above).

Territorial application

When some of the negotiating states have overseas territories, a clause providing for the treaty to be extended to one or more of them may be included (see pages 163–5 above), but it is not essential.[38]

---

[38] See pp. 165–8 above.

Reservations

Reservation clauses are found only in multilateral treaties, but not in all. When one is included, it may prohibit reservations:

No reservations may be made to this Convention.

Alternatively, the clause will specify those categories of reservations which are permissible. The content of the clause will depend entirely on the rest of the treaty. For examples and further details see pages 109–10 above.

Depositary

A clause about the depositary is only necessary for a multilateral treaty. It may be a separate article providing that, for example:

The Secretary-General of the United Nations shall be the depositary of this Agreement.

The article may include an illustrative list of the depositary's functions, though this should not be necessary if the depositary is the head of the secretariat of an international organisation which regularly acts as a depositary, and therefore needs no reminding of his duties. The main functions are set out in detail in Article 77. It should therefore be enough to specify only those functions which are peculiar to the treaty.

Often a separate article is dispensed with. Article 85 (Authentic texts) of the Vienna Convention provides simply that the original of the Convention 'shall be deposited with the Secretary-General of the United Nations'. For more details and examples, see pages 262–5 above.

Registration

It is not necessary to provide in a treaty that it shall be registered, since under Article 102 of the UN Charter there is already an obligation to do so. Nevertheless, some treaties, including even treaties for which the UN Secretary-General is the depositary, have a provision directing the depositary to register. Thus Article XV of the FAO Compliance Agreement 1993 provides that the FAO Director-General, as depositary, shall:

arrange for the registration of this Agreement, upon its entry into force, with the Secretariat of the United Nations in accordance with Article 102 of the Charter of the United Nations.

The advantage of such a clause is as a reminder to the depositary. The FAO formula is useful since it contains the further useful reminder that the treaty cannot be registered until it has entered into force.[39]

Authentic texts

Probably more than half of all modern treaties are in two or more languages, and these days multilateral treaties are very rarely in only one language. There is normally only one original copy of a multilateral treaty, which will contain all the authentic language texts.

Testimonium

'Testimonium' is the Latin name for the last, formal part of a treaty beneath which the representatives sign. It is not essential, and a treaty adopted at an FAO Conference will not have one since FAO treaties are not signed.[40] The Landmines Convention 1997 dispensed with a testimonium, the signature article merely noting that the Convention was 'done at Oslo, on 18 September 1997'. It is not clear if this innovation was intentional.[41]

A testimonium consists of the following formal statement:

> In witness whereof the undersigned, being duly authorised [by their respective Governments], have signed this [Agreement].
> Done at [place], this [   ] day of [   ], two thousand and [   ].

The reference to being authorised by their respective Governments can be omitted, and should be when a non-state entity is entitled to sign.

Sometimes the order of the two sentences is reversed, which would in fact appear to be the more logical order. The words 'In witness whereof' and 'Done' are often in capital letters, but this is purely a matter of style.

The Convention uses the term 'undersigned Plenipotentiaries', which means that the representatives are invested with full powers. Although this is sometimes still found today (e.g., the Straddling Stocks Agreement 1995), it is gradually falling into disuse (e.g., the CWC 1993). The term is anyway superfluous because of the inclusion of 'duly authorised'.

There then follow the 'signature blocks', that is the spaces in which

---

[39] See pp. 276–7 above.
[40] Compliance Agreement 1993 (ILM (1994), p. 968). See also p. 24 above.
[41] ILM (1997), p. 1509; UKTS (1998) 18. See Article 15.

representatives sign. Each block will begin with the words:

For [the Government of] Atlantis:

The name of the representative is *not* typed in. In the case of a multilateral treaty, the names of the states or governments are set out in alphabetical order according to the language of the treaty. When the treaty is in more than one language the different language texts (including any annexes, but not the testimonium) will follow, one after the other. The treaty will then end with the testimonium repeated in each of the language versions. In UN practice the states are then listed in English alphabetical order. There will be only *one* signature block. In other words, even when a multilateral treaty is in two or more languages, a representative signs only one original, and signs only once.

Bilateral treaties

If the treaty is to be signed in only one language, the testimonium will read:

In witness whereof the undersigned, being duly authorised thereto, have signed this [Agreement].
Done in duplicate at [place], this [   ] day of [   ], two thousand and [   ].
For the Government of   For the Government of
[   ]:   [   ]:
[signature]   [signature]

In one of the originals the name of one of the parties will be put before the name of the other in the title, preamble, main text, testimonium and signature blocks; in the other original the name of the other party will be put first. This alternating in the texts is known as the *alternat*.[42] Each representative will take away the original in which the name of his state is given precedence: a small, quintessentially diplomatic, touch.

If the treaty is in two languages the second sentence of the testimonium will read:

Done in duplicate at [place], this [   ] day of [   ], two thousand [   ], in the [   ] and [   ] languages, both texts being equally authentic.

The two originals will each include both language versions. One of the

---

[42] See *Satow*, para. 29.42.

originals will accord precedence to one of the states in *both* language versions, the precedence being reversed in the other original. Each representative will take away the original which gives precedence to his state. But if time is short, or it will not be easy to produce alternate texts in the two language versions (perhaps because one of the languages is 'difficult'), each party will be given precedence only in the versions of the text which are in its own language ('language precedence').[43] Note also that a bilateral treaty can be in three languages.[44]

It is no longer the practice to affix seals next to the signatures, except sometimes for heads of state treaties. In any case, sealing has no legal significance today.

Increasingly in bilateral treaties the testimonium is omitted. The testimonium of the UN–Iraq Memorandum of Understanding 1998 on weapons inspections reads:

> Signed this 23rd day of February 1998 in Baghdad in two originals in the English language.[45]

There are no final clauses, and no preamble. As for matters of form it is in some ways a model for bilateral treaties.

MOUs

An MOU does not have a testimonium as such. There is no standard form, but an MOU contained in a single document will usually end:

> The foregoing represents the understandings reached by the [Participants] [Governments].
> Signed in duplicate at [place], on [   ], in [[one language] *or* [in the [   ] and [   ] languages, each text having equal validity]].

There would then follow the same signature blocks as for a treaty.

Annexes

If a treaty has attachments it will usually provide that they are integral.[46] They will be named variously Annex, Protocol, Appendix or Schedule. Some treaties use more than one term. The Comprehensive Nuclear-Test-

---

[43] Today diplomacy *does* have other concerns as well. For an amusing account of the importance in the past of precedence and the *alternat*, see H. Nicolson, *The Congress of Vienna* (1946), pp. 217–20.   [44] See p. 202–4 above.

[45] ILM (1998), p. 501; UN Doc. S/1998/166. See also the Russia–Ukraine Treaty 1997 (UN Doc. A/52/174).   [46] See p. 348 above.

Ban Treaty 1996 (CTBT) has two Annexes (numbered 1 and 2) to the Treaty itself and a Protocol with two Annexes of its own (also numbered 1 and 2). This is unnecessarily confusing, since when referring to an annex one has to say always whether it is to the Treaty or to the Protocol. Unless there are good reasons for using different designations for the attachments to a treaty (and there may be political reasons in some cases), if an attachment is an integral part of the treaty it should be called an Annex, and if there are more than one they should all be called Annex and numbered. The name Protocol should be avoided, since it is used extensively as the title for amendment treaties (and sometimes even self-standing treaties), or for a treaty which is separate from but related to another new treaty. A typical example would be an optional protocol on settlement of disputes.[47] If it is necessary to have an attachment to an annex it should be named Appendix or Schedule.

Since some annexes are long and substantive, it is prudent to distinguish their provisions from those in the treaty itself. Since 'Article' should always be used in the treaty, it should *not* be used in an Annex. The Annex to the 1969 Vienna Convention is divided into seven *paragraphs*. If the Annex is much longer, it is better for it to be arranged as a series of 'Sections', each containing as few paragraphs as possible and with a heading to each Section. If desired, the Sections can be grouped into Chapters (or Parts if the main text is divided into Chapters, and *vice versa*).

Of course there may be other instruments which, although associated with the treaty, are not either expressly or by necessary implication integral to it, such as resolutions, and which may be attached to the Final Act. Although not part of the treaty as such, they may play a role in its interpretation.[48]

Exchange of notes

An exchange of notes (or letters) can constitute a treaty or an MOU.[49] The difference in status is indicated solely by the wording. An exchange of notes which constitutes a treaty will, in addition to usual treaty terminology in the body of the note (e.g., 'shall' rather than 'will'), have in the initiating note an opening paragraph ending with a formula such as:

I therefore have the honour to *propose*[50] the following:

The precise form of words will depend on the content. The note will end

---

[47] E.g., the Optional Protocol to the Vienna Convention on Diplomatic Relations 1961 concerning the Compulsory Settlement of Disputes (500 UNTS 241 (No. 7132); UKTS (1965) 19).
[48] See pp. 188–91 above.   [49] See p. 21 above.
[50] Remember, all emphasis is the author's unless otherwise indicated.

with a formula like:

> If the foregoing *proposals* are acceptable to the Government of Freedonia, I have the honour to *propose* that this Note and your reply in that sense *shall constitute an Agreement*[51] between our two Governments, which *shall enter into force* on the date of Your Excellency's reply.

The reply note will read:

> Your Excellency,
> I have the honour to refer to your Note No. [   ] of [date], which reads as follows:
>
> > [*The main text of the first note is then set out. If the reply note is in another language, the text of the first note will set out only in translation.*]
>
> I have the honour to confirm that the foregoing *proposals* are acceptable to the Government of Freedonia, and your Excellency's Note and this reply *shall constitute an Agreement* between our two Governments in this matter, which *shall enter into force* on [today's date].

See Appendix E. It is good practice to repeat the main text of the initiating note since this avoids any doubt as to what has been agreed, and especially if the reply is to be in a different language. It can sometimes be simpler for a bilateral treaty in two languages to be in the form of an exchange of notes. Although each state must check both language texts for accuracy, it may be easier for each to produce the text for signature in its own language, especially when the two languages (e.g., French and Arabic) do not share the same alphabet. It is not customary to provide, as one usually would in a single instrument treaty, that both texts are equally authentic.

MOUs

In contrast, an exchange of notes which amounts to no more than an MOU will, in addition to employing MOU terminology in the main text of the note (e.g., 'will' rather than 'shall', etc.), have an opening paragraph referring to discussions between the two governments and ending with a formula such as:

> As a result of these discussions it is the *understanding* of the Government of Utopia that the following *arrangements will* apply:

---

[51] Traditionalists do not use a capital A, but it is very common, and the point is not important.

The note will end with a formula such as:

If the *arrangements* set out above are acceptable to the Government of Freedonia, I have the honour to *suggest* that this Note and Your Excellency's reply to that effect *will place on record the understanding* of our two Governments in this matter which *will come into effect* on [the date of your reply or another date].

The reply note will read:

Your Excellency,
I have the honour to acknowledge receipt of your Note No. [   ] dated [   ] concerning [   ] and to *confirm* that the *arrangements* set out in your Note are acceptable to the Government of Freedonia, and that your Note and this reply will *place on record the understanding* of our two Governments in the matter, and which *will come into effect* on [today's date or another date].

Alternatively, the main text of the first note can be repeated (if necessary in translation) in the reply (see Appendix F).

Although an exchange of notes (whether constituting a treaty or not) can be in the third-person (and thus unsigned),[52] they are almost invariably in the first-person (and therefore signed). But they do not have to be signed and despatched separately. In practice, they are almost always signed and exchanged at the same time, usually in the foreign ministry of one of the states. The initiating note may be expressed to come from either the foreign ministry or the embassy, though it is more normal for the foreign ministry to *appear* as the initiator of the exchange, even if the initiative may have come from the embassy. 'Appear' has been emphasised to bring out the point that the exchange of notes form is by now artificial in that the reply note is rarely spontaneous. The practice is to agree *both* notes in draft, and so avoid the problem that can arise if the substance of the reply (and any translation) turns out to be not quite the same as in the initiating note. In that event the reply would amount to a qualified response. Even if it is acceptable to the initiating state, it should either send a further note confirming this or propose replacing the two notes with a fresh exchange. But this is untidy and therefore best avoided. Agreeing the texts in draft should also ensure that there is no misunderstanding as to the status of the exchange (i.e., treaty or MOU).[53]

---

[52] See the China–United Kingdom Exchange of Notes on the Establishment of Consulates-General 1996 (UKTS (1996) 100).   [53] See pp. 29–30 above.

If the notes are to be in different languages it is usually more convenient for the initiating note to be from the foreign ministry. If the embassy sends the initiating note it may feel obliged – as a courtesy – to write it in the language of the host state.[54] Since the host state will reply in its language, the initiating state will then have to translate it for its own domestic purposes. In such a case it would be desirable for the parties to agree the translation, as it would in a normal case.

Drafting techniques

Legal drafting is an art, not a science but, like any art, requires a disciplined ordering of material. Like managers, good drafters are born, not taught; but drafting technique can be improved by following some simple precepts. The basic rules for drafting treaties are essentially the same as for any legal instrument, whether a contract, legislation or a UN resolution:

(1) Keep it simple. The first draft should be as uncomplicated as possible; it will become more complex as the negotiations proceed.
(2) See the text as a whole. This is especially important during redrafting.
(3) Be consistent throughout the text. Do not use different forms of words to say the same thing. Adopt one (clear) system of numbering, and keep to it.
(4) Try to avoid drafting in a language with which you are not comfortable. And even if you are fluent in a foreign language, *always* have it checked by a native speaker. Negotiating problems can be caused by drafts done by non-native speakers.

How to begin

The initial draft should be done by *one* person. No good draft – and above all a first draft – ever emerged from a committee, even of two. Sometimes it is more sensible for the initial draft to be done by the policy-maker and then given to the legal adviser. The initial draft may be better done by hand rather than on a word processor, though it is more a matter of personal preference. If done by hand, use lined paper, double or treble spacing and generous margins. Write on one side only. Set aside time specially for the task. Draft at home if necessary.

Do not attempt to reinvent the wheel. Where possible, adapt prece-

---

[54] See a Czech–UK exchange of notes in UKTS (1997) 5.

dents, but only if they are clearly right for the purpose and you fully understand them. Have your draft read by a disinterested person. If he cannot understand it, start again.

Style

Use short sentences. Avoid unnecessary words, especially adjectives. Try to limit the number of cross-references.[55] Instead repeat the provision unless it is long. If there is a need to refer to the same provision several times, consider making it into a definition (e.g., the definition of 'party' in Article 2(2)(g)). Avoid 'and/or' if you really mean 'both or either'.

Numbering

Include a correct numbering scheme in the first draft, otherwise it will be difficult to renumber properly later. Once the initial draft has been presented, *do not change the numbering of the articles* unless the text becomes hopelessly complicated. Otherwise, leave renumbering until the end. The negotiations will go more smoothly if the representatives do not have to refer to 'Article 7, which used to be Article 5, and in the first draft was . . .'. If new articles have to be inserted, number them 5*bis*, 5*ter*, 5*quater* or 5A, 5B, 5C. If an article is deleted, leave a blank, and retain the article number.

Languages

If the draft is translated and there is no exact equivalent for a word, insert it after the approximate translation (e.g., 'public order (*ordre publique*)').

Amendment/consolidation

If the draft is of an amending treaty and the amendments will be extensive, consider a replacement treaty or attaching a consolidated text to the amending treaty, or to the Final Act 'for information'. The text of the Eurocontrol Convention 1960 was extensively amended by a Protocol in 1981, and a non-authoritative consolidated text of the amended convention was attached to the Final Act of the amendment conference.[56] Further

---

[55] Textbooks are different.   [56] Cmnd 8662, pp. 4 and 33.

amendments were made by a Protocol in 1997, which this time simply replaced the Convention by a consolidated text which incorporated all previous and new amendments.

Presenting the draft

Leave wide margins and use double-spacing *always*. Although it doubles copying costs, it will be much appreciated by the reader, who will certainly want to write between the lines. Include – as a temporary measure – either explanatory notes or footnotes, or both, to the articles, including references to precedents. Avoid endnotes, which only irritate the reader. Use square brackets liberally to indicate alternative formulations, doubts or disagreements. At the top of the front page of the first draft, and each redraft, put the date (and if necessary the time) when it was produced. This can avoid much confusion later. Include also the name of the originator (state or international organisation).

Have no fear, even if you follow all these precepts the text eventually adopted will bear little resemblance to your first draft, but at least you will have got the process off to good start, and the final text will be the better for your efforts.

APPENDIX A

VIENNA CONVENTION ON THE LAW OF TREATIES

CONTENTS

PART I. INTRODUCTION

PART II. CONCLUSION AND ENTRY INTO FORCE OF TREATIES

Section 1. Conclusion of Treaties

3

4

PART IV. AMENDMENT AND MODIFICATION
OF TREATIES

PART V. INVALIDITY, TERMINATION AND SUSPENSION
OF THE OPERATION OF TREATIES

Section 1. General Provisions

Section 2. Invalidity of Treaties

Section 3. Termination and Suspension of the Operation of Treaties

5

6

PART VII. DEPOSITARIES, NOTIFICATIONS, CORRECTIONS AND REGISTRATION

PART VIII. FINAL PROVISIONS

7

VIENNA CONVENTION ON THE LAW OF TREATIES

The States Parties to the present Convention,

Considering the fundamental role of treaties in the history of international relations,

Recognizing the ever-increasing importance of treaties as a source of international law and as a means of developing peaceful co-operation among nations, whatever their constitutional and social systems,

Noting that the principles of free consent and of good faith and the *pacta sunt servanda* rule are universally recognized,

Affirming that disputes concerning treaties, like other international disputes, should be settled by peaceful means and in conformity with the principles of justice and international law,

Recalling the determination of the peoples of the United Nations to establish conditions under which justice and respect for the obligations arising from treaties can be maintained,

Having in mind the principles of international law embodied in the Charter of the United Nations, such as the principles of the equal rights and self-determination of peoples, of the sovereign equality and independence of all States, of non-interference in the domestic affairs of States, of the prohibition of the threat or use of force and of universal respect for, and observance of, human rights and fundamental freedoms for all.

Believing that the codification and progressive development of the law of treaties achieved in the present Convention will promote the purposes of the United Nations set forth in the Charter, namely, the maintenance of international peace and security, the development of friendly relations and the achievement of co-operation among nations,

Affirming that the rules of customary international law will continue to govern questions not regulated by the provisions of the present Convention,

Have agreed as follows:

PART I

INTRODUCTION

ARTICLE 1

Scope of the present Convention

The present Convention applies to treaties between States.

ARTICLE 2

Use of terms

1. For the purposes of the present Convention:

(a) "treaty" means an international agreement concluded between States in written form and governed by international law, whether embodied in a single instrument or in two or more related instruments and whatever its particular designation;

(b) "ratification", "acceptance", "approval" and "accession" mean in each case the international act so named whereby a State establishes on the international plane its consent to be bound by a treaty;

(c) "full powers" means a document emanating from the competent authority of a State designating a person or persons to represent the State for negotiating, adopting or authenticating the text of a treaty, for expressing the consent of the State to be bound by a treaty, or for accomplishing any other act with respect to a treaty;

(d) "reservation" means a unilateral statement, however phrased or named, made by a State, when signing, ratifying, accepting, approving or acceding to a treaty, whereby it purports to exclude or to modify the legal effect of certain provisions of the treaty in their application to that State;

(e) "negotiating State" means a State which took part in the drawing up and adoption of the text of the treaty;

(f) "contracting State" means a State which has consented to be bound by the treaty, whether or not the treaty has entered into force;

(g) "party" means a State which has consented to be bound by the treaty and for which the treaty is in force;

(h) "third State" means a State not a party to the treaty;

(i) "international organization" means an intergovernmental organization.

2. The provisions of paragraph 1 regarding the use of terms in the present Convention are without prejudice to the use of those terms or to the meanings which may be given to them in the internal law of any State.

ARTICLE 3

International agreements not within the scope of the present Convention

The fact that the present Convention does not apply to international agreements concluded between States and other subjects of international law or between such other subjects of international law, or to international agreements not in written form, shall not affect:

(a) the legal force of such agreements;

(b) the application to them of any of the rules set forth in the present Convention to which they would be subject under international law independently of the Convention;

(c) the application of the Convention to the relations of States as between themselves under international agreements to which other subjects of international law are also parties.

ARTICLE 4

Non-retroactivity of the present Convention

Without prejudice to the application of any rules set forth in the present Convention to which treaties would be subject under international law independently of the Convention, the Convention applies only to treaties which are concluded by States after the entry into force of the present Convention with regard to such States.

ARTICLE 5

Treaties constituting international organizations and treaties adopted within an international organization

The present Convention applies to any treaty which is the constituent instrument of an international organization and to any treaty adopted within an international organization without prejudice to any relevant rules of the organization.

PART II

CONCLUSION AND ENTRY INTO FORCE OF TREATIES

Section 1. Conclusion of Treaties

ARTICLE 6

Capacity of States to conclude treaties

Every State possesses capacity to conclude treaties.

ARTICLE 7

Full powers

1. A person is considered as representing a State for the purpose of adopting or authenticating the text of a treaty or for the purpose of expressing the consent of the State to be bound by a treaty if:

(*a*) he produces appropriate full powers; or

(*b*) it appears from the practice of the States concerned or from other circumstances that their intention was to consider that person as representing the State for such purposes and to dispense with full powers.

2. In virtue of their functions and without having to produce full powers, the following are considered as representing their State:

(*a*) Heads of State, Heads of Government and Ministers for Foreign Affairs, for the purpose of performing all acts relating to the conclusion of a treaty;

10

(b) heads of diplomatic missions, for the purpose of adopting the text of a treaty between the accrediting State and the State to which they are accredited;

(c) representatives accredited by States to an international conference or to an international organization or one of its organs, for the purpose of adopting the text of a treaty in that conference, organization or organ.

ARTICLE 8

Subsequent confirmation of an act performed without authorization

An act relating to the conclusion of a treaty performed by a person who cannot be considered under article 7 as authorised to represent a State for that purpose is without legal effect unless afterwards confirmed by that State.

ARTICLE 9

Adoption of the text

1. The adoption of the text of a treaty takes place by the consent of all the States participating in its drawing up except as provided in paragraph 2.

2. The adoption of the text of a treaty at an international conference takes place by the vote of two-thirds of the States present and voting, unless by the same majority they shall decide to apply a different rule.

ARTICLE 10

Authentication of the text

The text of a treaty is established as authentic and definitive:

(a) by such procedure as may be provided for in the text or agreed upon by the States participating in its drawing up; or

(b) failing such procedure, by the signature, signature ad referendum or initialling by the representatives of those States of the text of the treaty or of the Final Act of a conference incorporating the text.

ARTICLE 11

Means of expressing consent to be bound by a treaty

The consent of a State to be bound by a treaty may be expressed by signature, exchange of instruments constituting a treaty, ratification, acceptance, approval or accession, or by any other means if so agreed.

ARTICLE 12

Consent to be bound by a treaty expressed by signature

1. The consent of a State to be bound by a treaty is expressed by the signature of its representative when:

(a) the treaty provides that signature shall have that effect;

11

(b) it is otherwise established that the negotiating States were agreed that signature should have that effect; or

(c) the intention of the State to give that effect to the signature appears from the full powers of its representative or was expressed during the negotiation.

2. For the purposes of paragraph 1:

(a) the initialling of a text constitutes a signature of the treaty when it is established that the negotiating States so agreed;

(b) the signature *ad referendum* of a treaty by a representative, if confirmed by his State, constitutes a full signature of the treaty.

ARTICLE 13

Consent to be bound by a treaty expressed by an exchange of instruments constituting a treaty

The consent of States to be bound by a treaty constituted by instruments exchanged between them is expressed by that exchange when:

(a) the instruments provide that their exchange shall have that effect; or

(b) it is otherwise established that those States were agreed that the exchange of instruments should have that effect.

ARTICLE 14

Consent to be bound by a treaty expressed by ratification, acceptance or approval

1. The consent of a State to be bound by a treaty is expressed by ratification when:

(a) the treaty provides for such consent to be expressed by means of ratification;

(b) it is otherwise established that the negotiating States were agreed that ratification should be required;

(c) the representative of the State has signed the treaty subject to ratification; or

(d) the intention of the State to sign the treaty subject to ratification appears from the full powers of its representative or was expressed during the negotiation.

2. The consent of a State to be bound by a treaty is expressed by acceptance or approval under conditions similar to those which apply to ratification.

ARTICLE 15

Consent to be bound by a treaty expressed by accession

The consent of a State to be bound by a treaty is expressed by accession when:

(a) the treaty provides that such consent may be expressed by that State by means of accession;

12

(b) it is otherwise established that the negotiating States were agreed that such consent may be expressed by that State by means of accession; or

(c) all the parties have subsequently agreed that such consent may be expressed by that State by means of accession.

ARTICLE 16

Exchange or deposit of instruments of ratification, acceptance, approval or accession

Unless the treaty otherwise provides, instruments of ratification, acceptance, approval or accession establish the consent of a State to be bound by a treaty upon:

(a) their exchange between the contracting States;

(b) their deposit with the depositary; or

(c) their notification to the contracting States or to the depositary, if so agreed.

ARTICLE 17

Consent to be bound by part of a treaty and choice of differing provisions

1. Without prejudice to articles 19 to 23, the consent of a State to be bound by part of a treaty is effective only if the treaty so permits or the other contracting States so agree.

2. The consent of a State to be bound by a treaty which permits a choice between differing provisions is effective only if it is made clear to which of the provisions the consent relates.

ARTICLE 18

Obligation not to defeat the object and purpose of a treaty prior to its entry into force

A State is obliged to refrain from acts which would defeat the object and purpose of a treaty when:

(a) it has signed the treaty or has exchanged instruments constituting the treaty subject to ratification, acceptance or approval, until it shall have made its intention clear not to become a party to the treaty; or

(b) it has expressed its consent to be bound by the treaty, pending the entry into force of the treaty and provided that such entry into force is not unduly delayed.

13

Section 2. Reservations

ARTICLE 19

Formulation of reservations

A State may, when signing, ratifying, accepting, approving or acceding to a treaty, formulate a reservation unless:

(a) the reservation is prohibited by the treaty;

(b) the treaty provides that only specified reservations, which do not include the reservation in question, may be made; or

(c) in cases not falling under sub-paragraphs (a) and (b), the reservation is incompatible with the object and purpose of the treaty.

ARTICLE 20

Acceptance of and objection to reservations

1. A reservation expressly authorized by a treaty does not require any subsequent acceptance by the other contracting States unless the treaty so provides.

2. When it appears from the limited number of negotiating States and the object and purpose of a treaty that the application of the treaty in its entirety between all the parties is an essential condition of the consent of each one to be bound by the treaty, a reservation requires acceptance by all the parties.

3. When a treaty is a constitutent instrument of an international organization and unless it otherwise provides, a reservation requires the acceptance of the competent organ of that organization.

4. In cases not falling under the preceding paragraphs and unless the treaty otherwise provides:

(a) acceptance by another contracting State of a reservation constitutes the reserving State a party to the treaty in relation to that other State if or when the treaty is in force for those States;

(b) an objection by another contracting State to a reservation does not preclude the entry into force of the treaty as between the objecting and reserving States unless a contrary intention is definitely expressed by the objecting State;

(c) an act expressing a State's consent to be bound by the treaty and containing a reservation is effective as soon as at least one other contracting State has accepted the reservation.

5. For the purposes of paragraphs 2 and 4 and unless the treaty otherwise provides, a reservation is considered to have been accepted by a State if it shall have raised no objection to the reservation by the end of a period of twelve months after it was notified of the reservation or by the date on which it expressed its consent to be bound by the treaty, whichever is later.

ARTICLE 21

Legal effects of reservations and of objections to reservations

1. A reservation established with regard to another party in accordance with articles 19, 20 and 23:

(a) modifies for the reserving State in its relations with that other party the provisions of the treaty to which the reservation relates to the extent of the reservation; and

(b) modifies those provisions to the same extent for that other party in its relations with the reserving State.

2. The reservation does not modify the provisions of the treaty for the other parties to the treaty *inter se*.

3. When a State objecting to a reservation has not opposed the entry into force of the treaty between itself and the reserving State, the provisions to which the reservation relates do not apply as between the two States to the extent of the reservation.

ARTICLE 22

Withdrawal of reservations and of objections to reservations

1. Unless the treaty otherwise provides, a reservation may be withdrawn at any time and the consent of a State which has accepted the reservation is not required for its withdrawal.

2. Unless the treaty otherwise provides, an objection to a reservation may be withdrawn at any time.

3. Unless the treaty otherwise provides, or it is otherwise agreed:

(a) the withdrawal of a reservation becomes operative in relation to another contracting State only when notice of it has been received by that State;

(b) the withdrawal of an objection to a reservation becomes operative only when notice of it has been received by the State which formulated the reservation.

ARTICLE 23

Procedure regarding reservations

1. A reservation, an express acceptance of a reservation and an objection to a reservation must be formulated in writing and communicated to the contracting States and other States entitled to become parties to the treaty.

2. If formulated when signing the treaty subject to ratification, acceptance or approval, a reservation must be formally confirmed by the reserving State

15

when expressing its consent to be bound by the treaty. In such a case the reservation shall be considered as having been made on the date of its confirmation.

3. An express acceptance of, or an objection to, a reservation made previously to confirmation of the reservation does not itself require confirmation.

4. The withdrawal of a reservation or of an objection to a reservation must be formulated in writing.

Section 3. Entry into Force and Provisional Application of Treaties

ARTICLE 24

Entry into force

1. A treaty enters into force in such manner and upon such date as it may provide or as the negotiating States may agree.

2. Failing any such provision or agreement, a treaty enters into force as soon as consent to be bound by the treaty has been established for all the negotiating States.

3. When the consent of a State to be bound by a treaty is established on a date after the treaty has come into force, the treaty enters into force for that State on that date, unless the treaty otherwise provides.

4. The provisions of a treaty regulating the authentication of its text, the establishment of the consent of States to be bound by the treaty, the manner or date of its entry into force, reservations, the functions of the depositary and other matters arising necessarily before the entry into force of the treaty apply from the time of the adoption of its text.

ARTICLE 25

Provisional application

1. A treaty or a part of a treaty is applied provisionally pending its entry into force if:

(a) the treaty itself so provides; or

(b) the negotiating States have in some other manner so agreed.

2. Unless the treaty otherwise provides or the negotiating States have otherwise agreed, the provisional application of a treaty or a part of a treaty with respect to a State shall be terminated if that State notifies the other States between which the treaty is being applied provisionally of its intention not to become a party to the treaty.

PART III

OBSERVANCE, APPLICATION AND INTERPRETATION OF TREATIES

Section 1. Observance of Treaties

ARTICLE 26

Pacta sunt servanda

Every treaty in force is binding upon the parties to it and must be performed by them in good faith.

ARTICLE 27

Internal law and observance of treaties

A party may not invoke the provisions of its internal law as justification for its failure to perform a treaty. This rule is without prejudice to article 46.

Section 2. Application of Treaties

ARTICLE 28

Non-retroactivity of treaties

Unless a different intention appears from the treaty or is otherwise established, its provisions do not bind a party in relation to any act or fact which took place or any situation which ceased to exist before the date of the entry into force of the treaty with respect to that party.

ARTICLE 29

Territorial scope of treaties

Unless a different intention appears from the treaty or is otherwise established, a treaty is binding upon each party in respect of its entire territory.

ARTICLE 30

Application of successive treaties relating to the same subject-matter

1. Subject to article 103 of the Charter of the United Nations, the rights and obligations of States parties to successive treaties relating to the same subject-matter shall be determined in accordance with the following paragraphs.

17

2. When a treaty specifies that it is subject to, or that it is not to be considered as incompatible with, an earlier or later treaty, the provisions of that other treaty prevail.

3. When all the parties to the earlier treaty are parties also to the later treaty but the earlier treaty is not terminated or suspended in operation under article 59, the earlier treaty applies only to the extent that its provisions are compatible with those of the later treaty.

4. When the parties to the later treaty do not include all the parties to the earlier one:

(a) as between States parties to both treaties the same rule applies as in paragraph 3;

(b) as between a State party to both treaties and a State party to only one of the treaties, the treaty to which both States are parties governs their mutual rights and obligations.

5. Paragraph 4 is without prejudice to article 41, or to any question of the termination or suspension of the operation of a treaty under article 60 or to any question of responsibility which may arise for a State from the conclusion or application of a treaty the provisions of which are incompatible with its obligations towards another State under another treaty.

Section 3. Interpretation of Treaties

ARTICLE 31

General rule of interpretation

1. A treaty shall be interpreted in good faith in accordance with the ordinary meaning to be given to the terms of the treaty in their context and in the light of its object and purpose.

2. The context for the purpose of the interpretation of a treaty shall comprise, in addition to the text, including its preamble and annexes:

(a) any agreement relating to the treaty which was made between all the parties in connexion with the conclusion of the treaty;

(b) any instrument which was made by one or more parties in connexion with the conclusion of the treaty and accepted by the other parties as an instrument related to the treaty.

3. There shall be taken into account, together with the context:

(a) any subsequent agreement between the parties regarding the interpretation of the treaty or the application of its provisions;

(b) any subsequent practice in the application of the treaty which establishes the agreement of the parties regarding its interpretation;

(c) any relevant rules of international law applicable in the relations between the parties.

4. A special meaning shall be given to a term if it is established that the parties so intended.

18

ARTICLE 32

Supplementary means of interpretation

Recourse may be had to supplementary means of interpretation, including the preparatory work of the treaty and the circumstances of its conclusion, in order to confirm the meaning resulting from the application of article 31, or to determine the meaning when the interpretation according to article 31:

(a) leaves the meaning ambiguous or obscure; or

(b) leads to a result which is manifestly absurd or unreasonable.

ARTICLE 33

Interpretation of treaties authenticated in two or more languages

1. When a treaty has been authenticated in two or more languages, the text is equally authoritative in each language, unless the treaty provides or the parties agree that, in case of divergence, a particular text shall prevail.

2. A version of the treaty in a language other than one of those in which the text was authenticated shall be considered an authentic text only if the treaty so provides or the parties so agree.

3. The terms of the treaty are presumed to have the same meaning in each authentic text.

4. Except where a particular text prevails in accordance with paragraph 1, when a comparison of the authentic texts discloses a difference of meaning which the application of articles 31 and 32 does not remove, the meaning which best reconciles the texts, having regard to the object and purpose of the treaty, shall be adopted.

Section 4. Treaties and Third States

ARTICLE 34

General rule regarding third States

A treaty does not create either obligations or rights for a third State without its consent.

ARTICLE 35

Treaties providing for obligations for third States

An obligation arises for a third State from a provision of a treaty if the parties to the treaty intend the provision to be the means of establishing the obligation and the third State expressly accepts that obligation in writing.

ARTICLE 36

Treaties providing for rights for third States

1. A right arises for a third State from a provision of a treaty if the parties to the treaty intend the provision to accord that right either to the

19

third State, or to a group of States to which it belongs, or to all States, and the third State assents thereto. Its assent shall be presumed so long as the contrary is not indicated, unless the treaty otherwise provides.

2. A State exercising a right in accordance with paragraph 1 shall comply with the conditions for its exercise provided for in the treaty or established in conformity with the treaty.

ARTICLE 37

Revocation or modification of obligations or rights of third States

1. When an obligation has arisen for a third State in conformity with article 35, the obligation may be revoked or modified only with the consent of the parties to the treaty and of the third State, unless it is established that they had otherwise agreed.

2. When a right has arisen for a third State in conformity with article 36, the right may not be revoked or modified by the parties if it is established that the right was intended not to be revocable or subject to modification without the consent of the third State.

ARTICLE 38

Rules in a treaty becoming binding on third States through international custom

Nothing in articles 34 to 37 precludes a rule set forth in a treaty from becoming binding upon a third State as a customary rule of international law, recognized as such.

PART IV

AMENDMENT AND MODIFICATION OF TREATIES

ARTICLE 39

General rule regarding the amendment of treaties

A treaty may be amended by agreement between the parties. The rules laid down in Part II apply to such an agreement except in so far as the treaty may otherwise provide.

ARTICLE 40

Amendment of multilateral treaties

1. Unless the treaty otherwise provides, the amendment of multilateral treaties shall be governed by the following paragraphs.

20

2. Any proposal to amend a multilateral treaty as between all the parties must be notified to all the contracting States, each one of which shall have the right to take part in:

(a) the decision as to the action to be taken in regard to such proposal;

(b) the negotiation and conclusion of any agreement for the amendment of the treaty.

3. Every State entitled to become a party to the treaty shall also be entitled to become a party to the treaty as amended.

4. The amending agreement does not bind any State already a party to the treaty which does not become a party to the amending agreement; article 30, paragraph 4 (b), applies in relation to such State.

5. Any State which becomes a party to the treaty after the entry into force of the amending agreement shall, failing an expression of a different intention by that State:

(a) be considered as a party to the treaty as amended; and

(b) be considered as a party to the unamended treaty in relation to any party to the treaty not bound by the amending agreement.

ARTICLE 41

Agreements to modify multilateral treaties between certain of the parties only

1. Two or more of the parties to a multilateral treaty may conclude an agreement to modify the treaty as between themselves alone if:

(a) the possibility of such a modification is provided for by the treaty; or

(b) the modification in question is not prohibited by the treaty and:

(i) does not affect the enjoyment by the other parties of their rights under the treaty or the performance of their obligations;

(ii) does not relate to a provision, derogation from which is incompatible with the effective execution of the object and purpose of the treaty as a whole.

2. Unless in a case falling under paragraph 1 (a) the treaty otherwise provides, the parties in question shall notify the other parties of their intention to conclude the agreement and of the modification to the treaty for which it provides.

PART V

INVALIDITY, TERMINATION AND SUSPENSION OF THE OPERATION OF TREATIES

Section 1. General Provisions

ARTICLE 42

Validity and continuance in force of treaties

1. The validity of a treaty or of the consent of a State to be bound by a treaty may be impeached only through the application of the present Convention.

21

2. The termination of a treaty, its denunciation or the withdrawal of a party, may take place only as a result of the application of the provisions of the treaty or of the present Convention. The same rule applies to suspension of the operation of a treaty.

ARTICLE 43

Obligations imposed by international law independently of a treaty

The invalidity, termination or denunciation of a treaty, the withdrawal of a party from it, or the suspension of its operation, as a result of the application of the present Convention or of the provisions of the treaty shall not in any way impair the duty of any State to fulfil any obligation embodied in the treaty to which it would be subject under international law independently of the treaty.

ARTICLE 44

Separability of treaty provisions

1. A right of a party, provided for in a treaty or arising under article 56, to denounce, withdraw from or suspend the operation of the treaty may be exercised only with respect to the whole treaty unless the treaty otherwise provides or the parties otherwise agree.

2. A ground for invalidating, terminating, withdrawing from or suspending the operation of a treaty recognized in the present Convention may be invoked only with respect to the whole treaty except as provided in the following paragraphs or in article 60.

3. If the ground relates solely to particular clauses, it may be invoked only with respect to those clauses where:

(*a*) the said clauses are separable from the remainder of the treaty with regard to their application;

(*b*) it appears from the treaty or is otherwise established that acceptance of those clauses was not an essential basis of the consent of the other party or parties to be bound by the treaty as a whole; and

(*c*) continued performance of the remainder of the treaty would not be unjust.

4. In cases falling under articles 49 and 50 the State entitled to invoke the fraud or corruption may do so with respect either to the whole treaty or, subject to paragraph 3, to the particular clauses alone.

5. In cases falling under articles 51, 52 and 53, no separation of the provisions of the treaty is permitted.

22

ARTICLE 45

Loss of a right to invoke a ground for invalidating, terminating, withdrawing from or suspending the operation of a treaty

A State may no longer invoke a ground for invalidating, terminating, withdrawing from or suspending the operation of a treaty under articles 46 to 50 or articles 60 and 62 if, after becoming aware of the facts:

(a) it shall have expressly agreed that the treaty is valid or remains in force or continues in operation, as the case may be; or

(b) it must by reason of its conduct be considered as having acquiesced in the validity of the treaty or in its maintenance in force or in operation, as the case may be.

Section 2. Invalidity of Treaties

ARTICLE 46

Provisions of internal law regarding competence to conclude treaties

1. A State may not invoke the fact that its consent to be bound by a treaty has been expressed in violation of a provision of its internal law regarding competence to conclude treaties as invalidating its consent unless that violation was manifest and concerned a rule of its internal law of fundamental importance.

2. A violation is manifest if it would be objectively evident to any State conducting itself in the matter in accordance with normal practice and in good faith.

ARTICLE 47

Specific restrictions on authority to express the consent of a State

If the authority of a representative to express the consent of a State to be bound by a particular treaty has been made subject to a specific restriction, his omission to observe that restriction may not be invoked as invalidating the consent expressed by him unless the restriction was notified to the other negotiating States prior to his expressing such consent.

ARTICLE 48

Error

1. A State may invoke an error in a treaty as invalidating its consent to be bound by the treaty if the error relates to a fact or situation which was assumed by that State to exist at the time when the treaty was concluded and formed an essential basis of its consent to be bound by the treaty.

23

2. Paragraph 1 shall not apply if the State in question contributed by its own conduct to the error or if the circumstances were such as to put that State on notice of a possible error.

3. An error relating only to the wording of the text of a treaty does not affect its validity; article 79 then applies.

ARTICLE 49

Fraud

If a State has been induced to conclude a treaty by the fraudulent conduct of another negotiating State, the State may invoke the fraud as invalidating its consent to be bound by the treaty.

ARTICLE 50

Corruption of a representative of a State

If the expression of a State's consent to be bound by a treaty has been procured through the corruption of its representative directly or indirectly by another negotiating State, the State may invoke such corruption as invalidating its consent to be bound by the treaty.

ARTICLE 51

Coercion of a representative of a State

The expression of a State's consent to be bound by a treaty which has been procured by the coercion of its representative through acts or threats directed against him shall be without any legel effect.

ARTICLE 52

Coercion of a State by the threat or use of force

A treaty is void if its conclusion has been procured by the threat or use of force in violation of the principles of international law embodied in the Charter of the United Nations.

ARTICLE 53

Treaties conflicting with a peremptory norm of general international law (jus cogens)

A treaty is void if, at the time of its conclusion, it conflicts with a peremptory norm of general international law. For the purposes of the present Convention, a peremptory norm of general international law is a norm accepted and recognized by the international community of States as a whole as a norm from which no derogation is permitted and which can be modified only by a subsequent norm of general international law having the same character.

24

Section 3. Termination and Suspension of the Operation of Treaties

ARTICLE 54

Termination of or withdrawal from a treaty under its provisions or by consent of the parties

The termination of a treaty or the withdrawal of a party may take place:

(a) in conformity with the provisions of the treaty; or

(b) at any time by consent of all the parties after consultation with the other contracting States.

ARTICLE 55

Reduction of the parties to a multilateral treaty below the number necessary for its entry into force

Unless the treaty otherwise provides, a multilateral treaty does not terminate by reason only of the fact that the number of the parties falls below the number necessary for its entry into force.

ARTICLE 56

Denunciation of or withdrawal from a treaty containing no provision regarding termination, denunciation or withdrawal

1. A treaty which contains no provision regarding its termination and which does not provide for denunciation or withdrawal is not subject to denunciation or withdrawal unless:

(a) it is established that the parties intended to admit the possibility of denunciation or withdrawal; or

(b) a right of denunciation or withdrawal may be implied by the nature of the treaty.

2. A party shall give not less than twelve months' notice of its intention to denounce or withdraw from a treaty under paragraph 1.

ARTICLE 57

Suspension of the operation of a treaty under its provisions or by consent of the parties

The operation of a treaty in regard to all the parties or to a particular party may be suspended:

(a) in conformity with the provisions of the treaty; or

(b) at any time by consent of all the parties after consultation with the other contracting States.

25

ARTICLE 58

Suspension of the operation of a multilateral treaty by agreement between certain of the parties only

1. Two or more parties to a multilateral treaty may conclude an agreement to suspend the operation of provisions of the treaty, temporarily and as between themselves alone, if:

(a) the possibility of such a suspension is provided for by the treaty; or

(b) the suspension in question is not prohibited by the treaty and:

(i) does not affect the enjoyment by the other parties of their rights under the treaty or the performance of their obligations;

(ii) is not incompatible with the object and purpose of the treaty.

2. Unless in a case falling under paragraph 1 (a) the treaty otherwise provides, the parties in question shall notify the other parties of their intention to conclude the agreement and of those provisions of the treaty the operation of which they intend to suspend.

ARTICLE 59

Termination or suspension of the operation of a treaty implied by conclusion of a later treaty

1. A treaty shall be considered as terminated if all the parties to it conclude a later treaty relating to the same subject-matter and:

(a) it appears from the later treaty or is otherwise established that the parties intended that the matter should be governed by that treaty; or

(b) the provisions of the later treaty are so far incompatible with those of the earlier one that the two treaties are not capable of being applied at the same time.

2. The earlier treaty shall be considered as only suspended in operation if it appears from the later treaty or is otherwise established that such was the intention of the parties.

ARTICLE 60

Termination or suspension of the operation of a treaty as a consequence of its breach

1. A material breach of a bilateral treaty by one of the parties entitles the other to invoke the breach as a ground for terminating the treaty or suspending its operation in whole or in part.

2. A material breach of a multilateral treaty by one of the parties entitles:

(a) the other parties by unanimous agreement to suspend the operation of the treaty in whole or in part or to terminate it either:

(i) in the relations between themselves and the defaulting State, or

(ii) as between all the parties;

26

(b) a party specially affected by the breach to invoke it as a ground for suspending the operation of the treaty in whole or in part in the relations between itself and the defaulting State;

(c) any party other than the defaulting State to invoke the breach as a ground for suspending the operation of the treaty in whole or in part with respect to itself if the treaty is of such a character that a material breach of its provisions by one party radically changes the position of every party with respect to the further performance of its obligations under the treaty.

3. A material breach of a treaty, for the purposes of this article, consists in:

(a) a repudiation of the treaty not sanctioned by the present Convention; or

(b) the violation of a provision essential to the accomplishment of the object or purpose of the treaty.

4. The foregoing paragraphs are without prejudice to any provision in the treaty applicable in the event of a breach.

5. Paragraphs 1 to 3 do not apply to provisions relating to the protection of the human person contained in treaties of a humanitarian character, in particular to provisions prohibiting any form of reprisals against persons protected by such treaties.

ARTICLE 61

Supervening impossibility of performance

1. A party may invoke the impossibility of performing a treaty as a ground for terminating or withdrawing from it if the impossibility results from the permanent disappearance or destruction of an object indispensable for the execution of the treaty. If the impossibility is temporary, it may be invoked only as a ground for suspending the operation of the treaty.

2. Impossibility of performance may not be invoked by a party as a ground for terminating, withdrawing from or suspending the operation of a treaty if the impossibility is the result of a breach by that party either of an obligation under the treaty or of any other international obligation owed to any other party to the treaty.

ARTICLE 62

Fundamental changes of circumstances

1. A fundamental change of circumstances which has occurred with regard to those existing at the time of the conclusion of a treaty, and which was not foreseen by the parties, may not be invoked as a ground for terminating or withdrawing from the treaty unless:

(a) the existence of those circumstances constituted an essential basis of the consent of the parties to be bound by the treaty; and

(b) the effect of the change is radically to transform the extent of obligations still to be performed under the treaty.

2. A fundamental change of circumstances may not be invoked as a ground for terminating or withdrawing from a treaty:

(a) if the treaty establishes a boundary; or

(b) if the fundamental change is the result of a breach by the party invoking it either of an obligation under the treaty or of any other international obligation owed to any other party to the treaty.

3. If, under the foregoing paragraphs, a party may invoke a fundamental change of circumstances as a ground for terminating or withdrawing from a treaty it may also invoke the change as a ground for suspending the operation of the treaty.

ARTICLE 63

Severance of diplomatic or consular relations

The severance of diplomatic or consular relations between parties to a treaty does not affect the legal relations established between them by the treaty except in so far as the existence of diplomatic or consular relations is indispensable for the application of the treaty.

ARTICLE 64

Emergence of a new peremptory norm of general international law
(jus cogens)

If a new peremptory norm of general international law emerges, any existing treaty which is in conflict with that norm becomes void and terminates.

Section 4. Procedure

ARTICLE 65

Procedure to be followed with respect to invalidity, termination, withdrawal from or suspension of the operation of a treaty

1. A party which, under the provisions of the present Convention, invokes either a defect in its consent to be bound by a treaty or a ground for impeaching the validity of a treaty, terminating it, withdrawing from it or suspending its operation, must notify the other parties of its claim. The notification shall indicate the measure proposed to be taken with respect to the treaty and the reasons therefor.

2. If, after the expiry of a period which, except in cases of special urgency, shall not be less than three months after the receipt of the notification, no party has raised any objection, the party making the notification may carry out in the manner provided in article 67 the measure which it has proposed.

3. If, however, objection has been raised by any other party, the parties shall seek a solution through the means indicated in Article 33 of the Charter of the United Nations.

4. Nothing in the foregoing paragraphs shall affect the rights or obligations of the parties under any provisions in force binding the parties with regard to the settlement of disputes.

5. Without prejudice to article 45, the fact that a State has not previously made the notification prescribed in paragraph 1 shall not prevent it from making such notification in answer to another party claiming performance of the treaty or alleging its violation.

ARTICLE 66

Procedures for judicial settlement, arbitration and conciliation

If, under paragraph 3 of article 65, no solution has been reached within a period of 12 months following the date on which the objection was raised, the following procedures shall be followed :

(*a*) any one of the parties to a dispute concerning the application or the interpretation of articles 53 or 64 may, by a written application, submit it to the International Court of Justice for a decision unless the parties by common consent agree to submit the dispute to arbitration;

(*b*) any one of the parties to a dispute concerning the application or the interpretation of any of the other articles in Part V of the present Convention may set in motion the procedure specified in the Annex to the Convention by submitting a request to that effect to the Secretary-General of the United Nations.

ARTICLE 67

Instruments for declaring invalid, terminating, withdrawing from or suspending the operation of a treaty

1. The notification provided for under article 65, paragraph 1 must be made in writing.

2. Any act declaring invalid, terminating, withdrawing from or suspending the operation of a treaty pursuant to the provisions of the treaty or of paragraphs 2 or 3 of article 65 shall be carried out through an instrument communicated to the other parties. If the instrument is not signed by the Head of State, Head of Government or Minister for Foreign Affairs, the representative of the State communicating it may be called upon to produce full powers.

ARTICLE 68

Revocation of notifications and instruments provided for in articles 65 and 67

A notification or instrument provided for in articles 65 or 67 may be revoked at any time before it takes effect.

29

Section 5.   Consequences of the Invalidity, Termination or Suspension of the Operation of a Treaty

ARTICLE 69

Consequences of the invalidity of a treaty

1. A treaty the invalidity of which is established under the present Convention is void. The provisions of a void treaty have no legal force.

2. If acts have nevertheless been performed in reliance on such a treaty:

(*a*) each party may require any other party to establish as far as possible in their mutual relations the position that would have existed if the acts had not been performed;

(*b*) acts performed in good faith before the invalidity was invoked are not rendered unlawful by reason only of the invalidity of the treaty.

3. In cases falling under articles 49, 50, 51 or 52, paragraph 2 does not apply with respect to the party to which the fraud, the act of corruption or the coercion is imputable.

4. In the case of the invalidity of a particular State's consent to be bound by a multilateral treaty, the foregoing rules apply in the relations between that State and the parties to the treaty.

ARTICLE 70

Consequences of the termination of a treaty

1. Unless the treaty otherwise provides or the parties otherwise agree, the termination of a treaty under its provisions or in accordance with the present Convention:

(*a*) releases the parties from any obligation further to perform the treaty;

(*b*) does not affect any right, obligation or legal situation of the parties created through the execution of the treaty prior to its termination.

2. If a State denounces or withdraws from a multilateral treaty, paragraph 1 applies in the relations between that State and each of the other parties to the treaty from the date when such denunciation or withdrawal takes effect.

ARTICLE 71

Consequences of the invalidity of a treaty which conflicts with a peremptory norm of general international law

1. In the case of a treaty which is void under article 53 the parties shall:

(*a*) eliminate as far as possible the consequences of any act performed in reliance on any provision which conflicts with the peremptory norm of general international law; and

(*b*) bring their mutual relations into conformity with the peremptory norm of general international law.

30

2. In the case of a treaty which becomes void and terminates under article 64, the termination of the treaty:

(a) releases the parties from any obligation further to perform the treaty;

(b) does not affect any right, obligation or legal situation of the parties created through the execution of the treaty prior to its termination; provided that those rights, obligations or situations may thereafter be maintained only to the extent that their maintenance is not in itself in conflict with the new peremptory norm of general international law.

ARTICLE 72

Consequences of the suspension of the operation of a treaty

1. Unless the treaty otherwise provides or the parties otherwise agree, the suspension of the operation of a treaty under its provisions or in accordance with the present Convention:

(a) releases the parties between which the operation of the treaty is suspended from the obligation to perform the treaty in their mutual relations during the period of the suspension;

(b) does not otherwise affect the legal relations between the parties established by the treaty.

2. During the period of the suspension the parties shall refrain from acts tending to obstruct the resumption of the operation of the treaty.

PART VI

MISCELLANEOUS PROVISIONS

ARTICLE 73

Cases of State succession, State responsibility and outbreak of hostilities

The provisions of the present Convention shall not prejudge any question that may arise in regard to a treaty from a succession of States or from the international responsibility of a State or from the outbreak of hostilities between States.

ARTICLE 74

Diplomatic and consular relations and the conclusion of treaties

The severance or absence of diplomatic or consular relations between two or more States does not prevent the conclusion of treaties between those States. The conclusion of a treaty does not in itself affect the situation in regard to diplomatic or consular relations.

ARTICLE 75

Case of an aggressor State

The provisions of the present Convention are without prejudice to any obligation in relation to a treaty which may arise for an aggressor State in consequence of measures taken in conformity with the Charter of the United Nations with reference to that State's aggression.

31

PART VII

DEPOSITARIES, NOTIFICATIONS, CORRECTIONS AND REGISTRATION

ARTICLE 76

Depositaries of treaties

1. The designation of the depositary of a treaty may be made by the negotiating States, either in the treaty itself or in some other manner. The depositary may be one or more States, an international organization or the chief administrative officer of the organization.

2. The functions of the depositary of a treaty are international in character and the depositary is under an obligation to act impartially in their performance. In particular, the fact that a treaty has not entered into force between certain of the parties or that a difference has appeared between a State and a depositary with regard to the performance of the latter's functions shall not affect that obligation.

ARTICLE 77

Functions of depositaries

1. The functions of a depositary, unless otherwise provided in the treaty or agreed by the contracting States, comprise in particular:

(a) keeping custody of the original text of the treaty and of any full powers delivered to the depositary;

(b) preparing certified copies of the original text and preparing any further text of the treaty in such additional languages as may be required by the treaty and transmitting them to the parties and to the States entitled to become parties to the treaty;

(c) receiving any signatures to the treaty and receiving and keeping custody of any instruments, notifications and communications relating to it;

(d) examining whether the signature or any instrument, notification or communication relating to the treaty is in due and proper form and, if need be, bringing the matter to the attention of the State in question;

(e) informing the parties and the States entitled to become parties to the treaty of acts, notifications and communications relating to the treaty;

(f) informing the States entitled to become parties to the treaty when the number of signatures or of instruments of ratification, acceptance, approval or accession required for the entry into force of the treaty has been received or deposited;

(g) registering the treaty with the Secretariat of the United Nations;

(h) performing the functions specified in other provisions of the present Convention.

32

2. In the event of any difference appearing between a State and the depositary as to the performance of the latter's functions, the depositary shall bring the question to the attention of the signatory States and the contracting States or, where appropriate, of the competent organ of the international organization concerned.

ARTICLE 78

Notifications and communications

Except as the treaty or the present Convention otherwise provide, any notification or communication to be made by any State under the present Convention shall:

(a) if there is no depositary, be transmitted direct to the States for which it is intended, or if there is a depositary, to the latter;

(b) be considered as having been made by the State in question only upon its receipt by the State to which it was transmitted or, as the case may be, upon its receipt by the depositary;

(c) if transmitted to a depositary, be considered as received by the State for which it was intended only when the latter State has been informed by the depositary in accordance with article 77, paragraph 1 (e).

ARTICLE 79

Correction of errors in texts or in certified copies of treaties

1. Where, after the authentication of the text of a treaty, the signatory States and the contracting States are agreed that it contains an error, the error shall, unless they decide upon some other means of correction, be corrected:

(a) by having the appropriate correction made in the text and causing the correction to be initialled by duly authorized representatives;

(b) by executing or exchanging an instrument or instruments setting out the correction which it has been agreed to make; or

(c) by executing a corrected text of the whole treaty by the same procedure as in the case of the original text.

2. Where the treaty is one for which there is a depositary, the latter shall notify the signatory States and the contracting States of the error and of the proposal to correct it and shall specify an appropriate time-limit within which objection to the proposed correction may be raised. If, on the expiry of the time-limit:

(a) no objection has been raised, the depositary shall make and initial the correction in the text and shall execute a *procès-verbal* of the rectification of the text and communicate a copy of it to the parties and to the States entitled to become parties to the treaty;

(b) an objection has been raised, the depositary shall communicate the objection to the signatory States and to the contracting States.

3. The rules in paragraphs 1 and 2 apply also where the text has been authenticated in two or more languages and it appears that there is a lack of concordance which the signatory States and the contracting States agree should be corrected.

33

4. The corrected text replaces the defective text *ab initio*, unless the signatory States and the contracting States otherwise decide.

5. The correction of the text of a treaty that has been registered shall be notified to the Secretariat of the United Nations.

6. Where an error is discovered in a certified copy of a treaty, the depositary shall execute a *procès-verbal* specifying the rectification and communicate a copy of it to the signatory States and to the contracting States.

ARTICLE 80

Registration and publication of treaties

1. Treaties shall, after their entry into force, be transmitted to the Secretariat of the United Nations for registration or filing and recording, as the case may be, and for publication.

2. The designation of a depositary shall constitute authorization for it to perform the acts specified in the preceding paragraph.

PART VIII

FINAL PROVISIONS

ARTICLE 81

Signature

The present Convention shall be open for signature by all States Members of the United Nations or of any of the specialized agencies or of the International Atomic Energy Agency or parties to the Statute of the International Court of Justice, and by any other State invited by the General Assembly of the United Nations to become a party to the Convention, as follows: until 30 November 1969, at the Federal Ministry for Foreign Affairs of the Republic of Austria, and subsequently, until 30 April 1970, at United Nations Headquarters, New York.

ARTICLE 82

Ratification

The present Convention is subject to ratification. The instruments of ratification shall be deposited with the Secretary-General of the United Nations.

ARTICLE 83

Accession

The present Convention shall remain open for accession by any State belonging to any of the categories mentioned in article 81. The instruments of accession shall be deposited with the Secretary-General of the United Nations.

ARTICLE 84

Entry into force

1. The present Convention shall enter into force on the thirtieth day following the date of deposit of the thirty-fifth instrument of ratification or accession.

2. For each State ratifying or acceding to the Convention after the deposit of the thirty-fifth instrument of ratification or accession, the Convention shall enter into force on the thirtieth day after deposit by such State of its instrument of ratification or accession.

ARTICLE 85

Authentic texts

The original of the present Convention, of which the Chinese, English, French, Russian and Spanish texts are equally authentic, shall be deposited with the Secretary-General of the United Nations.

IN WITNESS WHEREOF the undersigned Plenipotentiaries, being duly authorized thereto by their respective Governments, have signed the present Convention.

DONE AT VIENNA, this twenty-third day of May, one thousand nine hundred and sixty-nine.

ANNEX

1. A list of conciliators consisting of qualified jurists shall be drawn up and maintained by the Secretary-General of the United Nations. To this end, every State which is a Member of the United Nations or a party to the present Convention shall be invited to nominate two conciliators, and the names of the persons so nominated shall constitute the list. The term of a conciliator, including that of any conciliator nominated to fill a casual vacancy, shall be five years and may be renewed. A conciliator whose term expires shall continue to fulfil any function for which he shall have been chosen under the following paragraph.

2. When a request has been made to the Secretary-General under article 66, the Secretary-General shall bring the dispute before a conciliation commission constituted as follows:

The State or States constituting one of the parties to the dispute shall appoint:

(a) one conciliator of the nationality of that State or of one of those States, who may or may not be chosen from the list referred to in paragraph 1; and

(b) one conciliator not of the nationality of that State or of any of those States, who shall be chosen from the list.

The State or States constituting the other party to the dispute shall appoint two conciliators in the same way. The four conciliators chosen by the parties shall be appointed within sixty days following the date on which the Secretary-General receives the request.

The four conciliators shall, within sixty days following the date of the last of their own appointments, appoint a fifth conciliator chosen from the list, who shall be chairman.

If the appointment of the chairman or of any of the other conciliators has not been made within the period prescribed above for such appointment, it shall be made by the Secretary-General within sixty days following the expiry of that period. The appointment of the chairman may be made by the Secretary-General either from the list or from the membership of the International Law Commission. Any of the periods within which appointments must be made may be extended by agreement between the parties to the dispute.

Any vacancy shall be filled in the manner prescribed for the initial appointment.

3. The Conciliation Commission shall decide its own procedure. The Commission, with the consent of the parties to the dispute, may invite any party to the treaty to submit to it its view orally or in writing. Decisions and recommendations of the Commission shall be made by a majority vote of the five members.

4. The Commission may draw the attention of the parties to the dispute to any measures which might facilitate an amicable settlement.

5. The Commission shall hear the parties, examine the claims and objections, and make proposals to the parties with a view to reaching an amicable settlement of the dispute.

6. The Commission shall report within twelve months of its constitution. Its report shall be deposited with the Secretary-General and transmitted to the parties to the dispute. The report of the Commission, including any conclusions stated therein regarding the facts or questions of law, shall not be binding upon the parties and it shall have no other character than that of recommendations submitted for the consideration of the parties in order to facilitate an amicable settlement of the dispute.

7. The Secretary-General shall provide the Commission with such assistance and facilities as it may require. The expenses of the Commission shall be borne by the United Nations.

APPENDIX B

AGREEMENT
ON CO-OPERATION IN THE FIELD OF TOURISM BETWEEN
THE GOVERNMENT OF THE UNITED KINGDOM OF GREAT BRITAIN
AND NORTHERN IRELAND AND THE GOVERNMENT OF THE
REPUBLIC OF ALBANIA

The Government of the United Kingdom of Great Britain and Northern Ireland and the Government of the Republic of Albania (hereinafter referred to as "the Contracting Parties");

Desirous to further strengthen co-operation and to consolidate existing relations between the peoples of Albania and the peoples of the United Kingdom, and;

In order to further strengthen the relations that exist between them;

In view of the importance they attach to the exchange of information at the popular level, particularly in the field of tourism, the two sides have agreed as follows:

ARTICLE 1

The Contracting Parties undertake to facilitate tourist visits between the two countries.

ARTICLE 2

The Contracting Parties undertake to exchange material and publications on tourist information from their respective National Tourist Boards.

ARTICLE 3

The Contracting Parties shall allow the importation of such documents and material required for tourist promotion.

ARTICLE 4

The Contracting Parties shall encourage and create favourable conditions for nationals of the other side to participate in the construction, management and maintenance of tourist projects and other aspects of the tourism industry.

ARTICLE 5

(1) The Agreement shall enter into force upon signature.

(2) It shall remain in force for an indefinite period. Either side may terminate it by giving six months' advance notice in writing through diplomatic channels to the other side.

In witness whereof, the undersigned, being duly authorised thereto by their respective Governments, have signed this Agreement.

Done in duplicate at London this Thirtieth day of March 1994 in the English and Albanian languages, both texts being equally authoritative.

For the Government of the United Kingdom of Great Britain and Northern Ireland:

For the Government of the Republic of Albania:

DOUGLAS HURD

B KOPLIKU

APPENDIX C

MEMORANDUM OF UNDERSTANDING

ON DEFENCE CONTACTS AND COOPERATION BETWEEN

THE GOVERNMENT OF THE REPUBLIC OF AUSTRIA AND

THE GOVERNMENT OF THE

UNITED KINGDOM OF GREAT BRITAIN AND NORTHERN IRELAND

The Government of the Republic of Austria and the Government of the United Kingdom of Great Britain and Northern Ireland, being known hereafter as the Participants,

- acting in the spirit of partnership and cooperation,

- acting also in the interests of strengthening security and stability in Europe as a whole and in support of the work plan of the Euro-Atlantic Partnership Council and Partnership for Peace,

- sharing the aim of strengthening the good defence relations and increasing the understanding and confidence already established between their respective countries,

- with the aim of developing jointly programmes of practical cooperation on a wide range of defence related matters,

have identified, to fulfil these purposes, the following activities:

- exchanges between the staffs and students of military colleges and academies with the aim of strengthening confidence and cooperation in defence studies and military education for senior officers,

- consultations and exchanges between experts in the field of management of the armed forces in a democratic society,

- visits to exchange views on military doctrine, concepts of security and restructuring,

- visits to develop friendly relations between the personnel of the armed forces and to share experience of both operational and professional training,

- exchanges to share experience of the work of the Directorates of the Ministries of Defence,

- visits to discuss the current state of, and the future outlook for, UK-Austria relations in the defence field,

- visits to discuss possible future requirements in the defence equipment field,

- cooperation on military geography,

- and visits to establish personal contacts between the leadership and the command of the armed forces of the two countries.

The Participants have decided that, on the basis of this Memorandum of Understanding, the detail of a rolling two-year programme of defence contacts, for use as a flexible management tool, will be presented prior to the Defence Staff Talks, for discussion at the Talks.

They have further decided that each government is to bear its own administrative costs for implementation of the rolling two-year programme of defence contacts, as specified above. Specific financial procedures will be negotiated as part of the Implementing Arrangements, to be jointly determined by the Participants, if further cooperation of the type specified below is to take place.

The Participants have decided that the provisions of this Memorandum do not preclude other contacts and cooperation, including attendance on military training courses, joint exercises, use of military facilities or professional assignment to units, as may be mutually determined between the Participants in an Implementing Arrangement. The visits of Ministers of Defence will be arranged separately.

Information and documentation received by either of the Participants as a result of the programme will not be given to a third party without the prior written consent of the originator. Any classified information and material exchanged or generated in connection with this memorandum will be used, transmitted, stored, handled and safeguarded in accordance with the General Security Arrangement (GSA) between The United Kingdom of Great Britain and Northern Ireland and The Republic of Austria, concerning the Protection of Non-Atomic Classified Information Exchanged for the Purpose of Defence Production, Research and Procurement between the Two Countries dated 25 September 1995. International visits between the Participants will be covered in accordance with paragraphs 7.1 - 7.5 of the above mentioned GSA.

This Memorandum becomes effective upon the date of last signature, and will remain in operation until terminated by either Participant, giving the other three months written notice of termination.

The foregoing represents the understandings reached between the Government of the Republic of Austria and the Government of the United Kingdom of Great Britain and Northern Ireland upon the matters referred to herein.

Signed in duplicate in the English language at Vienna on 9 July 1997.

For the Government of the United
Kingdom of Great Britain & Northern
Ireland,

For the Government of the
Republic of Austria,

the Chief of the Air Staff of the Royal
Air Force

Chief of Defence

Sir Richard Johns
Air Chief Marshal

Karl Majcen
General

APPENDIX D

MEMORANDUM OF UNDERSTANDING
BETWEEN
THE GOVERNMENT OF [   ]
AND
THE GOVERNMENT OF [   ]
CONCERNING
[   ]

The Government of [   ] and the Government of [   ] ('the
Participants'),
Desiring to [   ];
Have reached the following understanding:

Section 1
Purpose
The Participants will seek to ....

Section 2
[heading]
The Participants will ....

Section [ ]
Amendment
This Memorandum may be amended at any time by the mutual written consent of the
Participants.

Section [ ]
Termination
This Memorandum may be terminated by either Participant giving six months written
notice. The Participants will consult to determine how any outstanding matters should
be dealt with. Termination will not effect the validity of any contract made under this
Memorandum.

Section [ ]
Disputes
Any dispute about the interpretation or application of this Memorandum will be
resolved by consultations between the Participants, and will not be referred to any
national or international tribunal or third party for settlement.

Section [ ]
Duration and effective date
This Memorandum will come into effect on [the date of signature].
The foregoing represents the understanding reached between the Participants on the
matters referred to in this Memorandum.

Signed in duplicate at [place] on [date] in [the   language] [in the   and
languages, both texts having equal validity].

For the Government of [   ]   For the Government of [   ]

APPENDIX E

No. 1

Her Majesty's Ambassador at Montevideo to the Secretary General at the Ministry of Foreign Affairs of the Oriental Republic of Uruguay

British Embassy
Montevideo
8 December 1997

Your Excellency,

I have the honour to refer to the hut at Hope Bay (Bahía Esperanza) in the Peninsula in Antarctica which is owned by the Natural Environmental Research Council (NERC), the parent body of the British Antarctic Survey (BAS). The British Government, having consulted both NERC and BAS is pleased to confirm that the hut is not being used, and that if the Uruguayan Government wish to take over the hut, free of charge and indefinitely, NERC would not assert any right or title to the hut, or its facilities, and would relinquish all responsibility for them.

If the Uruguayan Government, acting within the framework of the Antarctic Treaty[1], in particular Article II, is ready to take over the hut and its facilities on the above-mentioned basis, and accept responsibility for the future use and upkeep of the hut and its facilities, neither NERC nor the British Government would have any objection.

If the Government of Uruguay accepts this proposal, I have the honour to propose that this Note and your reply in the affirmative shall constitute an Agreement between our two Governments, and that the transfer of the hut and its facilities shall take effect on the date of your reply.

I avail myself of this opportunity to renew to Your Excellency the assurances of my highest consideration.

ROBERT HENDRIE

No. 2

The Secretary General at the Ministry of Foreign Affairs of the Oriental Republic of Uruguay to Her Majesty's Ambassador at Montevideo

Montevideo
8 de diciembre 1997

Señor Embajador:

Tengo el honor de dirigirme a Vuestra Excelencia en relación a su Nota del día de la fecha, por la que se propone el establecimiento de un Acuerdo entre la República Oriental del Uruguay y el Reino Unido de Gran Bretaña e Irlanda del Norte sobre la toma de posesión del refugio ubicado en Hope Bay (Bahía Esperanza) en la Península Antártica. El texto de su Nota ⁀e transcribe en idioma español como sigue:

"Su Excelencia:

"Tengo el honor de hacer referencia al refugio ubicado en Hope Bay (Bahía Esperanza)
"en la Península Antártica, que es propiedad del Consejo de Investigación del Medio

"Ambiente Natural (NERC), organismo rector del Instituto de Investigaciones
"Antárticas (BAS). Habiendo consultado tanto al NERC como al BAS, El Gobierno
"Británico tiene el placer de confirmar que dicho refugio no está siendo utilizado y que
"si el Gobierno Uruguayo deseara tomar posesión del mismo, libre de cargo y por
"tiempo indefinido, el NERC no hará valer sus derechos de propiedad sobre dicho
"refugio y renunciará a toda responsabilidad por el mismo.

"Si el Gobierno Uruguayo, actuando dentro del marco del Tratado Antártico, en
"particular del Artículo II, está dispuesto a tomar posesión del refugio y sus
"instalaciones en las condiciones arriba mencionadas y a aceptar toda responsabilidad
"por el futuro uso y mantenimiento del refugio y de sus instalaciones, ni el NERC ni
"el Gobierno Británico tendrán objeción alguna.

"Si el Gobierno de Uruguay acepta esta propuesta, tengo el honor de proponer que
"esta Nota y su respuesta afirmativa constituyan un Acuerdo entre nuestros dos
"gobiernos y que la transferencia del refugio y sus instalaciones entren en vigencia en la
"fecha de su respuesta.

"Me valgo de la oportunidad para reiterar a su Excelencia las seguridades de mi
"más alta y distinguida consideración."

Al respecto, cumplo en poner en conocimiento de Vuestra Excelencia la
conformidad del Gobierno de la República Oriental del Uruguay con las
disposiciones transcriptas, por lo que la presente Nota y la de Vuestra Excelencia
constituyen un Acuerdo entre nuestros dos Gobiernos que entrará en vigor en el día
de la fecha.

Reitero a Vuestra Excelencia las seguridades de mi más alta consideración.

G. LASARTE

TRANSLATION OF NO. 2

Ambassador:

I have the honour to write to Your Excellency regarding your Note of today's date, by
which an Agreement is proposed between the Oriental Republic of Uruguay and the
United Kingdom of Great Britain and Northern Ireland on the transfer of the hut located
in Hope Bay (Bahía Esperanza) in the Antarctic Peninsula. The text of your Note is
transcribed in Spanish as follows:

[As in No. 1]

With regard to the above, I wish to inform Your Excellency of the consent of the
Government of the Oriental Republic of Uruguay to the arrangements as set out, and
therefore this Note and Your Excellency's Note shall constitute an Agreement between our
two Governments which will come into force today.

I renew to Your Excellency the assurances of my highest consideration.

G. LASARTE

APPENDIX F

MODEL EXCHANGE OF NOTES RECORDING AN

UNDERSTANDING

[Initiating note]

Your Excellency,
I have the honour to refer to discussions which have taken place between our two Governments concerning [   ]. As a result of those discussions it is the understanding of the Government of [   ] that the following arrangements will apply:
1. The Government of [   ] will ....
2. The Government of [   ] will ....
3. These arrangements may be terminated if either Government gives three months written notice.
If the arrangements set out above are acceptable to the Government of [   ], I have the honour to suggest that this Note and your Excellency's reply to that effect will place on record the understanding of our two Governments in this matter, which will come into effect on [the date of your reply].
I avail myself etc.

[Reply note]

Your Excellency,
I have the honour to acknowledge receipt of your Note No. [ ] dated [   ] concerning [   ] and which reads as follows:

[*Text of the initiating Note set out in full, if necessary in translation*]

I have the honour to confirm that the above arrangements are acceptable to the Government of [   ], and that your Note and this reply will place on record the understanding of our two Governments in the matter and which will come into effect [today].
I avail myself ete.

APPENDIX G

TREATY AND MOU TERMINOLOGY

COMPARATIVE TABLE

TREATY	MOU
Article	paragraph
agree	decide, accept, approve
agreement	arrangement(s), understanding(s)
agreed	decided, accepted, approved
authentic	equally valid
authoritative	equally valid
clause	paragraph
conditions	provisions
continue in force	continue to have effect
Done	Signed
enter into force	come into effect, come into operation
mutually agreed	jointly decided
obligations	commitments
Parties	Participants, Governments
Preamble	Introduction
rights	benefits
shall	will
terms	provisions
undertake	carry out
undertakings	understandings

Note Treaty terms such as 'party' or 'rights' can, of course, be used in an MOU if the context requires it, e.g. 'third party' and 'intellectual property rights'.

APPENDIX H

March 1997

Mr Daniel Tarschys
Secretary General
Council of Europe

I have the honour to transmit to your Excellency the names of the Representatives who will represent Her Majesty's Government at the Diplomatic conference for the Adoption of the Draft Council of Europe/UNESCO Convention on the Recognition of Qualifications concerning Higher Education in the European Region to be held in Lisbon from 8 - 11 April 1997.

Miss Caroline Elisabeth Macready,

Divisional Manager
Higher Education Quality Division
Department for Education and Employment

Mr Nigel Acheson Drummond Lambert,

Legal Adviser
Legal Adviser's Office
Department for Education and Employment

I have the honour to convey to you, Sir, the assurances of my highest consideration.

MALCOLM RIFKIND

APPENDIX I

Sir Michael Hastings Jay, KCMG, Her Majesty's Ambassador at Paris, is hereby granted full powers to sign, on behalf of the Government of the United Kingdom of Great Britain and Northern Ireland, the Agreement between the Government of the United Kingdom of Great Britain and Northern Ireland and the Governments of the French Republic and the Federal Republic of Germany concerning scientific personnel at the Max Von Laue-Paul Langevin Institute.

In witness whereof I, Robin Cook, Her Majesty's Principal Secretary of State for Foreign and Commonwealth Affairs, have signed these presents.

Signed and sealed at the Foreign and Commonwealth Office, London, the Fourth day of September, One thousand Nine hundred and Ninety-seven.

GENERAL FULL POWERS FOR PERMANENT REPRESENTATIVE TO THE UNITED NATIONS

Her Excellency, Ms [full names], is hereby granted full powers to sign on behalf of the Government of [   ], subject if necessary to ratification, any treaty or other instrument deposited with the Secretary-General of the United Nations and any notification related thereto.

In witness whereof, I [full names], [President, Prime Minister or Minister of Foreign Affairs] have signed these presents.

Signed [and sealed] at [   ], this   day of   200[   ]

APPENDIX K

1. The General Assembly of the United Nations, having considered chapter II of the report of the International Law Commission on the work of its eighteenth session (A/6309/Rev.1,[1] Part II), which contained final draft articles and commentaries on the law of treaties,[2] decided, by its resolution 2166 (XXI) of 5 December 1966, to convene an international conference of plenipotentiaries to consider the law of treaties and to embody the results of its work in an international convention and such other instruments as it might deem appropriate. By the same resolution, the General Assembly requested the Secretary-General to convoke the first session of the conference early in 1968 and the second session early in 1969. Subsequently, the General Assembly, noting that an invitation had been extended by the Austrian Government to hold both sessions of the conference at Vienna, decided, by resolution 2287 (XXII) of 6 December 1967, that the first session should be convened at Vienna in March 1968. At its fifth meeting, held on 24 May 1968, at the conclusion of the first session, the Conference adopted a resolution[3] requesting the Secretary-General to make all the necessary arrangements for the Conference to hold its second session at Vienna from 9 April to 21 May 1969.

2. The first session of the United Nations Conference on the Law of Treaties was held at the Neue Hofburg, Vienna, from 26 March to 24 May 1968. The second session of the Conference was also held at the Neue Hofburg, from 9 April to 22 May 1969.

3. One hundred and three States were represented at the first session of the Conference, and one hundred and ten States at the second session, as follows: Afghanistan, Algeria, Argentina, Australia, Austria, Barbados (second session only), Belgium, Bolivia, Brazil, Bulgaria, Burma (second session only), Byelorussian Soviet Socialist Republic, Cambodia, Cameroon (second session only), Canada, Central African Republic, Ceylon, Chile, China, Colombia, Congo (Brazzaville), Congo (Democratic Republic of), Costa Rica, Cuba, Cyprus, Czechoslovakia, Dahomey, Denmark, Dominican Republic, Ecuador, El Salvador (second session only), Ethiopia, Federal Republic of Germany, Finland, France, Gabon, Ghana, Greece, Guatemala, Guinea (first session only), Guyana, Holy See, Honduras, Hungary, Iceland (second session only), India, Indonesia, Iran, Iraq, Ireland, Israel, Italy, Ivory Coast, Jamaica, Japan, Kenya, Kuwait, Lebanon, Lesotho (second session only), Liberia, Libya (second session only), Liechtenstein, Luxembourg (second session only), Madagascar, Malaysia, Mali (first session only), Malta (second session only), Mauritania (first session only), Mauritius, Mexico, Monaco, Mongolia, Morocco, Nepal, Netherlands, New Zealand, Nigeria, Norway, Pakistan, Panama (second session only), Peru, Philippines, Poland, Portugal, Republic of Korea, Republic of Viet-Nam, Romania, San Marino, Saudi Arabia, Senegal, Sierra Leone, Singapore, Somalia (first session only), South Africa, Spain, Sudan (second session only), Sweden, Switzerland, Syria, Thailand, Trinidad and Tobago, Tunisia, Turkey, Uganda (second session only), Ukrainian Soviet Socialist Republic, Union of Soviet Socialist Republics, United Arab Republic, United Kingdom of Great Britain and Northern Ireland, United Republic of Tanzania, United States of America, Uruguay, Venezuela, Yemen (first session only), Yugoslavia and Zambia.

4. The General Assembly invited the specialized agencies and interested intergovernmental organizations to send observers to the Conference. The following specialized agencies and interested intergovernmental organizations accepted this invitation:

Specialized and related agencies
International Labour Organisation
Food and Agriculture Organization of the United Nations
United Nations Educational, Scientific and Cultural Organization
International Civil Aviation Organization
International Bank for Reconstruction and Development and International Development Association
International Monetary Fund
World Health Organization
Universal Postal Union
Inter-Governmental Maritime Consultative Organization
International Atomic Energy Agency

Intergovernmental organizations
Asian-African Legal Consultative Committee
United International Bureaux for the Protection of Intellectual Property
Council of Europe
General Agreement on Tariffs and Trade
League of Arab States

5. The Conference elected Mr. Roberto Ago (Italy) as President.

6. The Conference elected as Vice-Presidents the representatives of the following States: Afghanistan, Algeria, Austria, Chile, China, Ethiopia, Finland, France, Guatemala (for 1969), Guinea, Hungary, India, Mexico, Peru, Philippines, Romania, Sierra Leone, Spain (for 1968), Union of Soviet Socialist Republics, United Arab Republic, United Kingdom of Great Britain and Northern Ireland, United States of America, Venezuela and Yugoslavia.

7. The following committees were set up by the Conference:

General Committee

Chairman: The President of the Conference

Members: The President and Vice-Presidents of the Conference, the Chairman of the Committee of the Whole and the Chairman of the Drafting Committee.

Committee of the Whole

Chairman: Mr. Taslim Olawale Elias (Nigeria)

Vice-Chairman: Mr. Josef Šmejkal (Czechoslovakia)

Rapporteur: Mr. Eduardo Jiménez de Aréchaga (Uruguay)

Drafting Committee

Chairman: Mr. Mustafa Kamil Yasseen (Iraq)

Members: Argentina, China, Congo (Brazzaville), France, Ghana, Japan, Kenya, Netherlands, Poland, Sweden, Union of Soviet Socialist Republics, United Kingdom of Great Britain and Northern Ireland, United States of America and, *ex-officio* in accordance with rule 48 of the Rules of Procedure, Mr. Eduardo Jiménez de Aréchaga (Uruguay), Rapporteur of the Committee of the Whole.

Credentials Committee

Chairman: Mr. Eduardo Suárez (Mexico)

Members: Ceylon, Dominican Republic, Japan, Madagascar, Mali (first session), Mexico, Switzerland, Union of Soviet Socialist Republics, United Republic of Tanzania (second session) and United States of America.

8. Sir Humphrey Waldock, Special Rapporteur of the International Law Commission on the law of treaties, acted as Expert Consultant.

9. The Secretary-General of the United Nations was represented by Mr. C. A. Stavropoulos, Under-Secretary-General, The Legal Counsel. Mr. A. P. Movchan, Director of the Codification Division of the Office of Legal Affairs of the United Nations, acted as Executive Secretary.

10. The General Assembly, by its resolution 2166 (XXI) convening the Conference, referred to the Conference, as the basis for its consideration of the law of treaties, chapter II of the report of the International Law Commission on the work of its eighteenth session (A/6309/Rev.1, Part II), containing the text of the final draft articles and commentaries on the law of treaties adopted by the Commission at that session. [4]

11. The Conference also had before it the following documentation:

(a) the relevant records of the General Assembly and of the International Law Commission relating to the law of treaties;

(b) comments and amendments relating to the final draft articles on the law of treaties submitted by Governments in 1968 in advance of the Conference in accordance with General Assembly resolution 2287 (XXII) (A/CONF.39/6 and Add.1-2);

(c) written statements submitted by specialized agencies and intergovernmental bodies invited to send observers to the Conference (A/CONF.39/7 and Add.1-2 and Add.1/Corr.1);

(d) a selected bibliography on the law of treaties (A/CONF.39/4), an analytical compilation of comments and observations made in 1966 and 1967 on the final draft articles on the law of treaties (A/CONF.39/5, Vols. I and II), standard final clauses (A/CONF.39/L.1), a guide to the draft articles on the law of treaties (A/C.6/376) and other pertinent documentation prepared by the Secretariat of the United Nations.

12. The Conference assigned to the Committee of the Whole the consideration of the final draft articles on the law of treaties adopted by the International Law Commission and the preparation of the final provisions and of any other instruments it might consider necessary. The Drafting Committee, in addition to its responsibilities for drafting, and for co-ordinating and reviewing all the texts adopted, was entrusted by the Conference with the preparation of the preamble and the Final Act.

13. On the basis of the deliberations recorded in the records of the Conference (A/CONF.39/SR.1 to SR.36) and the records (A/CONF.39/C.1/SR.1 to SR.105) and reports (A/CONF.39/14, Vols. I and II and A/CONF.39/15 and Corr.1 (Spanish only) and Corr.2) of the Committee of the Whole, the Conference drew up the following Convention:

Vienna Convention on the Law of Treaties

14. The foregoing Convention was adopted by the Conference on 22 May 1969 and opened for signature on 23 May 1969, in accordance with its provisions, until 30 November 1969 at the Federal Ministry for Foreign Affairs of the Republic of Austria and, subsequently, until 30 April 1970 at United Nations Headquarters in New York. The same instrument was also opened for accession in accordance with its provisions.

15. After 30 November 1969, the closing date for signature at the Federal Ministry for Foreign Affairs of the Republic of Austria, the Convention will be deposited with the Secretary-General of the United Nations.

16. The Conference also adopted the following declarations and resolutions, which are annexed to this Final Act:

Declaration on the prohibition of military, political or economic coercion in the conclusion of treaties

Declaration on universal participation in the Vienna Convention on the Law of Treaties

Resolution relating to article 1 of the Vienna Convention on the Law of Treaties

Resolution relating to the Declaration on the prohibition of military, political or economic coercion in the conclusion of treaties

Resolution relating to article 66 of the Vienna Convention on the Law of Treaties and the Annex thereto

Tribute to the International Law Commission

Tribute to the Federal Government and people of the Republic of Austria

IN WITNESS WHEREOF the representatives have signed this Final Act.

DONE at Vienna this twenty-third day of May, one thousand nine hundred and sixty-nine, in a single copy in the Chinese, English, French, Russian and Spanish languages, each text being equally authentic. By unanimous decision of the Conference, the original of this Final Act shall be deposited in the archives of the Federal Ministry for Foreign Affairs of the Republic of Austria.

ANNEX

Declarations and resolutions adopted by the United Nations Conference on the Law of Treaties

DECLARATION ON THE PROHIBITION OF MILITARY, POLITICAL OR ECONOMIC COERCION IN THE CONCLUSION OF TREATIES

The United Nations Conference on the Law of Treaties,

Upholding the principle that every treaty in force is binding upon the parties to it and must be performed by them in good faith,

Reaffirming the principle of the sovereign equality of States,

Convinced that States must have complete freedom in performing any act relating to the conclusion of a treaty,

Deploring the fact that in the past States have sometimes been forced to conclude treaties under pressure exerted in various forms by other States,

Desiring to ensure that in the future no such pressure will be exerted in any form by any State in connexion with the conclusion of a treaty,

1. *Solemnly condemns* the threat or use of pressure in any form, whether military, political, or economic, by any State in order to coerce another State to perform any act relating to the conclusion of a treaty in violation of the principles of the sovereign equality of States and freedom of consent,

2. *Decides* that the present Declaration shall form part of the Final Act of the Conference on the Law of Treaties.

DECLARATION ON UNIVERSAL PARTICIPATION IN THE VIENNA CONVENTION ON THE LAW OF TREATIES

The United Nations Conference on the Law of Treaties,

Convinced that multilateral treaties which deal with the codification and progressive development of international law, or the object and purpose of which are of interest to the international community as a whole, should be open to universal participation,

Noting that articles 81 and 83 of the Vienna Convention on the Law of Treaties enable the General Assembly to issue special invitations to States which are not Members of the United Nations or of any of the specialized agencies or of the International Atomic Energy Agency, or parties to the Statute of the International Court of Justice, to become parties to the Convention,

1. *Invites* the General Assembly to give consideration, at its twenty-fourth session, to the matter of issuing invitations in order to ensure the widest possible participation in the Vienna Convention on the Law of Treaties;

2. *Expresses the hope* that the States Members of the United Nations will endeavour to achieve the object of this Declaration;

3. *Requests* the Secretary-General of the United Nations to bring this Declaration to the notice of the General Assembly;

4. *Decides* that the present Declaration shall form part of the Final Act of the United Nations Conference on the Law of Treaties.

RESOLUTION RELATING TO ARTICLE 1 OF THE VIENNA CONVENTION ON THE LAW OF TREATIES

The United Nations Conference on the Law of Treaties,

Recalling that the General Assembly of the United Nations, by its resolution 2166 (XXI) of 5 December 1966, referred to the Conference the draft articles contained in chapter II of the report of the International Law Commission on the work of its eighteenth session, [a]

Taking note that the Commission's draft articles deal only with treaties concluded between States,

Recognizing the importance of the question of treaties concluded between States and international organizations or between two or more international organizations,

Cognizant of the varied practices of international organizations in this respect, and

Desirous of ensuring that the extensive experience of international organizations in this field be utilized to the best advantage,

Recommends to the General Assembly of the United Nations that it refer to the International Law Commission the study, in consultation with the principal international organizations, of the question of treaties concluded between States and international organizations or between two or more international organizations.

RESOLUTION RELATING TO THE DECLARATION ON THE PROHIBITION OF MILITARY, POLITICAL OR ECONOMIC COERCION IN THE CONCLUSION OF TREATIES

The United Nations Conference on the Law of Treaties,

Having adopted the Declaration on the prohibition of military, political or economic coercion in the conclusion of treaties as part of the Final Act of the Conference,

1. *Requests* the Secretary-General of the United Nations to bring the Declaration to the attention of all Member States and States participating in the Conference, and of the principal organs of the United Nations;

2. *Requests* Member States to give the Declaration the widest possible publicity and dissemination.

RESOLUTION RELATING TO ARTICLE 66 OF THE VIENNA CONVENTION ON THE LAW OF TREATIES AND THE ANNEX THERETO

The United Nations Conference on the Law of Treaties,

Considering that under the terms of paragraph 7 of the Annex to the Vienna Convention on the Law of Treaties, the expenses of any conciliation commission that may be set up under article 66 of the Convention shall be borne by the United Nations,

Requests the General Assembly of the United Nations to take note of and approve the provisions of paragraph 7 of this Annex.

TRIBUTE TO THE INTERNATIONAL LAW COMMISSION

The United Nations Conference on the Law of Treaties,

Having adopted the Vienna Convention on the Law of Treaties on the basis of the draft articles prepared by the International Law Commission,

Resolves to express its deep gratitude to the International Law Commission for its outstanding contribution to the codification and progressive development of the Law of treaties.

TRIBUTE TO THE FEDERAL GOVERNMENT AND PEOPLE OF THE REPUBLIC OF AUSTRIA

The United Nations Conference on the Law of Treaties,

Having adopted the Vienna Convention on the Law of Treaties,

Expresses its deep appreciation to the Federal Government and people of the Republic of Austria for making possible the holding of the Conference in Vienna and for their generous hospitality and great contribution to the successful completion of the work of the Conference.

APPENDIX L

WHEREAS a Convention on Prohibitions or Restrictions on the Use of certain Conventional Weapons which may be deemed to be excessively injurious or to have indiscriminate effects was open for signature by all States at the United Nations Headquarters in New York from the Tenth day of April, One thousand Nine hundred and Eighty-one until the Tenth day of April, One thousand Nine hundred and Eighty-two;

AND WHEREAS the Convention was signed by the Government of the United Kingdom on the Tenth day of April, One thousand Nine hundred and Eighty-one;

NOW THEREFORE the Government of the United Kingdom of Great Britain and Northern Ireland, having considered the Convention aforesaid, hereby confirm and ratify the same and undertake faithfully to perform and carry out all the stipulations therein contained, subject to the terms of the declaration contained in the accompanying Note.

411

In witness whereof this Instrument of Ratification is signed and sealed by Her Majesty's Principal Secretary of State for Foreign and Commonwealth Affairs.

Done at London the Ninth day of February, One thousand Nine hundred and Ninety-five.

APPENDIX M

CERTIFICATE OF EXCHANGE OF INSTRUMENTS OF RATIFICATION

The Undersigned having met together for the purpose of exchanging the Instruments of Ratification of a Convention relating to the Avoidance of Double Taxation and the Prevention of Fiscal Evasion with respect to Taxes on Income

which was signed at Pallanza on the 21st day of October, 1988, by representatives of the Government of the United Kingdom of Great Britain and Northern Ireland and the Government of the Italian Republic;

and the respective Ratifications of the said Convention having been found in good and due form, the said exchange took place this day.

In witness whereof the Undersigned have signed the present Certificate.
Done in duplicate at London the 30th day of November, 1990.

For the Government of the United Kingdom of Great Britain and Northern Ireland:

[signed]

For the Government of the Italian Republic:

[signed]

I sottoscritti che si sono incontrati al fine di scambiare gli strumenti di ratifica della Convenzione riguardante l'esenzione dalla Doppia Tassazione e la Prevenzione dell'Evasione Fiscale concernente l'imposta sul reddito

che è stata firmata a Pallanza il 21 ottobre 1988 da rappresentanti del Governo del Regno Unito della Gran Bretagna e dell'Irlanda del Nord, e del Governo Italiano.

Riconoscendo che le rispettive ratifiche della sopracitata Convenzione sono nella forma corretta e dovuta, hanno proceduto allo scambio degli strumenti di ratifica.
Predendo atto di quanto sopra, i sottoscritti hanno firmato il presente documento di ratifica, in duplicato, il giorno 30 November 1990.

Per il Governo del Regno Unito della Gran Bretagna e dell'Irlanda del Nord:

[signed]

Per il Governo Italiano:

[signed]

Reproduced with permission from Monroe Leigh and Merritt R. Blakeslee (eds.), *National Treaty Law and Practice* (Studies in Transnational Legal Policy No. 27, 1995), p. 255. © The American Society of International Law.

APPENDIX N

MODEL EXCHANGE OF NOTES CORRECTING AN ERROR IN AN EXCHANGE OF NOTES

[Initiating Note]

Your Excellency,
I have the honour to refer to the Exchange of Notes between our two Governments of [date] concerning [subject]. An examination of the text has revealed a clerical error in both Notes. It is proposed to correct this error before publication, as follows:

[In paragraph 1, replace '1 April 1900' by '1 April 2000'.]

I have the honour to propose that my Government make the above correction in the original copy of the Note from your Government and that your Government make the correction in the original Note from my Government, and that the Exchange of Notes be published as so corrected.
 I avail myself etc.

[Reply Note]

Your Excellency,
I have the honour to acknowledge receipt of your Note No.[   ] of [date] concerning correction of a clerical error in the Exchange of Notes between our two Governments of [date] concerning [subject]. I have the honour to confirm* that the proposal in your Note is acceptable to my Government and that it will make the correction in the original Note from your Government and publish the Exchange of Notes as so corrected .
 I avail myself etc.

* Note: this exchange of notes does not constitute a treaty and is not published.

APPENDIX O

I CERTIFY

(1) That the Protocol on Environmental Protection to the Antarctic Treaty, with four annexes, was done at Madrid on October 4, 1991, in the English, French, Russian and Spanish languages;

(2) That the Government of the United States of America, as depositary for the aforesaid Protocol, has received from the Government of Japan a communication drawing attention to an error in wording in the second sentence of Article 13, paragraph 1, of Annex 3 of the English language text of that Protocol;

(3) That an examination of the English language text of the aforesaid Protocol reveals that the use of the word "amendment" in Article 13 of Annex 3 is not consistent with amendment provisions in the French, Russian and Spanish language texts where a word equivalent to "measure" is used and therefore the Government of the United States of America believes that the use of the word "amendment" in Annex 3 is a typographical error and that the word "measure" should be substituted.

(4) That, accordingly, the English language text of the aforesaid Protocol shall be deemed to be corrected as set forth in Article 13, paragraph 1 of Annex 3, which appears below:

"1. This Annex may be amended or modified by a measure adopted in accordance with Article IX (1) of the Antarctic Treaty. Unless the measure specifies otherwise, the amendment or modification shall be deemed to have been approved, and shall become effective, one year after the close of the Antarctic Treaty Consultative Meeting at which it was adopted, unless one or more of the Antarctic Treaty Consultative Parties notifies the Depositary, within that time period, that it wishes an extension of that period or that it is unable to approve the measure."

IN TESTIMONY WHEREOF, I, WARREN CHRISTOPHER, Secretary of State of the United States of America, have hereunto caused the seal of the Department of State to be affixed and my name subscribed by the Authentication Officer of the said Department, at the city of Washington, in the District of Columbia, this twenty-fifth day of January, 1996.

Warren Christopher
Secretary of State

By _Annie R. Maddux_
Authentication Officer
Department of State

415

APPENDIX P

REGISTRATION AND PUBLICATION OF TREATIES AND INTERNATIONAL AGREEMENTS: REGULATIONS TO GIVE EFFECT TO ARTICLE 102 OF THE CHARTER OF THE UNITED NATIONS

Adopted by the General Assembly on 14 December 1946 [Resolution 97 (I)], *as modified by resolutions 364 B (IV), 482 (V) and 33/141 A, adopted by the General Assembly on 1 December 1949, 12 December 1950 and 18 December 1978, respectively.*

The General Assembly,

Considering it desirable to establish rules for the application of Article 102 of the Charter of the United Nations which provides as follows:

1. Every treaty and every international agreement entered into by any Member of the United Nations after the present Charter comes into force shall as soon as possible be registered with the Secretariat and published by it.

2. No party to any such treaty or international agreement which has not been registered in accordance with the provisions of paragraph 1 of this Article may invoke that treaty or agreement before any organ of the United Nations.

Recognizing, in making provision therefor, the importance of orderly registration and publication of such treaties and international agreements and the maintenance of precise records;

Adopts accordingly, having given consideration to the proposals of the Secretary-General submitted pursuant to the resolution of the General Assembly of 10 February 1946, the following regulations:

PART ONE

REGISTRATION

Article 1

1. Every treaty or international agreement, whatever its form and descriptive name, entered into by one or more Members of the United Nations after 24 October 1945, the date of the coming into force of the Charter, shall as soon as possible be registered with the Secretariat in accordance with these regulations.

2. Registration shall not take place until the treaty or international agreement has come into force between two or more of the parties thereto.

3. Such registration may be effected by any party or in accordance with article 4 of these regulations.

4. The Secretariat shall record the treaties and international agreements so registered in a register established for that purpose.

416

Article 2

1. When a treaty or international agreement has been registered with the Secretariat, a certified statement regarding any subsequent action which effects a change in the parties thereto, or the terms, scope or application thereof, shall also be registered with the Secretariat.

2. The Secretariat shall record the certified statement so registered in the register establishment under article 1 of these regulations.

Article 3

1. Registration by a party, in accordance with article 1 of these regulations, relieves all other parties of the obligation to register.

2. Registration effected in accordance with article 4 of these regulations relieves all parties of the obligation to register.

Article 4

1. Every treaty or international agreement subject to article 1 of these regulations shall be registered *ex officio* by the United Nations in the following cases:

   (a) Where the United Nations is a party to the treaty or agreement;

   (b) Where the United Nations has been authorized by the treaty or agreement to effect registration;

   (c) Where the United Nations is the depository of a multilateral treaty or agreement.

2. A treaty or international agreement subject to article 1 of these regulations may be registered with the Secretariat by a specialized agency in the following cases:

   (a) Where the constituent instrument of the specialized agency provides for such registration;

   (b) Where the treaty or agreement has been registered with the specialized agency pursuant to the terms of its constituent instrument;

   (c) Where the specialized agency has been authorized by the treaty or agreement to effect registration.

Article 5

1. A party or specialized agency, registering a treaty or international agreement under article 1 or 4 of these regulations, shall certify that the text is a true and complete copy thereof and includes all reservations made by parties thereto.

2. The certified copy shall reproduce the text in all the languages in which the treaty or agreement was concluded and shall be accompanied by two additional copies and by a statement setting forth, in respect of each party:

(a) The date on which the treaty or agreement has come into force;

(b) The method whereby it has come into force (for example: by signature, by ratification or acceptance, by accession, et cetera).

Article 6

The date of receipt by the Secretariat of the United Nations of the treaty or international agreement registered shall be deemed to be the date of registration, provided that the date of registration of a treaty or agreement registered *ex officio* by the United Nations shall be the date on which the treaty or agreement first came into force between two or more of the parties thereto.

Article 7

A certificate of registration signed by the Secretary-General or his representative shall be issued to the registering party or agency and also, upon request, to any party to the treaty or international agreement registered.

Article 8

1. The register shall be kept in the English and French languages. The register shall comprise in respect of each treaty or international agreement, a record of:

(a) The serial number given in the order of registration;

(b) The title given to the instrument by the parties;

(c) The names of the parties between whom it was concluded;

(d) The dates of signature, ratification or acceptance, exchange of ratification, accession, and entry into force;

(e) The duration;

(f) The language or languages in which it was drawn up;

(g) The name of the party or specialized agency which registers the instrument and the date of such registration;

(h) Particulars of publication in the treaty series of the United Nations.

2. Such information shall also be included in the register in regard to the statements registered under article 2 of these regulations.

3. The texts registered shall be marked *"ne varietur"* by the Secretary-General or his representative, and shall remain in the custody of the Secretariat.

Article 9

The Secretary-General, or his representative, shall issue certified extracts from the register at the request of any Member of the United Nations or any party to the treaty or international agreement concerned. In other cases he may issue such extracts at his discretion.

PART TWO

FILING AND RECORDING

Article 10

The Secretariat shall file and record treaties and international agreements, other than those subject to registration under article 1 of these regulations, if they fall in the following categories:

(a) Treaties or international agreements entered into by the United Nations or by one or more of the specialized agencies;

(b) Treaties or international agreements transmitted by a Member of the United Nations which were entered into before the coming into force of the Charter, but which were not included in the treaty series of the League of Nations;

(c) Treaties or international agreements transmitted by a party not a member of the United Nations which were entered into before or after the coming into force of the Charter which were not included in the treaty series of the League of Nations, provided, however, that this paragraph shall be applied with full regard to the provisions of the resolution of the General Assembly of 10 February 1946 set forth in the Annex to these regulations.

Article 11

The provisions of articles 2, 5 and 8 of these regulations shall apply, *mutatis mutandis*, to all treaties and international agreements filed and recorded under article 10 of these regulations.

PART THREE

PUBLICATION

Article 12

1. The Secretariat shall publish as soon as possible in a single series every treaty or international agreement which is registered or filed and recorded, in the original language or languages, followed by a translation in English and in French. The certified statements referred to in article 2 of these regulations shall be published in the same manner.

2. The Secretariat will, however, have the option not to publish *in extenso* a bilateral treaty or international agreement belonging to one of the following categories:

(a) Assistance and co-operation agreements of limited scope concerning financial, commercial, administrative or technical matters;

(b) Agreements relating to the organization of conferences, seminars or · meetings;

(c) Agreements that are to published otherwise than in the series mentioned in paragraph 1 of this article by the United Nations Secretariat or by a specialized or related agency.

3. In deciding whether or not to publish *in extenso* a treaty or international agreement belonging to one of the categories mentioned in paragraph 2 of this article, the Secretariat shall duly take into account, *inter alia*, the practical value that might accrue from *in extenso* publication. Treaties and international agreements that the Secretariat intends not to publish *in extenso* shall be identified as such in the monthly statements of treaties and international agreements provided for in article 13 of these regulations, it being understood that a decision not to publish *in extenso* may be reversed at any time.

4. Any State or intergovernmental organization may obtain from the Secretary-General a copy of the text of any treaty or international agreement which it has been decided, pursuant to paragraph 2 of this article, not to publish *in extenso*. The Secretariat shall likewise make a copy of any such treaty or agreement available to private persons against payment.

5. In respect of each treaty or international agreement registered or filed and recorded, the series referred to in paragraph 1 of this article shall include at least the following information: the registration or recording number, the names of the parties, the title, the date and place of conclusion, the date and method of entry into force, the duration (where appropriate), the languages of conclusion, the name of the State or organization that has registered it or transmitted it for filing and recording, and, if appropriate, references to publications in which the complete text of the treaty or international agreement is reproduced.

Article 13

The Secretariat shall publish every month a statement of the treaties and international agreements registered, or filed and recorded, during the preceding month, giving the dates and numbers of registration and recording.

Article 14

The Secretariat shall send to all Members of the United Nations the series referred to in article 12 and the monthly statement referred to in article 13 of these regulations.

APPENDIX Q

**SUBMISSION OF TREATIES FOR REGISTRATION AND PUBLICATION
IN ACCORDANCE WITH ARTICLE 102 OF THE U.N. CHARTER - REQUIREMENTS**

DOCUMENTATION/ INFORMATION TO BE PROVIDED	FORMAT / TYPE OF INFORMATION
1. Treaty/Agreement	• ONE certified true and complete copy of **all** authentic text(s), **and** • TWO additional copies **or** ONE electronic copy (on diskette)
2. All Attachments (annexes, minutes, procès-verbaux, etc.)	Same as (1) above
3. Text of reservations, declarations, objections	Same as (1) above
4. Translations of the Agreement and all attachments into English and/or French (if available)	One paper copy and one electronic copy, if available, where necessary
5. Title of Treaty/Agreement	If not printed as part of the text (eg: for exchange of notes)
6. Names of Signatories	If not appearing in typed form as part of signature block
7. Date of Signature	If not clear from the text
8. Place of Signature	If not clear from the text
9. Date of entry into force	In accordance with entry into force provisions
10. Method of entry into force	i.e., signature, ratification, approval, accession, etc. **including**: • date and place of exchange of the instruments of ratification or notifications for a bilateral agreement, **or** • in the case of a multilateral agreement, date and nature of the instruments deposited by each Contracting Party with the Depositary
11. Maps (if applicable)	In order of preference: • original document • facsimile document • high resolution scanned digital file • in the case of colour originals, either same-size, colour-separated film negatives or good quality, panchromatic, half-tone film negative • 4 x 5 inch colour slide (original to be photographed with standard colour bar and ruler) • high quality microfilm • same size, electrostatic, colour or black and white copies [oversized originals are to be copied with overlaps and left as separate sheets (not taped together)]

22 April 1996

421

OFFICE OF LEGAL AFFAIRS
Treaty Section

SUBMISSION OF TREATIES FOR REGISTRATION AND PUBLICATION
IN ACCORDANCE WITH ARTICLE 102 OF THE U.N. CHARTER

MODEL FOR THE CERTIFYING STATEMENT REQUIRED UNDER THE GENERAL ASSEMBLY
REGULATIONS TO GIVE EFFECT TO ARTICLE 102 OF THE CHARTER

I, THE UNDERSIGNED [--- name of the authority ---], hereby certify that the attached text is a true and complete copy of [--- title of the agreement---, --- name of the Parties ---, --- date and place of conclusion ---]; that it includes all reservations made by Signatories or Parties thereto (in the absence of any reservation, declaration or objection, the certifying statement would read "that no reservations or declarations or objections were made by the Signatories or Parties thereto"), and that it was concluded in the following languages: [.....]. **I further certify that the additional copy of this Agreement contained in the diskette is a true and complete copy of [---title of the agreement---].**[1]

I FURTHER CERTIFY that the Agreement came into force on [---date---] by [---method of entry into force---], in accordance with [--- article or provision in the agreement ---], and that it was signed by [.....] and [.....].

[Place and date of signature
of certifying statement]

[Signature and title of the
certifying authority]

---

[1]   The language in bold must be included when additional copies of a treaty are provided in a diskette.

APPENDIX R

OVERSEAS TERRITORIES

Australia
Ashmore and Cartier Islands
Australian Antarctic Territory
Christmas Island
Cocos (Keeling) Islands
Coral Sea Islands
Heard Island and McDonald Islands
Norfolk Island
Denmark
Faeroe Islands
Greenland
France
Clipperton Island
French Polynesia
French Southern and Antarctic Lands
Mayotte
New Caledonia
St Pierre and Miquelon
Wallis and Futuna Islands
Netherlands
Aruba
Netherlands Antilles
New Zealand
Cook Islands
Niue
Ross Dependency
Tokelau
Norway
Bouvet Island
Jan Mayen
Peter I Island
Queen Maud Land
Svalbard

United Kingdom

Crown dependencies

The Bailiwick of Guernsey

The Bailiwick of Jersey

The Isle of Man

Overseas territories

Anguilla

Bermuda

British Antarctic Territory

British Indian Ocean Territory

British Virgin Islands

Cayman Islands

Falkland Islands

Gibraltar

Montserrat

Pitcairn, Henderson, Ducie and Oeno Islands

St Helena and dependencies (Ascension and Tristan da Cunha)

South Georgia and South Sandwich Islands

The Sovereign Base Areas in Cyprus (Akrotiri and Dkehelia)

Turks and Caicos Islands

United States

American Samoa

Guam

Northern Mariana Islands

Puerto Rico

United States Virgin Islands

"Minor Outlying Islands" (Baker Island, Howland Island, Jarvis Island, Johnston Atoll, Kingman Reef, Midway Islands, Navassa Island, Palmyra Atoll, Wake Island)

Note Inclusion in this list does not necessarily reflect the views of other states, or, with the exception of United Kingdom territories, the parent state or the territory.

BIBLIOGRAPHY

Books

Bailey and Daws, *The Procedure of the UN Security Council* (1998)

Bengoetxea, J., *The Legal Reasoning of the European Court of Justice* (1993)

Birnie and Boyle, *International Law and the Environment* (1992)

Blaustein, *Constitutions of the World* (G. H. Flanz ed., looseleaf)

Blix and Emerson, *The Treaty Maker's Handbook* (1973)

Bloed, A., *The Conference on Security and Co-operation in Europe* (1993)

Chinkin, C., *Third Parties in International Law* (1993)

Denza, E., *Diplomatic Law* (2nd edn, 1998)

Dolzer and Stevens, *Bilateral Investment Treaties* (1995)

Elias, T., *The Modern Law of Treaties* (1974)

Evans, M. (ed.), *Remedies in International Law* (1995)

Gardner, J. (ed.), *Human Rights as General Norms and a State's Right to Opt Out* (1997)

Goodrich and Hambro, *The Charter of the United Nations* (3rd edn, 1969)

Higgins, R., *The Development of International Law through the Political Organs of the United Nations* (1963)

Problems and Processes (1994)

Horn, F., *Reservations and Interpretative Declarations to Multilateral Treaties* (1988)

International Law Association, *The Effect of Independence on Treaties* (1965)

Jacobs and Roberts (eds.), *The Effect of Treaties in Domestic Law* (1987)

Joyner and Chopra (eds.), *The Antarctic Legal Regime* (1988)

Keynes, J. M., 'The Economic Consequences of the Peace', (in *Collected Writings of John Maynard Keynes* (2nd edn, 1971)

Klabbers, J., *The Concept of Treaty in International Law* (1996)

Lee, L., *The Vienna Convention on Consular Relations* (2nd edn, 1991)

Leigh, M. (ed.), *National Treaty Law and Practice* (1995)

Lijnzaad, L., *Reservations to UN Human Rights Treaties* (1995)

Lowe and Fitzmaurice (eds.), *Fifty Years of the International Court of Justice* (1996)

MacLeod, Hendry and Hyett, *The External Relations of the European Communities* (1996)

Mann, F., *Studies in International Law* (1973)

McGoldrick, D., *International Relations Law of the European Union* (1997)

McNair, A., *Law of Treaties* (2nd edn, 1961)

Makarczyk, J., *The Theory of International Law at the Threshold of the 21st Century* (1996)

Matte, N., *Treatise on Air-Aeronautical Law* (1981)

Merrills, J., *The Development of International Law by the European Court of Human Rights* (2nd edn, 1993)

Michelmann and Soldatos (eds.), *Federalism and International Relations* (1990)

Mullerson, Fitzmaurice and Andenas (eds.), *Constitutional Reform and International Law in Central and Eastern Europe* (1998)

Nicolson, H., *The Congress of Vienna* (1946)

Nordquist, M. (ed.), *The United Nations Law of the Sea Convention: A Commentary* (1982)

O'Connell, D., *Law of State Succession* (1967)
    International Law (2nd edn, 1970)

Opeskin and Rothwell (eds.), *International Law and Australian Federalism* (1997)

Oppenheim's International Law (Jennings and Watts, eds., 9th edn, 1992)

Pictet, P. (ed.), *The Geneva Conventions 1949, Commentary* (4 vols., 1952–60)

Pini, G., *Mussolini* (1939)

Ragazzi, M., *The Concept of International Obligations Erga Omnes* (1997)

Reisenfeld and Abbott, *Parliamentary Participation in the Making and Operation of Treaties: A Comparative Study* (1993)

Reuter, P., *Introduction to the Law of Treaties* (2nd English edn, 1995)

Rosenne, S., *The Law of Treaties* (1970)
    Practice and Methods of International Law (1984)
    Breach of Treaty (1985)
    The Law and Practice of the International Court of Justice (3rd edn, 1997)

Sabel, R., *Procedure at International Conferences* (1997)

Satow's Guide to Diplomatic Practice (5th edn, 1979)

Schermers and Blokker, *International Institutional Law* (3rd edn, 1995)

Shaw, M., *International Law* (4th edn, 1998)

Shawcross and Beaumont, *Air Law* (P. Martin ed., looseleaf)

Sinclair, I., *The Vienna Convention on the Law of Treaties* (2nd edn, 1984)

Villiger, M., *Customary International Law and Treaties* (2nd edn, 1997)

Wade and Bradley, *Constitutional and Administrative Law* (10th edn, 1985)

Watts, A., *International Law and the Antarctic Treaty* (1992)

Wetzel and Rausching, *The Vienna Convention on the Law of Treaties: Travaux Préparatoires* (1978)

Whiteman, M., *Digest of International Law* (15 vols., 1963–73)

Woetzel, R., *The Nuremberg Trials in International Law* (1960)

Articles

Alen and Peeters, 'Federal Belgium within the International Legal Order', in K. Wellens (ed.), *International Law: Theory and Practice, Essays in Honour of Eric Suy* (1998), pp. 123–43

Anderson, D., 'Further Efforts to Ensure Universal Participation in the UN Convention on the Law of the Sea', ICLQ (1994), pp. 886–93

'Legal Implications of the Entry into Force of the UN Convention on the Law of the Sea', ICLQ (1995), pp. 313–26

Aust, A., 'Air Services Agreements: Current United Kingdom Procedures and Policies', *Air Law* (1985), pp. 189–202

'The Theory and Practice of Informal International Instruments' ICLQ (1986), pp. 787–812

Blum, Y., 'Russia Takes over the Soviet Union's Seat at the United Nations', EJIL (1992), p. 354

Bos, M., 'Theory and Practice of Treaty Interpretation', NILR (1980), pp. 3–38 and 135–70

Bowett, D., 'The Conduct of International Litigation', in Gardner and Wickremsinghe (eds.), *The International Court of Justice, Process, Practice and Procedure* (British Institute of International and Comparative Law, 1997), pp. 1–20

Bowman, M., 'The Multilateral Treaty Amendment Process – A Case Study', ICLQ (1995), p. 540

Caminos and Molitor, 'Progressive Development of International Law and the Package Deal', AJIL (1985), pp. 871–90

Chamberlain, K., 'Collective Suspension of Air Services', ICLQ (1983), p. 616

Cheng, B., 'Air Law' in *Max Planck Encyclopaedia of Public International Law* (1989), vol. 11

Chinkin, C., 'A Mirage in the Sand? Distinguishing Binding and Non-Binding Relations between States', *Leiden Journal of International Law* (1997), pp. 223–47

Chua and Hardcastle, 'Retroactive Application of Treaties Revisited', NILR (1997), pp. 414–20

Devine, D., 'The Relationship between International Law and Municipal Law in the Light of the Interim Constitution 1993', ICLQ (1995), p. 1

Evensen, J., 'Working Methods and Procedures in the Third United Nations Conference on the Law of the Sea', *Hague Recueil* (1986), vol. IV, pp. 483–6

Fitzmaurice, M., 'Modifications to the Principles of Consent in Relation to Certain Treaty Obligations', *Austrian Review of International and European Law* (1997), p. 275

Gardiner, R., 'Treaty Interpretation in the English Courts since Fothergill v. Monarch Airlines', ICLQ (1995), p. 620

'Treaties and Treaty Materials: Role, Relevance and Accessibility', ICLQ (1997), p. 643

'Revising the Law of Carriage by Air: Mechanisms in Treaties and Contract', ICLQ (1998), pp. 278–305

Greenwood, C., 'The Libyan Oil Arbitrations', BYIL (1982), pp. 27–81

Higgins, R., 'Human Rights: Some Questions of Integrity', *Modern Law Review* (1989), p. 1

'Some Observations on the Inter-Temporal Rule in International Law', in J. Makarczyk (ed.), *Theory of International Law at the Threshold of the 21st Century* (1996), pp. 173–81

'Time and the Law: International Perspectives on an Old Problem', ICLQ (1997), pp. 501–20

Howarth, D., 'The Compromise on Denmark', *Common Market Law Review* (1994), p. 765

Hutchinson, D., 'The Significance of the Registration or Non-Registration of an International Agreement in Determining Whether or Not it is a Treaty', *Current Legal Problems* (1993), pp. 257–90

Kamminga, M., 'State Succession in Respect of Human Rights Treaties', EJIL (1995), pp. 469–84

Kennedy and Specht, 'Austrian Membership in the European Communities', *Harvard International Law Journal* (1990), p. 407

Klabbers, J., 'The New Dutch Law on the Approval of Treaties', ICLQ (1995), pp. 629–43

'Les cimtieres marins sont-ils établis comme des régimes objectifs', *Espaces et Ressources Maritimes* (1997), pp. 121–33

'Protection of Legitimate Expectations in EC Law', *Kansainvälistä* (1997), pp. 732–42

'Some Problems Regarding the Object and Purpose of Treaties', *Finnish Yearbook of International Law* (1997), pp. 138–60

Kuner, C., 'The Interpretation of Multilateral Treaties: Comparison of Texts versus the Presumption of Similar Meaning', ICLQ (1991), pp. 953–64

Lauterpacht, E., '"Partial" Judgments and the Inherent Jurisdiction of the International Court of Justice' in Lowe and Fitzmaurice (eds.), *Fifty Years of the International Court of Justice* (1996), pp. 465–86

Lefeber, R., 'The Provisional Application of Treaties', in Klabbers and Lefeber (eds.), *Essays on the Law of Treaties* (1998), p. 82

Maluwu, T., 'Succession to Treaties in Post-Independence Africa', *African Journal of International and Comparative Law* (1992), p. 791

Marks, S., 'Reservations Unhinged: The Belilos Case before the European Court of Human Rights', ICLQ (1990), p. 300

McDade, P., 'The Interim Obligation between Signature and Ratification', NILR (1985), pp. 5–47

'The Effect of Article 4 of the Vienna Convention on the Law of Treaties 1969', ICLQ (1986), pp. 499–511

McHugo, J., 'The Judgments of the International Court of Justice in the Jurisdiction and Admissibility Phase of Qatar v. Bahrain', NYIL (1997), p. 171

McNeil, J., 'International Agreements: Recent US–UK Practice Concerning the Memorandum of Understanding', AJIL (1994), pp. 821–6

Mendelson and Hulton, 'La Revendication par l'Iraq de la Souveraineté sur le Koweït', *Annuaire Français de Droit International* (1990), p. 195

'The Iraq–Kuwait Boundary', BYIL (1993), pp. 135–95

Mikulka, V., 'The Dissolution of Czechoslovakia and Succession in Respect of Treaties', *Development and International Co-operation* (1996), pp. 45–63

Mullerson, R., 'The Continuity and Succession of States, by reference to the Former USSR and Yugoslavia', ICLQ (1993), p. 473

'NATO Enlargement and Russia', ICLQ (1998), pp. 192–204

Mus, J., 'Conflicts between Treaties in International Law', NILR (1998), pp. 208–32

O'Connell, D., 'A *Cause Célèbre* in the History of Treaty-Making', BYIL (1967), p. 156

Opeskin, B.,'Federal States in the International Legal Order', NILR (1996), pp. 353–86

Parry, C., 'Where to Look for Your Treaties', *International Journal for Law Libraries* (February 1980)

Pickelman, M., 'Draft Convention for the Unification of Certain Rules for International Carriage by Air: The Warsaw Convention Revisited for the Last Time?', *Journal of Air Law and Commerce* (1998), pp. 273–306

Richard, G., 'KAL 007: The Legal Fallout', *Annals of Air and Space Law* (1983), p. 146

Rogoff, 'The International Legal Obligations of Signatories to an Unratified Treaty', *Maine Law Review* (1980), pp. 263–99

Rosenne, S., 'The Qatar/Bahrain Case', *Leiden Journal of International Law* (1995), p. 161

Rowe and Meyer, 'The Geneva Conventions (Amendment) Act 1995: A Generally Minimalist Approach', ICLQ (1996), pp. 476–84

Schabas, W., 'Reservations to Human Rights Treaties: Time for Innovation and Reform', *Canadian Yearbook of International Law* (1994), pp. 39–81

Schachter, O., 'The Twilight Existence of Non-Binding International Agreements', AJIL (1977), pp. 296–304

Schwebel, S., 'May Preparatory Work be Used to Correct Rather than Confirm the "Clear" Meaning of a Treaty Provision?', in J. Makarczyk, (ed.), *Theory of International Law at the Threshold of the 21st Century*, (1996), pp. 541–7

Schwelb, E., 'The Nuclear Test Ban Treaty and International Law', AJIL (1964), p. 642

Shaw, M., 'State Succession Revisited', *Finnish Yearbook of International Law* (1994), p. 34

Sinclair, I., 'The Principles of Treaty Interpretation and their Application by the English Courts', ICLQ (1963), pp. 508–51

Slinn, P., 'Le Règlement Sino-Britannique de Hong-Kong', *Annuaire français de Droit International* (1985), p. 167

'Aspects Juridiques du Retour de Hong-Kong à la Chine', *Annuaire français de Droit International* (1996), p. 273

Sloss, D., 'The Domestication of International Human Rights: Non-Self-Executing Declarations and Human Rights Treaties', *Yale Journal of International Law* (1999), pp. 129–221

Sprudzs, A., 'Status of Multilateral Treaties: Researcher's Mystery, Mess or Muddle?', AJIL (1972), p. 365

Tabory, M., 'Registration of the Egypt–Israel Peace Treaty: Some Legal
    Aspects', ICLQ (1983), p. 981

Thirlway, H., 'The Law and Procedure of the International Court of Justice
    1960–1989', BYIL (1989), p. 1; BYIL (1990), p. 1; BYIL (1991), p. 1; and
    BYIL (1992), p. 1

Treves, T., 'Codification du droit international et pratique des Etats dans le
    droit de la mer', *Hague Recueil* (1990), IV, vol. 223, pp. 25–60

Vierdag, E., 'The Time of the "Conclusion" of a Multilateral Treaty', BYIL
    (1988), pp. 75–111

    'The International Court of Justice and the Law of Treaties' in Lowe and
    Fitzmaurice (eds.), *Fifty Years of the International Court of Justice*
    (1996), pp. 145–66

Vogts, D., 'Taking Treaties Less Seriously', AJIL (1998), pp. 458–62

Watts, A., 'The Legal Position in International Law of Heads of States, Heads
    of Government and Foreign Ministers', *Hague Recueil* (1994), III, pp.
    114–28

Widdows, K., 'The Unilateral Denunciation of Treaties Containing No
    Denunciation Clause', BYIL (1982), p. 83

Williams, P., 'The Treaty Obligations of the Successor States of the Former
    Soviet Union, Yugoslavia, and Czechoslovakia: Do They Continue in
    Force?' *Denver Journal of International Law and Policy* (1994), pp. 1–37

Wolfe, K., 'Treaties and Custom: Aspects of Interrelation', in Klabbers and
    Lefeber (eds.), *Essays on the Law of Treaties* (1998), pp. 31–9

Wood, M., 'Participation of Former Yugoslav States in the United Nations
    and in Multilateral Treaties', *Max Planck Yearbook of United Nations
    Law* (1997), pp. 231–58

Substantial citations are in italics.

INDEX